Ultimate Handbook of Urban Warfare

Attention Authors

'We Convert Fighters into Writers'. That's the motto of Manas Publications since more than four decades. Our message to the world is that India can win the battle not only by the bullet but also by the pen. There is no dearth of intellectuals in our country, but their knowledge is confined to them only. No sincere effort has been made by any other publisher to channelise their knowledge in national interest. That is why the talent of a large number of intellectuals remains latent. An author transforms his knowledge into a manuscript, and it is our job to spread his/her knowledge by converting it into a beautiful book. For over four decades, Manas has been motivating the intellectuals by publishing their manuscripts and would like to publish your manuscript too. So if you or your colleagues have any manuscript ready for publication or are working on it, kindly contact us with detailed synopsis and list of contents. We will transform your work into a valuable publication. If you wish, we can also suggest you the suitable subjects for writing the books related to your area of expertise. Manas is known for its publishing quality and commitments. We take utmost care in production and give wide publicity to the book as well as its author through our national and international distribution network.

Ultimate Handbook of Urban Warfare

Dr NC Asthana, IPS

Manas Publications
(We Convert Fighters into Writers)
New Delhi-110002 (INDIA)

MANAS PUBLICATIONS
(We Convert Fighters into Writers)
(Publishers, Library Suppliers, Importers & Exporters)
4402/5-A, Ansari Road (Opp HDFC Bank)
Darya Ganj, New Delhi-110 002 (India)
Off. ☏ 23260783, 23265523, Fax: 011-23272766
E-mail: manaspublications@vsnl.com
manaspublications@yahoo.com
manaspublications@gmail.com

ISBN 978-81-7049-442-3
₹ 995/-

Designed at
Manas Publications

Printed in India at
RK Offset, Delhi
and published by Mrs Suman Lata for
Manas Publications, 4402/5-A, Ansari Road
(Opp HDFC Bank), Darya Ganj,
New Delhi-110 002 (INDIA)

Contents

*"When a soldier says
that he learnt that in the basic training;
when a sergeant says trust me;
when a young officer says
that based upon his experience;
and when a senior officer says
that he thinks that;
they are all going to land you
in very very deep shit".*

Acknowledgements

An unprecedented work of this sort could be accomplished only by the grace of the Almighty God and nothing else. Man can only aspire and strive to acquire knowledge; the intellect to comprehend, it is given by Him. Equally important is the capability to present knowledge in such a form so that it becomes comprehensible to others also—that's how knowledge is preserved and perpetuated, one of the sacred duties that have been cast upon the human race. This capability too is given by Him. I thank God that in my life He gave me the opportunities and the resources to acquire knowledge and also the intelligence to comprehend it. I have made an all-out effort to present the subject in such a way that it becomes a source of knowledge and inspiration for posterity. If this work reflects genius and scholarship, the source is none but Him; if some mistakes are left, they are entirely mine. I humbly offer this treatise at His feet for all the kindness He has bestowed upon me.

Preface

There is no avoiding war; it can only be postponed to the advantage of others.

Life was simple only when regular armies fought regular armies in fields. It became complex when armies started fighting in the jungles and urban areas. I have discussed jungle warfare at length in my treatise "Ultimate Handbook of Jungle Warfare". Fighting in urban areas is equally complex. Remember the Battle of Stalingrad and the Battle of Berlin—how they fought bitterly for every single house? Since they were doing so for the first time, most of the methods of fighting were improvised right then and there. The tank and the field guns played an important role. But still, the basic idea of fighting was simple. There is a building held by the enemy. Most probably, they would have fortified the firing positions therein. There could be snipers too. The presence of snipers meant that you could not afford to take chances loitering around. How do you take the building? If you have field guns, you could shoot at them and try to reduce it. If you had tanks, you would do the same thing. The infantry could try to advance to the building behind the cover of the tanks. If you had ground attack aircrafts, or aircrafts that could drop precision-guided bombs to flatten the building, it would be very good. However, if you did not have field guns, tanks or ground attack aircrafts; or, more probably, did not have the liberty to use them, things became greatly difficult. Such a situation could easily arise in a civil war-like situation; in an urban insurgency; in an urban guerrilla warfare situation, or in anti-terrorist operations. Much later, such limitations led to the development of the science of house intervention—that is, how to approach and kill the enemy who could be firing at you from inside the house without blasting the house by artillery or tanks.

As such, most of the armies, paramilitary forces and police forces of the world are unprepared for fighting an unconventional war in an urban environment. Unconventional warfare includes a broad spectrum of military and paramilitary operations, ranging from terrorist bombs, snipers, ambushes, and landmines, to use of improvised mortars and even regular artillery; from terrorist attacks on civilian targets to guerrilla warfare, and pitched battles with regular armies. Do not confuse urban guerrilla warfare with 'terrorism' alone as many people do; terrorism is simply one of the means adopted in urban guerrilla warfare, as is sabotage. Urban guerrillas have often employed novel unconventional tactics in order to surprise and deceive enemy forces—tactics which often left regular armies totally confounded and flummoxed. Although traditional guerrilla warfare had been primarily a rural endeavour, as populations have gravitated to the cities on every continent, it is but natural for the guerrilla to conduct combat operations in these environments. As the communities have shifted from rural-based to urban-based societies, the guerrilla must and will do the same if he is to gain their material and moral support. Hence modern state versus non-state actor conflict will necessarily involve a significant urban warfare component.

You have had, for example, the Irish Republican Army (IRA); the Afghan mujahideen during the Soviet occupation; and the Chechen rebels during the Battles for Grozny in 1994 and 2000. I have chosen them as case studies for their relatively modern time frames, which allowed for more availability of resources detailing the tactics used, and their particularly unique aspects of urban warfare. The IRA operated in essentially peacetime conditions and almost completely covertly, rarely taking up direct combat with the British military or security forces—they exemplified attacks from a distance or by remote control; and the British suffered from limitations imposed upon their response in neutral populated areas. It was no holds barred for the mujahideen—they did not give a quarter and did not expect a quarter from the Soviets either. The Soviets felt free to use any weapon short of nukes on them and the mujahideen fought back with everything they had, including Stinger missiles. The mujahideen operated primarily in rural areas, but moved liberally into the cities to conduct specific combat operations as their needs called for. The Chechens lived, operated, and fought within Grozny, and were in near constant violent contact with the Russians. Almost every infantry weapon was used in this combat.

Unconventional warfare in an urban environment is a game that even relatively small groups can play. It is cheap and therefore many do choose to play it. It requires no masses of troops, armament, equipment, specialised units or complex organisation as a conventional rural or jungle guerrilla warfare would demand. No nation of the world has prepared itself for the complex situations that may unfold in an unconventional war in an urban environment by way of preparing a comprehensive urban guerrilla warfare combat operations TTP (tactics, technique and procedures). Precisely for this reason, the British were at their wits' end in fighting the IRA, and the mighty Soviet war machine eventually beat a very costly retreat from the rugged land of Afghanistan. In Chechnya also, the Russians had eventually to forget all about collateral damage and fall back on their heavy artillery and air power to scrape their way through against the Chechen rebels. It was extremely heavy firepower from artillery, tanks and aircrafts that could eventually suppress the Chechen guerrillas. The Indians, on the other hand, have neither any significant experience nor any institutional doctrine in this regard. Whenever they have been obliged to operate in urban areas, they have fumbled and messed up. Their first exposure of urban warfare was during the Operation Blue Star at the Golden Temple Complex in Amritsar in 1984. They messed it up badly—eventually the tanks had to be called in and the repercussions of the extensive collateral damage were heavy—one prime minister got assassinated and thousands of innocent people were killed in the communal riots that immediately followed the assassination. In almost all the operations they have undertaken against terrorists in Kashmir, they end up blasting the entire house with explosive charges after suffering a few casualties because they do not know the science of house intervention. This habit of blasting houses actually led to a great deal of alienation there and has thus complicated the problem as no one, not even a child, ever believed in their pet theory of some brick-cement house catching fire from small arms fire touted for the benefit of ignorant journalists. Everybody knows that bullets don't start fires or collapse walls. Obviously there is much to be learnt. This treatise addresses that universal need.

Indians have a habit of desiring simple explanations and simple solutions—no one has the patience or the intellectual capacity to grapple with complexity. The Indians react only for the present because as a system they are intellectually bankrupt. Knee-jerk reactions have taken such complete control of the collective psyche of the nation that the system is utterly unable to think beyond the last method of attack. Bombay (26/11) was a rifle-cum-grenade attack. Then it was presumed that all future attacks would also be rifle attacks and hence the demand that there should be commandos in all the major towns. Fine, you may have it. The next could be a bomb attack. What would the commandos do then? You may station the commandos in major towns; the terrorists would attack small towns. You may deploy police in places of religious worship; the terrorists would attack markets. People refuse to understand that there is no way in which every possible target in the country could be protected unless you recruit three-fourth of the population in the security forces to protect the remaining one-fourth round-the-clock in three shifts! Before 26/11 the Indian security establishment thought in terms of bombs planted on bicycles. No one has the intellectual capacity to realise that the terrorist is not short of methods of attack. Indians love to splurge on costly gadgets that the unscrupulous suppliers dump on them—they have money to spend and the companies have some stuff to sell—a perfect symbiotic existence; the stupidity of one is fed by the cupidity of the other and *vice versa*. What would the metal detectors and the terribly costly backscatter imaging systems do if the terrorists choose to lob shells from improvised mortars (as the IRA had done in firing at 10, Downing Street) kept in the back of vans or improvised rockets like the Palestinian Qassam?

Urban guerrilla warfare has been a popular subject for authors, either in general or concerning a specific case. It is also a favourite topic for the media. Urban terrorists and the media are locked together into an inexorable symbiotic partnership of mutual need and benefit because violence is news. Most of them have, however, focused on 'what' the guerrillas did, and 'why' they did it—a matter not difficult for political scientists and even journalists to dabble into it. Not one of them could get into the details of 'how' the government forces or the guerrillas conducted their operations because they are not military scientists themselves. Military scientists or military officers, on the other hand, do not understand the mind of the guerrilla and cannot think beyond military hardware. In this treatise, I have made good for the respective deficiencies of both. Urbanisation of the battleground requires the development of new skills and core competencies. A critical analysis of urban unconventional warfare requires intimate knowledge of the conditions in which the combat operations have hitherto been conducted by both the guerrillas and the security forces, and what aspects of those conditions were critical to their success or failure. Only then you can formulate and evaluate measures of effective urban guerrilla combat operations.

Dr NC Asthana, IPS

PS: The views expressed in the book are my own and have nothing to do with the Government of India or my official capacity.

1

Anatomy of Urban Guerrilla Warfare

War is a game that is played with a smile. If you cannot smile, grin; if you cannot grin, keep out of the way till you can.

(1.1) How an Urban Attack Impacts Us?

Killing for peace is like screwing for virginity.

On that fateful day 9/11, previous attacks and urban terrorism outrages were eclipsed by a few orders of magnitude. It was not only George Bush who was flabbergasted; the entire nation of USA was stunned, dumbfounded, and stupefied. Americans have a morbid fascination with all sorts of calamities and disasters and it is amply reflected in over 467 disaster films made in Hollywood on every imaginable type of disaster ranging from earthquakes, asteroids, volcanoes, tsunamis, epidemics, chemical accidents, nuclear accidents, aircraft accidents, and alien attacks to monsters. Yet when the real calamity of 9/11 struck nobody knew how to react to that sort of crisis. You have only to recall the visuals of frightened people running in panic to wherever they could even as the World Trade Tower buildings crumbled behind them raising great clouds of dust and debris. What they could have done after all? The old defensive responses to them—CCTV, road blocks, heavily controlled street spaces, immigration controls—suddenly became comically irrelevant in this new age of threat. These traditional practices concentrate either on the micro spaces and practices of the street and averting the car or suicide bomb, or on the macro-scale of international migration controls and geo-political espionage focused on stopping terrorists from moving around the world. But no one had bothered with the middle scale—the relatively free and unpoliced mobilities within nation-states.

The events of 9/11 were a macabre yet subtle exploitation of the multiple and interconnected mobilities, continuously telescoping between the local and global that sustain global urban capitalism: mobilities of people and machines; mobilities of images and media; mobilities of electronic finance and capital. They provided the latest in a long line of dawning realisations that urban modernity, despite its promises of absolute technological and material progress, is actually utterly interwoven with fragility and vulnerability.

A strategic urban site, as throughout urban and military history, has been an overwhelmingly tempting target in war. Even before 9/11, Martin Pawley had predicted that "fear of the dislocation of urban services on a massive scale is now endemic in the populations of all great cities". Now, such fear threatens to be pathological and paralysing. This is especially so in the cosmopolitan cities where the popular culture of prosperity has long perpetuated the myth in their make believe world that war, risks and instant urban devastation are the domains of the rest of the planet, and not the blessed rich, powerful and the beautiful people with their 'manifest destiny' of prosperity peace and superiority. The 9/11 thunderbolt ate away at the very iconic and geographic cores

A tidal wave of dust and debris roars through lower Manhattan as the World Trade Center collapses on September 11, 2001 – a stunning photo taken by Greg Semedinger of the New York police aviation unit – 2752 people perished in the attack

of US economic and military hegemony. As *Newsweek* reported the week after, "September 11th ended the illusion that Americans could somehow float above the hatreds of the world".

Deepening fears of the inherent vulnerability of strategic cities, of course, are fed by the attacks themselves. They are also fuelled by a media culture which endlessly analyses and dissects such risk. But such fears are also growing because the technological mobilities that cross-cut cities – of machines, people, computer communications, and potential biological pathogens – now threaten apparently unopposable carnage at any instant, at any turn. As Paul Virilio has repeatedly reminded us, urban walls, whether physical, electronic, electromagnetic or psychological, are no longer tenable. "From here on", he wrote in 1991 itself, "urban architecture has to work with the opening of a new 'technological space-time' " based on unstoppable flow, unpredictable mobility, and the risk of these enormously complex technological systems being perverted to disrupt, destroy and kill.

The attacks of 9/11 were the result of three pre-existing conditions.

Exploiting the inherent fragilities of urban technological mobilities: First, the fragile and subtle mobilities and technologies that underpin and sustain global urban capitalism were forcibly redirected, perverted, and turned in on themselves. The strikes therefore mocked the political fantasies of the Bush regime that suggested – until 9/11 – that major urban catastrophes could be kept at bay through defensive missile shields laid out along Cold War, geo-political, lines. Instead of 'rogue states' aping the superpowers and acquiring intercontinental nuclear, biological or chemical weapons, the equivalent of a nuclear impact was produced by the simple expedient of a few 'stone age' paper-cutting knives, supposedly used to hijack the planes.

Offering choreographies of carnage for global media: In this age of televised urban wars, the mass appropriation of airliners within poorly-protected US domestic airspace allowed events to be timetabled, with sickening logic, as precisely as any conventional airliner or television schedule, to have maximum global impact. This allowed the iconic and unforgettable moments of mass casualties and urban devastation to be beamed live to a terrified, but transfixed, global TV audience, many of whom were brought up on the staples of hyper-real video games, science fiction urban dystopias and disaster movies. One of the most common responses, either amongst those that lived through and saw the horror first hand or those who watched on TV, was "it was just like in a movie".

As Martin Amis observed in the *Guardian*, the four planes were carefully co-ordinated so that "the first plane would crash into the northern tower just as the working day hit full stride. Then a pause for 15 minutes, to give the world time to gather round its TV sets. With that attention secured, the second plane would crash into the south tower, and in that instant America's youth would turn into age". The actual implementation of a million simulations of urban devastation perfectly mocked the urban culture in the West which endlessly recycles images of its own destruction. In fact, the events were a kind of carefully staged reverse hyper-reality: they enacted events which had been endlessly simulated before but which had never actually happened.

Of course the choice of New York—arguably the world's media capital—meant that the entire world would hear of little else for months. The Western media complex will inevitably be obsessed by carnage and devastation within its own backyard. It has been shown countless times, though, that, at the same time, it systematically ignores or downgrades the much higher casualty figures of many ongoing wars and crises in the global South (Sudan, Colombia, Indonesia, Somalia, Rwanda, the Congo, Sierra Leone, and, of course, Afghanistan). It has been repeatedly and unfailingly seen that the huge numbers of avoidable deaths, directly implicating the United States and its allies, through Iraqi sanctions or global structural adjustment programmes, merit barely a line in even the most highbrow newspapers. And it has been proven beyond doubt that the Western media operates on an informal and unwritten system of valuing human beings, and their deaths, extremely unequally: affluent employees of the global financial services industry in New York are near the top and the global majority in the so-called developing world—including the huge numbers who have perished in Afghanistan—are near the bottom. Thus, yet another irony of the 9/11 attacks is that the perpetrators chose their targets to directly demonstrate the huge asymmetries and biases in global media and representational power that accompany the economic and cultural globalisation that they are trying to undermine and destroy.

It has also been alleged that the co-ordination of events surrounding the attacks also stretched to the more bizarre manipulation of the other key mobility system underpinning global urban capitalism: the electronic financial system (which, ironically, provided the very rationale for the World Trade Center's construction). Considerable evidence is now emerging that the terrorist network behind the attacks participated in a major series of insider trading deals by using their knowledge of forthcoming events to make millions of dollars exploiting the inevitable volatilities that resulted in airline, insurance, gold and oil stock values and commodity prices.

Exploiting the concentrating logics of global city development: The third and final facilitating factor, of course, was the intense concentrating logic of global city development. The world's most strategic urban sites—global city cores like lower Manhattan—have grown ever-more concentrated over the last thirty years as they take advantage of the economic spin-offs of global economic liberalisation, the explosion of financial markets and the remote control capabilities of information and communication technologies.

The iconic power of the skyscraper—a symbol of urban 'progress' and modernisation for a century—was irrevocably reversed in an instant on that day. From an icon of power, progress and the dynamism of urban America it has been transmuted into a symbol of fragility which builds deep vulnerability into the cityscape. Thus, one or two precision strikes could bring down two of the world's tallest buildings and kill over 6,000 people whilst a plane hitting the relatively low-level Pentagon killed less than 200. Incredibly, the New York impacts have meant that the entire fragile apparatus of the global capitalist

Smoke and debris swallows the surrounding areas following the collapse of the south tower – The intrinsic vulnerability and fragility of urban areas was exposed in all starkness

system was pushed over the brink into deep recession. Some of the world's largest and most powerful companies were brought to the brink of bankruptcy. A possibly fatal blow was delivered to many of the companies that profit from global mobilities (tourism operators and, especially, airlines). And a new era of global geopolitics was ushered in.

(1.2) Resorting to Terrorism as a Means to a Political End: The Fundamental Reasons

War is hell and all that, but it has a good deal to recommend it. It wipes out all the small nuisances of peace-time.

(1.2.1) One's admittedly weak position *vis-à-vis* the State

Terrorism is one of the numerous means which an urban guerrilla may employ in his struggle. He has many other means also of waging his war. In this work, however, the word 'terrorism' is often used synonymously with 'urban guerrilla warfare'. I have done this in deference to the fact that the word 'terrorism' is found much more frequently in popular usage and people often relate more quickly to the context when one speaks of terrorism. The simplest way to understand terrorism is to regard it as a form of coercive intimidation. Terrorism exists for some simple reasons. Firstly, there are non-state actors or even state actors who feel that they need justice and that the system would simply not deliver it to them for whatever reason. Secondly, they are convinced that the disparity in their strength and the strength of those whom they despise is so great that they cannot exert any pressure upon them through conventional or 'constitutional' means. When non-state actors have problems with states, they know that they have neither the organisation, public support or military strength to launch an insurgency and that if they have to exert any pressure, it must come from unconventional means; when nation-states support terrorism in some other nation, they find that they are much weaker than the states they have to settle scores with and that they cannot even think of going to war as the proverbial last argument of the kings.

(1.2.2) *Because it can create impacts much bigger than its real strength*

The methods which a terrorist or urban guerrilla can adopt are limited only by his imagination. Repressive terror is directed by the guerrilla movement against members of the population for the purpose of enforcing guerrilla directives. Structural terror is the terror employed against the government, police, army and civilian structure which supports the government. It is designed to systematically terrorise members of the establishment in order to paralyse its operations. But what is of greater consequence is the impact of his actions. The impact of a terrorist act is both physical and psychological. The physical element is impermanent or may be even immaterial. When a bomb explodes, there is physical damage. It is also possible that there is no significant damage. But the psychological impact is always there and its overall effect may be greater than that of the physical impact. Even if a bomb does not result in many casualties or extensive damage to property, the very fact that a bomb could be planted at a certain place goes on to show that the terrorists could breach the security of the state and thus the act damages the credibility of the state. A terrorist act which does not result in psychological impact on the enemy is a waste of time and effort. A terrorist strike is therefore necessarily intended to create worry, fear, or panic in the minds of the target.

Terrorists do select soft targets for the simple reason that is expedient to do so. A terrorist has no misgivings about his strength. He never intends to take on the might of the military or the police of the nation-state he is targeting. He makes no claims to the concepts of honour in battle either. He knows that he is fighting an unequal battle and in that battle he feels justified to employ any means available.

All terrorist strikes have an eventual political goal in mind though it may not be apparent to the target. The exact objective is known only to the terrorist—you cannot penetrate his mind. Some terrorist acts may appear quite senseless or even perverse to you—they may not appear to be so to the terrorist. You do not have any means of understanding his thought process. You never know what has made his mind what it is. For all you know, he could be genuinely sick—he is also likely to be a man who has suffered great injustice in his life.

Western scholars have tried to limit the objectives of terrorism to secession of a territory to form a new sovereign state; dominance of territory or resources by various ethnic groups; imposition of a particular form of government; economic deprivation of a population; or opposition to a domestic government or occupying army. Such straitjacketing is unnecessary. A terrorist is not bound to take up arms only when his grievances fall in one of these categories.

Yes, a nation must address the root causes of any conflict but it is a long-drawn out endeavour. What do you do in the interregnum? Wait for the roots of conflict to wither away on their own? Certainly not!

Left to themselves, things only go from bad to worse—this is the law of nature. This book tells you what to do when you are faced with urban terrorism and urban guerrilla warfare.

(1.3) Why and how Terrorism becomes a Preferred Option?

Sometimes, being good and lucky still is not enough.

(1.3.1) The Travails of being a Soft State

Soft states are characterised not only by weak-kneed governments; they are also characterised by a highly immature public and an utterly irresponsible media. A soft state not only lacks resolve, it also lacks proper understanding. The people and the media fail to understand that in a modern state it is impossible to protect the myriads of targets that it presents. They expect that the government should be able to protect everything by a magic wand. In soft states, the government becomes the default target of every terrorist activity because an immature society and an even more immature media blame the government for every terrorist act by over-reacting. Terrorists know that killing a few people or damaging some property is not going to take them anywhere near their objective. But they know it well that all such acts make a dent on the credibility of the government in the eyes of the people and the media who expect the impossible from the government. Terrorists bank on this and hope that a beleaguered government would go out of the way to grant them some concessions. It is with this belief that they kidnap important personalities or hijack a plane.

Crozier described it in the following words: "A common purpose is to make life unendurable for the enemy". Terrorising the key institutions of the government and thus bringing about a paralysis in the functioning of the administration has manifold results. If the police are the target, terror causes a sort of disillusionment to set in, leading the force to a state of shock and inactivity. Conversely, if the government persists in trying to stamp out terrorism under the pressure of the people and the media, the resources of the police and the army are greatly stretched, making them even less effective. At the same time it imposes a heavy financial burden on the system as extra security measures are put in place. Moreover, there is a clamoring from a large section of the people, the media and even the ruling group for what they perceive as a panacea in the days of participative democracies, that is, a dialogue, which is essentially nothing but a tacit admission that the regime has buckled up and is prepared to grant some concessions. As the Governor General of Algeria Jacques Soustelle had described it,

"Terror is a psychological weapon of unbelievable power. Before the bodies of those whose throats have been cut and the grimacing faces of the mutilated, all capacity for resistance lapses; the spring is broken".

Terrorism is thus found to be a particularly potent tool against regimes which lack resolve, which are weak-kneed, and which lack the moral courage to face some of the harsh realities built in their socio-political system. As we have had occasion to witness time and again, down from the release of terrorists following certain kidnappings in the early days of insurgency in Kashmir to the release of foreign mercenaries following the hijacking of IC-814, a soft state is particularly prone to this sort of blackmail. There is a profound psychological reason for it. Since unlike most of the countries of Europe and even some of Asia which have gone through a horrific amount of human suffering and bloodshed in the wars of the twentieth century, this country has not had a real baptism through blood, the Indian society has developed a morbid fear of violence and the great middle-class reacts to it in a most irrational manner. This has made the Indian society particularly vulnerable to acts of terrorism—intelligent terrorists can certainly extort more out of the Indian state than they can ever expect from a principled and resolute state. The bomb blasts in Delhi in July 2008, created tremendous furor in the country—the media got it had dissected from every angle possible by arm-chair theorists sitting in TV studios. This over-reaction could be compared with even neighbouring Pakistan where a higher number of casualties were inflicted in the Marriott hotel bomb blast but there was no such furor in the media. The Indian society and political system have inherent cracks that stand to get magnified under the stress of a determined and sustained phase of terrorism.

(1.3.2) How the media makes a Soft State softer

The people, the pseudo-intellectuals amongst them and the media of a soft state are frequently responsible for making it even softer. Before anybody else cracks up, the people and the media crack up. Public opinion in this country, for example, is determined largely by the trash which is fed to the public by the print and electronic media. Since they are the most irresponsible and intellectually the most bankrupt lot, they take the lead in softening the resolve of the people. Let no one forget that it is the same media which has not only failed in condemning our acts of capitulation before terrorism, but has had gone to the extent of suggesting that for the sake of peace we could pardon all the terrorists who have killed thousands of people! It is the same media which exulted in eulogising terrorists like Abdul

Majid Dar in Kashmir the moment he showed the slightest inclination of talking with the government. It is the same media which started referring to the Hizb-ul-Mujahideen insurgents of Kashmir as 'Hizb-ul-Mujahideen commanders' when they came for talks and accorded them a respect which would have been due only to representatives of a sovereign nation at war with us. The pseudo-intellectuals of the country, who have excellent relations with the media, both react to a sustained phase of terrorism in such an effeminate manner that their collective wailing builds up an unbearable pressure on the leaders who too have no dearth of people with essentially the same bent of mind and character, and it predisposes them to react in a very predictable manner. Knee-jerk reactions are common.

No responsible citizen should ever forget the most shameful manner in which we had capitulated before the hijackers of flight IC-814. The terrorists knew that eventually we would capitulate. In a way, it contained the seeds of some very bad omens – we are inherently capable of doing that again. Trust me, I know the Indians. Intelligent terrorists have only to maintain a certain level of terrorist violence to make the people, the pseudo-intellectuals, the media and the leaders sick of it. That would usher in the 'climate of collapse' much before it actually arrives. After that the developments would take care of themselves. For example, foreign investors would lose no time in running away the moment their interests start getting systematically targeted. Then at isolated places there may be such police or army excesses as to lead to mass protests. In short, if the guerrilla or terrorists are able to use terrorist violence in such a manner as to act as a catalyst for the innate disruptive tendencies in the country or goad certain important people into taking certain decisions, an uncontrollable and unpredictable chain reaction may result which will bring us perilously close to a climate of collapse. Then they may take advantage of it in bargaining from a position of strength and extracting concessions or acceptance of demands which they could have never hoped for otherwise.

(1.4) Why Unconventional Warfare in Urban Environment Makes Great Sense?

If you find yourself in a fair fight, you didn't plan your mission properly.

Urban terrorism or urban guerrilla warfare is the most effective tool which disgruntled elements may employ against a state. Classical insurgencies of the communist type are frequently obliged to be based in rural areas because they need support of the traditionally poor, exploited and marginalised sections of the society, and also require an environment to thrive where the obstructive presence of the state and its administrative apparatus is relatively thinner. Rural areas fit into the bill perfectly. But the intrinsic disadvantage of actions in rural areas is that they may often fail to create the desired ripples in the society. The media has a pronounced urban bias and their OB vans have no interest in rushing to rural areas. To their utter dismay, the not-so-dumb terrorists realise that the killing of even 75 personnel of the security forces in a single strike in remote areas like the jungles of Chhattisgarh of central India neither creates any waves in the urban-centric Indian media nor does it lead to a spate of TV discussions and coverage in the print medium. If some film actor called Shahrukh Khan reportedly slapped the husband of some dance director called Farah Khan, it became national news in India—long stories were printed in the papers and the idiot box of course, went ballistic—who in the hell is interested in the 'killing' of some personnel of security forces? Thus the terrorists' effort goes waste for all practical purposes. On the other hand, given the way the media behaves with all its upper-middle class biases, even a firecracker blast in Sarojini Nagar market of Delhi creates a terrible noise across the country. Indian readers may also recall the terrorist attack on the five-star hotels in Bombay on 26/11. There was a tremendous outrage because it was for the first time that the rich people were targeted.

On February 10, 2012 the naxal insurgents in India used a landmine on the vehicle carrying BSF (Border Security Force) officers in a remote area in Malkangiri, Orissa and killed four, including two senior officers, one of them being the commandant of the BSF battalion operating in the area—a daring challenge to the might of the nation which has deployed 86 battalions to combat the insurgency. Yet, this received much less coverage in the *Times of India* than other incidents in urban areas on that very day—some of the urban incidents included the following reports: "Girl injured in stampede at Ramjas College annual fest" (dateline New Delhi); and 'Four youths drive away with 18-year old" and 'Girl knew an abductor: Cops' (both dateline New Delhi). Similar examples are found in other countries also. A major strike somewhere deep in Waziristan goes unnoticed whereas even a failed bomb blast in front of a hotel in Islamabad where foreigners stay, attracts attention of the world media.

In most of the countries, the interests of the ruling class are aligned with the urban upper or upper-middle classes. Thus, urban terrorist strikes produce impacts far greater on them than that by similar strikes in rural areas. Hence, for a terrorist who understand the psyche of a nation, its people, its media and its ruling class, urban terrorism makes eminent sense. The returns of urban terrorism are certainly disproportionately higher than its innate worth. Its strength lies in two words: anytime and anywhere. The fear that they can strike you anytime and anywhere makes them larger than life. The secret of the power of urban terrorism lies in the fact that they are able to create a climate of fear, panic, disorientation and capitulation out of all proportion to their actual strength courtesy an irresponsible media and an effete population under its influence.

Then there are tactical advantages also that the urban environment offers to the guerrillas. Getting lost after perpetrating a crime in the urban areas is easy—rural guerrillas will have to run scores of miles to their inaccessible refuges in the mountains or jungles. In an urban setting, the guerrilla could be living in the same apartment building as you! The urban guerrilla finds it much easier to keep in touch with his comrades in an urban setting. Further, should he be making something technically advanced, be it bomb or whatever, the technical support in an urban area is much better. Above all, the very nature of an urban area denies the use of artillery and aircraft, etc. by the government there which they can possibly use on insurgents operating from jungles or rural areas.

The urban guerrilla does not really need the support of a large number of people for shelter, logistic support and base of operations as his rural counterpart necessarily does. In fact, a few guerrillas can operate entirely on their own and commit terrible acts without even their next door neighbours getting suspicious. The EOKA in Cyprus chose to maintain a small organisation. The EOKA's active membership never exceeded 350 people, few of whom were full time. In fact, the backbone of the EOKA consisted mainly of 85 members in Nicosia, and another 34 in Limassol at the height of its power. The Basque Fatherland and Liberty had just about 200 members; so had the FLN in Algiers. If in due course, they happen to get the support of a section of the population, it is a bonus. But it also comes with the increased risk of infiltration by the security forces and intelligence operatives. The Tupamaros in Uruguay were quite successful when they were a small organisation—when their ranks swelled to about 3000, infiltration did them in. This is an operational or strategic advantage to guerrilla warfare in urban areas but can assist the tactical operations also by increased recruiting, support from outside organisations or nations, and increased internal or external pressure on the enemy to resolve the conflict on terms favourable to the guerrillas.

Bullet for bullet; shot for shot; and bomb for bomb, the asymmetric war of the urban guerrilla is the most efficient way of waging war

The expenditure is minimal and the gains are enormous. The goals of the urban guerrilla movement differ radically from the goals of the conventional military force. The secret of urban guerrilla warfare or urban terrorism is that the guerrilla or the terrorist refuses to fight on the terms of the enemy. And why should he? An urban guerrilla would be committing suicide if he were to launch himself against the overall military might of the Leviathan that is the government. Nay, nay. He must fight on his own terms. He should only create such a situation that the government, panicked in view of the brouhaha created by the media, buckles and comes to negotiate with the guerrilla on terms favourable to them. The guerrilla has to act only as the catalyst—the government would wind up out of its own weaknesses.

There could be a non-political dimension also to urban guerrilla. Organised criminal elements like the narco-terrorists in Latin American and the Russian Mafia are good candidates, for example. These organisations use violence to achieve political ends. Narco-terrorists of the Medelin drug cartel in Colombia instigated a campaign of car bombing and murder in the 1980s. This campaign eventually culminated in 1991 with the Colombian government amending the constitution to forbid extraditing drug lords to the United States as well as backing away from a crackdown on the cocaine industry. Over a 24-month period, this campaign cost more than a thousand lives and did millions of dollars worth of property damage. The rival Cali Cartel even maintains a distinct military wing. In a similar fashion, the governments of Pakistan and Brazil had to use the army to reassert control over parts of Karachi and Rio de Janeiro after they fell under the *de facto* administrative control of Organised criminal gangs. A 'criminal revolution' in Russia is also seeking to claim political power, especially at local and regional levels. This even includes the use of murder and physical intimation to influence the official process of privatising former Soviet State resources. Organised criminal groups also use widespread violence to intimidate prosecutors, judges, juries and well-known political figures from the public and private sectors that opposed them.

(1.5) The Strategy of the Urban Guerrilla

You're only better than your enemy if you kill him first.

The spectrum of urban guerrilla activities range from the most conventional to the most unusual—from demonstrations and strikes to riots; from kidnappings to assassinations; from bank robberies to looting of armouries; from terrorist bombs to raids on the establishments of the security forces; from sniper attacks to large-scale sabotage; and from ambushes to military-scale battles in the streets, the urban guerrilla has the field wide open for him.

The first thing an urban guerrilla or terrorist does is to abandon any pretense to heroism, popular support, or fair play. Urban terrorism is for the cold, calculating, ruthless men who do not mind if they are called cowards, inhuman or butchers. To him only the impact of his strikes matters. They strike at the softest of the soft targets; if they have to make a selection they make it according to the psychological impact it would produce and not by the considerations of the material damage caused. Western nations had developed elaborate doctrines on dealing with insurgencies because that was their main problem during the Cold War. Urban terrorism has flummoxed them as they cannot find doctrines to combat it. There are a large number of people involved in insurgencies and many of them could lend themselves to manipulation; the number of actors in terrorism is so small that manipulating them is more or less impossible. An insurgency can be fought to some extent on an ideological plane as well as on a very tangible plane, such as by offering a better life under the current regime by focusing on development, etc. An urban terrorist does not even make an effort to change the views or perception of the masses or bring them over to his side.

An insurgent needs to build himself to the level of his adversary; an urban terrorist never bothers to do so. He is the ultimate predator who attacks only the soft underbelly of his target however large or powerful it be. He plays upon the weaknesses of the target people. He brings their hidden fears to the fore. The upper-middle and the upper classes fear nothing more than any damage to their privileged positions and possessions. Urban terrorism threatens them right there. Shopping may no longer be enjoyable because a bomb could explode there. Somebody may start shooting at a hotel or crash a car bomb; somebody may fire at some party. Worse, political instability may result as a result of the brouhaha and the stock market may plunge. In short, urban terrorism threatens to screw their happy and cocooned existence.

The urban guerrilla is a die-hard realist. He knows that that defeating the resources of a large nation-state through guns or bombs would be impossible. On the other hand, they also realise that given the fundamentally flawed approach of the security establishment they are not likely to be faced with the prospect of immediate extinction either. Hence, he makes the best of the situation available. He measures his success in terms of how effective he is in creating havoc, a general feeling of insecurity and a loss of confidence in the government besides taxing the resources of the government in chasing shadows. Urban strikes are perfectly suited for a terrorist organisation which is low on resources. Fewer men are required; they can conceal themselves easily in an urban environment and there is little which the police can do to secure the myriads of targets which an urban area presents to the urban guerrilla even if the police are deployed very heavily. The urban terrorist approach does not require an extensive political apparatus either; rather, closely knit cells do the job.

He knows that even small urban attacks lead to a great deal of:

- Noise in the media and thus impart a larger-than-life image to the terrorists
- Panic amongst the urban population which is not used to such acts; once again helping their image
- Consequent effect on the governments because the urban-centric media and the urban population are key opinion-builders
- Knee-jerk reactions from the governments and possibly wasteful decisions
- Perfectly useless diversion of police manpower and resources to urban areas which, in any case, fails to add to their security

- The resulting depletion in the other areas which increases their vulnerability even more
- India is a particularly vulnerable target in this regard. The media here is habitually given to making more noise than anywhere else in the world for the smallest thing.

The actual physical damage caused by an attack is a bonus – what really matters is its psychological impact

(1.6) Organisation of Urban Guerrillas

Most of urban guerrilla and terrorist organisations are organised in a non-hierarchical fashion. Even where vertical definition exists, it generally consists of relatively few layers. Typically, such groups are composed of several three to ten person cells that are tightly compartmented from each other in the interest of security. (This pattern is pretty consistent across time, regardless of the nature of the group, or its location). The FLN in Algeria during the late 1950s and early 1960s provides a good example of such organisation. An FLN military director in each region headed an organisation consisting of three 11-man groups. Each group was composed of three 3-person cells plus a chief and a deputy. Additionally, there was a 50 to 150-person bomb network that was responsible directly to the zonal commander. Similarly, the Tupamaros in Uruguay were organised into two to six member cells linked together to form 'columns' that operated in particular geographic areas. All the columns were then subordinated to an overall executive committee. The IRA had an 'Army Council' that served much the same function as the executive committee of the Tupamaros and had 'Active Service Units' instead of cells. In some cases, there is also functional specialisation among the cells. Some groups, for example, appear to have maintained separate cells devoted exclusively to activities like intelligence, sniping, executions, bombings, propaganda, and robberies. Actual control is typically diffuse with each cell having a good bit of operational autonomy.

The operational cells within the 'columns' of the Italian Red Brigades were known for enjoying considerable operational autonomy. When the Northern Command of IRA wished to raise campaign funds for an upcoming election, it apparently issued instructions for all Active Service Units to raise the money, but issued no instructions as to how they were to go about doing so. Thus, questions of interpretation and implementation were left up to individual local commanders. In a sense, the relationship between the command elements of many of these organisations can best be described as one of influence more than control at the tactical level. Command elements seem to have much greater influence in determining overall objectives and strategies.

There are, however, some notable exceptions. The Greek EOKA was a thoroughly centralised and authoritarian organisation being, in the words of one observer, merely "an extension of the leader's will and personality". This same observer goes on to describe the EOKA's command structure as consisting of "one Field Marshal, a score of lieutenants, and the rest privates—and not too many privates". The small size of the EOKA, coupled with the fact that it was primarily concentrated in two cities on a small island, made such centralised command and control possible.

(1.7) Finances for an Urban Movement

Urban insurgents and terrorists cannot live by enthusiasm alone. Even Marxist idealists need a great deal of money because urban operations are expensive. A couple of historical examples shed light on the extent of this problem. The small Jewish Irgun that operated in Palestine during the 1940s needed 2,500 British pounds per month in 1945 just to meet normal operating expenses—no small sum for those times. Special operations (which were often crucial to the Irgun's success) were extra. Just one spectacular escape, for instance, might (at 3,000 pounds) cost more than the normal operating budget of an entire month. The amount needed for large groups to keep operating is sometimes staggering. The 1983 battle for Tripoli lasted 45 days and cost the PLO more than $26 million. The PLO spent approximately

$580,000 each day to pay its soldiers as well as to purchase extra arms and ammunition to continue that battle. The PLO had to spend $100 million per year on its military wing Al Fatah. Even the small, ultra-leftist German Red Army Faction needed lots of cash. This group is estimated to have raised 1.7 million Deutsche Marks from robbery and extortion by the mid-1970s. The Italian Red Brigades, for example, spent one entire million-dollar ransom within a year.

Based on debriefing of LTTE activists detained or co-operating, and LTTE financial reports recovered by governments worldwide, the LTTE was a very wealthy terrorist and insurgent group. The LTTE raised $ 25 million to 50 million per year from 1987 to 1993, $ 50 to 75 million per year from 1993 to 2002 and $ 200 million per year from 2002 to 2008. At its peak the LTTE was worth $ 300 million. The LTTE had multiple sources of income. The principal sources were individual collection and LTTE businesses. The businesses included investment in real estate, shipping, grocery stores, gold and jewellery stores, gas stations, restaurants, production of films, mass media organisations (TV, radio, print), industries, and in several other sectors. By creating front, cover and sympathetic organisations, the LTTE accessed government and NGO funding under the guise of reintegrating new migrants to host society. For example, LTTE affiliates in Canada used deception to access several million dollars from metro, provincial and federal governments. The LTTE's premier front Tamil Rehabilitation Organisation raised millions of dollars that went into procuring arms, ammunition and explosives from North Korea, the principal supplier of weapons to the LTTE since 1997. Unfortunately, it took several years for governments worldwide to work together to dismantle the LTTE international network.

Largely due to the good work of the western security and intelligence services in the West, the LTTE international network was rendered almost bankrupt by early 2009. Although unacknowledged, the LTTE cells were disrupted globally starting with the US. The disruption of the three LTTE fund-raising and procurement cells in the US monitored by the FBI even before 9/11 created the impetus for Canada, Europe and Australia to share information and intelligence on the LTTE. This spate of operations led the US, India and a few other countries to share intelligence on the LTTE ships transporting weapons from North Korea to the LTTE leading to their destruction. Due to financial difficulties, the LTTE found it exceptionally difficult to organise even the last shipment of weapons transported on board MV Princess Easwary in early 2009.

Urban groups need such large amounts of money in part because of inefficiencies in their collection and distribution process. Sometimes, a group must split the 'take' with its criminal partners. For example, the Red Brigades in Italy had to divide one $2 million ransom evenly with the Camorra criminal syndicate. Ransom money and the proceeds from bank robberies usually must be laundered through professionals because the authorities have a list of the serial numbers of the individual bills. The cost of doing so is high – usually a running 30 per cent of every note exchanged.

The Red Army Faction described bank robberies in the following way: "No one claims that bank robbery of itself changes anything. For the revolutionary organisation it means first of all a solution of its financial problems. It is logistically correct, since otherwise the financial problem could not be solved at all. It is politically correct because it is an act of dispossession. It is tactically correct because it is a proletarian action. It is strategically correct because it serves the financing of the guerrilla".

Kidnapping for ransom has remained one of the most popular and enduring techniques for raising money everywhere, especially in Latin America and Europe. Businesses often do not admit to kidnapping since to do so would invite government pressure to withhold the ransom. Also, firms have an interest in denying payoffs both to discourage imitators and to hide the extent of their business losses. Some multi-national companies stated policy of not ransoming kidnapped employees is actually no more than a public gesture to appease the local government. The ransom provides essential operating funds to the group at considerably less risk than bank robberies. But equally important, such actions are seen as striking powerful psychological blows at the social hierarchy of the state, the detested capitalist system in general, and/or at the 'international imperialism' of multi-national corporations in specific. This offers the secondary benefit of increasing the political standing of the group among its main target audience. Thus, ideology and financial gain coalesce into a single act whereby the state is weakened and the urban revolutionary's coffers are filled.

Marxist groups in Latin America have often shaken the money tree vigorously in the past through hostage and ransom schemes. The US State Department calls ransom one of the major sources of finance for such Latin American groups and claims that guerrillas in Colombia earn "millions of dollars" each year in this way. In 1994, kidnappers in Guatemala earned more than $35 million by seizing 3 to 4 wealthy people per month on average. The Exxon Corporation paid $14.2 million to a Marxist group in Argentina to release Victor Samuelson, one of their executives. The all time record, however, is $60 million paid to the Monteneros in Argentina for returning the Juan and Jorge Born who owned the grain- exporting firm of Bunge & Born. In addition to the $60 million ransom, the group insisted that the company distribute $1 million in food and clothing to the poor. The Argentine government for example complained that the $60 million paid for the return of Juan and Jorge Born equaled one third of the national defence budget. Basque Fatherland and Liberty also often engages in kidnapping for ransom schemes and, on several occasions, has received ransoms of more than $1 million.

Groups have long strong-armed "revolutionary taxes" from local businesses, the general population, and ex-patriots abroad through threats and violence. Sometimes, friendly third-party states have even assisted the group in collecting such "taxes" from local immigrants. During the 1970s and 1980s, every Palestinian was obliged to donate 5 to 10 per cent of his income to the PLO. In two places (Libya and Algeria), the government permitted this amount to be deducted before the worker received his pay. The Kurdistan Workers Party follows the same practice of "taxing" Kurdish "guest workers" in Germany today. Loyalist and Catholic paramilitary groups in Northern Ireland had advanced the protection racket to a veritable art form. In the north-eastern states of India, this extortion has been a very old racket. The paper *Hindustan Times* had estimated in 2008 that the naxal insurgents were raising as much as Rs 3200 million per year from extortions – the victims being mining companies, and local industries.

The transportation, distribution, and sales of illegal drugs have become another major source of funds for many urban insurgent and terrorist groups. The profits from such efforts are so large that, in some cases, the potential for personal profits in drug-trafficking was a major recruiting incentive in places like Turkey and Northern Ireland. Predictably, the groups with the strongest ties to the drug-trafficking business come from Latin America. M-19 and FARC from Colombia both get a large per centage of their funds from drugs. Both groups provide protection to drug producers in exchange for large payments.

(1.8) Psychological Make-up of Urban Guerrillas

Culture shapes the values of many urban paramilitary groups and sometimes motivates them to actions that seem unreasonable to foreign observers. One of the major cultural determinants of behaviour is the perception of 'outsiders' and the expected threat they pose to an ethnic group's survival. Fear of cultural extermination often leads to violence that may seem irrational to those outsiders. Also in societies in which people identify themselves in terms of group membership (e.g., family, clan, tribe) there may be a willingness to self-sacrifice seldom seen elsewhere.

Religion may be the most volatile of cultural identifiers because it encompasses deeply held values. Also religion can reinforce ethnicity to make a conflict more intractable. This sentiment is echoed in an interview with Abu Mohammed, a prominent member of a radical Islamic group in Algeria today. As he explains to the interviewer, "According to Islamic Law you cannot negotiate with apostates". Abu Mohammed goes on to say even more succinctly: "no talks with heretics". The religiously motivated see violence first and foremost as a sacramental act or as a divine duty executed in direct response to some theological imperative. Their actions are morally certain and divinely sanctioned.

The behaviour of individual urban guerrillas and terrorists is also shaped by certain psychological traits. Usually, for example, they are motivated to act in response to a real or perceived grievance. They are very sensitive to the injustices done to them and quick to accuse others. They become, in the words of one psychologist, insatiable 'justice collectors' who seek retribution and amelioration of that grievance. That is, they respond to what they perceive as an 'intolerable' injustice by taking matters into their own hands.

Urban guerrillas and terrorists also project their own anti-society motivations onto others, thereby creating a dualistic 'us versus them' outlook. The motives of those outside the group are evil. Those of the group are righteous. According to this way of thinking, there is only one path to correct behaviour – the one sanctioned and approved by the group. The group reserves to itself the right to judge and punish the behaviour of others. This also allows members of the group to dehumanise their victims and remove any sense of ambiguity from their minds. This, in turn, permits the group to justify violence against virtually any target outside itself.

Predictably, activists are often absolutists and 'true believers' who reject the idea of compromise and lean toward maximalist positions. They also demand unanimity and are intolerant of dissent within the group. This explains why urban guerrilla and terrorist groups are prone to splintering and why those breakaway groups tend to be more intellectually rigid and violence prone than the parent organisation.

Individual urban guerrillas and terrorists also have a deeply rooted psychological need to belong to a group. Group acceptance is often a stronger motive for joining than the stated political objectives of the organisation. In such circumstances, individuals tend to define their social status in terms of group acceptance. Perhaps because of the powerful psychological attraction of belonging, some groups lose their focus and the struggle eventually becomes more important than attaining their stated objectives. For this reason (and also because the original aim may be elusive in any case), the struggle must never end. Consequently, announced aims may change just at the point where victory appears in sight. This behaviour pattern may explain why the IRA abruptly returned to violence in 1997 just when, in the words of *The Economist*, "many of its demands [for inclusion in the political process] were being met".

At the rational level, violent acts attract the world's attention to the group's cause, intimidate its foes, and demonstrate the impotence of the government to provide security. At the subconscious level, violence relieves an urban guerrilla's or terrorist's constant sense of anger about his personal condition. They come to believe that one must destroy in order to save.

Violence is directed both inwardly and outwardly. Indeed, violence is often used against members of the group who do not conform to the 'party line' or who are wavering in their commitment. Inwardly directed violence against a wayward member also provides a powerful warning for others. Members often find that is much easier to join such an organisation than to leave it. Violence also provides a way of reinforcing the loyalty of people in the target constituency and of distancing them from government authorities.

Higher casualty rates from religious and cult groups are not accidental. They consciously strive to kill all of their enemies, in part because God has sanctioned it and in part because they see their enemies as non-people. This point is illustrated by the chilling words of senior Islamic cleric Imam Sheikh Ahmad Ibrahim's oft repeated call to arms: "Six million descendants of monkeys [i.e., Jews] now rule in all the nations of the world, but their day, too, will come. Allah! Kill them all, do not leave even one".

Action is also important as a means of maintaining group self-esteem, sense of purpose, and legitimacy. Additionally, action provides a way of building more intensely personal loyalties and group solidarity through mutually shared experiences. In small organisations led by charismatic father-figures, action provides a vehicle for revalidating his authority and claim on the loyalty of his followers. Eventually, some urban guerrillas and terrorists become, in the words of one psychologist, 'action addicts' who crave the action 'high' in the same way that other addicts long for drugs or alcohol.

(1.9) How the Targets Play into the Hands of the Urban Terrorist?

As the famous adage "Kill one, terrorise a thousand" beautifully illustrates, albeit somewhat simplistically, the real or perceived success of a terrorist depends essentially on the reaction of the target to his acts or threats. Therefore, in order to understand the advantage which terrorists have, we must first understand the behavioural patterns of the targets. Once we understand how and why terrorism works, the knowledge can be used by the targets or potential targets of terrorism to ultimately beat terrorism in its psychological game. If the target is fully aware of the perceptions that eventually lead to the response that corresponds with the purpose of the terrorists, it can be made to alter its perceptions and respond in a different way. The mere act of doing this will be tantamount to a defeat of the terrorist because he would have failed in eliciting the desired response from the target. In the following paragraphs we present an analysis of the factors and phenomena which make urban terrorism effective.

The theory of over-reaction: Over-reaction by a target is a very familiar pattern of behaviour. When a target perceives itself to be righteous, the terrorists to be the epitome of evil, and maintains that in terms of its power to respond it is in an overwhelmingly superior position, it is likely to over-react. The target may over-react in two ways. If it prefers extensive and ostentatious protective measures, it unknowingly and unwittingly exaggerates the political stature and threat capability of the terrorists. India is a classic example of this phenomenon. Further, if the target resorts to an indiscriminate use of force, it may quite possibly harm even the innocents. Such victims are quite likely to become more and more receptive to the terrorists. In both situations, the advantage goes to the terrorists.

The theory of power deflation: A target that is somehow incapable of responding effectively to terrorism lands itself in a vicious circle. It loses the support and the confidence of the people which ultimately reduce its capabilities and confidence to cope with terrorism in future. In this case the target perceives itself to be harassed by its enemies and lacking the public support it thinks it deserves; it also perceives the terrorists as rather clever and formidable foes. Further, even if the target knows that its overall military might is excessive in comparison to that of the terrorists, it finds itself weakened and handicapped by a lack of intelligence or viable military options thereby finding itself unable to act effectively against the terrorists. The simple fact is that if the regime cannot protect its people then it loses all moral claims to legitimacy. The success of the terrorists is even greater and plain for all to see if they are able to choose the timing and victims of their strikes without any hindrance, and then successfully secure the release of prisoners, have their manifestos or demands publicised in the media, or even kill the victims. The ignominy of the state is compounded if the terrorists are able to completely avoid any effective retaliation by the state, especially if the target is shameless enough to persist in publicly speaking of all sorts of anti-terrorist motions and proclamations. Only a completely shameless state can live with such a situation. If it survives the opprobrium it is only because the people of the nation are as indifferent to the honour of the nation as their government. Really, people get the government they deserve. If the people do not condemn their governments for its acts of capitulation, the governments persist in disgraceful acts. A soft state, by its repeated acts of capitulation before the terrorists, not only deflates its power and disorientates itself in its approach to terrorism; it helps in making the terrorists far bigger than what they really are.

The theory of failed repression of the moderates: In this case the target suffers from the mental state of a besieged person. Finding itself unable to cope with the terrorists directly, it vents its ire on the moderate, non-violent opposition as well. Actually, it becomes a last ditch effort to preserve its authority. The target comes to believe that reforms or buying off the opposition will not suffice and repression is the only solution. It may then go on to ban political parties, NGOs, institute censorship, increase surveillance, go for large-scale arrests of protesters and even secretly eliminate some leaders as a veiled threat. Little does it realise that repression is an act of desperation and has a high probability of failure. The problem is that though the regime tries to be ruthless, it really finds itself unable to become sufficiently ruthless as it, at the same time, does not want to shed its cloak of liberalism for the world to see. The result of such a use of insufficient and inefficient force is that the moderates become more prone to be driven into the folds of the terrorists. They may very well conclude that moderation is untenable and in order to protect themselves, switch their allegiance to the terrorists. Thus, the target finds itself in a position where the mild opposition converts into militant opposition thereby strengthening the terrorists and, at the same time, weakening itself as a result of the physical and mental costs of repression.

The theory of appeasing the moderates: This situation is really a euphemistic way of describing the beginning of the capitulation of a regime. It is essentially a face-saving device. The target, deep down its heart, admits that it cannot cope with the terrorists. Yet it finds itself ashamed of admitting it openly as that would involve an enormous loss of face. The target gets prepared to accede to some or all of the demands of the terrorists. However, instead of giving in directly to the terrorists, it seeks to accomplish the same effect by granting essentially the same things to the moderates. The regime thus saves face by bowing before the moderates, claiming that it has bowed before a legitimate entity and not the illegitimate entity, that is, the terrorists. The facade is only for the rest of the world. The terrorists know it very well that it is because of them that the concessions have been granted. Their purpose is served—it is quite possible that they had been using the moderates all along as a legitimate 'front' to deal with precisely such a situation. Let us be very clear—granting political reforms, autonomy, special status or all sorts of largesse is not an immoral thing by itself. It becomes immoral when it is done under coercion from the terrorists. It becomes all the more immoral when the state does not have enough moral integrity to admit its failure and the reforms are instituted indirectly in the name of the moderates. Terrorists all over the world understand this weakness of the states and always keep some moderates, intellectuals or political fronts handy to extract the maximum advantage for them in the negotiations. In effect it boils down to the terrorists achieving their purpose through some middlemen who could be treated as legitimate by the state.

The theory of intimidation: This is a variation of the theory of power deflation, but with a subtle difference. In the case of power deflation, the target is unable to respond to terrorism. In the case of intimidation, the target is able to respond but does not because of several reasons. In the first place the target does not have any scientific and well-conceived political strategy to deal with terrorism. Secondly, the target is not only unsure of its convictions but is also quite apprehensive of the consequences of any possible actions it might take, either elsewhere in the nation or in the international arena. Thirdly, the target seems to have an underlying fear that the terrorists could outmanoeuvre it, and thus feels vulnerable. Thus, the target is intimidated into inaction or obedience of the terrorists.

(1.10) The Key to Combating Terrorism

Terrorism becomes effective only if the target makes it so. When a nation responds to a few small blasts as if a national calamity has struck; when a nation describes small blasts as 'highly sophisticated blasts' caused by a mysterious thing called 'embedded chips'; when a nation attributes goddamn everything to the ISI, a couple of leaders of the LeT, Dawood Ibrahim or CAM Basheer, it unknowingly adorns the culprits with an aura which they don't deserve. If at all it shows anything, it is sheer ignorance. These characters have been out of the reach of the Indian law for years and we have not been able to do anything. But by invoking their name all the time, we help create a larger-than-life image of these people which is, in fact, detrimental to the morale of the nation. To make the people believe that just a couple of individuals are able to strike in India at will is to announce the impotence of the nation-state and make people lose confidence in it.

Terrorists will shift even the theater of operations to stay in news. The Provisional Irish Republican Army's out-of-theater operations against British interests in England and Europe are an example of this phenomenon. They apparently realised that bombings in Northern Ireland had lost much of their shock value after two decades of violence. Therefore the PIRA shifted their bombing campaign to Britain proper and to Europe since targeting these sites still had the capacity to disturb people and grab the attention of the news media. Chechen groups also realised the psychological shock value of operating on Russian soil. Therefore, they sent a 100-man raiding party to seize hostages in the Russian town of Budyonnovsk in June 1995, and then followed that operation seven months later by capturing a hospital and maternity home in the town of Kizlar. Botched rescue attempts by Russian security forces in both cases led to an even greater propaganda victory for Chechen paramilitary forces.

The effectiveness of Israeli security forces also probably explains why Islamic fundamentalist groups so often strike outside Israel. Out-of-theater operations offer one more way to demoralise military personnel by demonstrating to them that they can never truly escape the battle zone. As one pro-IRA newspaper so eloquently explained in 1980: "Overseas attacks also have a prestige value and internationalise the war in Ireland. We have kept Ireland in the world headlines".

Proper timing is another central feature in the strategies of urban paramilitary and terrorist groups. The news value of an event often hinges on its timing. The timing of the attack (e.g., a religious holiday, a weekend, or immediately following a successful government operation) may catch the security forces in a lower state of readiness and its people less alert. This explains why Algeria's Armed Islamic Group (GIA) hijacked an Air France Airbus A 300 on Christmas Eve 1994 to demonstrate its demands that France stop supporting the

Algerian government. Proper timing can also heighten the shock value of an event such as when the Irish Republican Army consciously chose to bomb Harrods Department Store in London during the 1983 Christmas season. Nations must not over-react to these things.

Terrorism, to be successful, expects that the target must respond in a certain manner. The fact of responding in an expected manner is such that it weakens the target, both in image and reality. Deny the terrorist the pleasure of the expected response and you have beaten him. One should always keep in mind that while the root causes of terrorism could be political, sociological or whatever, the impact of terrorism is determined to a great extent by the target's behaviour, which is largely psychological in character. The design of the terrorist is to manipulate the target's psychological perceptions to induce it to act in the way it is predisposed to act.

The effort of those who have to combat terrorism must be to refuse to act in a predictable or expected manner, and least of all in a manner that serves the purpose of the terrorists. Prudent targets must not behave as automatons. For example, if the terrorists perceive a target as powerful and self-righteous, they should expect it to over-react; certainly they would not expect it to suffer from power deflation, repress moderates, appease moderates, or be intimidated. Now, if the target, despite being powerful and self-righteous, has over-reacted, it has played into the hands of the terrorists. To avoid this, the target must not over-react. It is only through knowledge of one's own perceptions and how they can be manipulated that one learns to avoid the propensity to make particular mistakes. There is no way a modern large nation can prevent a terrorist from striking, whatever we may try; we can, however, learn to react in a more mature way.

And remember that lack of fancy equipment and harsh laws is not to be blamed for your failure in handling terrorism. This is throwing the blame of your intrinsic weaknesses on to something utterly simplistic. This is the most favourite theory of the establishment, the media, the politicians, the police officers and the intelligence agencies—we have the problem of terrorism because we do not have adequate number of policemen and sufficiently harsh laws! Simple! Give us enough powers and resources and we will root it out! Unfortunately, it is not true. It only betrays an extremely poor understanding of the phenomenon of terrorism. You can make every single cop in the country a commando; you can equip him with the best that money can buy (as dumb journalists are fond of suggesting)—from passive night vision device, blast-proof eyewear, helmet with built-in hands-free communication, Nomex overall, body-worn camera, Level 3 bullet-proof vest, knee pad, non-skid shoes, Kevlar tactical gloves, hydraulic ram for building intervention, corner-shot for pistol, helicopter drone with shotgun, free fall parachute, mobile command post, anti-material rifle, and Gatling gun; the works—still that would not solve the problem. These guys look up things over the Internet or Discovery Channel's 'Future Weapons' programme and think that fancy items are the solution to everything. They lamented that the average cop does no firing practice. No problem, sir, we will make him a marksman. But will that prevent the other guy from becoming a terrorist in the first place? After all, how many we can kill or convict? Terrorism, by its very nature, defies such gung-ho police solutions—those who have any faith in this have not risen above the intellectual level of police sub-inspectors!

Terrorism defies standard 'police' solutions or short-term solutions—we must learn to attack it at its roots. One journalist has offered a 'clever' solution: "In the long run, terrorism of the kind we are experiencing can only be defeated if the people on whose behalf the terrorists claim they are acting repudiate them and force them to stay away, or inform the police of their plans. But for this the community as a whole must feel that the police and the majority community are their friends". How simple! In effect the journalist is advising that if the police become people-friendly, the people will become informers and we will be able to defeat terrorists. Isn't it a revelation? You never knew that the root of the problem lay at the bad behaviour of the police.

2

Minimanual of the Urban Guerrilla: Marighella's Detailed Roadmap

Disguise fair nature with hard-favour'd rage.

(2.1) The Giant is Known by his Toe

Never forget that no military leader has ever become great without audacity. If the leader is filled with high ambition and if he pursues his aims with audacity and strength of will, he will reach them in spite of all obstacles.

Carlos Marighella (d.1969), was a Brazilian Marxist revolutionary and writer. Marighella's most famous contribution to guerrilla literature was the 'Minimanual of the Urban Guerrilla', from which the excerpts are reproduced here. It consists of advice on how to disrupt and overthrow an authoritarian regime aiming a revolution. He also wrote 'For the Liberation of Brazil'. The theories laid out in both books have greatly influenced contemporary ideological activism. Unlike Ernesto 'Che' Guevara, who argued for guerrilla activity in the countryside in the classical communist fashion, Marighella's theories on urban guerrilla warfare envisaged cities as the source of rebellion. Written in 1969, it is still a source of inspiration to innumerous romantic revolutionaries across the world. As he says in the introduction to the work: "The accusation of 'violence' or 'terrorism' no longer has the negative meaning it used to have. It has acquired new clothing; a new colour. It does not divide, it does not discredit; on the contrary, it represents a center of attraction. Today, to be 'violent' or a 'terrorist' is a quality that ennobles any honourable person, because it is an act worthy of a revolutionary engaged in armed struggle against the shameful military dictatorship and its atrocities". Readers would admire the cold-blooded ruthlessness with which he describes the actions that he prescribes for the urban guerrilla—leaders and strategists of the nations battling urban guerrillas must study this if they ever hope to fight them credibly. The following are excerpts from the famous 'minimanual'.

The urban guerrilla follows a political goal, and only attacks the government, the big businesses and the foreign imperialists. The urban guerrilla is an implacable enemy of the regime, and systematically inflicts damage on the authorities and on the people who dominate the country and exercise power. The primary task of the urban guerrilla is to distract, to wear down, to demoralise the military regime and its repressive forces, and also to attack and destroy the wealth and property of the foreign managers and the upper class. The urban guerrilla is not afraid to dismantle and destroy the present (Brazilian) economic, political and social system.

(2.1.1) *Personal Qualities of the Urban Guerrilla*

A leader is a man who had the ability to get other people to do what they don't want to do, and like it.

The urban guerrilla must be a person of great cleverness to compensate for the fact that he is not sufficiently strong in weapons, ammunition and equipment. The guerrilla may also be a convicted person or one who is out on parole, and must then use false documents. Because his weapons are not uniform, the urban guerrilla faces the problem of a variety of weapons and a shortage of ammunition. Moreover, he has no place in which to practice shooting and marksmanship. These difficulties have to be overcome, forcing the urban guerrillas to be imaginative and creative. The urban guerrilla must possess initiative, mobility and flexibility, as well as versatility and a command of any situation. Initiative especially is an indispensable quality. It is better to err acting than to do nothing for fear of making a mistake. Without initiative, there is no urban guerrilla warfare.

(2.1.2) *How the Urban Guerrilla lives and Operates*

The urban guerrilla must know how to live among the people, and he must be careful not to appear strange and different from ordinary city life. The urban guerrilla must make his living through his job or his professional activity. If he is known and sought by the police, he must go underground, and sometimes must live hidden. Under such circumstances, the urban guerrilla cannot reveal his activity to anyone, since this information is always and only the responsibility of the revolutionary organisation in which he is participating.

The armed struggle of the urban guerrilla points towards two essential objectives:

1. The physical elimination of the leaders and assistants of the armed forces and of the police because men of the government, agents of the dictatorship and of foreign imperialism, especially, must pay with their lives for the crimes they have committed against the people.
2. The expropriation of government resources and the wealth belonging to the rich businessmen, the large landowners and the imperialists, with small expropriations used for the sustenance of the individual guerrillas and large ones for the maintenance of the revolutionary organisation itself.

The fruit of these expropriations has been devoted to the tasks of learning and perfecting urban guerrilla techniques, the purchase, production and transportation of weapons and ammunition for the rural areas, the security precautions of the guerrillas, the daily maintenance of the fighters, those who have been liberated from prison by armed force, those who have been wounded, and those who are being persecuted by the police, and to any kind of problem concerning comrades liberated from jail or assassinated by the police and the military dictatorship. The bank robberies carried out by the (Brazilian) urban guerrillas hurt big businesses and others, the foreign companies which insure and re-insure the banking capital, the imperialist companies, the federal and state governments.

(2.1.3) *Technical Preparation of the Urban Guerrilla*

Be polite. Be professional. But have a plan to kill everyone you meet.

No one can become an urban guerrilla without paying special attention to technical preparation. It is very important to learn how to drive a car, pilot a plane, handle a motor boat and a sailboat, understand mechanics, radio, telephone, electricity and have some knowledge of electronics. In the area of 'makeshift' medicine, the urban guerrilla has the special role of being a doctor or understanding medicine, nursing, pharmacology, drugs, basic surgery and emergency first-aid. Among the explosives, the use of incendiary bombs, smoke bombs, and other types is also indispensable prior training. They must know how to improvise explosives, grenades, mines and weapons; how to blow up bridges; and tear up and put out of service railroads and railroad cars.

Experience in metallurgy and on the mechanical lathe is basic skill the urban guerrilla should incorporate into his manufacturing plans for the construction of homemade weapons. Courses in explosives and sabotage must be organised. The primary materials for practice in these courses must be obtained ahead of time, to prevent an incomplete apprenticeship—that is to say, so as to leave no room for experimentation. Molotov cocktails, gasoline, homemade contrivances such as catapults and mortars for firing explosives, grenades made of pipes and cans, smoke bombs, mines, conventional explosives such as dynamite, plastic explosives, gelatin capsules, and ammunition of every kind are indispensable to the success of the urban guerrilla's mission.

To prevent his own death, the urban guerrilla must shoot first, and he cannot err in his shot. The urban guerrilla can lose no time, and thus has to be able to shoot at once. Shooting must be practiced until it becomes a reflex action on the part of the urban guerrilla. Shooting and marksmanship are the urban guerrilla's water and air. His perfection of the art of shooting may make him a special type of urban guerrilla—that is, a sniper, a category of solitary combatant indispensable in isolated actions.

(2.1.4) The Firing Group

In order to function, the urban guerrillas must be organised into small groups. A team of no more than four or five is called a firing group. The firing group plans and executes urban guerrilla actions. A minimum of two firing groups, separated and insulated from other firing groups, directed and co-ordinated by one or two persons, this is what makes a firing team.

There is no such thing as a firing group without its own initiative. For this reason, it is essential to avoid any rigidity in the guerrilla organisation, in order to permit the greatest possible initiative on the part of the firing group. The old-type hierarchy, the style of the traditional revolutionaries, doesn't exist in our organisation. This means that, except for the priority of the objectives set by the strategic command, any firing group can decide to raid a bank, to kidnap or execute an agent of the dictatorship, a figure identified with the reaction, or a foreign spy, and can carry out any type of propaganda or war of nerves against the enemy, without the need to consult with the general command. No firing group can remain inactive waiting for orders from above. Its obligation is to act.

This method of action eliminates the need for knowing who is carrying out which actions, and thus helps greatly when you run the risk of being captured by the police.

(2.1.5) Logistics of the Urban Guerrilla

Logistics for the 'gorillas' (forces of the government) can be expressed with the formula FFEA:

- F – food
- F – fuel
- E – equipment
- A – ammunition

For the urban guerrilla, however, logistics are expressed by the formula MMWAE, which is:

- M – mechanisation
- M – money
- W – weapons
- A – ammunition
- E – explosives

Revolutionary logistics takes mechanisation as one of its bases. Every good urban guerrilla must be a driver. An experienced driver is not made in one day, and apprenticeship must begin early.

Once he has weapons, ammunition and explosives, one of the most serious logistics problems facing the urban guerrilla is a hiding place in which to leave the material, and appropriate means of transporting it and assembling it where it is needed. This has to be accomplished even when the enemy is alerted and has the roads blocked. The knowledge that the urban guerrilla possesses of the terrain, and the devices he uses or is capable of using, such as scouts specially prepared and recruited for this mission, are the basic elements in solving the eternal logistics problems faced by the guerrillas.

(2.1.6) *Characteristics of the Urban Guerrilla's Tactics*

The tactics of the urban guerrilla have the following characteristics:

1. It is an aggressive tactic, or, in other words, it has an offensive character. As is well-known, defensive action means death for us. Since we are inferior to the enemy in firepower, and have neither his resources nor his power base, we cannot defend ourselves against an offensive or a concentrated attack by the 'gorillas'. That is the reason why our urban technique can never be permanent, can never defend a fixed base nor remain in any one spot waiting to repel the circle of repression.
2. It is a tactic of attack and rapid withdrawal, by which we preserve our forces.
3. It is a tactic that aims at the development of urban guerrilla warfare, whose function will be to wear out, demoralise and

distract the enemy forces, permitting the emergence and survival of rural guerrilla warfare, which is destined to play the decisive role in the revolutionary war.

(2.1.7) *The Initial Advantages of the Urban Guerrilla*

The dynamics of urban guerrilla warfare lie in the guerrilla's violent clash with the military and police forces of the dictatorship. In this conflict, the police have superiority. The urban guerrilla has inferior forces. The paradox is that the urban guerrilla is nevertheless the attacker. The military and police forces, for their part, respond to the conflict by mobilising and concentrating greatly superior forces in the pursuit and destruction of the urban guerrilla. The guerrilla can only avoid defeat if he depends on the initial advantages he has and knows how to exploit them to the end, to compensate for his weakness and lack of material. The initial advantages are:

1. He must take the enemy by surprise.
2. He must know the terrain of the encounter.
3. He must have greater mobility and speed than the police and other repressive forces.
4. His information service must be better than the enemy's.
5. He must be in command of the situation, and demonstrate decisiveness so great that everyone on our side is inspired and never thinks of hesitating, while on the other side the enemy is stunned and incapable of acting.

The enemy has no way to combat surprise and becomes confused and is destroyed. The technique of surprise is based upon four essential requirements:

1. We know the situation of the enemy we are going to attack, usually by means of precise information and meticulous observation, while the enemy does not know he is going to be attacked and knows nothing about the attackers.
2. We know the strength of the enemy we are going to attack, and the enemy knows nothing about our strength.
3. Attacking by surprise, we save and conserve our forces, while the enemy is unable to do the same, and is left at the mercy of events.
4. We determine the time and place of the attack, fix its duration and establish its objectives. The enemy remains ignorant of all of this information.

To have the terrain as an ally means to know how to use with intelligence its paths and shortcuts; its empty lots; its underground passages; its pipes and sewer systems; its fixed and secret passages; its abandoned areas; its thickets; streets under repair; police checkpoints; military zones and closed-off streets; entrances and exits to tunnels and those that the enemy can close off; corners controlled or watched by the police; traffic lights and signals; etc. The guerrilla must take maximum advantage of all of this for the success of armed actions, escapes, retreats, covers, and hiding places. Being familiar with the places with which the police is unfamiliar, the urban guerrilla can surprise the police in a fatal ambush; and never be trapped himself.

Acting in small groups with only a few people, the guerrillas can rendezvous at a time and place determined beforehand, following up the initial attack with new guerrilla operations, or evading the police cordon and disorienting the enemy with their unexpected audacity. It is an impossible problem for the police, in the labyrinthine terrain of the urban guerrilla, to catch someone they cannot see, to repress someone they cannot catch, and to close in on someone they cannot find. The police pursue the urban guerrilla blindly, without knowing which road he is using for his escape. While the urban guerrilla escapes quickly because he knows the terrain, the police lose the trail and give up the chase.

Mobility requires mechanisation and an extensive knowledge of the terrain. If he can disrupt enemy transport and communications, it will be good for him. By carefully carrying out operations that last only a few moments, and leaving the site in mechanised vehicles, the urban guerrilla beats a rapid retreat, escaping capture. The urban guerrilla must know the way in detail, and, in this manner, must go through the schedule ahead of time as a training, to avoid entering alleyways that have no exit, or running into traffic jams. Tangled and treacherous traffic is a disadvantage for the enemy, as it would be for us if we were not ahead of him. Do not be afraid of the helicopter because it will never succeed in hitting from above a target that is lost among the crowds and street vehicles.

By whatever means, the sources of information at the disposal of the urban guerrilla are potentially better than those of the police. The enemy is observed by the people, but he does not know who among the people transmits information to the urban guerrillas. Information represents an extraordinary potential in the hands of the urban guerrilla. The creation of an intelligence service, with an organised structure, is a basic need for us. The enemy also wants to know what actions we are planning, so he can destroy us or prevent us from acting. The enemy therefore encourages betrayal and infiltrates spies into the guerrilla organisation. The urban guerrilla's technique against this enemy tactic is to denounce publicly the spies, traitors, informers and provocateurs. For his part, the urban guerrilla must not evade the duty—once he knows who the spy or informer is—of physically wiping him out. For complete success in the battle against spies and informers, it is essential to organise a counter-espionage or counter-intelligence service.

It is impossible to carry out any action, however well-planned, if the urban guerrilla turns out to be indecisive, uncertain, and irresolute. Decisiveness means to put into practice the plan that has been devised with determination, with audacity, and with an absolute firmness. It takes only one person who hesitates to lose all.

(2.1.8) Objectives of the Guerrilla's Actions

With his tactics developed and established, the urban guerrilla trains himself in methods of action leading to attack, and has the following objectives:

1. To weaken the security systems of the regime, given the fact that we are attacking and the 'gorillas' defending, which means catching the government in a defensive position with its troops immobilised in the defence of the entire complex of national maintenance, with its ever-present fears of an attack on its strategic nerve centers, and without ever knowing where, how or when the attack will come.
2. To attack every area with many different armed groups, small in size, each self-contained and operating independently, to disperse the government forces in their pursuit of a thoroughly fragmented organisation, instead of offering the regime the opportunity to concentrate its forces in the destruction of one tightly organised system operating throughout the country.
3. To give proof of its combativenes, decision, firmness, determination, and persistence in the attack on the regime, in order to allow all rebels to follow in our example and to fight with urban guerrilla tactics. Meanwhile, the government with all of its problems, incapable of halting guerrilla actions within the cities, will lose time and suffer endless attrition, and will finally be forced to pull back its repressive forces in order to mount guard over all the banks, industries, armouries, military barracks, prisons, public offices, radio and television stations, big firms, gas storage tanks, oil refineries, ships, ports, airplanes, airports, hospitals, health centers, blood banks, stores, garages, embassies, residences of high-

ranking members of the regime such as ministers and generals, police stations, official organisations, etc.

4. To increase urban guerrilla actions gradually into an endless number of surprise raids, such that the government cannot leave the urban area to pursue guerrillas in the rural interior without running the risk of abandoning the cities and permitting rebellion to increase on the coast as well as the interior of the country.
5. To force the Army and the police, their commanders and their assistants, to give up the relative comfort and tranquility of their barracks and their usual rest, for a state of fear and growing tension in the expectation of attack, or in a search for trails which vanish without a trace.
6. To avoid open battle and decisive combat with the government, limiting the struggle to brief, rapid attacks with lightning results.

(2.1.9) Tactics of the Urban Guerrilla

"The giant is known by his toe." The same can be said of the urban guerrilla, who is known from afar by his correct tactics and his absolute fidelity to principle. In order to achieve the objectives previously listed, the urban guerrilla is obliged, in his tactics, to follow missions whose nature is as different or diversified as possible. Some of the missions the urban guerrilla can undertake are described below.

Assaults are the armed attacks which we make to expropriate funds, liberate prisoners, and capture explosives, weapons and ammunition. Targets are selected on the basis of their vulnerability and must include financial institutions. Raids and penetrations are rapid attacks on establishments located in neighbourhoods, or even in the center of the city, such as small military units, commissaries, hospitals, to cause trouble, seize weapons, punish and terrorise the enemy, take reprisals, or to rescue wounded prisoners or those hospitalised under police guard. Raids and penetrations are also made on garages and depots to destroy vehicles and damage installations. When they take place on certain stretches of highway or in certain distant neighbourhoods, these raids can serve to force the enemy to move great numbers of troops, a totally useless effort since when they get there they will find nobody to fight.

(2.1.10) Bloody, Bold and Resolute

The occupation of factories and schools during strikes, or at other times, is a method of protest or of distracting the enemy's attention. The

If the urban guerrillas know their job, they would be bloody, bold and resolute

occupation of radio stations is for propaganda purposes. Occupation is a highly effective model for action but, in order to prevent losses and material damage to our forces, it is always a good idea to plan on the possibility of a forced withdrawal. It must always be meticulously planned, and carried out at the opportune moment. Occupations always have a time limit, and the swifter they are completed, the better.

The principle object of the ambush is to capture enemy weapons and to punish him with death. Ambushes to halt passenger trains are for propaganda purposes, and, when they are troop trains, the object is to annihilate the enemy and seize his weapons. The urban guerrilla sniper is the kind of fighter specially suited for ambush, because he can hide easily in the irregularities of the terrain, on the roofs and the tops of buildings and apartments under construction. From windows and dark places, he can take careful aim at his chosen target.

Street tactics have revealed a new type of urban guerrilla who participates in mass protests. This is the type we designate as the "urban guerrilla demonstrator", who joins the crowds and participates in marches with specific and definite aims in mind. The urban guerrilla demonstrator must ransack government vehicles, official cars and police vehicles before turning them over or setting fire to them. Street tactics are used to fight the enemy in the streets, utilising the participation of the population against him and stones as the universal projectiles. When the police troops come wearing helmets to protect them against flying objects, we have to divide ourselves into two teams—one to attack the enemy from the front, the other to attack him in the rear—withdrawing one as the other goes into action to prevent the first from being struck by projectiles hurled by the second. The roads followed by police vehicles must be mined at key points along the way and at forced roadblocks. The police will be caught in the trap and will suffer losses and be victims of an ambush. Snipers are very good for mass demonstrations, and can easily cause losses among the enemy. A strike is successful when it is Organised by a small group, if it is carefully prepared in secret using the most clandestine methods. Weapons, ammunition, Molotov cocktails, homemade weapons of destruction and attack, all of these must be supplied beforehand in order to meet the enemy. So that the action can do the greatest possible amount of damage, it is a good idea to study and put into effect a sabotage plan.

In daily struggle against the enemy, the urban guerrilla is subject to arrest, and can be sentenced to unlimited years in jail. This does not mean that the battle ends here. There is no jail, either on an island, in a city penitentiary, or on a farm, that is impregnable to the slyness, cleverness and firepower of the rebels. The guerrilla operations that can be used in liberating prisoners include: riots in penal establishments, in correctional colonies or camps, or on transport or prison ships; assaults on urban or rural prisons, detention centers, prison camps, or any other permanent or temporary place where prisoners are held; assaults on prisoner transport trains or convoys; raids and penetrations of prisons; and ambushing of guards who move prisoners.

Execution is the killing of a foreign spy, of an agent of the regime, of a police torturer, of a dictatorial personality in the government involved in crimes and persecutions against patriots, of a stool pigeon, informer, police agent or police provocateur. Those who go to the police of their own free will to make denunciations and accusations, who supply information and who finger people, must be executed when they are caught by the urban guerrillas.

Kidnapping is capturing and holding in a secret place a spy, political personality or a notorious and dangerous enemy of the revolutionary movement. Kidnapping is used to exchange or liberate imprisoned revolutionaries or to force the suspension of torture in jail by the regime. The kidnapping of personalities who are well-known artists, sports figures or who are outstanding in some other field, but who have evidenced no political interest, can be a useful form of propaganda for the guerrillas, provided it occurs under special circumstances, and is handled so the public understands and sympathises with it. The kidnapping of foreigners or visitors constitutes a form of protest against the penetration and domination of imperialism in the country.

When the urban guerrilla uses sabotage, the first step is isolated sabotage. Then comes the step of dispersed and general sabotage, carried out by the population. Well-executed sabotage demands study, planning and careful action. The objective of sabotage is to hurt, to damage, to make useless and to destroy vital enemy points such as the following:

- The economy of the country
- Agricultural or industrial production
- Transport and communication systems
- Military and police systems and their establishments, and depots
- The repressive military-police system
- The firms and properties of exploiters in the country

The urban guerrilla should endanger the economy of the country, particularly its economic and financial aspects, such as its domestic and foreign banking network, its exchange and credit systems, its tax collection system, etc. Public offices, centers of government and government depots are easy targets for sabotage. Nor will it be easy to prevent the sabotage of agricultural and industrial production by the urban guerrilla, with his thorough knowledge of the local situation. Factory workers acting as urban guerrillas are excellent industrial saboteurs, since they, better than anyone, understand the industry, the factory, the machinery or the part most likely to destroy an entire operation, doing much more damage than a poorly-informed layman could do. Telephone and telegraph lines can be systematically damaged, their towers blown up, and their lines made useless.

With respect to the enemy's transport and communications systems, beginning with railway traffic, it is necessary to attack them systematically with sabotage. The only caution is against causing death and injury to passengers, especially regular commuters on suburban and long-distance trains. Attacks on freight trains, rolling or stationary stock, stoppage of military transports and communications systems, these are the major objectives in this area. Sleepers can be damaged and pulled up, as can rails. A tunnel blocked by a barrier of explosives, or an obstruction caused by a derailed car, causes enormous harm. The derailment of a train carrying fuel is of major damage to the enemy. So is dynamiting a railroad bridge. In a system where the size and weight of the rolling equipment is enormous, it takes months for workers to repair or rebuild the destruction and damage.

Oil lines, fuel plants, depots for bombs and ammunition arsenals, military camps and bases must become targets for sabotage operations, while vehicles, army trucks and other military or police vehicles must be destroyed wherever they are found. Foreign firms and properties in the country, for their part, must become such frequent targets of sabotage that the volume of actions directed against them surpasses the total of all other actions against enemy vital points.

Terrorism is a weapon the revolutionary can never relinquish. Terrorism is an action which the urban guerrilla must execute with the greatest calmness and determination. Although terrorism generally involves an explosion, there are cases in which it may be carried out through executions or the systematic burning of installations, properties, plantations, etc.

Propaganda—even though exercised in the heart of the people by every possible means, does not indicate that our forces have everyone's support. And it is not necessary either. It is enough to win the support of a portion of the population, and this can be done by popularizing the motto, "Let he who does not wish to do anything for the guerrillas do nothing against them."

The war of nerves or psychological warfare is an aggressive technique, based on the direct or indirect use of mass media and rumours in order to demoralise the government. The objective of the war of nerves is to mislead, spreading lies among the authorities in which everyone can participate, thus creating an atmosphere of nervousness, discredit, insecurity, uncertainty and concern on the part of the government. The best methods used by urban guerrillas in the war of nerves are the following:

- Using the telephone and the mail to announce false clues to the police and government, including information on the planting of bombs and any other act of terrorism in public offices and other places - kidnapping and assassination plans. etc.—to force the authorities to wear themselves out by following up on the false information fed to them;
- Letting false plans fall into the hands of the police to divert their attention;
- Planting rumours to make the government uneasy;
- Exploiting by every means possible the corruption, the mistakes and the failures of the government and its representatives, forcing them into demoralising explanations and justifications in the very communication media they wish to maintain under censorship.

(2.1.11) Rescue of the Wounded

The problem of the wounded in urban guerrilla warfare merits special attention. During guerrilla operations in the urban area, it may happen that some comrade is wounded by the police. When a guerrilla in the firing group has a knowledge of first-aid, he can do something for the wounded comrade on the spot. Under no circumstances should the wounded guerrilla be abandoned at the site of the battle or left in the enemy's hands. One of the precautions we must take is to set up first-aid courses for men and women, courses in which guerrillas can learn the rudiments of emergency medicine. The houses in which the wounded are made to stay should not be known to anyone but a small group of comrades responsible for their care and transport. Sheets, bloody clothing, medicine and any other indications of treatment of comrades wounded in combat must be completely eliminated from any place they visit to receive treatment. When all else fails, it is often necessary to resort to legal clinics, using armed force if necessary to force a doctor to treat our wounded.

(2.1.12) Guerrilla Security

The urban guerrilla lives in constant danger of the possibility of being discovered or denounced. The primary security problem is to make certain that we are well-hidden and well-guarded and that there are secure methods to keep the police from locating us. The worst enemy of the urban guerrilla, and the major danger that we run into, is infiltration into our organisation by a spy or informer. The spy trapped within the organisation will be punished with death. The same goes for those who desert and inform to the police. The fundamental way to defeat infiltration of the ranks is to be strict and cautious in recruiting. Nor is it permissible for everyone to know everything and everyone.

3

Major Urban Attacks in India

I'm an urban guerrilla; I make bombs in my cellar.

(3.1) Analysis of the Attacks and their Portents

Always cheat; always win. The only unfair fight is the one you lose.

In this chapter we present a year-wise chronological record and analysis of the major urban attacks in India. The analysis shows how the attacks were mounted; what were the intrinsic advantages which the terrorists enjoyed; what were the intrinsic handicaps faced by the security forces; what were the mistakes committed by the terrorists; what were the mistakes committed by the security forces; how they could have responded better; and what can possibly be done to reduce the occurrence of such attacks in future.

(3.1.1) *Punjab: Killings of Hindu Bus Passengers*

Thirty-four Hindu bus passengers were killed in July 1987 by suspected Khalistani terrorists. The buses were stopped by creating roadblocks with a car and a jeep. They singled out Hindu passengers, dragged them off and shot them. From the point of view of security planners it is important to understand that for the terrorists it was an easy job; can be repeated anytime, anywhere, and there is little which the nation-state can do to prevent it. The impact is great.

(3.1.2) *Kashmir: Rubaiya Sayeed's Kidnapping*

Rubaiya Sayeed was kidnapped in Srinagar on December 8, 1989 by the Jammu Kashmir Liberation Front. Rubaiya is the daughter of Mufti Mohammad Sayeed, the then Home Minister of India. She was then a 23-year-old medical intern at Lal Ded Memorial Women's Hospital. Rubaiya was kidnapped within five days of her father becoming the minister. The kidnappers demanded the release of five of their comrades (Sheikh Abdul Hameed, a JKLF 'area commander' Ghulam Nabi Butt, younger brother of the late Maqbool Butt; Noor Muhammad Kalwal; Muhammed Altaf; and Javed Ahmed Zangar) in exchange for Rubaiya's release. The government accepted their demands and freed the jailed terrorists. Political kidnappings are fun for the terrorists and can be done anytime. Nobody can keep himself in an armoured capsule all the time. There will be necessarily some time when the target would be exposed and vulnerable. The terrorists have only to monitor the target closely.

(3.1.3) Punjab: Massacres of Train Passengers

On June 15, 1991 the terrorists killed at least 80 passengers travelling in two trains near the city of Ludhiana. The militants stopped the two trains about a kilometer from Ludhiana station by applying the emergency brakes provided in the passenger compartments and then opened fire. The survivors stated that on one of the two trains Hindu passengers were identified before being shot. On the second train the militants fired indiscriminately and many Sikhs as well as Hindus were killed. In the same year in December 1991 they further killed 49 passengers, mostly Hindus, travelling on train from Ludhiana to Ferozepur. From the point of view of security planners, armed guards can be provided on trains. However, the point to be noted is that the guards on a train are in uniform and hence easily identified—unlike the marshals on an airplane who dress like ordinary passengers. Hence, the guards can be easily picked by terrorists disguised as passengers and systematically taken out before the actual attack commences.

(3.1.4) Bombay 1993 Bombings

A series of thirteen bomb explosions on March 12, 1993 was the most destructive bomb explosions in Indian history. The single-day attacks resulted in up to 257 civilian casualties in dead and 700-1400 in injured. The attacks are popularly believed to have been Organised by Dawood Ibrahim, gang leader of an organised crime syndicate. It is also believed that the attacks were carried out in retaliation for widespread massacre of Muslims in Bombay during December 1992 and January 1993, and also the demolition of the Babri Masjid (Mosque) in Uttar Pradesh. It may be recalled that in December 1992 and January 1993, there was widespread rioting in Bombay following the December 6 destruction of the Babri Mosque in Ayodhya, UP. Between 1:30 p.m. and 3:40 p.m. a total of 13 bombs exploded throughout Bombay. Most of the bombs were car bombs, but some were in scooters also.Three hotels, namely, Hotel Sea

Rock, Hotel Juhu Centaur, and Hotel Airport Centaur, were targeted by suitcase bombs left in rooms booked by the perpetrators. Grenades were also thrown at Sahar International Airport and at the Fishermen's Colony, apparently targeting Hindus at the latter. A double-decker bus was very badly damaged in one of the explosions and that single incident accounted for the greatest loss of life—perhaps up to 90 people were killed. Several days later, unexploded car bombs were discovered at a railway station.The buildings, markets and places attacked included the Bombay Stock Exchange Building; the Hotel Sea Rock; the Hotel Centaur, Juhu; the Hotel Centaur, Santa Cruz; the Plaza Cinema; the Shiv Sena Bhawan; the Zaveri Bazaar; the Century Bazaar; the Passport Office; the Air India Building; the Sahar Airport; and the Plaza Theatre, Dadar. From the point of view of terrorists, it was an easy job. In fact, there is nothing easier than planting bombs in vehicles in an urban area and detonating them by timer or command. After all, whatever you do, there will be numerous place where cars would be parked on the streets—you cannot have underground parking everywhere. Then you cannot check the things carried by all sorts of millions of people. Anybody can conceal a bomb in his handbag or wherever.

This attack had one more thing of significance. It was perpetrated with the collusion of government officials in it who were simply

The 1993 Bombay bomb blasts: the scene at the Gateway of India

bribed. Five of them, all custom officials, were convicted for having facilitated the smuggling of explosives. One sub-inspector of police and four constables were also convicted for facilitating the passage of the explosives. This could happen anywhere—Indians, being some of the most corrupt people in the whole world, have a known weakness for bribes. Moreover, they could be subverted too on religious or some ideological ground.

(3.1.5) *Kashmir: Kidnapping and Killing of Western Tourists*

Six foreign tourists were kidnapped by Al Faran, a hitherto unknown terrorist organisation, from the Liddarwat area of Pahalgam in Anantnag district in south Kashmir on July 4, 1995 while they were trekking there in the forest. The six victims included two British tourists, Keith Mangan and Paul Wells; two Americans, John Childs and Donald Hutchings; a German, Dirk Hasert; and a Norwegian, Hans Christian Ostro. Childs managed to escape and was rescued four days later. Ostro was beheaded by his abductors and his body was found near Pahalgam on August 13, 1995. Mangan, Wells, Hutchings, and Hasert have never been found are presumed to have been killed and their dead bodies disposed off.

The kidnappers had demanded the release of Maulana Masood Azhar and 20 other terrorists. Several national and international organisations issued appeals to Al Faran to release the tourists. Representatives of the embassies of the victims' countries also visited Kashmir frequently to seek their release, but all without success. Al Faran was never heard of again after that.

This incident is very important because it exposes a weak underbelly of the system. That foreign tourists could be kidnapped is not significant. Anybody can be kidnapped. The portents are far more serious. Intelligent terrorists can use the technique to great effect. It pays to kill tourists as a way of embarrassing the government, internationalizing the conflict, and reeking economic havoc. For example, they can take a busload of foreign tourists, single out American tourists out of them and kill them after brutalising them—all professedly as a revenge for what the Americans have done in Iraq, Afghanistan and Waziristan. This will have immediate consequences. The Americans will issue an advisory to their citizens that India is not a safe zone for American tourists. This will hit Indian tourism financially. Next time they can single out British tourists also and say that they have been punished for Britain's role in the Coalition Forces. Similarly, the interests of Israeli, French or any other nation aligned with the

USA could be targeted. Further, given the legendary ineptitude of the Indian police and deep-rooted corruption therein, it will be difficult to even locate the criminals, not to speak of bringing them to book quickly—the Americans may then accuse India of being a place where Islamic fanatics have a free run. Naturally, India will protest this and a round of mutual incriminations will follow. The Islamic Group in Egypt, for example, has aggressively targeted foreign visitors on tour buses and Nile cruise ships as well as at historical sites, restaurants, and hotels. Between 1992 and 1993, these attacks cost Egypt half of its earnings from tourism. Islamic groups in Algeria have also targeted foreigners, killing 100 between 1993 and 1995. The Basque Fatherland and Liberty has done much the same.

The terrorists can also search and single out American businessmen or diplomats in India for kidnapping and brutal killing. They can also attack those industries or businesses where American money has been invested or which are popularly identified with America. This will have an adverse impact on American investment in India—once again with serious consequences for Indian economy. It can even strain Indo-American relations. And remember, India is not a place where, like Pakistan, the FBI or the American Special Forces agents may just move in and take over the investigation or shoot people in the markets. The inability to do this will irk the Americans all the more. Thus, the consequences of a few but properly selected murders would be far-reaching and there is little which the system can do to prevent it.

Typically, assassinations by the urban guerrilla are meticulously planned and carefully choreographed. The victim is carefully watched for some period to determine his habits, schedule, as well as the extent of his personal security arrangements. Often the assassination takes place in a public place. This both maximises the shock value of the attack as well as offers the perpetrator a chance to slip away unnoticed into the rapidly dispersing and panic-stricken crowd.

(3.1.6) Assam: Brahmaputra Mail Train Bombing

In this incident the Brahmaputra Mail train travelling in Lower Assam on 30 December, 1996 was attacked. The bomb was of unknown composition, and had been left next to the track between Kokrajhar and Fakiragram stations. The explosion also caused the derailment of six carriages—at least 33 people were killed. It is likely the bomb was detonated by a remote control device, and timed precisely to cause maximum destruction, as the train was moving at a high speed.

Bombing trains is an old thing, and very easy too. The psychological impact is great. It is dwarfed only by the impact which the bombing of an aircraft would produce. They have not yet been able to do that in India. But there is no reason to become complacent on that score. A few Sikhs could bomb the Air India plane Kanishka. Somebody else can very well do that again. Yes, airport security has been tightened since then. But that's largely show, not substance. It does nothing for what goes in the cargo hold. A bomb can be easily smuggled in that and exploded in mid-air to bring the aircraft down. The only problem is that the bomber may not be able to get off the aircraft—so what, they can always find some fool who would be prepared to give up his life in return for glory or compensation to his family. Remember, Arthur Hailey's 'Airport'? The Glasgow airport bomber Kafeel was a fool who thought that he could ram a jeep inside the airport building and blow it up. Poor fellow had no idea of what it takes to blow up a building that size—in the end, he only blew himself up. No intelligent terrorist would try that. He would do something better. The airport security does nothing to those who enter the airport building as passengers. At any time hundreds of people are to be found before the counters. Terrorists can simply open fire on them with automatic weapons and kill hundreds there besides damaging the computers and other equipment and thereby rendering the airport dysfunctional for quite some time. All those scores of security forces personnel whom the imbeciles put up so ceremoniously there would not be able to do a thing in such a situation because they will have to shoot at the innocent people from amongst whom the terrorists would be firing at others. Now, you understand why I call the Indians dumb?

(3.1.7) Kashmir: Attack on the Army's 15 Corps HQ, Srinagar

At about 5:30 p.m. on November 3, three terrorists alighted from a bus near the so-called Batwara gate, one of the several gates of the Badami Bagh cantonment in Srinagar, the HQ of the 15 Corps. They threw two hand grenades on a BSF vehicle parked near the gate and also fired in which the driver of the vehicle was killed. Taking advantage of the confusion and panic thus created, the terrorists entered through the gate and ran inside the Army Public Relations Officer's (PRO) office, adjacent to the Batwara Gate inside the boundary wall. Inside the office, the terrorists shot dead a major, the PRO, at point blank range and also killed five other army personnel. Later, during the night the terrorists managed to enter the adjacent cantonment board office where they remained holed up for the entire night and fought from there till they were killed by 5:30 a.m. the next day. At the end of the encounter, two terrorists were killed. Nine security forces personnel also lost their lives and five were injured. One terrorist managed to escape—that was the worst part of it. The incident showed that security in the establishments of Indian forces is largely for the show of it and determined terrorists could not only easily breach them but manage to successfully run away also after that. Above all, it punctured the inflated ego of the Indian army. Obviously, the Indian security establishment had never learnt to expect the unexpected. They do not have the slightest idea of what ought to be done in such situations. Ask any Indian soldier what he would do and he would say: "*fire ka jawaab fire se denge*", that is, he would retaliate bullets by bullets. Ask any officer what he would do and he would say: "*position le ke fire karenge*", that is, they would take up positions and fire. Duffers don't have horns on their heads.

(3.1.8) *Hijacking of the Flight IC-814*

The Indian Airlines flight IC-814 was to fly from Kathmandu to Delhi. It was hijacked on December 24, 1999, shortly after the aircraft entered Indian airspace at about 5:30 p.m. by five men. Ultimately, the plane landed in Afghanistan, where the hijackers agreed to release their hostages in exchange for the release of three terrorists. Anil Sharma, the chief flight attendant on IC-814, later recalled that a masked, bespectacled man threatened to blow up the plane with a bomb and ordered the pilot to 'fly west'. Nobody knows how he came in contact with the pilot—or was it merely the stupid crew which dutifully conveyed the information to the pilot. As it befits the dumb Indians eminently, they accepted his threat on its face value! The hijackers apparently wanted to take the aircraft to Lahore, but the Pakistani authorities quickly refused permission. The pilot apparently told the hijackers that they would have to land in Amritsar instead.

The hijackers asked for the plane to be refueled. At first the Indian Government did not agree, but after the hijackers stabbed a passenger named Rupin Katyal, they agreed to refuel the plane. However, for reasons unknown, the plane was not refueled. The hijackers threatened the crew that they would kill everyone on board if the pilot did not take off within 30 seconds. In any case, the Airbus A 300 took off for Lahore with almost no fuel. When the aircraft reached near Lahore the ATC did not allow the plane to land. Instead, lights and other navigational instruments were switched off. The ATC gave the permission to land in Lahore when the pilot apparently mistook the lights on a road to be the runway and was about to land there. A few seconds after touchdown, the right engine of the aircraft flamed out due to fuel starvation. The plane was quickly re-fuelled and took-off, bound for Dubai, UAE. Katyal died on the way to Dubai. In Dubai some 25 passengers were released along with Katyal's body. From UAE the plane headed for Afghanistan, then under the Islamic regime of the Taliban.

The Taliban authorities argued that they would not allow a foreign military outfit to operate in Afghanistan. They even encircled the plane with tanks and heavily armed militia in a bid to stop any forceful storming by Indian Special Forces. Negotiations opened up between the Indian embassy officials and the hijackers. By that time the media outcry in India was so great that a quick resolution to this crisis was needed as a political face-saving exercise. Eventually, the government accepted the demand to release Maulana Masood Azhar, Mushtaq Ahmed Zargar and Ahmed Omar Saeed Sheikh in exchange for the release of the passengers and crew of flight IC - 814. The erstwhile Indian foreign minister Jaswant Singh went personally to Kandahar to deliver the prisoners over to the hijackers and receive the passengers back in exchange for a safe passage to the hijackers. The hostages were freed after eight days. Take my word; the same thing would happen if somebody hijacked a plane again. We are all aware of how we speak of not giving in to any demand of the terrorists but those who know the Indians know better—you know we can always invoke the plea of saving innocent lives; how lives of women and children are important; how we are committed in our fight against terrorism; how we follow Gandhiji's principles; how we do not want any blood to be shed; how we will raise the issue at various international forums; and how we can always punish the terrorists later.

IC-814 hijacking: how a nation capitulated—possession of nuclear weapons and massive armed forces do not give balls to a nation

(3.1.9) *Kashmir: Attack on the Police Special Operations Group Complex, Srinagar*

Eleven security men were killed and 20 injured in this incident. At about 5:05 p.m. on December 27, 1999 two terrorists in police uniform arrived at the gate of the SOG (Special Operations Group) complex, Srinagar and entered through the single-entry inlet built into the main gate. This single entry inlet was open at that time. After entering the complex the two terrorists informed the sentry on duty, who came out from his bunker, that they wanted to meet 'Saheb'. As soon as the sentry came out of the bunker; the terrorist shot him. A large number of SOG and CRPF personnel were there in the open in front of the building within the complex at that lime. The terrorist fired at them. Thereafter, one of the terrorists spotted a DySP who was in-charge of the SOG and shot him too. After that, one terrorist moved to the first floor of the building while the other terrorist took position on the staircase. The terrorists on the first floor located the armoury and broke it open. The terrorists held out against the forces by using grenades, arms and ammunition available in the armoury. They could be killed only when the portion of the building in which the terrorists were holed up was blown up by the forces. The incident also shows, quite like the attack on the Badami Bagh cantonment, how the Indian security establishment is completely flummoxed when they are faced with something unexpected. If the terrorists had found the armoury by chance and used the material, it was great improvisation—if they had intelligence about it, this speaks volumes about their preparation. Further the fact that mere police uniform was enough to secure entry for them in a high-profile place, shows that while the Indians have managed to acquire a lot of security systems and gadgets, they still do not have the 'security consciousness'.

(3.1.10) *Kashmir: Attack on the Rashtriya Rifles Sector HQ, Khanabal, Anantnag*

This attack was mounted in a direct fashion sans any stratagem. Three terrorists arrived in a dark blue Maruti van (a snatched one) in the evening on January 12, 2000 near the Rashtriya Rifles Sector HQ, Khanabal, Anantnag. They stopped the car a little away from the gate and attacked directly by hurling grenades/smoke bombs at the entry gate. One of the terrorists got injured right away when the sentry returned fire. He took shelter in a building outside and was shot later – even in that process one man was killed. The other two terrorists entered into the RR camp and took position in a two-storey building of the MES, where three civilian employees were also staying. In the encounter that ensued, one major was killed and two men injured.

Even these terrorists could be killed only when the building was blown up using Carl Gustaf anti-tank warheads. This is important. This showed that Indian forces have really no tactical solution to the problem of terrorists firing from well-defended positions. The only solution is to blow up the building—a rather costly solution. As we saw above, the attack on the SOG complex in Srinagar was also resolved in this manner only. Years later, when terrorists would attack the Taj hotel in Bombay, the forces would not have the liberty of destroying the building and that's one of the reasons that the operation stretched to nearly 54 hours! Further, in this incident, the forces spoke of smoke as if it was the most infallible thing in the world which left them clueless. This incident too illustrated how we could be taken by surprise.

(3.1.11) Kashmir: Attack on the Rashtriya Rifles Coy HQ, Ganderbal, Srinagar

They struck in the early hours of morning this time. On March 5, two-three terrorists entered the Coy HQ of the RR at Badampora, Srinagar. As soon as they entered the main gate, they poured heavy fire at a barrack. Six army personnel were killed and several others injured in tins firing. The terrorists managed to escape in the confusion and panic created. A very disturbing example, indeed—we can only lament at the gross incompetence of the security planners! Worst of all, they managed to escape as if to add insult to injury!

(3.1.12) Kashmir: Attack on the BSF Coy. HQ, Natipora, Srinagar

Yet another evening attack—this time two terrorists attacked the sentries at the main gate of the BSF Coy. HQ, 173 Bn at the SICOP complex, Natipora. After injuring the sentries, the terrorists managed to enter the complex and ran inside and hid themselves in one of the rooms. The forces were flummoxed again. Eventually, a part of the building had to be blown up.

(3.1.13) Kashmir: Attack on the Army's 15 Corps HQ, Srinagar

On April 19, 2000 a car tried to gain entry into the Badami Bagh cantonment, the HQ of the 15th corps, through its main gate located on the national highway. When the car crossed the first barrier, it was signalled to stop by the man on duty. However, the vehicle continued to move towards the main gate and would have succeeded but for an army vehicle which was parked outside. As soon as the vehicle stopped, it was blown up by the driver. Five Army personnel were injured in the blast. The army had learnt little from the earlier attack on the same cantonment—that time men firing guns had flummoxed them; this time an explosive-laden car confounded them. But for the fortuitous presence of the parked vehicle that had effectively blocked the road, the car would have crashed inside.

(3.1.14) Kashmir: Massacre of Amarnath Pilgrims

Thirty Hindu pilgrims were massacred by terrorists on August 1, 2000 in Pahalgam town located in Anantnag. The pilgrims were on their way to the Amarnath temple deep into the hills on annual pilgrimage. The target was carefully chosen. By choosing pilgrims, the terrorists also ought to communalise the issue.

(3.1.15) Kashmir: Attack on the Rashtriya Rifles HQ, Beervah, Budgam

This attack came deep into the night at about 2:30 a.m. on September 12. A single terrorist killed the sentry at the main gate of the 34 Bn RR (Rashtriya Rifles) HQ complex and entered inside. Two other terrorists, believed to have gained access through some other direction, subsequently joined him. Nobody knows how and from where they came—a terrible state of affairs. The terrorists then went inside a barrack and after opening fire at the inmates, took up positions. They managed to kill 11 security men including a major and injured 10 others before getting killed.

(3.1.16) Delhi: Attack on the Red Fort

The attack on the Red Fort is a terrible blot on the Indian army and leaves most of the vital questions unanswered. In a terrible affront to the might of the nation, just two men dressed in jeans and jackets sneaked into the Red Fort at about 9:30 p.m on December 22, 2000. Two soldiers and one civilian employee of the army were killed in the attack. More than the casualties, the Red Fort is the symbol of the sovereignty of the nation; a place on which the national flag was hoisted first when India became independent in 1947. Even now the Indian prime minister addresses the nation from its ramparts every Independence Day. The place is under the protection of the Indian army. That the terrorists could enter surreptitiously in itself is a serious insult. One version is that there were six of them and all of them had gained entry into the Red Fort on the pretext of watching the English version of the light-and-sound show which is held from 7:30 p.m. to 8:30 p.m. It is said that all the terrorists had entered the Red Fort through the Lahori Gate with assault rifles, magazines and hand-grenades hidden under their jackets. After the show, two of them sneaked into the military area under the cover of darkness and carried out the strikes. Thereafter, they fled through the Fort's rear wall and escaped in auto-rickshaws. The army and the police have no answer as to how the terrorists could have entered with all that weaponry through the elaborate checking, frisking and metal detectors at the so-called Lahori Gate? They want us to believe that? It is possible that the two had scaled the wall at some place and thus entered the Fort. It is also surmised that they had inside help and that they had hidden weapons inside the Fort earlier. The arms were claimed to have been retrieved after they gained entry. Even if we accept that there was some inside help, it is a great failure of the system that no insider was ever caught for this. And, in any case, how could civilian insiders have ever carried arms inside?

The army says that they switched off the lighting system inside the Fort. A party of the Rajputana Rifles was going on in the Fort at that time. They fired at the army pickets within the Fort and ran around firing. They engaged the army men at three places inside the Fort and fought for 45 minutes. After that they made good their escape! They escaped by scaling the high wall on the ring road side of the Fort. How could they easily scale the rather high wall of the fort without any implement is also a mystery? And if the army speaks of their having been confounded because the terrorists had switched of the lights, it means that they had neither prepared for such an eventuality in terms of backup lighting systems nor they had any tactical solutions to fighting in such a situation. A most ignoble security failure—the simple fact is that the attack bewildered them so greatly that they could not do anything.

(3.1.17) Kashmir: Attack on the Srinagar Airport

On January 16, 2001, the convoy of a minister of the state government was passing through a newly erected barrier (called gate number 0) by the police about 500 m short of the old barrier (gate number 1) at the Srinagar airport. A group of six terrorists in a hardtop jeep that appeared to be a government jeep managed to get into the convoy of the minister. Policemen on duty, however, became suspicious and taking lift in a civilian Maruti car of a Rural Bank Manager followed the terrorists. They overtook the terrorists' jeep and stopped it some distance short of gate number 1 of airport for checking. The terrorists, after getting down from the jeep, started running towards the gate. Four of them were shot immediately. One of the terrorists succeeded in entering the cabin of the X-Ray machine and threw a grenade injuring

CRPF personnel in the cabin. One terrorist hid near the adjoining shops. They were killed shortly thereafter. The terrorists killed three security men and a civilian and injured 12 security men. As such the attack was not well-planned. The point to be noted, however, is that, as in the attack on the SOG complex, in this case also, an official appearance did the trick.

(3.1.18) *Kashmir: Attack on the Police Control Room, Srinagar*

This was a night attack. At around 7:15 p.m. on February 9, 2001 two terrorists, one of whom was wearing police uniform, arrived at the main gate of the PCR, Srinagar, in a taxi. On being stopped at the main gate, the man in the police uniform told the sentry that he was called by some officer, on which he was allowed to go to room of the 'Munshi' (writer). While going towards the room, he lobbed a grenade and upon reaching the room, started firing in which five police personnel were killed inside the room. In the ensuing confusion the other terrorist waiting at the gate was also able to enter inside the PCR. The man inside the Munshi room continued to fire for over seven hours! The police could extract eight of their comrades who were trapped in an adjacent room with the help of two improvised armoured vehicles. In all, eight policemen were killed and six injured. It is all too obvious that once again an officious appearance defeated the system. Of course, at all times, the forces try to explain things by saying that there was confusion. What else do you expect in such a situation? It is the job of the security planners to evolve such systems and procedures that confusion and panic do not consume the men. 'Security consciousness' was again found to be missing.

(3.1.19) *Kashmir: Attack on the Legislative Assembly, Srinagar*

On October 1, 2001 terrorists carried out an attack on the Jammu and Kashmir State Legislative Assembly complex in Srinagar using an explosive-laden car, one 'suicide' bomber and three others who rode the same car till the last moment. Thirty-four people and four terrorists were killed in this attack. Four terrorists in police uniforms hijacked a Tata Sumo vehicle belonging to the Telecom department from Jehangir Chowk in Srinagar earlier during the day. Explosives were packed in it and they drove it towards the Assembly. Three of them got down about 100 m away from the main gate. The driver then accelerated the vehicle and rammed it into the main gate. At the same time he detonated the explosives. A conundrum resulted and taking advantage of that the remaining three sneaked into the premises.

They started firing indiscriminately and also lobbed grenades. They entered the Assembly Annexe building. The Speaker and the MLAs were, however, evacuated safely. Eventually, all the terrorists were killed but not before they managed to kill 34 and injure 70.

The point to be noted is that an officious appearance once again secured entrance. Ramming of an explosive-laden car into the security barrier was tried for the first time, and successfully. We would not be surprised if this is tried again later also. The Assembly had been in session since September 25, but was adjourned the day when the attack took place. Not knowing this was an intelligence failure on the part of the terrorists; otherwise, the casualties could have been higher.

(3.1.20) Delhi: Attack on the Parliament

On December 13, 2001, five terrorists infiltrated the Parliament House in a car on the strength of Home Ministry and Parliament labels which managed to befool the security personnel there. Upon entering they started racing towards one of the gates of the building. While both the Rajya Sabha and the Lok Sabha had been adjourned forty minutes before the incident, many MPs and government officials were believed to have still been in the building at the time of the attack.

The car of the terrorists happened to collide with the rear of the car of the Indian vice president. That seems to have upset their plans and confound them. Then they got out, and began firing. The vice president's guards and a large number of security personnel present in the campus shot back at the terrorists. All of them were killed before they could enter the Parliament main building. Five policemen, a Parliament security guard, and a gardener were killed, and 18 others were injured. No members of the government were hurt. Once again it can be seen how an officious appearance defeated the system.

The terrorists were said to be in possession of four AK-rifles with Urdu markings and green stickers thereon, 15 hand grenades, one grenade launcher, three 7.62 mm pistols, 15 kg plastic explosive, 12 spare magazines, two IEDs and 30 detonators made in Pakistan's Wah Nobel factory. They were also claimed to have planned it meticulously for eight months.

In my considered opinion, daring though the attack was, a simple analysis shows that the execution of the strike was not all commensurate with the claimed planning and resources. It has been a regular practice with even the most inexperienced terrorists that they file away all the markings on their weapons. Scores of thousands of AK-rifles have been recovered in Kashmir and not one of them had any markings on it. Usually, this is got done even before the weapons are supplied to the terrorists. For a very special operation of this kind, it is difficult to believe how could the terrorists be so stupid as to carry all that telltale evidence of their trans-border connections with them? No terrorist should and would ever mount an attack believing that it would be nothing but a success. He must always keep the possibility of death or capture in mind. For these eventualities, they normally destroy all the evidence of their preparatory activities and connections before going in for the attack—only a fool would leave incriminatory files stored in his laptop, or would not take a new cell phone instead of keeping the old phone with him which would reveal all the calls that he had made.

There were ten thousand ways of attacking a building with the kind of weaponry they were claimed to have. The modus operandi adopted by them was the most amateurish. They were claimed to be meticulous enough to keep dry fruits worth Rs 2000 to keep them going in a hostage-taking situation. How could they be so careless in certain other vital aspects? If the other claims are correct, it would only show that the terrorists were not really as meticulous, skilled and well-organised as they were made out to be by the media. This means that a wrong perception was projected regarding the capabilities of the terrorists and a larger-than-life image of the terrorists was unnecessarily created.

An attack of that sort by intelligent professionals should have been planned only after procuring a detailed layout of the interior of the building—photos of the exterior, even if they were 21 in number, would not be of any help. If one ventured into the attack based on only that sort of information, he had to be one of the biggest fools among the terrorists.

(3.1.21) Jammu: Attack on the Raghunath Temple

There were two attacks on the Raghunath Temple in Jammu in 2002. The first attack took place on March 30, 2002. Three-four terrorists lobbed a grenade in the Raghunath Bazar and then started firing. After that they entered the temple which was later surrounded by the forces. Seven persons including three security forces personnel were killed and 20 injured. The terrorists attacked the temple again on November 24, 2002 when two terrorists stormed the temple and killed 13 devotees and injured 45 others. All such attacks on places of religious worship have the potential of having communal ramifications elsewhere in the country; something that would add to the worsening of public order and development of anarchy. If communal riots follow any such attack, the terrorist has achieved more than his purpose.

(3.1.22) *Jammu: Kaluchak Massacre and Attack on the Army Camp*

On May 14, 2002 near the town of Kaluchak in Jammu, three terrorists attacked a tourist bus coming from Himachal Pradesh. The terrorists boarded the bus at Bari-Bramahana about 14-km from Jammu on the Jammu-Pathankot highway. When the bus reached near Kaluchak, they shot the driver and the conductor and opened fire on the passengers killing seven passengers. The terrorists then entered the nearby army camp of 196 Field Regiment and rushed in the direction of the Army's family quarters, located on the main road. They also threw grenades on some vehicles parked in the vicinity. Upon entering the family quarters they again fired on the people there. The terrorists were eventually cordoned off and killed by 10 a.m. A total of 32 persons were killed, including three army personnel, 18 army family members and 10 civilians. There were 47 wounded including 12 army personnel, 20 army family members and 15 civilians. The very fact that the terrorists could enter an army camp so easily speaks volumes about how dumb the army men are.

(3.1.23) *Jammu: Qasimnagar Massacre of Hindus*

On July 13, 2002 eight terrorists walked into the Qasimnagar slum on the outskirts of Jammu and threw three or four grenades before opening fire with automatic weapons. Within minutes 24 people, all Hindus, were dead. Three more died later in hospital and at least 30 were injured. The dead included 13 women and a child. The terrorists then escaped into the thickly wooded hills nearby. The victims were, incidentally, listening to the commentary of Indian-England cricket match. The incident shows how easy it is to commit mayhem with soft targets.

(3.1.24) *Gujarat: Attack on the Akshardham Temple*

On September 25, 2002 two heavily armed terrorists arrived at the Akshardham Temple in Gandhinagar at around 4:30 p.m.—this also happens to be a popular tourist spot. How the terrorists gained entry is still not very clear. One account says that they scaled the perimeter fence and opened fire, killing a woman and a temple volunteer right away. According to the temple administration, the terrorists had tried to enter the complex through Gate 3, but the volunteer security guards stopped them for a security check. Then they jumped the fence, firing their guns as they walked. After that they began throwing grenades into the Hindu crowd at the temple. About 600 Hindu visitors were in the temple at the time.

The National Security Guards (NSG) had to mount an elaborate operation to kill the terrorists. About 50 people were trapped inside the building, but the quick action of the volunteers in the temple prevented the terrorists from gaining access to more people inside. They were later rescued safely. By the end of the attack, 28 people were killed and another 79 wounded. Apart from the 25 people killed in the first assault, one state police officer and one commando also died in the action. One more seriously injured commando died after about two years of remaining in coma.

This mode of entry adopted by the terrorists in this case was quite amateurish. More mayhem and panic would have been caused had they fired right at the gate and forced their way in because the guards were unarmed—there was no point arguing with them. This shows that terrorists were not as good or intelligent as they are generally made out to be by an ignorant media and the security forces. It also shows that the elaborate security arrangements which such premises make are actually of no use—there is nothing in them which deters an armed man prepared to die.

(3.1.25) Bombay: 2003 Train Bombing

At 9:45 p.m. on March 13, 2003 a bomb exploded as a train pulled into the Mulund station. The bomb was placed in the first class ladies' compartment and killed 10 people and injured 70. Among the ten killed were four women who were in the first class compartment and six men who were in the adjoining second class compartment. As I mentioned earlier, there is nothing easier than planting bombs in trains. The terrorist has the natural camouflage of all sorts of bags which people carry and it is not difficult to quietly leave a bag somewhere and disappear on the pretext of going to the toilet or simply getting down in the hustle and bustle—there is such a tremendous crowd that one would not even notice that somebody has left his bag and disappeared.

(3.1.26) Delhi: 2005 Bombings

Three bomb explosions occurred in Delhi on October 29, 2005 just two days before the major Hindu festival of Diwali when people traditionally flock to markets for shopping. The explosions killed 62 people and injured at least 210 others. The bombs were triggered in two busy markets in central and south Delhi and in a bus in the

Govindpuri area in the south of the city. The first explosion occurred in the Paharganj market outside the New Delhi Railway Station. The explosive device was planted in a scooter. The Govindpuri explosion took place inside a bus with about 40 people on board. The bomb was left in a bag which the crew and the passengers even tried to throw out of the bus. The third and the most devastating explosion took place in a very crowded corner of the busy Sarojini Nagar market. Eyewitnesses claim that the bomb was placed in a white Maruti van. The bomb went off near a vendor using a LPG cylinder which ruptured and the gas caught fire, leading to an outbreak of fire in a row of shops—43 people were killed in Sarojini Nagar alone. Busy markets are most vulnerable to a bomb attack. As with a train; the bomber can conceal, and leave his bomb anywhere with almost complete impunity in a market also. You introduce too many checks and the shoppers would be deterred—the shopkeepers themselves would protest.

Delhi bombing: terror writ large on the people's faces

(3.1.27) Bombay: 2006 Train Bombings

There was a series of seven bomb blasts that took place over a period of 11 minutes on the Suburban Railway in Bombay on July 11, 2006 in which 209 people lost their lives and over 700 were injured. Pressure cookers filled with explosives, were placed on trains plying on the western line of the suburban train network (popularly called 'local trains'), which forms the backbone of the city's transport network. The blasts took place in the evening, the first one being at 6:24 p.m. when the rush of people returning from work makes the passenger crowd densest. All the bombs had been placed in the first-class 'general' compartments where anyone can travel as against the 'reserved' compartments which require prior reservation. The bombs exploded at or near the suburban railway stations of Matunga Road, Mahim, Bandra, Khar Road, Jogeshwari, Bhayandar and Borivali. Terrorists used pressure cookers because it provides an easily available and naturally strong vessel to keep the explosive—moreover, being an item of domestic use, it does not arouse suspicion either.

The bomb literally rips through the train compartment

(3.1.28) Hyderabad: Lumbini Park Bombings

Two bombs exploded almost simultaneously in the evening of August 25, 2007 in Hyderabad. The first bomb exploded in the Lumbini Amusement Park. The second bomb exploded five minutes later in Gokul Chaat Bhandar, a popular restaurant about 5-km away. At least 42 people were killed in the two bombings. Two more bombs were defused in other parts of the city. In these attacks in Hyderabad and subsequently in the Jaipur bomb blasts, the terrorists had selected the targets with great care—places with high crowd density. There is little that can be done to protect such targets—even a stampede would claim many lives.

(3.1.29) UP: Bombings at Lucknow, Faizabad and Varanasi

Six consecutive serial blasts took place in Lucknow, Varanasi and Faizabad courts in UP on November 23, 2007 afternoon in a span of 25 minutes, in which at least 15 people were killed and over 60 injured. Three bomb blasts took place in Varanasi in the premises of the civil court. Two blasts occurred in the Faizabad district court. In Lucknow two bombs were found; one triggered panic after explosion and other was deactivated. All the bombs were planted on bicycles. In Varanasi at least 11 people were killed including four lawyers and 42 injured. In Faizabad blasts at least four people were killed on spot and about 15 were injured. The Lucknow blast was mildest of the three. There was nothing sophisticated about the bombs; they were quite crude devices. But the fact that they were placed in a crowded place like court complexes, made their news value great. Courts are associated with the state, as a symbol of its power—an attack there, even if it killed and injured ordinary citizens was an affront to the might of the state.

(3.1.30) Jaipur Bombings

There was a series of nine synchronised bomb blasts that took place within a span of fifteen minutes at various locations in Jaipur on May 13, 2008. A tenth bomb was found and defused. Sixty-three people were killed with 216 or more injured. The group called Indian Mujahideen had claimed responsibility through an elaborate email sent to the media. The bombs were mostly planted on bicycles.

The terrorists applied a great deal of mind in selecting the locations of the bombs and their timings of explosion. The terrorists displayed remarkable skill in observation and planning. The bombs were placed in a most strategic manner. The first two blasts occurred at Manak Chowk and as the crowd ran towards Johri Bazar another two blasts near the National Handloom Centre blocked the exit point, pushing back the panicked crowd towards Tripolia Bazar and Chandpol area, where subsequent blasts caused maximum fatalities. The placement of the bombs was critical. The walled city of Jaipur is a bewildering maze of shops and it is only a local man who could know where and when the crowds would be at their peak capacity; it is only a local who could know fine details such as when the evening 'aarti' in that particular Hanuman temple takes place. It is not possible that someone came from outside a couple of days ago and worked out the details by himself. Even if the perpetrators came from outside, all this crucial intelligence had to be given by his local contacts. And it had to be an extensive local support network. That also explains how they got several women and children to purchase the cycles so that the process of purchase did not appear unnatural to any shopkeeper. One may call them sleeper cells in fashionable jargon; but there is no running away from the fact that logistic and intelligence support was extended to the perpetrators by the locals and that could have been only on communal grounds. This shows how terrorists can exploit communal divide to their advantage.

The media was not able to notice a very important fact that out of the nine bomb blasts, four took place quite near the police offices. One thing which is proved from this is that the presence of the police is no deterrent to the urban terrorist. This should open the eyes of those who start demanding that the police presence must be increased following every terrorist attack. The police cannot protect the myriads of targets that are presented in a civilised society—in fact they cannot protect even themselves.

(3.1.31) Ahmedabad Bombings

A series of 21 bomb blasts hit Ahmedabad in the evening of July 26, 2008, within a span of 70 minutes. Fifty-six people were killed and over 200 people were injured. The bombs were planted in tiffin carriers on bicycles and were placed in busy markets, a pattern similar to the Jaipur bombings. Many of the blasts targeted the city bus service; two blasts took place inside the premises of two hospitals, about 40 minutes after the initial series of blasts. One of the blasts in the hospitals occurred when injured victims of the initial series of blasts were being admitted there, a very clever and devious design. One bomb was found and defused on the following day in the Hatkeshwar area.

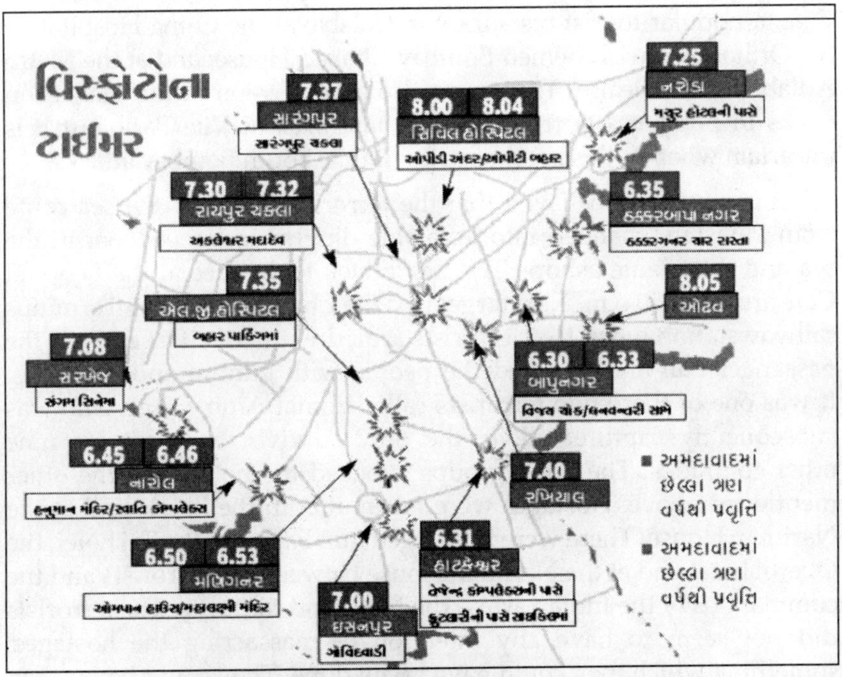

The biggest serial bombing in India: note the timing co-ordination and wide dispersal of the attacks in the city

(3.1.32) Delhi 2008 Bombings

Five synchronised bomb blasts took place within a span of few minutes on September 13, 2008 evening at various busy markets or commercial locations in Delhi. Thirty people were killed and over 100 injured. The casualties were rather disproportionate to the strength of the bombs because the crowd density was high at all the places.

(3.1.33) Bombay: 26/11 Attacks

There were ten co-ordinated terrorist attacks across Bombay on November 26, 2008. The terrorists fought pitched battles with the security forces and could be overcome only by November 29 after over 54 hours of fighting. The attacks have been dubbed by the media as "India's 9/11". This once again shows the bootlicking nature of the Indian media with respect to the West. Anything in India assumes significance only when it is measured with respect to something in the West. At least 173 people, including at least twenty-two foreign nationals, were killed and 308 people were injured. Most of the attacks took place in South Bombay; at the crowded Chhatrapati Shivaji Terminus (CST) railway station; at two five-star hotels: the Oberoi Trident at Nariman Point, and Taj Mahal Palace & Tower near the Gateway of India; at the Leopold Café, a popular tourist restaurant in Colaba; at the Cama Hospital; at the Orthodox Jewish-owned Bombay Chabad House; and at the Metro Adlabs movie theatre. There was also an explosion at the Mazagaon docks in Bombay's port area, and a taxi blast at Vile Parle but it is uncertain whether this is connected with the South Bombay attacks.

It is popularly believed that the terrorists came by the sea route from Pakistan, changed into inflatable dinghy and speedboat in the sea and then came ashore. The first attack took place at the Leopold Café around 9:50 p.m. Next target was the Chatrapati Shivaji Terminus railway station when two terrorists armed with AK-rifles entered the passenger hall and attacked the people with gunfire and grenades. It was one of these two terrorists called Ajmal Amir Kasab who was subsequently captured alive, the only survivor amongst his nine other comrades. The other groups attacked the hotels and the other mentioned above. Hostages were taken at both the hotels and at the Nariman House. There were prolonged gun battles at the Taj hotel, the Oberoi hotel and at the Nariman House between the terrorists and the commandos of the Indian army, the NSG, and the navy. The terrorists did not seem to have any intention of massacring the hostages, something which they could have easily done. They could have taken a manageable number as hostages to be kept as shields and massacred the rest. They did not do that—obviously they were not very clear about what they had to do. At the Nariman House, due to the densely populated locality, the NSG was obliged to insert commandos in the building by helicopter, a first in the history of terrorism in India, and much to the delight of the idiot box. In any case, that fancy job did not help much as the terrorists killed all the hostages in the Nariman House—let no one boast about any 'surgical operation'.

26/11: A relatively simple attack that left an entire nation utterly dazed and flummoxed

(3.2) Utterly Dazed and Flummoxed

The incident brought out the difficulties of urban combat, particularly when the opponent happens to be well-armed and also with some cover. As I have pointed out earlier, the forces have become used to blasting buildings in Kashmir, something which could not be done in Bombay for obvious reasons and that made the job even more difficult.

In the mass hysteria generated by the brouhaha in the media over the attacks nobody appreciated the importance of the terrorists' prior familiarisation with the target places and the necessity of a strong local support network. The police investigation also missed the line completely. If the terrorists ventured into this without prior familiarisation, they are hopelessly dumb. As I have pointed out above in connection with the Jaipur bomb blasts, there has to be a very committed local support network. I dismiss it straightaway that the terrorists had set foot on the soil of Bombay for the first time for this attack—there are no such smart people in real life who could execute a plan like this with the help of tourist maps or GPS. Leave that to the half-educated hacks in the TV. If they had come earlier and had stayed for quite some time, we must ask about their mode of transport and infiltration, a question that has not been raised so far. They might have hijacked MV Kuber this time but what was the mode earlier? If they stayed in the town earlier, it also means that there were many families who kept them in a manner that would not arouse suspicion and helped them familiarise with the town. A stranger requires the support of many people—down from the boys who would bring tea, to drivers and people who would keep their weapons safely. And all such people have to be absolutely trustworthy otherwise the operation would be blown up prematurely. The terrorists are said to have used at least three SIM cards purchased on the Indian side of the border with Bangladesh—this also requires local support. Two guys including one from Srinagar were arrested for having supplied them with SIM cards; one from Calcutta and the other from Delhi. The net result is that we have closed our eyes to the presence of a large number of subverted people amidst us and whose network remains intact.

The targets were as soft as they could be—anybody could attack them. As Chrtistine Fair, senior political scientist and a South Asia expert at the RAND Corporation also pointed out, disagreeing with the requirement of extensive training: "This wasn't something that required a logistical mastermind. These were not hardened targets. A huge train station with zero security. Two hotels with no security, both owned by Indians. Leopold's Café. How hard is it, really? It's not rocket science". In fact, had they been intelligent professionals, they could have caused much greater mayhem. In both the hotels, if they were really keen on taking hostages, they should have assembled them in a central place as the Chechen terrorists had done in the Moscow theater siege so that they could inflict greater casualties. They seemed to be keen on engaging the forces rather—that was a classic mistake. They geared the attacks more with its shock value in mind and not with the number of casualties that could be inflicted. Had they intended so, they could have collected some hotel guests in one place and shot them to prove their intent and capability and then held another set of them hostage for negotiation. Fighting the forces or holding them for long may be glamorous but serves no purpose because the forces have unlimited ammunition and even at the cost of some casualties, would eventually kill you. Had they taken hostages properly, perhaps they could have even negotiated for some demands. The demands which they made were too generalised in character and they never seemed keen on it. They did so just for the heck of it.

As I have mentioned repeatedly, the success or failure of a terrorist attack is to be judged by the overall psychological impact it creates. By that standard, the Bombay attack was a complete success. Bruce Hoffman, a professor at the School of Foreign Service at Georgetown University and the author of the book "Inside Terrorism" also pointed out: "These attacks show how a handful of men, basically using weapons off the shelf, can paralyse a city and frustrate highly-trained security forces. These attacks were calculated to spread alarm and anxiety—to put it quite frankly, to unhinge things—and that's exactly what they've done".

4

Major Urban Attacks in Rest of the World

In ten years nobody will remember the details of calibre, stance, or tactics. They will only remember who lived.

(4.1) Analysis of the Attacks and their Portents

(4.1.1) Pakistan: The Lal Masjid Operation

On July 3, 2007, the militant supporters of the brothers Maulana Abdul Aziz and Abdul Rashid Ghazi who ran the Lal Masjid seminary and Pakistani security forces clashed in Islamabad after the students from the mosque attacked a nearby government ministry building. The brothers had been challenging the government for long in their call to impose Islamic law and way of life. The Pakistani security forces finally laid a siege around the mosque complex which lasted until July 11. In the assault by the troops 154 people were killed and the Masjid finally liberated. This operation, codenamed Operation Sunrise, turned out to be the proverbial last straw leading to the eventual breakdown of the truce that had existed between Pakistan and the Taliban and the Waziristan Accord was scrapped by them. In retaliation of the army operation, suicide attacks on forces and civilians increased nearly ten-fold throughout the country.

(4.1.2) Pakistan: Benazir Bhutto's Assassination

The two attacks on Benazir Bhutto in Pakistan after her return from exile forcefully drove the point home that the façade of security works only as long as the terrorists are dumb. If the terrorists are intelligent, there is nobody in the world who cannot be killed without much difficulty.

Contrary to popular myth, protection does not lie in the number of security men surrounding you—what we euphemistically call 'multiple layers' of security. Even a stun grenade would disorientate them—a real grenade would either distract their attention sufficiently for the terrorist to strike or kill them outright. Men with handguns are of use only against fools who might try to shoot the protected person.

Another myth is that security can be guaranteed by technical devices like jammers. They do not know that there are scores of ways in which jammers can be beaten—the simplest of them, as the Benazir assassination and numerous killings in Sri Lanka have shown, a suicide bomber! A terrorist requires brains and nothing else. If he has brains which the security establishment has not, he will beat them anytime. We tend to forget that a bullet-proof car is not bomb-proof! A VIP carcade on a road could be slowed down or forced to brake by something as simple as driving a few cattle on the road or pushing a child on the road; after that a proper attack could then be mounted on the carcade.

(4.1.3) *Pakistan: Attack on the Marriott Hotel*

On September 20, 2008, a dump truck filled with explosives detonated in front of the Marriott Hotel in Islamabad, killing at least 54 and injuring at least 266. The majority of the casualties were Pakistanis; although about fifteen foreigners have also been reported injured. The Marriott was the most prestigious hotel in the capital, located near government buildings and diplomatic missions. It was popular with foreigners and the Pakistani elite. The hotel had previously been the target of militants. In 2007, a suicide bomber had killed himself and another person in an attack at the hotel. From the terrorists' point of view, the choice of the target was alright but the attack was made in an unprofessional manner and failed to achieve the desired objective.

(4.1.4) *Afghanistan: Attack on the Indian Embassy*

It was a suicide bomb attack on the Indian embassy in Kabul, Afghanistan on July 7, 2008 at 8:30 a.m. local time. The suspected suicide car bombing took place near the gates of the embassy. The bombing killed 58 people and wounded 141. It occurred on a busy, tree-lined street where people usually line up at the embassy gates to apply for visas to India. An explosive-packed Toyota Camry, driven by the suicide bomber, rammed into two Indian diplomatic vehicles entering the embassy and detonated. The gates to the embassy were blown off and the walls of some buildings in its compound were damaged. People around the shops nearby also became immediate victims of the attack, and the Indonesian embassy in the vicinity also suffered some damage.

The casualties could have been higher but for the sand filled blast barriers. Much of the impact was taken up by the sand filled blast barriers. These barriers, which were built across the embassy for added protection just one week before the blast, saved it from structural damage. The HESCO barrier or HESCO bastion is a modern gabion for military fortification. It is made of a collapsible wire-mesh container and heavy duty fabric liner, and used as a temporary blast or small-arms barrier. One of the less heralded life-and labour-saving devices of war, it is used on nearly every US Military base in Iraq as well as on NATO bases in Afghanistan. It is named after the British company that developed it over a decade ago.

(4.1.5) Sri Lanka: Assassination of MP Neelan Thiruchelvam

The TULF MP was assassinated by a LTTE suicide bomber in July 1999. The incident happened at 9:30 a.m. as Thiruchelvam was going from his home to his office. Both located within a kilometer of each other and in the immediate vicinity of Prime Minister Sirimavo Bandaranike's home. The suicide bomber was riding pillion on a motorcycle which slowly edged its way to the MP's car waiting to take a turn at a busy junction not far from the leader's home in a high-security neighbourhood of the Capital. The bomber got off the bike, ran to the car's rear left where Thiruchelvam was seated, threw himself on the car and exploded himself. While Thiruchelvam's driver and his bodyguard were critically wounded, three policemen in an escort jeep behind the car were also injured.

This was quite a novel technique and shows what a determined attacker can do. For most people traffic cannot be stopped. This means that it is not possible for a vehicle from coming close to the protected person's vehicle—if it comes to that he can even force his way through—and then explosives would do their job. In this case, the attacker selected a turn where the target's car had slowed down; it helped him because he was riding pillion on a bike and he had to get down—had the attacker been also in a car, he could have simply pulled parallel to the target car and detonated.

(4.1.6) Sri Lanka: Assassination of Minister Dassanayake

On January 8, 2008 the Minister for Nation Building DM Dassanayake was killed in a bomb blast. The attack took place at a place called Ja-Ela near the famous statue of Rukmani Devi about 19-km from Colombo. He was going to Colombo to attend the first day of the parliament. Besides the minister, one of his bodyguards also died, whereas 11 others were injured.This was one of the cleverest attacks in the history of terrorism. The terrorists scored one hundred per cent marks for the neatness of execution, precision of the attack, meticulous planning and reconnaissance, and use of appropriate technology; the only department in which they scored less than one hundred per cent was the lethality of the attack—the minister was not killed outright but died in the hospital.

The attack was mounted using a directional mine exploded from the side of the road. The shrapnel hit the target vehicle with such precision that hardly any blood was spilled on the road! The mine had been set up on a tree in a bare land on the side of the road. The land was covered with thick bush and separated by a barbed wire fence. A remote control device had triggered the blast from the land located around seven meters from the ill-fated vehicle. This particular mode of attack becomes all the more significant because they could plant the device in a busy area, yet conceal it well, and activate it remotely with such great precision on a moving vehicle.

The incident is an eye-opener for all those stupid bosses of VIP security who create their entire façade of security on the presumption that someone would try to shoot the protected person, or that a large number of security men around would be of any help. The entire system of security works only as long as the terrorists are dumb; they do not bother to attack; or as long as your luck holds out. Intelligent terrorists will beat all those systems of security which are essentially ceremonial in character. In this case, his security personnel in the motorcade could not do a thing—there was simply no target on which they could fire! The entire motorcade remained absolutely intact and in position and could not do a thing because the terrorists outsmarted them. Dassanayake even got medical aid in time. The traditional system of security had worked as good as it could—unfortunately it was simply not good enough for the intelligent terrorists.

(4.1.7) *Sri Lanka: Assassination of Minister Jeyaraj*

On April 6, 2008, the Sri Lankan Chief Government Whip and Minister of Highways and Roads Development Jeyaraj Fernandopulle was killed at a place called Welliweriaya just outside Colombo. The minister was killed in a bomb blast as he was about to flag off a marathon race to mark the celebration of the Sinhala New Year. Thirteen more persons were killed and over 80 injured. The bomb was exploded by a suicide bomber.

This incident showed that even a not-so-sophisticated bomb could inflict so many casualties and effectively achieve its purpose. His security personnel were not able to do anything because the attacker had no intention of shooting at the target, something for which the security men so dutifully prepare all their lives. The prevailing security system is of no defence against a bomber. If there is one principle that can be derived from the assassination of Jeyaraj, it is: "One who goes close to unchecked people, shall be killed very easily irrespective of the number of security personnel guarding him". The corollary of the above principle is: "Such a person shall not be killed only as long as the terrorists are utterly dumb or do not have a man who is prepared to sacrifice his life".

This incident and the principles derived from it has great importance. It is common for protected persons in the Indian sub-continent to lean out of their bullet-proof cars to approach the crowds on the roadside for cheap popularity even as they are travelling. While crowds coming to a function could be checked by metal detectors, those on the roadside (even if they are kept behind some barricades) cannot be checked—it is just not possible. Benazir Bhutto became a victim of the same problem—the bullet-proof car was of no value if she had to stand through the hatch in the roof the car.

(4.1.8) Sri Lanka: Assassination of Admiral Clancy Fernando

Admiral Clancy Fernando, the chief of the Sri Lankan Navy was assassinated by the LTTE in 1992, as the most senior officer in the Sri Lankan armed forces to be killed in the line of duty. The suicide bomber drove an explosives-laden motorbike into his official vehicle on November 16, 1992 when he was on his way to the Naval Headquarters from his official residence. Lt Gen Parami Kulatunga, the Deputy Chief of Army staff was killed in a manner very similar to that used for Admiral Clancy Fernando. On the morning of June 26, 2006 he was killed by a suicide bomber who drove an explosives-laden motorbike into his official vehicle as it was driving to a military base at Panipitiya near Colombo.

From the point of view of terrorists, that was an excellent technique and can be repeated anywhere. Let us face it; you cannot have barricades all along the route—this is not the era of some maharaja! There will necessarily be gaps somewhere as the public also has to use the road. It is easier for a motorcycle to be hidden somewhere close to the road for breaking in but theoretically even a car, truck, tractor, anything may be used. It is just not difficult for someone to barge on the road just in time to crash with the target vehicle. They may keep the engine running and compensate for any mismatch in timing with a larger quantity of explosives. Cops, bereft of any brains as they are, tend to man intersections little realising why a terrorist should be obliged to barge from an intersection only; don't we have off-roaders now in the world? Further, what prevents them from driving a herd of cattle or some animals on to a road from the side so as to make the target carcade brake and slow down? As it slows down, it can be conveniently attacked.

(4.1.9) *Palestinian Attacks*

Palestinian tactics has ranged from carrying out mass protests and general strikes, as in the First Intifada, to armed attacks on security forces, mounting suicide bombing attacks, and firing Qassam rockets into Israeli residential areas. Most suicide bombing attacks (although not all) are targeted against civilians, and conducted on crowded places in Israeli cities, such as public transportation (buses), restaurants and markets. Use of remote-controlled landmines has been noticed. The youngest Palestinian suicide bomber was 16-year-old Issa Bdeir, a high school student from the village of Al Doha, who shocked his friends and family when he blew himself up in a park in Rishon LeZion, killing a teenage boy and an elderly man. The youngest attempted suicide bombing was by a 14-year-old captured by soldiers at the Huwwara checkpoint before managing to do any harm.

(4.1.10) *The Qassam Rocket and its Capabilities*

The rocket gets its name from Sheikh Izz ad-Din Al Qassam, a militant Syrian preacher who advocated rebellion against European colonial powers in the Middle East during the 1920s and 1930s. He was killed in action on November 19, 1935 in the first Palestinian guerrilla action against British forces. His martyrdom triggered the Great Revolt of 1936-39.

The Qassam rocket: a weapon of great potential and future for the urban guerrilla

The invention of the Qassam rocket is attributed to Adnan Al Ghoul, known as the "Father of the Qassam," who was killed by the Israeli military in October 2004. The solid motor uses a fuel as elementary as potassium nitrate and sugar. The Qassam-1, first launched against an Israeli target in October 2001, is capable of an approximate range of 4.5 kilometers (2.796 miles). The Qassam-2 is approximately 2.2 meters (7.22 feet) in length, has a range of up to 9.5 kilometers (5.9 miles), and can carry a payload of 5-9 kilograms of explosives. The more advanced Qassam-3 is capable of achieving a range of approximately 10-12 kilometers, and carries a payload of 10-20 kilograms of explosives. The Qassam-4, developed in September 2005, is expected to have a range of 17 kilometers. The extended-range Qassam perhaps contained an increased explosives payload and standard fuzes. This places the Ashkelon's power station and Netivot within striking distance of the Gaza Strip.

There are reports of a Qassam with two engines also, developed in June 2006. This dual-engine Qassam was seen fired in July 2006 and impacted against the ORT Ronson High School building in central Ashkelon. Hamas claimed the missile was an upgraded Qassam capable of a 15-kilometer range. The Qassam was apparently launched from the northern-most point of the northern Gaza town of Beit Hanun (between the former Israeli communities of Nisanit/Dugit) and traversed the longest distance of a projectile ever launched from the Gaza Strip.

The technical details of the various models are given below.

	Qassam-1	**Qassam-2**	**Qassam-3**
Width:	~80 cm	~180 cm	~200 cm
Diameter:	~60 mm	~150 mm	~170 mm
Weight:	~5.5 kg	~32 kg	~90 kg
Payload:	0.5 kg	5-9 kg	10-20 kg
Max. Range:	3-4.5 km	8-9.5 km	10-20 km

The iron sheet used in the tubing is 2.5-3 mm thick.

It is a terrorist weapon alright and even a small payload of 5-9 kg can cause some casualties, but it remains a terrorist weapon only. Given its inaccuracy, it would still be a weapon of frustration that can irritate but not inflict any significant damage. There is no way it is going to change the balance of power—any claim to the contrary must be dismissed as western propaganda to justify Israeli oppression of the Palestinians.

If the Qassam shows one thing, it is that rocket science is not really as difficult as it is generally believed to be. If Tipu Sultan could make rockets called Tagraq (hailstones) with propellant as elementary as a pyrotechnic mixture or black powder in the 19th century, and the design of which eventually led Col William Congreve to create modern military rockets, what prevents a man in the 21st century to make such small rockets when a tremendous amount of knowledge regarding propellants, explosives and aerodynamics is freely available in public domain? It is interesting to note that Col Congreve's rockets ranged in size from 3 lbs to 300 lbs. The 24 lbs rocket with a 15 feet guide pole was very common and easily got a range of up to 2 miles! The casing, even in that era for a 32 lbs rocket was a tube of three-and-a-half feet by four inches – what is so difficult in this era to make a rocket with a body of seven feet or so? Amateur rocketry is a popular hobby in the USA and Canada. Rocketry enthusiasts like Richard Nakka maintain elaborate websites [www.nakka-rocketry.net] giving full details of every aspect of amateur rocketry, including principles and design.

Information about a host of propellant combinations for amateur rocketry is available in the public domain. Typical amateur formulations in use today are: sugar (sucrose, dextrose, and sorbitol are all common)/ potassium nitrate, zinc-sulfur, HTPB (a rubber like epoxy)/magnesium/ ammonium nitrate, and HTPB or PBAN/aluminium/ammonium perchlorate (APCP). In fact, there is a programme called SS2S (Sugar Shot To Space, http://sugarshot.org/). The goal of the Sugar Shot to Space programme is to loft a rocket powered by "sugar propellant" into space, officially defined as 100-km (62 miles) above the earth's surface. Well, if people can legitimately try to send a rocket 100-km up in space, what business people have bothering about throwing a sugar-powered rocket 20-30 km on ground! And if it comes to that, who said that one cannot make proper military-grade propellant at home – it requires rather high skills, still it can be done.

We must admit the fact that it is extremely easy for modern terrorists to devise such elementary things. We will have to learn to live with that. In fact, therein lies the strength of modern terrorism. Even the naxal insurgents of India had tried making what appeared to be their own version of a RPG-7. It would not have flown like a RPG when fired from the shoulder but, fired from a makeshift launcher at 45 degrees or so, it could have flown like Tipu's rockets. The Hamas are certainly better-equipped than the naxals of India.

(4.1.11) UK: The 7/7 London Bombings

Forty-nine people were killed in four bombing attacks on the London Public Transportation System on July 7, 2005. The first explosion occurred on a Circle Line train in a tunnel between Liverpool Street and Aldgate East underground stations at 8:51 a.m. The train was just approaching Liverpool Street station coming from Aldgate. Circle Line trains run at an average depth of 21 feet. The explosive device was placed on the floor of the third carriage. Seven people died and estimated 100 were injured. The second explosion occurred in the Piccadilly Line Subway train travelling between King's Cross and Russell Square Station at 8:56 a.m. The device was placed in the first carriage by the first set of double doors. The Piccadilly Line is 70 feet deep at the blast site. At least 21 people died. The third explosion hit a west-bound Circle Line train just leaving Edgware Road Underground station for Paddington at 9:17 a.m. The device was on the floor of the second carriage close to the first set of double doors. The blast blew through a wall and hit a second train on an adjoining platform. Seven people died in the blast. The fourth explosion took place on a bus in Woburn Place, close to Tavistock Square and Russell Square at 9:47 a.m. The roof of a double-decker bus (Hackney to Marble Arch) was blown off. Some cars nearby were also damaged. Thirteen people died in the bus blast.

The western world tried to make it appear that it was a great terrorist attack. Fact is, they were crude bombs. As it has been shown at great length in 'Urban Terrorism: Myths and Realities', all that they could make was a dust bomb with hydrogen peroxide as oxidizer and wheat flour as fuel.

(4.1.12) Russia: Moscow Theater Hostage Crisis

The Moscow theater hostage crisis, also known as the 2002 Nord-Ost siege, was the seizure of a crowded Moscow theater on October 23, 2002 by about 40-50 armed Chechen rebel fighters who claimed allegiance to the separatist movement in Chechnya. They took 850 hostages including members of the audience and performers, among them a MVD general, and demanded the withdrawal of the Russian forces from Chechnya and an end to the Second Chechen War. The siege was led by Movsar Barayev, aged 22 at the time. All the hostages were kept in the auditorium and the orchestra pit was used as a lavatory. After a two-and-a-half day siege, Russian OSNAZ forces pumped a hitherto unknown chemical agent into the building's ventilation system and raided it. Officially, 39 of the terrorists were killed by Russian forces, along with at least 129 and possibly many more of the hostages. All but two of the hostages who died during the siege were killed by the toxic substance pumped into the theater to subdue the militants.

This operation was a good example of out-of-the-box thinking by the Russians. Nothing would have been easier than a full-scale assault on the building with armour as the Indians did in their Operation Blue Star. However, that would have led to considerable collateral damage. Yes, civilian casualties did result in their method also but the reason was different. Fentanyl was being used for the first time and enough scientific literature was just not available regarding the correct amount to be administered with some exactitude. Hence, overdosing took place, leading to the casualties. Several Russian Special Forces operatives were also poisoned by the gas during the operation. The Russians have an old culture of secrecy—hence there were no further reports on studies pertaining to effect of the gas on humans.

The Russians went about the whole thing in a very clever manner. They leaked information that the storming of the place would take place at three in the morning. The Chechen fighters expected a usual commando raid and they were on their guard. Two members of the Alpha forces moving around in the no-man's land were seriously wounded by a grenade fired from the building by the rebels. But the raid did not take place. Then there was the natural reaction—a relaxation. And at 5:00 a.m. the place was attacked.

Early in the morning before dawn at around 5:00 a.m. Moscow time, the searchlights that had been illuminating the main entrance to the theatre went out. Inside, although many hostages at first took the gas to be smoke from some fire, it soon became apparent to gunmen and hostages alike that a mysterious gas had been pumped into the building. Different reports said it came either through the specially-created hole in the wall, that it was pumped through the theater's ventilation system, or that it emerged from beneath the stage. It is thought that the security services pumped an aerosol anesthetic, later conjectured to be weaponised fentanyl (or an FSB-made aerosol version of carfentanyl, an artificial, powerful opium-like substance), into the theater through the air conditioning system.

The entire hostage-taking operation, from the point of view of the terrorists, was conducted in a most amateurish manner. This is important because it proves that they were not as good, deadly or professional as they are generally made out to be. They could have killed some of the hostages to build up pressure on the government. Cell phone conversations between the hostages trapped in the building

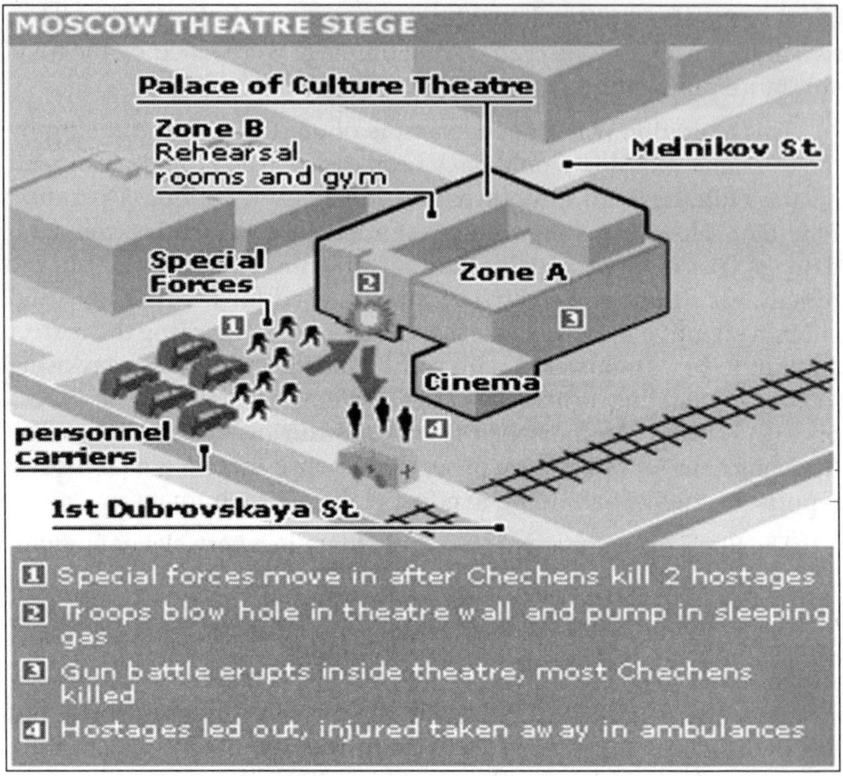

The Moscow Theater Siege Operation: A good example of some quick out-of-the-box thinking by the Russians, something which the Indians could not do in Operation Blue Star

and their family members gave the impression that the hostage-takers had grenades, mines and improvised explosive devices strapped to their bodies, and had deployed more explosives throughout the theater. A majority of these explosives (including all those worn by the female fighters) were later found to be military dummies. The remaining ones had no detonators or the batteries were taken out. In other words, the so-called terrorists had actually been play-acting! They were also using Arabic names among themselves, and the female rebels wore Arab-style *burqas* which is highly unusual in the North Caucasus region—a very childish thing to do.

The Chechens, some of whom were equipped with gas masks, did not set off any explosives or fire on their hostages once the storming got under way. That was an obvious mistake. Either, as discussed above, they did not have explosives or they did not have the resolve to kill the hostages. Instead, the rebels responded with firing blindly at the

Russian positions outside. After thirty minutes, when the gas had taken effect, a physical assault on the building commenced. The combined forces entered through numerous building openings, including the roof, the basement, and finally the front door. After nearly one and a half hours of sporadic gun battles, the Russian Special Forces blew open the doors to the main hall and poured into the auditorium. In a fierce firefight, they gunned down the terrorist who were still conscious and systematically executed those who had succumbed to the gas.

(4.1.13) Indonesia: 2002 Bali Bombing

The 2002 Bali bombings occurred on October 12, 2002 in the tourist district of Kuta on the Indonesian island of Bali. The attack was the deadliest act of terrorism in the history of Indonesia, killing 202 people, 164 of whom were foreign nationals (mostly from Australia), and 38 Indonesian citizens. A further 209 people were injured. The attack involved the detonation of three bombs: a backpack-mounted device carried by a suicide bomber; a large car bomb, both of which were detonated in or near popular nightclubs in Kuta; and a third much smaller device detonated outside the United States consulate in Denpasar, causing only minor damage.

At 11:05 p.m. in the night, a suicide bomber inside the nightclub Paddy's Pub detonated a bomb in his backpack. Fifteen seconds later, a second and much more powerful car bomb hidden inside a white Mitsubishi van, was detonated by another suicide bomber outside the Sari Club, located opposite Paddy's Pub. Damage to the densely populated residential and commercial district was immense, destroying neighbouring buildings and shattering windows several blocks away. A comparatively small bomb detonated outside the US consulate in Denpasar, which is thought to have exploded shortly before the two Kuta bombs, caused minor injuries to one person and property damage was minimal. It was reportedly packed with human excrement to express disgust with the Americans.

The Mitsubishi L300 van bomb was initially thought to have consisted of C4, a military grade plastic explosive. However, investigators subsequently discovered the bomb was made from something as simple as potassium chlorate, aluminium powder, and sulfur. For the Sari club bomb with the L300 van, the terrorists assembled 12 plastic filing cabinets filled with explosives. The cabinets, each containing a potassium chlorate, aluminium powder, sulfur mixture with a TNT booster-cum-primer, were connected by 150 meters of detonating cord. Ninety-four electric detonators were

The Bali bombing

used for the TNT boosters. The total weight of the van bomb was 1.125 tons. This shows what terrible damage can be inflicted by even low explosives if used in large quantities and proves that, against the popular misconception created by the media, explosives like RDX, C4 or Semtex are not the only explosive which the terrorists are obliged to use all the time.

(4.1.14) Indonesia: 2003 Marriott Hotel Bombing

The 2003 Marriott Hotel bombing took place on August 5, 2003 in Mega Kuningan, South Jakarta. A suicide bomber detonated a car bomb outside the lobby of the JW Marriott Hotel, killing 12 people and injuring 150. The hotel was viewed as a Western symbol, and had been used by the United States embassy for various events. A Toyota Kijang was loaded with explosives and driven through the taxi stand in front of the Marriott Hotel. The vehicle stopped briefly in front of the lobby and CCTV cameras show a security guard approaching the vehicle, briefly speaking to the driver. The security guard then turned and suddenly the car exploded. It is still not clear if the explosion was accidental; set off by remote detonation; by a timer that set off prematurely; or by the suicide bomber himself who somehow panicked and set it off prematurely. If the vehicle had kept a course heading straight for the lobby the damage would undoubtedly have been more severe. According to the Indonesian police, the car bomb contained the same mixture as used in the 2002 Bali bombing.

(4.1.15) Indonesia: 2004 Australian Embassy Bombing

The 2004 Australian embassy bombing took place on September 9, 2004 in Jakarta. Jemaah Islamiyah is suspected to be the culprit. This time also they used a fairly big car bomb. A one-ton car bomb, packed into a small Daihatsu delivery van, exploded outside the Australian embassy, killing 9 people, and wounding over 150 others. Damage was also reported to the nearby buildings—window glasses were shattered up to half-a-km away. The explosive used in this attack was probably TNT.

(4.1.16) Indonesia: 2005 Bali Bombings

The 2005 Bali bombings were a series of suicide bomb attacks that occurred on October 1, 2005, in Bali. Bombs exploded at two sites in Jimbaran and Kuta, both in south Bali. Twenty people were killed, and 129 people were injured by three bombers who killed themselves in the attacks. One of the blasts struck Raja's Restaurant at the Kuta Square shopping mall in central Kuta. Another two bombs exploded at Warungs along the Jimbaran beach, one of which was near the Four Seasons Hotel. These areas are generally popular with Western tourists—the dead included four Australians. The wounded included many Indonesians, 19 Australians, 6 South Koreans, 6 Americans, 4 Japanese, 3 Canadians, and 1 Briton.

According to Indonesia's head of counter-terrorism, Maj Gen Ansyaad Mbai, the attacks were carried out by at least three suicide bombers in a fashion similar to the 2002 bombings. The remnants of backpacks and excessively mutilated bodies are believed to be evidence of suicide bombings. There remains also a possibility that backpacks were hidden inside the target restaurants before detonation.

(4.1.17) USA: 9/11 Attacks

The 9/11 attacks had great show value—but going by the principles of terrorism they were a terrible folly. It provoked the USA into launching a full-scale war against Afghanistan which nearly destroyed the Taliban. Could not al-Qaeda foresee such a direct consequence? They should have known that after such a demonstrative strike the people would rally behind the 'Stars and Stripes' and the clarion call would be for vengeance—immediate and blood red. Could they be such fools as to believe that the Americans would be too stunned to do anything and would only cry haplessly? Could they be so naïve as to not understand that the most readily available target would be Afghanistan only as there was little evidence against anyone of the 'respectable' nation-states? Further, if it is to be believed that al-Qaeda was utilising Afghanistan and the hospitality of the Taliban as a safe sanctuary, they were bound to lose it as a result of the American attack on the Taliban. Why would they have chosen to deprive themselves of this? If an organisation could plan such a spectacular strike and carry it out with such great precision, it is difficult to believe that they would be so stupid as to invite destruction of their sanctuary as a result of that. Such great tactical finesse that resulted in the most spectacular terrorist attack in the history of mankind and such poor strategic vision are mutually irreconcilable. In all probability, al-Qaeda was not the culprit!

The US says that al-Qaeda did it. For a moment let us assume that they did it. The immediate question would be: "What was their motive"? Nearly a decade later also, even now there is no clue as to what would al-Qaeda have hoped to achieve by the 9/11 strike, if at all they did it. Osama never claimed responsibility for the attack but is said to have acknowledged his support for the 9/11 hijackers and repeated his claim that strikes on American targets should be viewed by Muslims and Americans as a defensively motivated response to perceived American aggression in the Islamic world. The first reports had said that as soon as he heard of that, he went on to perform a '*sajda*' (Muslim act of kneeling and bending to touch the ground with the head) as an act of thanksgiving to Allah. This is important—had al-Qaeda engineered it, Osama would have had heard of it through his own sources—not the world media. If you could arrange 19 men to carry out the attacks, you could have arranged one more man to report on the carnage through a network of calls.

The US has never furnished conclusive proof of the involvement of al-Qaeda in the WTC towers/ Pentagon attacks. Note that here we are speaking of legally tenable evidence and not beliefs or presumptions. No evidence worth its name was ever produced in public; the Americans took refuge behind the plea of protecting intelligence sources. The British Prime Minister had, however, issued a public document entitled "Responsibility For The Terrorist Atrocities In The United States, 11 September, 2001" which was based on evidence supplied by the USA. It states in the beginning itself (and the Brits must be given some credit for not being as shameless as the Americans): "This document does not purport to provide a prosecutable case against Osama bin Laden in a court of law. Intelligence often cannot be used evidentially, due both to the strict rules of admissibility and to the need to protect the safety of sources. But on the basis of all the information available HMG is confident of its conclusions as expressed in this document".

- The document consists of 74 paragraphs but most of these pertain to al-Qaeda and Osama's previous strikes and atrocities. On the September 11 attacks, the document offers the following as evidence:

- That three of the 19 hijackers have been identified as associates of al-Qaeda;
- Intelligence sources have been cited to claim that bin Laden himself asserted that he was preparing for a major attack on the USA; and
- That al-Qaeda's associates were asked to return to Afghanistan by September 10.

It needs no great legal knowledge to convince oneself that the evidence is just not convincing. Paragraph Number 73 of the document says: "No other organisation has both the motivation and the capability to carry out attacks like those of September 11—only the al-Qaeda network under Osama bin Laden"! The logic is nothing but absurd. It amounts to saying that if a woman 'A' has been ravished by someone and if there was a neighbour 'B' who was known to like her (that is, allegedly had some motive) and who was potent too (that is, had the capability of performing the sexual act), then it is to be presumed that it was 'B' who had committed the crime—no other evidence need be taken into account! It does not matter that 'A' could have been ravished by anybody in the world—they have 'B' right there and they don't like 'B' and hence 'B' is the criminal. These guys do not understand that the desire to commit a crime does not mean that one could have committed a crime.

The Guardian, in its editorial "Still No Smoking Gun" had concluded that the case against bin Laden as published by the British Government "would be almost worthless from a legal point of view". Similarly, the foreign editor of *The Times*, London, Bronwen Maddox, described the document as a "puzzling and worrying piece of work" and preferred the opinion that "only if it is read as a political text does it seem shrewd".

The FBI investigation into the attacks, code named operation PENTTBOM, was able to identify the 19 hijackers within days, as the hijackers are said to have made little effort to conceal their names on flight, credit card, and other records. Thus, as far as the FBI is concerned, they solved such a complicated case within a few days! And how did they arrive at their conclusions? Identical handwritten letters (in Arabic) were found in three separate locations: the first, in a suitcase of hijacker Mohamed Atta that did not make the connection to the American Airlines Flight 11 that crashed into the North Tower of the World Trade Center; the second, at Washington Dulles International

Airport, in a vehicle that belonged to hijacker Nawaf al Hazmi; and the third at the crash site of United Airlines Flight 93 in Shanksville, Pennsylvania. Translations indicate that the hijackers were willing to die. Surprised? No—only the greatest duffers could think otherwise—they had to be willing to die—nothing new in it! Well, be prepared for the mother of all surprises!

The Americans say that rescue workers sifting through the tons of rubble discovered a passport belonging to one of the hijackers, Satam Al Suqami, a few blocks from the World Trade Center a passerby picked it up and gave it to a NYPD detective shortly before the World Trade Center towers collapsed. According to the 9/11 Commission, the passports of two of the hijackers Flight 93 were also found intact at the crash site, and the passport of hijacker Abdul Aziz Alomari was found in Mohamed Atta's left-behind luggage.

The very first premise is questionable. Who would be so dumb as to not try to conceal his identity when taking a ticket? Who would be so stupid as to leave identical handwritten letters at three locations, and why? If the plan was to eventually deny al-Qaeda's involvement, who could commit such elementary mistakes? On one hand, we claim to have the world's best terrorists in them; on the other hand, you have people who commit such mistakes as if they wanted to tell the whole world that they had done it. Unbelievable! And then we have the matter of the alleged recovery of the passports? Who would be such a fool as to carry it on his person on the flight when it was not supposed to be necessarily required for inland travel? And to believe that of all the myriad things that perished in the crash, what was slated to survive was the passport of the perpetrator—surely someone in the American establishment is a strong believer in divine justice! If at all the passports were required to be carried by them, they must have been on their person—the bodies were incinerated but the passports survived—outrageous, isn't it! Who in the world would believe in it?

The Washington Post reported that by checking flight manifests and comparing them with other information, like watch lists, customs officials were able to find the names of all 19 hijackers by 11:00 a.m. When examining Mohamed Atta's left-behind luggage, the FBI found important clues about the hijackers and their plans. His luggage contained papers that revealed the identity of all the 19 hijackers, and provided information about their plans, motives, and backgrounds. The FBI was able to determine details such as dates of birth, known and/or possible residences, visa status, and specific identity of the suspected pilots. However, the fact is that none of these documents have been scrutinised by independent legal experts. And why should

Atta leave all that documentary evidence in the left-behind luggage? If an organisation had commissioned him, the organisation would have known the identities of everybody else involved too—if Atta wanted honours for all of them and pensions for their families, the organisation could have done that—why should he leave the papers? Surely he did not intend to survive the crash and retrieve it later? Or do the Americans think so? On September 27, 2001, the FBI released photos of the 19 hijackers, along with information about the possible nationalities and aliases of many.

Thus, we are supposed to believe that a gang of 19 people who pulled off the biggest, the most spectacular hijacking and terrorist strike in human history were so dumb that Atta had left the details of each one of them in his left-behind luggage! Obviously, this is a fabricated thing.

While the hijacking was in progress, two flight attendants on American Airlines Flight 11, Betty Ong and Amy Sweeney, are said to have contacted airline personnel on the ground and identified Mohamed Atta al Sayed as one of five individuals who had hijacked the plane. A flight attendant on United Airlines Flight 175 is said to have called a United Airline mechanic and reported that hijackers had killed the crew. While the hijacking was in progress on American Airlines Flight 77, several passengers, including a flight attendant, Renee May, are said to have contacted and reported details of the hijacking to persons on the ground. Sales clerks are said to have identified two individuals to whom they sold tickets for Flight 77 as the hijackers Hani Hanjour and Majed Moqed. During the hijacking of United Airlines Flight 93, Jeremy Glick identified the hijackers as Arabic-looking and carrying knives. Thus, the evidence is sought to be built on such flimsy testimonies of people who get to see hundreds of people in a day and who have, in any case, very little knowledge of the appearance and mannerisms of Arabs? Is there any reason for them to have remembered their faces? Does anyone in his right mind think that such determined, skillful and meticulous hijackers would have been so stupid as to make their appearance obviously conspicuous? Americans are so stupid that in hate crimes they are known to have attacked Sikhs, mistaking their turbans and beards for Arabs and here you have some not-so-smart clerks who remember everything? By God, if someone was staying in the USA and learning flying, he could have acquired some American mannerisms also.

And is it so easy to hijack a plane with knives of permitted length of blades? If you have permitted a certain length, this means you have determined that nothing much can be done with that and that it is harmless. Then how could they be used for hijacking? Obviously, either you, as a nation, were a fool before 9/11 in permitting them or you are telling a lie. And if the knives were longer, how did the knives get through the security checks in the first place? Why is the FBI silent on that? There are reasons to believe that such elementary checks were very much in place at all the airports in question? Why don't they tell how did the security violation take place and who were responsible? How did they kill the crew? Using the same knives? How the cockpit doors were got opened? Obviously they could not be forced open so easily? And surely the Americans are not so dumb that their pilots would have opened the doors merely on hearing that a flight attendant or a passenger is being held hostage on knife point? It is precisely the thing that they have been teaching to their pilots for the last several decades.

The investigators claim that they were quickly able to link the 19 men to the terrorist organisation al-Qaeda, by accessing their intelligence agency files! *The New York Times* reported on September 12 that: "Authorities said they had also identified accomplices in several cities who had helped plan and execute Tuesday's attacks. Officials said they knew who these people were and had important biographical details about many of them. They prepared biographies of each identified member of the hijack teams, and began tracing the recent movements of the men". Well, well, you had all the details on them and yet, in the first place, you could not spot them in your country, and secondly, you did nothing to nab them during all those months even as they stayed comfortably, moved around comfortably, and even attended flight training courses? Both things cannot be true simultaneously. If you knew that they were there, you are guilty of not having acted against them or monitored them; or you are simply telling a lie. FBI agents in Florida investigating the hijackers are said to have quickly 'descended on flight schools, neighbourhoods and restaurants in pursuit of leads'. At one flight school, "students said investigators were there within hours of Tuesday's attacks". *The Washington Post* later reported that "In the hours after Tuesday's bombings, investigators searched their files on [Satam] Al Suqami and [Ahmed] Alghamdi, noted the pair's ties to [Nabil] al Marabh and launched a hunt for him. The whole thing is so unnatural—there was no fumbling—they seem to have zeroed on to the accused as if they knew what exactly they had to look for and the things were simply waiting for them to come and pick them up!

The planes that struck the WTC towers were different models of the Boeing 767 (one was -222 and the other was -223ER). Everybody in the world who sucks up to the West has believed without asking a single question that a few months in a flight school would have been enough to fly the planes with such great precision. This could only mean two things. These guys were exceptionally talented flying geniuses or that all the formal pilot training and all the sophisticated equipment used in training are a farce.

Most people do not have any idea of how long and arduous the training of an airline pilot is. Pilot training in the USA entails a series of steps one must accomplish before you are employable as an FAA Certified Pilot. Most, if not all, Flight Colleges and Universities in the USA require that you have your Private Pilot Certificate completed before you commence their programme. In comparison whatever flying training these guys had received was extremely perfunctory that would not have enabled them to fly a single-seater properly, not to speak of a 767! Why does someone else not demonstrate that he could fly a 767 merely by reading its manual privately?

Well, well, if you believe in the story concocted by the FBI, hijacking and flying a Boeing 767 had never been so easy! Either the Americans must admit that these Arabs had some unimaginable talent or they should stop wasting the great deal of time and money that they do in producing 767 pilots—one could as well learn flying on a Cessna, spend some time in front of the simulator and voila—you are fit to fly the 767 and land it with great precision! Those who flew the two huge commercial airliners into the WTC towers flew it with great precision. It amounted to landing the plane in a strip of the width of the towers and that too without the aid of any guidance system which the aircrafts necessarily receive when they land at an airport—even their speed was far in excess of the normal landing speed. This means that they did it with simple visual control. Who in the world can believe that these guys, who were below average even in the most elementary training which they are said to have received, could have pulled it off? You have to be dumb like the Americans to believe in it.

Secondly, the story of a flight manual in Arabic having been found in an abandoned car is unbelievable. One who is able to fly a Boeing 767 with great precision obviously knows his job. He does not need to read a flight manual till he enters the airport building—only weak and nervous students are seen to be mugging till the last moment before entering the examination hall! Thirdly, an organisation that could muster the services of about 20 men or so for an operation, could easily muster the services of one more man to take out the car that they used for going to the airport. Only a fool would leave tell-tale evidence like that for the police to discover! All along my years in the Indian police, I have known the Indian police for fabricating such absurd lies for nailing some poor guy- now I am convinced that policemen are equally crooked all over the world—they tell the same lies, with same crudity!

The Americans only passed judgment; they did not produce any evidence. As late as June 2002, the FBI Director Robert S. Mueller III, in testimony before a Senate committee, reported on the then-current speculation: "We think the masterminds of it were in Afghanistan, high in the al-Qaeda leadership. Plotters and others—the principals—came together in Germany and perhaps elsewhere". The evidence, as even men like Noam Chomsky pointed out, was never even remotely adequate, not to speak of a definitive proof, to show that bin Laden or al-Qaeda in Afghanistan were directly responsible for the 9/11 attacks.

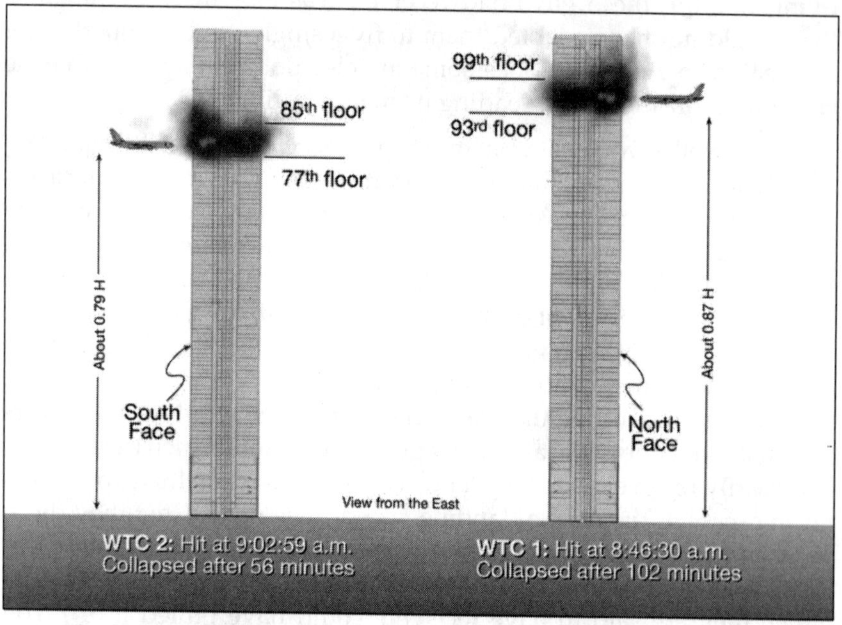

The 9/11 attack—conspiracy theories may be wrong, but the so-called evidence presented by the US against al-Qaeda is pure trash

Al-Qaeda had the motive and the desire to hurt the USA—but such a flawless execution of the most spectacular hijacking-cum-crashing of several flights simultaneously was way beyond their capability—none of their earlier feats had ever indicated even a hint of such finesse, sophistication and near perfection that was so eloquently demonstrated in the 9/11 attacks. I have analysed each one of the major attacks attributed to them across the world and they are all characterised by sheer amateurishness, lack of technical knowledge, lack of professional planning, and poor execution. In fact, the technical capability and perfection evident in the 9/11 attacks is just not reconcilable with what they had displayed in the years preceding that and also in the incidents following that. In any case, as I argued above, it never made any sense for them to attack the USA in such a manner and invite disaster for themselves.

They have attributed the bombings of the US military complex at Khobar (Saudi Arabia, June 1996), the US embassies in Kenya and Tanzania (August 1998) and the USS Cole (Aden, October 2000) all to the al-Qaeda. The embassy bombings involved car bombs—quite a simple thing. Although the targets of the attacks were US government facilities, most of its victims were African civilians: about 200 Kenyans were killed at the embassy in Nairobi, and 11 Tanzanians were killed in Dar-es-Salaam—so much so for the planning by al-Qaeda. The motive never made any sense to anybody. Bin Laden is reported to have initially said that the sites had been targeted because of the `invasion` of Somalia; then he described an American plan to partition Sudan, which he said was hatched in the embassy in Nairobi. He also told his followers that the genocide in Rwanda had been planned inside the two American embassies. Lawrence Wright says that bin Laden's actual goal was "to lure the United States into Afghanistan, which was already being called 'The Graveyard of Empires'. We regard it as outrageous. Could Osama ever hope to finish off the USA in Afghanistan? They had not finished off even the Soviet Union there. The covert operation, sustained mainly on the strength of the massive pumping of arms and ammunition by the USA directly or through purchases afforded in the illicit arms market and guided ably by the CIA-ISI combine, had merely made it untenable for the Soviets to continue occupation there. The Soviet Union was not defeated there, in the much the same way that the USA was not defeated in Vietnam—the only thing is that the occupation or intervention could no longer remain a viable or profitable proposition. Hence, the theory of Osama intending to provoke the USA into entering Afghanistan does not hold water. The USA did enter there and bombed the shit out of them—how did it help Osama—did it trigger a world-wide Muslim uprising? No! Osama could not have been such a fool. It had to be something else.

In October 2000, suspected al-Qaeda militants in Yemen attacked the missile destroyer USS Cole in a suicide attack with an explosive-laden dinghy, killing 17 US servicemen and damaging the vessel while it lay offshore. This was a classic example of the stupidity of the terrorists and shows how ignorant they were. These guys thought that by just exploding a dinghy close to a destroyer they would be able to sink it. How foolish! Obviously, they had no idea of the compartmentalised structure of the ship nor did they know that for a ship anchored in harbour, a hole in the port side was not going to sink it anyway. This speaks volumes about their so-called training and their technical capabilities. It further strengthens our assertion that the West has been presenting a grossly inflated picture of the capabilities of the terrorists and the dangers arising out of them so that it may, under the cover of the bogey, continue its hegemonic agenda. The blast had hit the ship's galley, where crew was lining up for lunch. The crew fought flooding in the engineering spaces and had the damage under control by the evening. Divers inspected the hull and determined the keel was not damaged. The target was far too big (8886 tons) for the explosives contained in the small dinghy that had to explode without penetrating the hull first as a missile does. The LTTE knew the job better. When they use explosive-laden suicide boats, they attack usually small vessels of the Dvora class patrol boats of 45-60 tons.

There is no reason to believe that guys who did the above, could do something as flawless as the 9/11 attacks?

5

Bombs: The Urban Guerrilla's Ever-faithful Companion

There is no human problem that cannot be solved with a proper application of high explosives.

(5.1) General Ignorance about Explosives in the Media

If there is to be found one word that could describe the ignorance of the media and the security forces about the entire business of explosives, bombs and IEDs, it is 'terrible'—in fact the subject has given a license to cub reporters and old hacks alike to indulge in all sorts of wild speculations. Examples of ignorance regarding explosives are legion. We will cite but a few to illustrate the point.

That the terrorists have invented such mysterious explosives which they can make on board aircrafts using innocuous ingredients. The ingredients will be smuggled in bottles of cold drink etc. and the explosive will be made in the toilets of the aircrafts. After that they will blow up the aircrafts in mid-air. (And hence liquids must be banned on flights. Have you forgotten? They had indeed banned all liquids in cabin baggage on aircrafts! They could have at least considered a Nobel Prize in chemistry for such a wonderful discovery!)

That terrorists are coming by the sea route in dinghies and with just a few pounds of explosives carried in their backpacks they will be able to breach our dams, and destroy vital installations like power stations, etc. (Yeah, you know the Arabian sea is their backwater anyway and these old dams are really fragile! A few pounds are all that they will need and you will have a veritable deluge! Strike off dams from the list of picnic spots! By God, if the stupid Indians could be scared of a film called Dam999 which imagined the consequences of a dam-break, they would surely believe that terrorists could bust dams!)

That the terrorists are able to make 'deadly explosives' from things as simple as hair bleach, nail polish remover and battery acid. (How ingenious! Smart guys, isn't it? They should have banned such things immediately! Find some herbal solution quickly, please.... otherwise what will happen to the fashion industry and the millions of cars?)

That if there is a bomb blast, RDX must have been used. The only explosive terrorists now use is RDX. (Incidentally, it was Semtex in the days of terrorism in Punjab. The al-Qaeda has decreed that any terrorist using any other explosive shall be excommunicated from the fraternity and his license to practice terrorism shall be revoked!)

Forensic experts have identified the explosive material used in the 'landmine' as ammonium nitrate. (Yeah, just ammonium nitrate and you did not know all these years that it was a bloody explosive? These fertilizers must be banned! We support organic farming!)

That the terrorists are able to make 'high intensity' explosives using substances as simple as aluminium powder. (Looks like even paint shops will have to be banned! Next they will make explosives out of thin air!)

That the terrorists can simply shoot at the lakhs of LPG and petrol tankers moving across the country and blow them up. Or they will strap small charges to them and they will have 'huge bombs on wheels'. Have they not been showing this in films all along? (What do we do now, momma? Never knew bombs could be soo... big! Stay away from them, baby! Shall we suggest underground gas pipelines all over the country?)

That the terrorists have made explosives which also release poisonous fumes after explosion, thereby invoking a chemical warfare aspect to it. (Now these guys are really getting nasty, isn't it? Adding insult to injury—as if the blast itself was not enough? Where do they learn their chemistry—CBSE ought to have a rethink on their stupid chemistry texts.)

That they use a timer circuit called ABCD timer in their time bombs. (Ever heard of it; even if you have a Ph.D. in electronics? And you thought the ISI was teaching them English alphabet? That's the wonder timer, baby!)

That the terrorists have only to carry a couple of LPG cylinders in a car and crash it—they will be able to blow up entire airport buildings. (They do invent such brilliant things. You know, the Glasgow bomber Kafeel was doing PhD in aeronautical engineering in UK? And your stupid son-in-law? The bugger did not learn a thing all these years with Microsoft!)

That the IED (which was no bigger than a cricket ball), if it had succeeded in exploding, would have demolished a three-storey building. A major tragedy was thus averted. (Thank God! Had it been of the size of a football it would have taken the entire town down!)

That the explosive used in the pressure cooker bomb was a high explosive as well as incendiary and that's why it had set the train compartment ablaze. (You know, what these American scientists will ever invent? The ISI knows how to invent explosives! They are the real master blasters! And you thought a master blaster is a batsman?)

Do not be surprised, dear readers. Einstein had said once: "Only two things are infinite, the universe and human stupidity; and I'm not sure about the former". I have not cooked up the list. If you have been monitoring the media closely, you too would have seen such gems some time or the other. Such outrageous notions are held not only by the Indian media, intelligence and security agencies but also by premier agencies across the world including the FBI, the British police and the German police. For some it is pure ignorance; for some it is prejudice that has closed the mind to reason; and for some it is both.

(5.2) The Outrageous Advice Given by the Media for Combating the 'Menace' of Explosives

The following is a typical example of the advice tendered by the media on the subject of combating the menace of explosives: "India's failure to develop modern inventory-management and security procedures for its civilian explosives stockpile is undermining efforts to build a credible case that Islamist terror groups are receiving external sponsorship... While most major terror strikes a decade ago relied on military-grade explosives like RDX, PETN or Semtex that could be obtained only from a military or covert service attacks are now most often carried out with ammonium nitrate-based explosives pilfered from legitimate dealers... For example, NeoGel a commercial mix of nine parts of ammonium nitrate to one part of an emulsifier was used in last week's blasts in Hyderabad. Investigators believe that the explosive was most likely stolen from a quarry in Andhra Pradesh and eventually purchased by terrorists from the flourishing local black market...India's efforts to address the problem, experts say, are deeply flawed. In 2004, the Union Home Ministry imposed a comprehensive ban on the manufacture of nitroglycerine-based explosives for civilian purposes. In their place, users like the mining and construction industry adopted ammonium nitrate-based explosives...Our idea, said one official involved in the decision, was to try and deny terrorists the option of building up large caches of nitroglycerine-based explosives. Unlike nitroglycerine-based explosives, ammonium nitrate based explosives are very vulnerable to moisture retention. In field conditions, they have a shelf life under two months...But the ban was subverted by the proliferation of production facilities. While just three large factories produced civilian-use explosives till 2004, there are now 73 manufacturers. Many of the factories have come up in anarchic parts of Bihar and Jharkhand since end-users like the mining industry have a significance presence in these regions...Although explosives users must possess license to make purchases and adhere to strict protocols for securing stocks, preventing pilferage has proved impossible. Fishermen, for example, buy explosives for stunning underwater prey, while farmers frequently make crude bombs to scare away predators and pests...We urgently need to improve the system for auditing stocks of explosives and fertilizers with dual-use potential, a Home Ministry official told *The Hindu*. But without electronic inventory-management and well-secured storage facilities, there is no way to do this. Everyone wants security but no one wants to pay the bill for it...Explosives pilferage is not the only area of concern. Intelligence and police officials have long been calling for design changes in detonators the thin, thumb-length tubes that initiate an explosion. Experts want detonators fitted with hard-wired fuse which will ensure that an explosion takes six seconds after the completion of the electrical circuit...Such fuses, the experts say, will make precision attacks on security force convoys or VIPs almost impossible since terrorists will no longer be able to set off explosions at the exact moment their targets pass by. For precision strikes, terrorists will be forced to rely on detonators provided by their foreign sponsors...Across the world, terror groups have come to rely on locally-manufactured explosives and detonators. Ammonium nitrate-based explosives were used to execute the Istanbul bombings of 2003, the Bali nightclub attack in 2002 and the al-Qaeda strike on the US embassy in Nairobi in 1998...Western governments have tightened controls on both ammonium nitrate-based explosives and fertilizers. Police in the United Kingdom prevented a major terror strike in 2004 as a consequence. In 2006, the Royal Canadian Mounted Police broke up an al-Qaeda inspired terror group, after the men purchased three tonnes of ammonium nitrate".

Let us rip it apart point-by-point. Is an inventory-management of our civilian explosive production really feasible? Do they have an idea of how much explosives we produce? According to the latest Annual Report of the Petroleum and Explosives Safety Organisation, Nagpur (Formerly Department of Explosives), Government of India: "There are 71 factories licensed under Explosives Rules in the medium and Small Scale Sector, engaged in the production of explosives, having an installed capacity of 2,117 MT of gunpowder, 18,90,931 MT of High Explosives, 246 million meters of safety fuze, 543 million meters of detonating fuze, 906 million numbers of detonators, 2911 MT of booster and 8457 MT of PETN".

That is to say, we produce 1.89 billion kilos of explosives and 906 million detonators for civilian purposes like mining, quarrying, construction, etc. every year. A terrorist needs to 'procure' only a few kilos out of that at a time. One bomb needs just one detonator. There is no way the nation can keep track of every kilo of explosive produced and every detonator sold. For once, if there is any practical way of doing it, let the media people tell it. After all, are they there only to make demands that such-and-such should be done? Does the word practicability not exist in their dictionary? Detonators are so cheap that even petty criminals have been found in possession of thousands of detonators—they purchase them for Rs 1.50 a piece and sell them for Rs 5 a piece to fishermen and the like. If terrorists obtain even a few hundreds of detonators right now from anywhere, it will be enough to carry on terrorism for several decades!

There is no reliable evidence that till a decade ago only RDX, PETN or Semtex was being used. It is actually a figment of imagination of the media. It was the media which had cooked up the Semtex theory during the days of terrorism in Punjab. Forensic analysis of explosives in this country is a massive fraud—they claim to find traces from properly detonated high explosives also which is scientifically not even possible. For unexploded explosives, police claims of identification are made by visual inspection as soon as recovery is shown and then the material is destroyed 'in the interest of safety'!

And what is wrong with the explosive production in the country going up and the responsibility being taken up by more and more companies? Would this journalist like our requirement of nearly two million tons to be met by just three companies? Can they do so? Is he not regressive—even anti-growth? Does he mean to say that states like Bihar and Jharkhand should not be trusted with any explosive production because parts of them are anarchic? So we still have a nation in which certain states are considered 'anarchic'—at least in the opinion of this journalist! For his information, it is not a subversion of the ban—it is growth. The ban was on NG-based explosives—do we not require sufficient AN-based explosives for our growth-related requirements?

For the information of the media every explosive is dual use—even the explosive used in the firecrackers used in the festival of Diwali in India, notably the so-called 'cherry bomb' can be converted into quite effective grenades by those who know the tricks. Even simple gunpowder could be put to very effective use by terrorists provided they know how to use it properly. Incidentally, as I have mentioned earlier, the Bali bombing had not used ammonium nitrate. As for his lamenting about fertilizers, perhaps the poor fellow does not know that even urea can be got converted into urea nitrate which can be used in lieu of ammonium nitrate in IEDs. We produce well over 10 million tons of urea every year. Would he like the use of even urea to be restricted?

The media does not understand that there is very little pilferage of explosives—there is only diversion. There is no way this can be stopped. We do have a system of the legitimate users keeping a register in respect of their stock of explosives. That system does not and cannot monitor the actual use of explosives. Suppose he writes in the register that he charged a bore hole with 10 kg of explosive. Suppose, he actually used only 2 kg and diverted the remaining 8 kg. A system of registers will not and cannot prevent him from selling off the balance. How in the world are the police supposed to stop this? Given the fact that India has only 122 policemen per 100,000 people and they have to perform myriad duties, most of them being mandatory to boot. Is it possible for them to check and monitor the actual use of explosives? Such impractical dreams are for those who do not have the slightest idea of the practical problems involved in policing—the journalists being foremost amongst them.

The most outrageous suggestion is regarding changing the design of the detonator so that it has a delay of six seconds. We can only pity the ignorance of the media. They have no idea at all of the science of detonators and mining. They are sincerely advised to read some treatises on explosives. Unfortunately, most of the journalists are arts or commerce graduates and hardly have the knowledge to understand them. Detonators are made so because the current design makes them immensely cheap—obviously the media does not know that electronic detonators have already been made. It is possible to keep track of them as each one of them carries an ID number. Yet they could not become popular because it is difficult to use them and they are much costlier too. Presently, even practically illiterate self-trained people can use the detonators—this guy would expect electronic engineers to be appointed in the jungles of Jharkhand in quarries at a princely salary of Rs 49 a day! These guys would not let even poor quarry workers to survive! Then it is utterly puerile to think that terrorists could be prevented from making bombs to target VIP cars if the detonators have a delay of six seconds. The poor journo does not know that if someone is serious, he can easily convert a detonator with a built-in delay to one without a delay—it is only a matter of bypassing the delay circuit!

Or for that matter, one can simply take the 'explosive train' out of any detonator and fabricate his own detonator using that. Any electrician worth his salt can do the necessary soldering!

A terrorist does not need great money for procuring explosives. He does not need ISI training either for making timers—timer circuits that can give a delay of over six months, can be made for as low as Rs 43 by any knowledgeable electronics enthusiast. The technology of making bombs is not a secret—it does not help us to blame everything on the invisible hand of some terrorist groups operating from the dark areas of Pakistan or Afghanistan, or the ISI.

(5.3) Does it Help to Worry so much about the Type of Explosive used?

The media has a morbid fascination with the type of explosive used or the design of the bomb. After every blast they harass the police to disclose the type of explosive used and the design of the bomb. It is this pressure of the media which makes the police claim that RDX was used without even seeing the place of explosion. The media is visibly disappointed if the police do not claim RDX immediately. Following the Bangalore blasts, the TV reporter of a channel repeatedly asked the DIG Bangalore (Deputy Inspector General of Police—a one-star officer) as to what could have caused the explosion. The poor DIG said that it was an explosive substance! How profound!

The terrorists have a long shopping list for their explosives and all of them are available in India. They do not have to wait for a shipment of RDX to arrive from somewhere. Civilian explosives available in India are more than adequate for terrorist purposes and there is no need to look for RDX. What can be done by half a kilo of RDX can be done equally well a little larger quantity of commercial emulsion like Neogel, and the terrorist is not designing a beauty that refuses to take an extra half kilo in the packet. Furthermore, no terrorist holds a patent on the design of a bomb. Anyone can design a bomb in any manner—how does it help to identify the bomber by the design of the bomb?

(5.4) IEDs: Three Letters that Spell Danger

There's something about a good bomb.

(5.4.1) What are IEDs?

As the name suggests, Improvised Explosive Devices are those explosive devices which are not produced in a proper factory which normally produces munitions. Following the American propaganda, people have started taking IEDs to be synonymous with non-state actors at the best and terrorists at the worst. In principle, the IED requires only two things; the explosive charge and the firing device. The bomber has the field wide open for both the things. He can use any explosive he gets. Why? The reason is that military explosives are selected with several factors in mind, such as stability. The IED-maker need not bother about such niceties. Even if the explosive is not good in storage, who cares? He does not have to store it for long in any case. Most IEDs are made just hours before the use. If he is prepared to take some risk, he can use even those explosives which are not very safe in handling either. All he requires is an explosive substance. He would like to have a powerful one but he would settle for any explosive he is able to get or make. Different explosives have been found to be popular in different regions at different times, depending on the availability. It is in respect of the firing device that a serious bomber exercises his ingenuity to the fullest extent.

Let no one be under the impression that IEDs are poorly made bombs and lack sophistication. It all depends on who is making it and how intelligent or dumb he is. The Harvey's Casino bomb made by John Birges was more sophisticated than any bomb ever made by any nation in any factory and defeated all the attempts of even the scientists from the US Navy's Explosive Ordnance Disposal Facility, the US Army's 34th Explosive Ordnance Disposal Team and Lawrence Livermore Laboratory towards defusing it! By definition, it was also an IED! Bombing is actually a battle of wits between the bomber and the security forces.

(5.4.2) IEDs Using Non-electrical Detonators in Firing Devices

The basic objective in designing an IED-based on non-electrical detonator is to ignite the safety fuse after a delay or when tripped or when a command is given. The safety fuse would, of course, be connected to the detonator. The delay could be purely mechanical—clockwork delays were once popular. A chemical (straight) delay uses some reaction or even a physical phenomenon to start a chemical reaction after a certain length of time. This chemical reaction would then result in production of heat or flame sufficient to ignite a fuse or could result in a small explosion that would set off other explosives. A chemical (mechanical) firing device does not require a heat-producing or exothermic reaction. All that it requires is that the chemical reaction should release a mechanical device. Then something as simple as a percussion cap can take over. This is the mechanism used in the so-called 'timer pencils' quite popular with militaries of the world and made in factories.

(5.4.3) *The Extreme Versatility of IEDs-based on Electrical Detonators*

An electrical detonator requires a certain amount of current to detonate. Hence, all that an IED-based on electrical detonator requires is that current of a sufficient magnitude should flow through the detonator. What do you require for current to flow in a circuit? The circuit should be complete. That is if all other things like the power source (battery, for example) and wirings, etc. are in place, a circuit requires nothing but a switch to make it complete. That is an electrical IED requires nothing but an electrical contact to be made or broken for the device to be triggered. The ways in which it can be done are limited only by imagination. You can construct the most sophisticated devices; you can also construct very simple devices with the help of household things. The basic objective of the device is to send current to the detonator at the desired moment, either after a delay or on command, or on tripping. You can have a mechanical completion of circuit—it also lends itself to booby trap devices—that is, the circuit activating with some mechanical action, such as pressing of an object, pulling of a wire or whatever. You can also have an automatic electronic completion of circuit after a certain lapse of time (as in a time bomb) or when some stimulus triggers it (such as some light flashing or some infrared beam breaking).

Light sensitive switches are triggered by the flash of camera or some light falling on it. Many switches have been made based on infrared light. We are all aware of infrared alarms; the type used for security of valuables—they are commercially available for about $15. They can be easily converted into triggers for bombs. In Iraq they used it for attacking vehicles also. The infrared emitter and receiver are placed on each side of the road—that forms an invisible barrier. The moment a vehicle crosses it the device is triggered. Then there could be sound-actuated switches. For example, they could be made to respond to the sound of gunfire or grenade explosions. They could be used to booby trap rooms and corridors etc. for urban combat situations. The devices would go off as soldiers would enter there firing and throwing grenades. The soldiers may take all the care in the world to not trigger trip wires etc. as they enter the building but the natural soldierly action of shooting may doom them. Now, you understand how dangerous this switch could be?

(5.4.4) *Collapsing Circuits and Anti-disturbance Switches*

The ingenuity of the designer does not end here. This field has received the loving attention of numerous geniuses. Particularly in the West, bombers have been found to suffer from a massive ego problem and the biggest trip of their life is to make the other guy admit that they are geniuses. They know that the security forces try to defuse bombs. Collapsing circuits are designed to defeat attempts at defusing bombs. In technical language we would say that the collapsing of the first circuit would trigger a relay in another circuit and that would send current to the detonator. Collapsing circuits can be made to incorporate delays also. Intelligent bombers may easily devise secondary and tertiary collapsing circuits also or various combinations of collapsing and non-collapsing circuits. You trip a wire and one collapsing circuit is activated. But it does not set off the device as yet. The personnel defusing the bomb may be led into believing that the device has malfunctioned. To confuse them further, the bomber could have very well made dummy connections to a detonator and explosive from the first collapsing circuit. As the personnel disconnect some wire in the secondary circuit, it could activate a third circuit which will actually send current to the detonator.

One could devise bombs with anti-disturbance switches or even switches that would be activated the moment somebody came close to them. Nothing in the world is more frustrating than anti-disturbance switches. Just touch the bomb or even come close to it and it goes off! In October 1940 the British found one 'butterfly cluster bomb' of the Germans that had failed to explode. That particular piece had an anti-disturbance fuze. The British could disarm it only by making a clay wall around the weapon and pouring liquid nitrogen over it, thus freezing the mercury in the mercury anti-disturbance switch! Perhaps you might be wondering how they plant a bomb with an anti-disturbance switch under field conditions. Good question! The basic precaution which must be taken with such circuits is that one must provide for an arming switch. This switch must be kept off till the very last moment lest there is any mistake in the circuit and the detonator goes off. They also test the circuit with a flashlight bulb in place of the detonator.

(5.4.5) Time Bombs

Who does not know the legendary time bomb with the clock ticking away? In fact, it is the most enduring symbol of a bomb and immortalised by innumerous films! Even the dumbest of the security forces officers recognise it. The downside is that all the time they keep on looking for a bomb with a clock, little realising that hardly anybody makes it anymore! The problem with the mechanical delays are that they are relatively large in size, can be easily detected and the delay offered is necessarily small.

Electronic delay circuits rule the roost now. They are very neat devices—a bomber's delight in fact! The electronic delay circuits use electronic devices or circuits to initiate current in a circuit immediately upon tripping, on command, or after a delay which could be very long also. They can be made extremely small and hence very easily concealed. They can offer delays of months and that too very precisely. This means that the bomber can hide the device months before the bombing and go home. The best thing about electronic timers is that the components required for most of them are commercially available and all that the bomber needs is knowledge of electronic circuits. Electronics buffs who have been taking up all sorts of electronics projects as a hobby since their adolescence, find it easy.

Some of the finest electronic delays are based on the famous IC - 555. This integrated circuit chip was introduced in 1971 by the Signetics Corporation and was found to be so versatile that it instantly became famous as 'The IC Time Machine'. Timer circuits based on the Motorola MC 14536B chip are also very versatile. The circuit can provide delays ranging from 8.5 minutes to 194 days. We are making a special reference to it because in the Indian context it seems quite popular with the terrorists. The bombs used in Jammu and Jaipur were buried in place several months ago when there was no reason for the security to be tight. The bombers took the risk of burying them and leaving them because it could be reasonably well presumed that given the venue being stadiums, the rostrum etc would be constructed in fixed places only. They escaped detection when anti-sabotage checks were carried out before the Republic Day because in a place like a stadium there is always a considerable quantity of metal at the site on account of the poles and steel used in the reinforced cement concrete—the mine-sweepers therefore get confused.

(5.4.6) Command Actuated Devices

The great advantage of command actuated devices is that they enable the bomber to select the optimal moment of bombing. Thus, they are preferred when a bomb has to be exploded, say only when a car passes a certain point or when a person appears at some place. Time bombs won't work reliably in such situations and you do need command actuated devices. The downside of command-actuated devices is that the bomber cannot afford to be very far from the IED whereas for a time-delay device he can plant the device and disappear conveniently. They are therefore not for the chicken-hearted. Once again the manner in which the command can be given is limited only by the ingenuity of the bomber. Now, commands could be given in two basic manners;

wired and wireless. Thus, the two most common types of command-actuated IEDs would be: Command Wire IEDs (CWIED) and Remote (or Radio) Control IEDs (RCIED).

If a device is wired you could send an electrical current in it and to the detonator. Nothing could be simpler. The advantage of a wired device is that it is almost foolproof. The disadvantage of a wired device is that it is difficult to employ, takes time and even more difficult to conceal. However, where the surroundings and the terrain permit it, people have drawn wires over 600 feet long!

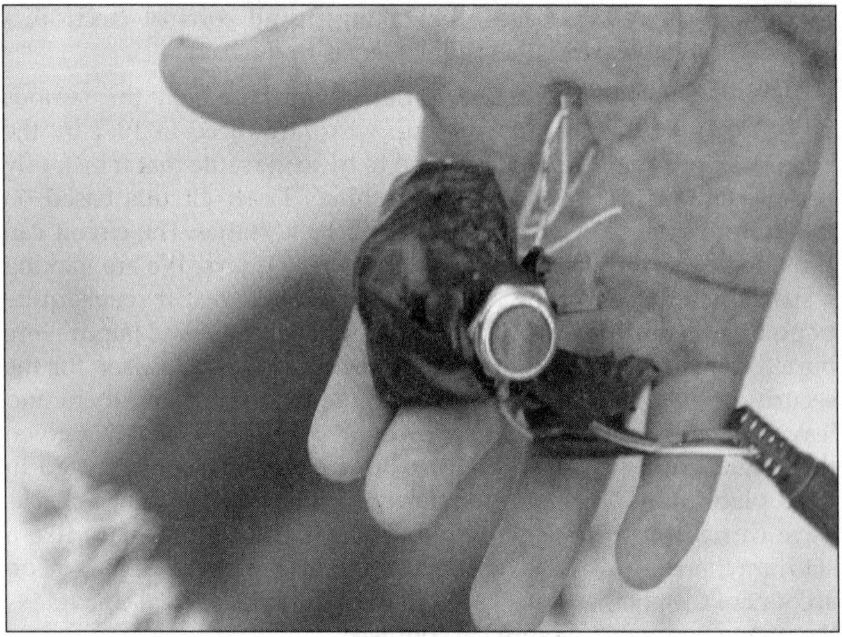

The switch of a remote controlled IED recovered in Afghanistan

A remote control or a wireless device must have two things: a transmitting device and a receiving device. The transmitter remains with the bomber. The receiver is attached to the IED. The transmitting device must be capable of sending a signal to the receiver in the IED without wires. The receiver must be able to convert the received signal into say, an electrical signal. This signal triggers an electronic circuit which sends the required current to the detonator. For wireless devices, you could give the command by regular radio transmission in MW/SW or FM, mobile telephone, infrared rays, microwaves, visible light rays, or for that matter even audible sound or ultrasound waves. Subsequent circuitry in a command controlled device is essentially the same as in a regular electronic timed device.

(5.4.7) *Practical RCIEDs made from commercially available Items*

IEDs based on mobile phones have become popular because they are almost readymade and very little modification needs to be done to make the IED functional. The mobile phone functions as the receiver in the IED. The phone must, of course, be left 'on'. There is absolute selectivity also. However, the device cannot be used for blowing up vehicles because one cannot ensure split-second timing when making a call on a mobile. The great advantage of a mobile phone actuated IED is that the bomber can activate it from thousands of miles away from any part in the world. The disadvantage of a mobile phone actuated IED is that it can be used only in those areas where mobile network is there. Further, since getting a connection through may take some time which even though small cannot be controlled; the system cannot be used in applications requiring split-second timing. On exactly the same principle, IEDs based on pagers and cordless phones can also be made. The problem of timing is solved by using commercially available VHF sets (walkie-talkies). Two sets are to be used. A large number of Red Scorpio and Falcon car alarm pager receivers have been recovered. The car alarm pager is a much more sensible device than an ordinary pager.

Some bombers have been found triggering their RCIEDs using DTMF codes from VHF sets. Many companies such as Kenwood, ICOM, Alinco, Yaesu, Vertex, and Hy-com make VHF/UHF sets from which DTMF (dual tone multi-frequency) calls may be made. To make a DTMF call all one has to do is to press the PTT (press to talk) button and press the numeric keys. One could use one, two digits or three digits. The risk with two digits is that of accidental pressing of the keys. That risk is reduced with three digits. The set mutes the microphone and transmits the DTMF tones. The receiver with DTMF decoder will be with the IED. The moment it receives the signal, it will generate an alert signal. This alert signal can be used to activate a relay circuit in the standard manner and that can be connected to the detonator.

For terrorists, the simplest remote control devices are those based on commercially available systems like remote call bells, garage door openers, or remote control toys. They have a problem of limited range but the cost is very low and that makes them attractive. Several models of Qusan wireless doorbells have been employed as IED triggers in the Middle East. The circuit base is Type 2262 encoder IC (transmitter) and type 2272 decoder IC (receiver). They operate in the frequency range of 307 to 319 MHz. Qunxing QX-2218 TX RC Toy Transmitter has found application numerous times. Several models of the Qunxing RC toy receiver have been used in various devices. All of them are commercial receivers operating in the RC hobbyist frequency range of 26 to 28 MHz. A large number of Cora keyless entry systems have been used as triggers. The system consists of a key fob transmitter and receiver with two relay outputs. The circuit base is Type 2262 encoder IC (key fob transmitter) and type 2272 decoder IC (receiver). They operate in the frequency range of 310 to 315 MHz.

All radio-based systems are prone to jamming. To circumvent that the terrorists could use improvised MW/SW or FM transmitter/receiver systems; or for that matter, even a microwave-based system could be used. To beat jammers, they have also used laser based devices such as commercially available laser speed radars and infra-red based systems. One can also design an ultrasound transducer or use even simple ultrasound whistles which are commercially available and are used for calling dogs because dogs can hear ultrasound. All he has to do is to install a microphone-like receiver which converts sound into electrical signal. The rest follows.

(5.5) Car Bombs

(5.5.1) Give them hell

Though invented much earlier, car bombs became popular in a big way in 1972, when the Provisional Irish Republican Army (IRA) accidentally, so the legend goes, improvised the first ANFO car bomb. These new-generation car bombs, requiring freely available fertilizer and fuel, were very cheap to fabricate. They elevated urban terrorism to an industrial level from the level of an artisan! They got a revival in post-defeat Iraq and Afghanistan.

The car bomb is a semi-strategic weapon that quite like aerial bombs is able to bring down huge structures. After all it was the truck bomb attack on the US Marine Landing Team barracks in Beirut in 1983 that eventually forced the Americans to get the hell out of Lebanon, their fighters and warships of the Sixth Fleet notwithstanding. Two-hundred-and-forty-one Marines were killed in the attack! It is estimated that in this attack the truck was carrying about 12,000 to 18,000 lbs of high explosive—almost as much as a Daisy Cutter bomb (or perhaps even more) that only a nation like the US possesses. Precisely for this reason car bombs have been described as the poor man's air force!

There are basically two types of car bombs. They are differentiated by the intended mode of use and not so much by the design of the initiating devices. Car bombs have been made using all the initiating

The scene of devastation at the US embassy, Tanzania caused by car bomb – that's why they call it 'poor man's air force'

devices that we have discussed so far. Timothy McVeigh, the Oklahoma bomber who destroyed the Alfred P Murrah Federal Building used something as simple as safety fuze to trigger his bomb used in the Oklahoma City Center bombing. No electrical or electronic device was used in his bomb! In the first type the explosive-laden vehicle is left stationary at some place and then detonated either by command or by a time delay device. In this case, the car bomb is just a large bomb with the car or the vehicle providing a large and yet inconspicuous container for the huge quantity of explosives. People have used such diverse vehicles as even a concrete mixer! In the other type, the moving car bomb is used as the tool of a suicide attack to force its way in a protected location such as in the attack on the US Marine barracks in Beirut. In this type, use is made of the strength of the body of the car and its momentum in crashing through barriers. For this type of attack, heavy vehicles are naturally preferred.

When a car bomb is being used in the suicide mode, then the terrorist has to contend with the possibility of getting shot even before he has the time to command detonate the bomb. To counter this, they have devised several means. One of the simplest means is to provide a sound-actuated switch which triggers by a certain sound which the terrorist can emit even as he is dying. The bomb can be given a time delay or a 'dead man's switch' also. Alternatively, these switches can be provided as a back up to the command actuation so that they swing into operation only when command detonation fails or when the engine of the vehicle stops due to bullets or grenades fired on it. There is one more way of ensuring detonation. The detonation can be made remote controlled and the remote can be operated by a man outside the area of operation but in sight of the proceedings. In fact, several American authorities suspected that this last method was used in the attack on the Marines' barracks. What is of more concern to the terrorist is that even if the driver is shot up, the vehicle should keep on moving in a certain direction for it to reach where it originally intended to reach. This is not very difficult because if the vehicle intends to ram into a barrier or barriers, it must be moving at a high speed in a straight line. Some armour-plating on the vehicle has been tried to protect the driver but unless done in a professional manner, that makes the vehicle conspicuous and thus takes away the element of surprise. To ensure that the vehicle keeps on moving irrespective of the condition of the driver, they have devised mechanisms by which both the steering and the accelerator pedal can be jammed so that even the death of the driver does not affect the motion of the vehicle. Security forces which think that the best way of dealing with a car boring down on them is to shoot at the driver, may be in for some rude surprise!

A third use of large truck bombs is also possible. As we saw, the truck that attacked the US Marines' barracks was carrying 12,000 to 18,000 lbs of high explosive. Used properly, this kind of charge can be extremely effective for sabotage of a very serious kind. A truck full of explosives, if exploded inside an important tunnel could inflict irreparable damage to it and may well put it out of action for long. Remember that the tunnel could be an arterial one linking two important areas and its closure or loss could have catastrophic consequences even during normal times, not to speak of during a war. The 2.5 mile long Salang tunnel in Afghanistan, the world's highest road tunnel, is one such arterial tunnel that connects northern Afghanistan with southern Afghanistan. During the Soviet occupation, there was a devastating fire in this tunnel in 1982 in which 1000 to 2000 people had perished. A Soviet military convoy was passing through the tunnel at that time on its way to the south. The exact cause of the fire could never be ascertained given the cult of secrecy amongst the Soviets. Several theories were advanced. One was that a fuel tanker had exploded; the other was that a munitions truck had exploded as a result of another vehicle crashing into it. Yet another theory was that the munitions truck was actually attacked by the Mujahideen and that's why it exploded. The tunnel's entrances and ventilation system were destroyed again in 1996 in the course of the fighting between the Taliban and the Northern Alliance and it could be cleared for traffic only in 2002. Whether the Mujahideen had a hand in the Salang tunnel fire of 1986 remains uncertain but it is certain that an attack of that sort can be very much made with catastrophic consequences. Security planners must therefore be ever alive to the possibility of such an attack.

(5.6) What Makes the Car Bomb such an Attractive Option?

By them we live; for them we would die – whatever the mission; we'll give it a try.

What makes the car bomb such a favourite weapon of the urban guerrilla? Well, from the point of view of the bomber, there are several reasons.

- The first is the enormous load of explosives that can be used in it. Trucks, vans, or even SUVs can easily transport the equivalent of several conventional 1,000-pound bombs to the doorstep of a prime target. There is no other way in which the bomber can deliver this quantity of explosives at the target.
- The second is stealth. Who knows what you are carrying in a vehicle? No government can check all the vehicles plying on the roads. And nothing prevents the bomber from using even a trailer full of explosives either.
- Thirdly, it is dirt cheap, thanks to the introduction of the ANFO car bomb. Fertilizer and fuel worth just $400 are enough to take care of 40-50 people. Ramzi Yousef, the mastermind of the 1993 attack on the World Trade Center, bragged that his most expensive outlay was in long-distance phone calls. The explosive itself (one half ton of urea) cost $3,615 plus the $59 per day rental for a ten-foot-long Ryder van.
- Fourthly, car bombings are operationally simple to organise. Just two individuals Timothy McVeigh and Terry Nichols could do in the Oklahoma City bombing and with what resources!
- Fifthly, if the purpose is not very specific and it is just a terror weapon, even then it is the ideal choice. Explode a parked car in a market and you inflict casualties indiscriminately.
- Sixthly, car bombs are highly anonymous and leave practically no forensic evidence. Even in the 1920s, Buda had managed to quietly slip out to home in Italy, leaving William Burns, J Edgar Hoover, and the Bureau of Investigation (later, to be renamed the FBI) to make fools of themselves as they chased one false lead after another for a decade. Ideally, they use stolen vehicles.

Timothy McVeigh was not a professional criminal and hence he was fool enough to neither erase the engine and chassis numbers nor did he bother to not hire the van in his own name.

- Seventhly, the car bomb lends itself to safe and assured delivery. The IRA had made a habit of kidnapping the family of one of the employees of the target and then forcing him to take the car to the target – great idea! This also ensures that the car will get past the usual checks.
- Eighth, car bombs have the great advantage of having one of the most sophisticated guidance systems available: human beings. This allows for last-minute changes to the location and detonation of the explosive as conditions dictate.
- Ninth, the mobility of car bombs also affords certain flexibility in operation to groups that employ them; if the location or circumstances of the target change prior to the execution of the operation, car bombs grant their user an ability to adjust and develop alternate plans in a way that stationary IEDs do not.
- Tenth, they allow the bomb to be assembled at a safe location, for example, and then driven to the target area, as opposed to 'roadside bombs' that have to be placed on routes routinely travelled by enemy personnel.

(5.7) Defence Against Car Bombs

The only surefire defence against car bombs is to not allow cars at all in the vicinity. Nations usually do it for the residences of their highly protected persons or for very important offices. The next best option is to increase the standoff distance as much as possible under the given circumstances. Standoff distance is the distance that is allowed to be maintained between the target and the last point accessible to a potential vehicle bomb. This depends on where your building is located. If you are erecting a new building then this can, of course, be incorporated in the site layout itself. The options get limited if the building is located in a congested area. The basic principles of security in respect of car bombs for a target having a campus of its own pertain to strength and negotiability of barriers and to restricting the speed of incoming vehicles. If you find a car bomb that has not yet exploded or is about to explode, try to keep a safe distance. The very minimum distance you should find is 600 feet.

Vehicle type	TNT equivalent explosive possible	Building evacuation distance	Outdoor evacuation distance
Compact Sedan	500 lbs	320 feet	1500 feet
Sedan	1,000 lbs	400 ft	1,750 ft
Passenger/Cargo van	4,000 lbs	640 ft	2,750 ft
Small Moving van/ Delivery Truck	10,000 lbs	860 ft	3,750 ft
Moving van/Water Truck	30,000 lbs	1,240 ft	6,500 ft
Semi-trailer	60,000 lbs	1,570 ft	7,000 ft

(5.8) How to Improve Blast Resistance of Buildings?

Once you accept that a dog is a dog, you can't get upset when it barks.

You cannot design a building to resist all possible explosive threats for the simple reason that it would not be economical! How much you would like to protect a building must depend on the threat you perceive for the building. It is a different thing that you may reduce some of the threats by taking suitable precautionary measures. For example, if you secure a large perimeter, you reduce the threat from car bombs. If you institute screening procedures at entrance, you reduce the threat from bombs carried in briefcases. None of these would, however, protect your building from an aerial bomb attack! Details of the structural engineering aspects can be had from my treatise 'The Ultimate Book of Explosives, Bombs, and IEDs'.

Façade Protection: The building's exterior is its first real defence against the effects of a bomb. If you want to harden the façade fully, it may require a dramatic change to the exterior appearance of the structure such as smaller *window* sizes and more rugged attachments. Most people would not accept it. It serves little purpose to make changes which would protect only partly. Hence, most experts would concentrate on improving the post-damage behaviour of the façade. To improve the post-damage behaviour of the glazing system, one could use laminated glass for new construction or apply anti-shatter film to existing glazing. While these features do little to improve the strength of the glass, they attempt to hold the shards of glass together and better protect the occupants from hazardous debris.

Curtain walls and Energy-absorbing Catch Systems: A curtain wall is a non-load-bearing exterior enclosure that is supported by a building's structural steel or concrete frame and holds either glass, metal, stone, or pre-cast concrete panels. An alternative approach takes the concept one step further by making full use of the flexibility and capacity of all the window materials to absorb and dissipate large amounts of blast energy while preventing debris from entering the occupied space. Energy-absorbing catch systems or the so-called Cable Protected Window Systems (CPWS) work in such a way that as the glass is damaged it bears against a cable catch system, which in turn deforms the window frames.

Floor Slab Reinforcements: A reinforced-concrete, flat-plate structural slab is an economical system that provides for maximum use of vertical space, particularly for buildings in areas with height restriction. Increased protection against blasts can be obtained by paying more attention to the conventional flat-plate design and detailing of exterior bays and lower floors, which are the elements most susceptible to a bomb exploding outside the building, and the design of the spandrel beams, which tie the structure together and enhance the response of the slab edge. The slab should be designed to prevent a punching shear failure that may in turn develop into a progressive collapse.

Column Reinforcements: Due to direct blast pressures, the columns of a typical building, which are designed primarily to resist gravity loads with no special detailing for ductility demands, may experience severe bending deformations in addition to the axial loads that the columns support. To enhance protection, the columns must be designed to be sufficiently ductile to sustain the combined effects of axial load and lateral displacement. Existing concrete columns may be encased in a steel jacket or wrapped with a composite fiber to confine the concrete core and increase the shear capacity. On the other hand, existing steel columns may be encased in concrete to add mass and prevent a premature buckling of the thin flanges.

Preventing Progressive Collapse: Progressive collapse occurs when an initiating localised failure causes adjoining members to be overloaded and fail; resulting in an extent of damage that is disproportionate to the originating region of localised failure. A protective design must avoid structural systems that either facilitate or are vulnerable to a progression of collapse resulting from the loss of a primary vertical load-bearing member. New facilities may be designed to accept the loss of an exterior column for one or possibly two floors above grade without precipitating further collapse. But the upgrading of existing structures to prevent localised damage from developing into a progressive collapse may not be easily accomplished through the alternate path method. If a transfer girder is required and is vulnerable to an explosive loading, then the girder should be designed to be continuous over several supports.

Overall Lateral Resistance: The ability of structures to resist a highly impulsive blast loading depends in great measure on the structural detailing of the slabs, joists, and columns that provides for the ductility of the load-resisting system. The structure has to be able to deform inelastically under extreme overload (i.e., dissipate large amounts of energy) prior to failure. In addition to providing ductile behaviour, there needs to be a well-distributed lateral-load resisting mechanism in the horizontal floor plan. The use of several shear walls or a combined lateral-load resisting mechanism throughout the building will improve the overall seismic as well as the blast behaviour of the building.

Using Alternative Construction Materials to Resist Explosive Threats: A variety of materials, not traditionally used in building construction, may provide alternatives to conventional blast hardening solutions. Among these alternatives there are Shock Attenuating Chemically Bonded Ceramics (SA/CBC), and composite systems comprised of carbon, aramid and polyethylene fibers and resin.

(5.9) IEDs Made by Cannibalizing Artillery Shells and other Military Warheads

If you survive the extraordinary things, it will often be the little things that will kill you.

An artillery shell, mortar bomb or the warhead of a shoulder-fired rocket provides a readymade source of factory-made high explosive of excellent quality. Not only that, the explosive is packed in a case which is designed for proper fragmentation! Thus two of the biggest worries of making IEDs are taken care of. What more he could ever ask for? You have high explosive and you have proper containment also. A large number of unexploded ordnance is easily found in a war zone. Even unexploded aerial bombs can be found. Non-state actors look for them and make good use of them. The Iraqi resistance fighters, for example, used them extensively. The Iraqis have been using even anti-tank mines as IEDs because they can convert them into command-actuated devices, a role in which they would be more useful than as a merely dumb anti-tank mine waiting for some tank to come up, and which may never come up in an urban situation. When command-detonated, it can be effectively used against other types of vehicles also. The intended use of the IED will depend on the size of the warhead. If the bomber has got just the bomb of a 61 mm or 81 mm mortar or has taken out the warhead of a shoulder-fired rocket, he can make only an AP device. If he has got bigger things such as a 155 mm artillery shell or aerial bombs he can make anti-tank devices also. They would be great as AP devices and would work very satisfactorily as AT devices.

The catch lies in removing the fuze of the warhead safely. That demands some specialised tools and some mechanical skill. Even those tools can be improvised, however. Once that is done, priming the shell with one's own detonators is easy and one has his own IED! He can make a booby trap device, time delay device, command actuated device or whatever he wants out of that. However, suitable detonators are required as the explosives in the shell are rather insensitive. The bomber must know the strength of detonator or the amount of detonating cord required or else he would be wasting that precious warhead!

US Marines rush to evacuate a comrade wounded by IED in Afghanistan

(5.10) Improvised Barbed Wire Anti-personnel Device

This takes the cake amongst the IEDs. A brilliant idea! One can make an excellent anti-personnel device by this stratagem. One roll of standard barbwire (weight about 50 lbs and of the size of a basketball) is placed into position, and 1.25 lbs of C4 or an equivalent quantity of some other high explosive is placed in the center of the roll and primed. This device must be command-detonated. The barbwire AP device can be made somewhat directional by placing the wire against an embankment or a fixed object. This causes the force of the explosion to expel the barbwire fragments in the desired direction.

(5.11) Improvised Firebombs and Incendiaries

In spite of what they have been showing you in the films, the traditional Molotov Cocktail (or Molly as the West Germans called them) consisting of a glass bottle filled with petrol, rags and a burning wick is a fairly useless device in the open. It is of use only when it is used in a confined space. Then it inflicts burn injuries and can also ignite other inflammable materials present there. For the serious terrorist, firebombs are adolescent pranks. Don't even think that you could throw one on a tank and it would harm the tank—what is there on the outside of a steel hulk to burn, dear?

As long as someone is trying to throw a bottle of thickened fuel or gel, it is no better than a nuisance. A much more sensible idea in the context of urban guerrilla warfare was the invention of the incendiary mines. This is something the security forces should be really concerned about. The guerrilla takes a petrol drum and fills it with napalm mixture. Then they either bury it in the path of advancing troops or hang them from the trees at a height of about 2 meters. You can make a chain of them and trigger them remotely. You will have to give them an igniter of white phosphorous or thermite and a high explosive bursting charge. US forces in Korea had made them even better by tightly winding barbed wire over the drums and hanging the mines from the trees. When the drum exploded, the barbed wire also got broken into fragments making up a large amount of shrapnel to boot.

Incendiaries produce intense, localised heat designed to ignite adjacent combustible target materials. The true incendiary produces no fireball and relatively little flame. They are highly effective against fuel and other flammable targets. Incendiaries lend themselves eminently to sabotage operations also. The idea is to make a small incendiary device that could be surreptitiously placed on the target. Obviously this should have some delay element in it. Fieser, the inventor of napalm, himself had made such a device for the US Army in the WWII. It was known as the Harvard Candle. It consisted of a cylinder of celluloid filled with napalm. It was ignited by a red phosphorous composition in a metal pull cap which served as a scratching disc.

The main incendiary agents are thermite, magnesium, white phosphorus (WP), and oil-based incendiaries including combustible hydrocarbons and gelled ones. Aluminium can be used as a pure metal; as an alloy with magnesium; in the form of napthenate, palmitate or laurate in napalm; or in organometallic compounds such as triethyl aluminium.

Thermite incendiaries are a mixture of powdered aluminium metal and ferric oxide and are used in bombs for attacks on armoured fighting vehicles. Another composition consists of 2.75 parts of black iron oxide (ferrosoferric oxide) and 1.0 part of granular aluminium. Yet another composition used was three parts of aluminium powder, six parts of barium nitrate and eight parts of ferrous oxide. Interestingly, thermite was used before the WWI for welding railway lines. For military purposes it is necessary to use a binder like sodium or potassium silicate or even sulfur. Sulfur is used when you intend to scatter the thermite; otherwise silicate is better. Thermite requires an igniter. One popular igniter consisted of magnesium (9 parts) and potassium perchlorate (13 parts).

Pyrogels: The properties of oil-based and metal-based incendiaries are different. Oil-based incendiaries give a spreading effect. Metal-based incendiaries increase the burning temperature and prolong the effect by producing hot slags of solid oxides. It was therefore thought desirable to combine the two. Pyrogels serve this purpose. They are essentially thickened gasoline in which the thickener is usually isobutyl metacrylate and may include natural rubber also. A metal incendiary is added to it later which increases the burning temperature to up to 1600 degrees. The dissemination of this mixture is similar to conventional napalm compositions when the bursting charge bursts it. Asphalt may, however, be added to the mixture to overcome the shearing strains resulting from high altitude bombing.

(5.12) Demolitions and Disruptions in Mind?

Improvised Shaped Charges: Shaped charges can be improvised but because of the many variables (configuration, explosive density, liner cavity density, and so forth), consistent results are impossible to obtain. The most popular item for making a shaped charge are bottles that come equipped with built-in cavity liners, such as champagne or cognac bottles. With the ends removed, the container is ready for a cavity liner and explosive. People have used even dynamite and molten TNT in the absence of plastic explosive. Liners are made from copper, tin or zinc. Bombers have worked out some expedient formulas for using the shaped charge. Cavity angle is sought to be 42-45 degrees but anything between 30 to 60 degrees does the job in a pinch. The explosive height is two times the cone height, measured from the base of the cone to the top of the explosive. The normal standoff distance is one and one-half cone diameters.

Improvised Plastic Explosives: Improvised plastic explosives have been made in a pinch using any regular high explosive and mixing it with potassium chlorate and vaseline.

Power Disruption Bombs: How do rioters or saboteurs disrupt power supply? Well, they simply lob a long chain on to some overhead electric wires. The chain hangs from one of the wires and its hanging parts short circuits the wires. The Americans do everything seriously – even the job of a rioter or saboteur! So they developed a sophisticated bomb to disrupt power supplies also. This was first used in the NATO air campaign against the Serbs in the spring of 1999. In the first attack itself they knocked out 70 per cent of the power supply in Serbia. It took 500 people and 15 hours to get just one transformer yard back into operation!

This is a cluster bomb called CBU-94/B. Its sub-munition is called BLU-114/B. They are about the size of two beer cans stacked on top of each other. After the sub-munitions are scattered by the TMD, they pop off a nose cap. 147 spools of conductive fibers are then shot out with a small explosive charge to unravel into a tangle that falls on power lines and other power-distribution equipment, short circuiting them. Now, wires can be cleaned even if it takes hours. So the Americans applied some more mind to it. An improvement is said to form a sort of conductive cloud that gets into every opening and is very difficult to clean up.

6

Stealthy Sniping and Suicidal Attacks: Two Diametrically Opposite yet Popular Modes

Anything worth fighting for is worth fighting dirty for.

(6.1) Snipers in Urban Warfare

(6.1.1) Snipers in Conventional Combat

The utility of snipers in urban combat is well documented throughout the spectrum of conflict from low intensity conflicts to total war. The use of precision long and short range fires can have a devastating effect on an enemy's morale and initiative. Generally, a sniper's primary function in warfare is to provide detailed reconnaissance from a concealed position and, if necessary, to reduce the enemy's fighting ability by striking at high value targets (especially officers, communication and other personnel) and in the process pinning down and demoralising the enemy. If you have rifles of larger calibers such as the .50 BMG, like the Barrett M82, McMillan Tac-50, and Denel NTW-20, you can try destruction of enemy military equipment also. A careful sniping strategy can use a few individuals and resources to thwart the movement or other progress of a much better equipped or larger force. Because of this perceived difference in force size, the sniping attacks may be viewed as the act of a few persons to terrorise (earning the moniker 'terrorists') a much larger, regular force—regardless of the size of the force the snipers are attached to. These perceptions stem from the precept that sniping, while effective in specific instances, is much more effective as a broadly deployed psychological attack—a very important factor in low-intensity conflict, guerrilla warfare and terrorism as the governments tend to panic quickly.

Military snipers from the US, UK, and other countries that adopt their military doctrine are typically deployed in two-man sniper teams consisting of a shooter and spotter. A common practice is for a shooter and a spotter to take turns in order to avoid eye fatigue. In most recent combat operations occurring in large densely populated towns such as Fallujah, Iraq, two teams would be deployed together to increase their security and effectiveness in an urban environment. A sniper team would be armed with their long range weapon, and a shorter ranged weapon to engage and protect the team should enemies come in close contact. German doctrine of largely independent snipers and emphasis on concealment developed during the Second World War have been most influential on modern sniper tactics, currently used throughout Western militaries (examples are specialised camouflage clothing, concealment in terrain and emphasis on coup d'œil). Soviet-Russian and derived military doctrines include squad-level snipers.

During the pursuit to Dunkirk, British snipers were able to significantly delay German infantry's advance. During the Winter War, Finnish snipers took a heavy toll of the invading Soviet army. Simo Häyhä is credited with 505 confirmed kills, most with the Finnish version of the iron-sighted bolt action Mosin-Nagant. One of the best known battles involving snipers, and the battle that made the Germans reinstate their specialised sniper training, was the Battle of Stalingrad. Their defensive position inside a city filled with rubble meant that Soviet snipers were able to inflict significant casualties on the Wehrmacht troops. Because of the nature of fighting in city rubble, snipers were very hard to spot and seriously dented the morale of the German attackers. The best known of these snipers was probably Vassili Zaitsev, immortalised in the novel 'War of the Rats' and the subsequent film 'Enemy At The Gates'. The US Army's lack of familiarity with sniping tactics resulted in disastrous effects in Normandy and the campaign in Western Europe where they encountered well trained German snipers. In Normandy, German snipers remained hidden in the dense vegetation and were able to encircle American units, firing at them from all sides. The American and British forces were surprised by how near the German snipers could safely come and attack them, as well as by their ability to hit targets at up to 1,000 m. A notable mistake made by the green American soldiers was to lie down and wait when targeted by German snipers, thus allowing the snipers to pick them off one after another. In the Pacific War, the Empire of Japan trained snipers. In the jungles of Asia and the Pacific Islands, snipers posed a serious threat to the US, British, Canadian and Australian troops. Japanese snipers were specially trained to use the environment to conceal themselves. They used foliage on their uniforms and dug well-concealed hide-outs that were often connected with small trenches. There was no need for long range accuracy because most combat in the jungle took place within a few hundred meters. Japanese snipers were known for their patience and ability to remain hidden for long periods. They almost never left their carefully camouflaged hiding spots. This meant that whenever a sniper was in the area, the location of the sniper could be determined after the sniper had fired a few shots.

The legendary Carlos Hathcock of the US Marines in Vietnam: 93 kills to his credit

In the Vietnam War, Carlos Hathcock, a US Marine Corps Gunnery Sergeant, had 93 confirmed kills of North Vietnamese Army and Viet Cong personnel. Hathcock's record and the extraordinary details of the missions he undertook made him a legend in the Marine Corps. The North Vietnamese Army placed a bounty of $30,000 on Hathcock's life for killing so many of their men. Hathcock held the record for highest bounty and killed every Vietnamese marksman who sought it. The Viet Cong and NVA called Hathcock Lông Trang, translated as "White Feather", because of the white feather he kept in a band on his bush hat. He was honoured by having a rifle named after him: a variant of the M-21 dubbed the Springfield Armoury M-25 White Feather. After a platoon of trained Vietnamese snipers was sent to hunt down "White Feather", many Marines in the same area donned white feathers to deceive the enemy. These Marines were aware of the impact Hathcock's death would have and took it upon themselves to make themselves targets in order to confuse the counter-snipers. One of Hathcock's most famous accomplishments was shooting an enemy sniper through the enemy's own rifle scope, hitting him in the eye and killing him. Hathcock and John Roland Burke, his spotter, were stalking the enemy sniper in the jungle near Hill 55, the firebase from which Hathcock was operating. The sniper had already killed several Marines and was believed to have been sent specifically to kill Hathcock. When Hathcock saw a flash of light (light reflecting off the enemy sniper's scope) in the bushes, he fired at it, shooting through the scope and killing the sniper. Surveying the situation, Hathcock concluded that the only feasible way he could have put the bullet straight down the enemy's scope and through his eye would have been if both snipers were zeroing in on each other at the same time and Hathcock fired first, which gave him only a few seconds to act. During a volunteer mission days before the end of his first deployment, he crawled over 1,500 yards, of field to shoot an NVA commanding general. He was not informed of the details of the mission until he accepted it. This effort took four days and three nights, without sleep, of constant inch-by-inch crawling. Hathcock said he was almost stepped on as he lay camouflaged with grass and vegetation in a meadow shortly after sunset. At one point, he was nearly bitten by a bamboo viper but had the presence of mind to avoid moving and giving up his position. As the general exited his tent, Hathcock fired a single shot that struck the general in the chest, killing him. He had to crawl back instead of run when soldiers started searching, and later regretted taking the mission, for in the aftermath of the assassination the NVA doubled their attacks in the area, apparently in retaliation for their general being killed and leading to an increase in American casualties. In 1967, Hathcock set the record for the longest combat kill. He used a M-2 Browning machine gun mounting a telescopic sight at a range of 2,286 yard (2,090 m), taking down a single Viet Cong guerrilla. This was not exceeded until Canadian snipers from the 3rd Bn PPCLI during the War in Afghanistan in 2002.

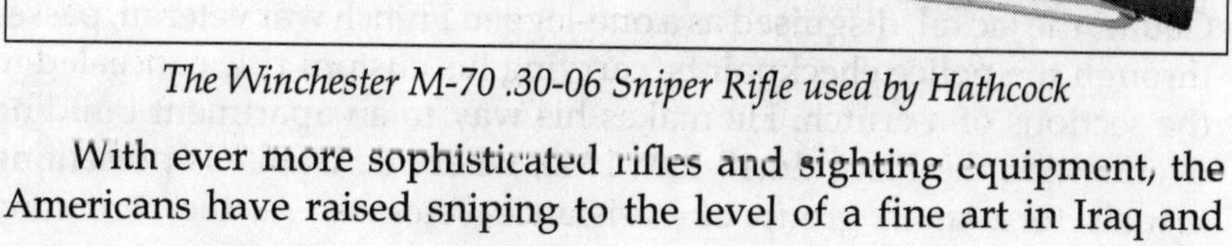

The Winchester M-70 .30-06 Sniper Rifle used by Hathcock

With ever more sophisticated rifles and sighting equipment, the Americans have raised sniping to the level of a fine art in Iraq and

Afghanistan. The other side also used snipers. One Juba in Iraq is said to have killed as many as 37 American soldiers. Whilst in Helmand Province, two British snipers (part of the Welsh Guards Battle group) shot dead a total of 75 Taliban in only 40-days during the summer of 2009. On the other hand, over a four-month period in early 2011, two Taliban snipers have shot dead two British soldiers and wounded six others at an outpost in Qadrat, Helmand province.

(6.1.2) Snipers in Urban Guerrilla Warfare

Don't one of you fire until you see the whites of their eyes.

Surprise is vital to urban guerrilla warfare. Attacking the enemy when least expected is critical to successful guerrilla combat operations. This requires rapid force concentration, operations during limited visibility, hasty reorganisation after an engagement, and a prompt withdrawal to avoid unwanted contact. It can also involve deception operations. The urban environment can be advantageous to gaining surprise through the increased cover and concealment and three-dimensional terrain. Sniping offers excellent surprise and all of the above advantages. As distances between enemy units in contact and possible reinforcement are generally quite less in urban areas, guerrillas are generally prepared to close off their objectives to maintain surprise and mobility.

In the Northern Ireland Troubles in 1972, the bloodiest year of the conflict, the majority of the soldiers killed were shot by concealed IRA riflemen. There were some instances in the early 1990s of British soldiers and RUC personnel being shot with .50 caliber Barrett rifles by sniper teams collectively known as the South Armagh sniper. In Northern Ireland, in addition to the uses listed above, a sniper was quite often a form of bait called a 'come-on', whereby the sniper's position would be made obvious to a British patrol so as to draw them into an ambush in their attempt to close with the sniper.

Guerrillas using snipers in an urban environment do know one thing. While in the hustle and bustle of an urban environment, it is difficult to quickly work out from where the shot would have come. But it can also put a guerrilla at a disadvantage because getting in unnoticed to the firing spot with a big weapon is not easy and getting out is even more difficult. Remember the famous novel and film 'The Day Of The Jackal'? On the day of the planned assassination of de Gaulle, the Jackal, disguised as a one-legged French war veteran, passes through the police checkpoints, carrying his custom rifle concealed in the sections of a crutch. He makes his way to an apartment building overlooking the Place du 18 Juin 1940, where de Gaulle is presenting medals to a small group of Resistance veterans. As the ceremony begins, the detective Lebel is walking around the street on foot, questioning and re-questioning every police checkpoint. When he hears from one CRS officer about a one-legged veteran with a crutch, he realises what the Jackal's plan is, and rushes into the apartment building, yelling for the CRS man to follow him. In his sniper's nest, the Jackal readies his rifle and takes aim at de Gaulle's head. Yet his first shot misses by a fraction of an inch, when de Gaulle unexpectedly leans forward to kiss the cheeks of the veteran he is honouring. The Jackal begins to reload. Outside the apartment, Lebel and the CRS officer arrive on the top floor in time to hear the sound of the first, silenced shot. The CRS man shoots off the lock of the door and bursts in. He falls to Jackal who is waiting with the loaded rifle. However, Jackal needs time to reload his third and last bullet—in the meantime he is killed by automatic fire of Lebel. A real life guerrilla may find it difficult to fabricate a sniper rifle that could be concealed in a crutch—guerrillas do not have time for such fancy work; assassins have. A true guerrilla sniper will first perfect his getaway plan. Once he has that, he is a deadly enemy to contend with.

Famous fictional characters like 'The Jackal' have helped weave numerous myths surrounding snipers

(6.2) Suicidal or 'Fidayeen' Attacks

Onward we stagger, and if the tanks come, may God help the tanks.

(6.2.1) How the Role of Religion has been in it?

Suicidal attacks are not a new concept in warfare. There have been very many suicidal charges in the history of warfare of all races and religions; some of them heroic, some desperate, some intended, some unintended, and some simply foolish.

Suicide terrorism is the use of suicidal operations by terrorist groups. It is not unique to Muslim terrorists as some ill-informed journalists in the West and their bootlickers in the rest of the world would have you believe. It has been witnessed in Sri Lanka, India, Lebanon, Kuwait, Israel, Panama, Algeria, Pakistan, Argentina, Croatia, Turkey, Tanzania, Kenya and the USA. The LTTE in fact has conducted the highest number of suicide operations in the world, followed by the Hizbullah, Hamas and the PKK (Kurdistan Workers' Party, Turkey).

Of late, the media has started making indiscriminate use of the word '*fidayeen*', particularly in respect of Islamic terrorists and those in the Middle East. The Indian media uses this very frequently for Kashmiri terrorists. This word is being used to describe those terrorists who are supposed to be members of mysterious things called 'suicide squads'. The word is being used out of context and the usage is not correct. '*Fidayeen*' is the plural of '*fidayee*'. Its root word in Arabic is '*fida*' which means enamoured, in love, captivated, or totally devoted. From '*fida*' we get '*fidayee*' which means a lover, devotee, faithful or one who would even give up his life for another person on for a cause. The word drifted into popular usage in the 1950s when it was used to describe Arab guerrillas, especially those operating against Israel. It must be kept in mind that a *fidayee* should be prepared to sacrifice even his life for his love. If his love is for a cause, he should be prepared to lay down his life, if it comes to that, for the cause. The emphasis is on his willingness to sacrifice his life; it does not mean that he should necessarily sacrifice his life. The simple idea is that his devotion ought to be of such a high degree that he should not hesitate from paying the highest price for it. It does not say that he has to commit suicide in the process. Islam values martyrdom but there is no religious approbation for achieving martyrdom in a suicidal fashion.

The decision to commit suicide for a cause or thought is something which the Western mindset is never able to comprehend. And that's why they think that the suicide bombers are either crazy in an inexplicable manner or so vehemently fired by some obscure religious philosophy that they are able to do so. The very idea of giving up one's life voluntarily for a cause is abhorrent to their deep-rooted culture and societal mores. They are wrong on both counts. The suicide bomber is neither crazy nor he is necessarily steeped in Wahabi philosophy. There are things which the Westerners would never understand because one has to belong to a certain society to understand them. Since they are not able to understand them, they find simplistic explanations for them. Wahabi philosophy is one of them. Little do they realise that there are any number of Muslim suicide bombers who have not had even heard of Wahabi philosophy, not to speak of Hindu suicide bombers amongst the LTTE and suicide attackers amongst the followers of other religions. Many of the Islamic suicide bombers are well-educated and even technically qualified too. The Glasgow airport bomber (2007) Kafeel Ahmed had an MPhil in aeronautical engineering from the Queen's University, Belfast and was pursuing PhD in computational fluid dynamics. The Haifa bomber (2003) Hanadi Taysser Darajat was a law graduate from Jareesh University, Jordan, a rather unusual distinction for a Palestinian girl. It is utterly simplistic to say that: "The profile of a suicide-bomber is that of a young man from a religious home who has been approached by a mosque, then recruited and finally trained". It can be easily seen that such simplistic theories would fail to explain the use of suicide terrorism by groups like the LTTE. The role of religion in suicide terrorism has obviously been greatly overstated with vested political interests in mind and to propagate the current American world-view.

(6.2.2) The True Concept of Martyrdom in Islam

A martyr in Arabic is called a '*shaheed*'. The word '*shahada*' is derived from the Arabic verbal root '*shahada*', which means to 'see', to 'witness', to 'testify', to 'become a model and paradigm'. '*Shahada*' therefore literally means to 'see', to 'witness', and to 'become a model'—from it we get the word '*shaahid*' for a witness. Interestingly, the English word 'martyr' comes from the Greek word '*martur*' which also means witness. The connection between a witness and a martyr is that a witness sees and witnesses. A martyr, on the other hand, not only sees the truth (*haqq*) physically or testifies to it verbally, he is also prepared to struggle and fight and give up his life for the truth. In this way, and by his struggle and sacrifice for the sake of the truth, he becomes a model, a paradigm, and an example for others, worthy of being copied, and worthy of being followed [2:185]. The term '*shahada*' was used in the Qur'an for those who were martyred too. *Istishhad* means the seeking of or the act of martyrdom. The goal, motive, and the whole aim are the establishment of the truth. He is a Mujahid while he lives and a martyr if he dies or is killed for it. The concept of martyrdom is of crucial importance in all the major monotheistic religions. It serves as an advertising tool and attests to the truth of the faith. Sheikh Yusuf al-Qaradawi, sometimes called "the world's most quoted independent Islamic jurist", has called martyrdom operations the greatest of all sorts of '*Jihad* in the cause of Allah'. He says that a martyr operation is carried out by a person who sacrifices himself, deeming his life less value than striving in the cause of Allah, in the cause of restoring the land and preserving the dignity.

(6.2.3) Immediate Motivating Factors for Suicidal Operations: Western Perception versus Reality

While moral obligations derived from a rigid adherence to sacred values has its place, in reality the immediate motivation of many suicide bombers is their desire to seek revenge for humiliation inflicted upon himself or whom he considers of his side or upon his entire community. In Iraq, for example, the theme of humiliation, such as well-publicised atrocities committed at the Abu Ghraib prison, is important to understanding their rage. Next comes the question of how some people react to the treatment they find being meted out to their people by the American soldiers and other officials. Once again, it is a question of Oriental sensibilities and the westerners find it almost impossible to understand. Witnessing the abuse of elders in front of their children, whether verbal insults at roadblocks or strip-downs during house searches, indelibly stains the memory and increases popular support for martyrdom actions. This can be true even if the person is witness only to an injured party living thousands of miles away, for example, an Indonesian observing events in the Palestinian territories on television or through the Internet. What may be considered standard police practice in the United States may warrant undying calls for revenge in another society. It must be kept in mind that the Americans in particular are known for the most insulting behaviour during the so-called strip-down searches. Their junior staff behaves as if they are zombies, completely impervious to any human argument. Readers may also recall the well-publicised photo of Saddam Hussain immediately following his capture in which a medic was examining his teeth as if he were cattle! The excuse given was that it was a routine check-up for prisoners and they wanted to check for some gum disease or that he could have hidden some poison capsule—these guys did not realise that if he really had a poison capsule, he would have bitten it the moment they barged in! The purpose was essentially to insult him and nothing else.

The severed foot of a suicide bomber lying at the site of attack – a grim reminder of their fierce motivation

(6.3) Different Methods of Suicidal Attacks

They include the following:

Suicidal attacks on foot using explosive belt, satchel charge or any explosive device carried on the person of the attacker. The attack requires that the entry must be gained through surreptitiously or through some subterfuge. The target could be humans or even a vehicle, such as in the case of the assassination of Neelan Thiruchelvam, TULF MP in Sri Lanka. (What is popularly known as an explosive belt or jacket is simply an improvised belt or jacket in which a complete IED has been concealed. A serious suicide bomber would make the explosive belt or jacket with plastic explosives so that they may be given the desired shape. The idea is that it should blend into the clothing as much as possible. Sophisticated explosive belts or jackets should have the explosive in the form of sheets or plates. The most popular shrapnel still remains ball bearings and with good reason. Those who use nails, nuts and bolts deserve to be beaten up first. The use of the words 'human bomb' for a suicide bomber is so atrocious English that I would not even mention it again).

- Suicidal attacks on foot using firearms. In this type of attack a forced entry can be made.
- Vehicle-borne IED—also known as car bomb or truck bomb
- Suicidal attack made using a boat. The attack on the USS Cole was made this way. The LTTE have used it numerous times with great success.
- Suicidal attack can be made using a small submarine or human-steered torpedo also. The Japanese had done it in the WW-II—the torpedoes were called Kaiten.
- Suicidal attack mounted using airplanes—who does not know the famous 'Kamikaze' attacks?
- Suicidal attacks made using animals as carriers of explosives. Donkey bombs were a specialty of the Sendero Luminoso (Shining Path) in Peru.
- Explosives can be carried on bicycles also. The most famous example is the assassination of the Sri Lankan President Ranasinghe Premadasa.
- In the 9/11 type of attack an airplane itself could be used as a weapon with its great momentum and fuel load.
- A suicidal attack can also be made by forcefully diverting a vehicle to an abyss, e.g., the Tel Aviv Jerusalem bus 405 massacre in which a Palestinian travelling in a crowded bus en route from Tel Aviv to Jerusalem seized the steering wheel from the driver and crashed the bus over a steep precipice in the area of Qiryat Ye'arim.

(6.4) When Terrorist Organisations may Resort to Suicide Terrorism?

Terrorists resort to suicide terrorism for a variety of reasons. Agreed, that all of them stem from an implicit admission that they are desperate. Nobody loves to blow himself up. They are obliged to do so when, at a military or operational level, they find that their usual repertoire of numerous terror tactics or other tactics of unconventional warfare is not proving sufficiently effective. One should always keep in mind that suicidal attacks are normally against the basic tenets of warfare. It they are forced to adopt unconventional means to keep the group or the movement going, it can only mean that they are desperate. Terrorists who are using suicidal techniques are doing it simply because they have, at that particular juncture in their struggle, found it expedient to do so. It is incorrect to say, as most people seem to believe, that they do it under the influence of some fundamentalist indoctrination or some sort of religious brainwashing. The cause comes first, the religion later. The point being made is that suicide terrorism is both a tactical as well as emotional decision. While the West can possibly understand the former, it is difficult for them to understand the latter. In the following I list the reasons due to which a person or group decides that it would be expedient to resort to suicide attacks.

- Suicide attacks have got a certain shock value attached to them. They send the target into a state of shock much beyond the actual damage inflicted upon him.
- Suicide attacks are sure-fire methods. The chances of the attacks succeeding and inflicting considerable damage on the enemy are quite high.
- As such they are very cost-effective. The same amount of damage to the target's military resources (such as aircrafts and ammunition dumps), men (such as the US Marines in Beirut) and economic resources (such as fuel depots) cannot be easily inflicted through conventional means of attack. Hence, it makes them particularly attractive to the non state actors. When non-state actors find that militarily they cannot take on the military might of a state, they may resort to suicide attacks.
- They are a cost effective means of countering sophisticated weapons at the disposal of the state, particularly air force, armour and heavy artillery, things which non-state actors lack, either in the combat zone or outside it. The destruction of more than a dozen aircraft including eight military and some civilian aircrafts by the LTTE in a single suicidal attack on the Katunayake military airbase is a good example.
- Suicide attacks are much simpler to plan. They do not have to concern themselves with making an escape plan, often the most difficult part of an operation. They have only to worry about penetration.
- They do not have to worry about some member getting caught and revealing sensitive information in the course of interrogation or torture.
- It has great psychological impact on the enemy.
- At times, if properly executed it can even result in strategic advantage to the non-state actor particularly if they have taken out some important leaders, vital for the conduct of operations against them. While a state can recover from any such

elimination and introduce substitutes, there is undoubtedly some dislocation both in terms of time and planning of subsequent moves.

- It also makes the state waste its manpower and material resources in strengthening the security of its top functionaries, vital installations and public places.
- In fact the non-state actors can force the state to squander its resources merely by propagating a 'hit list' of their real or imaginary targets. Once that list is out, there are few governments which can afford to think rationally and most of them are forced to protect even those things which they would have never protected otherwise.
- Not only that, it forcefully introduces widespread panic and feeling of insecurity amongst the people and towards this end they are aided by the media which is keen only on sensationalisation. Further, over-reaction from the government aggravates the feeling of insecurity and indirectly fosters the image of the group being almost invincible if not into an all-pervading force. They get a larger-than-life image at a very low cost.
- They can deliver maximum shock to the enemy in a single attack. That is to say, they do not have to worry about conserving their resources for some other day.
- The fact that, in a suicidal attack, even high security places can be attacked, serves as a great morale booster to them. It has great propaganda value too.
- Suicide attacks are living examples of the supreme sacrifice. They constitute the most convincing proof of the dedication and devotion of those who took part in it for their 'cause'. Thus, they act as a source of inspiration to all those who find their resolve wavering and that they are lacking in the fervour which they had once.
- They can hope to gain some sympathy amongst their covert or half-hearted supporters by such acts of daring and 'bravery'. Every movement looks for and eulogizes its martyrs.

Terrorists know that this is a technique that cannot be used indiscriminately; otherwise the movement will soon run out of members. The idea is to keep a sufficiently motivated cadre ready for the act and use them whenever the leadership feels like it, keeping the above-mentioned reasons in mind.

(6.5) Intrinsic Difficulties in Dealing with a Suicide Bomber

Float like a butterfly, sting like a bee; you can't hit what you can't see.

There is nothing you can do if the bomber does his job undetected. Then you are taken by absolute surprise and cannot do anything. However, if you spot him then don't pounce on him in some mistaken notion of bravery. They won't be able to count the number of pieces in which your body will be blown up. Hold it, dear, life is precious! If the bomber has any brains he can even pretend to surrender so as to draw security personnel closer to him. Worst, the bomb could be under the remote control of somebody else! They invented this mechanism so as to counter the Western security forces who insisted that the bomber wishing to surrender must remove himself first to an isolated place, keep the stand-off distance and then remove the bomb from his person. His remote controller would activate the bomb the moment he suspected that the suicide bomber is losing resolve or is being taken away! Terrorists might incorporate plastic explosives into brassieres which could, in a cursory examination, easily pass off as padded or sports bras—there are, in any case, many designs of wired bras for push-up—hence presence of metal in the bra is not that unusual to security personnel.

Western forces have developed a notion that one should shoot or nab the bomber. Little do they realise that the bomber could have easily made the device in such a way that it went off with an audio command which he could give when he got nabbed or could be linked to his pulse so that it went off the moment he dies and so on! These are known as 'dead man's switches'. The phrase comes from 'dead man's handle'. An intelligent suicide bomber could have easily provided for secondary and tertiary devices; or for that matter there could be multiple suicide bombers in one place!

A somewhat more intelligent way of dealing with a suicide bomber is to fire a TASER at him. That would leave him immobilised and yet leave him alive so that a dead man's switch is not activated. It could be countered only by making a spring loaded switch which would require to be kept pressed as long as the bomb were to remain un-triggered. The moment the bomber would be immobilised, paralysed or become unconscious; he could lose muscle control over the switch and set it off. More intelligent bombers could make his body sensitive to the receipt of electrical current also.

The first thing that must be admitted in planning security measures against suicide attacks is that terrorists would not go for a suicide attack unless they have adequate information about the target. If they have that intelligence it can only mean that there has been breach of security. Security managers should constantly search for such present or likely breaches. In other words, a greater emphasis on OPSEC (Operations Security) is required to deny vital information to terrorists.

Safe distances to be observed

Device carried	TNT equivalent explosive	Building evacuation distance	Outdoor evacuation distance
Suicide belt	10 lbs	90 ft	1080 ft
Suicide Vest	20 lbs	110 ft	1,360 ft
Briefcase/ Suitcase Bomb	50 lbs	150 ft	1,850 ft

Those who are interested in protecting certain facilities and premises from suicide attacks should be prepared to introduce fundamental and scientific changes in the physical security measures so as to prevent vehicles from crashing through. This would be an elaborate exercise and would require measures like concrete ditches, drawbridges, and bollards etc.

(6.6) Mortar and RPG Attacks

The Irish Republican Army deployed several types of homemade, throwaway mortars "to devastating effect" against a wide range of targets over the years. Press releases by the Royal Ulster Constabulary even go so far as to describe these mortars as the undoubted "favourite weapon of the Provisional IRA". This assertion is reinforced by the fact that IRA used its homemade mortars on average of once every ten days in the six months prior to the 1994 cease-fire. The targets of IRA mortar attacks include reinforced police and military compounds, British military facilities outside Northern Ireland, Heathrow airport outside London, and once against the British Prime Minister's official residence at 10, Downing Street during the Gulf War. Members of IRA Active Service Units have also used their mortars in a direct-fire mode against police and military vehicles as surrogates for RPG anti-tank weapons.

Although the IRA has field up to 17 different mortar variants, they all are constructed in basically the same way. A number of homemade mortar tubes are mounted on the back or inside of a hijacked truck or van. These tubes are sealed on one end and fitted with an electrically detonated charge that launches the projectile out of the tube.

They are usually one-shot weapons because they are very difficult to reload quickly, but have considerable destructive effect because several tubes are fitted together and fired salvo fashion. Typically, these mortars fire 40-60 pound projectiles from 80 to 300 yards. The 'Mark 10' version which was used against 10, Downing Street, for example, could have a six-inch shell containing 24 pounds of explosives up to 300 meters.

The IRA's 'Mark 10' improvised Mortar that was used to fire on the 10, Downing Street, London installed in a Ford transit van

The RPG-7 is the signature weapon of the guerrilla. Before the Afghan Mujahideen made it iconic, it was a favourite of the PLO. The PLO frequently ambushed Israeli M-113 armoured personnel carriers in Lebanon in 1982. These PLO ambushes with Soviet-designed RPGs produces extensive casualties in part because of the tendency of the M113-s aluminium armour to catch fire after being hit by an RPG round. In some Israeli units, men became so frightened at the possibility of RPG induced fire that they simply walked next to their M-113 or rode outside rather than risk being burned to death. An unidentified group fired 3 RPGs at a limousine carrying Georgian President Eduard Shevardnadze in February of 1998. And who does not know the world famous Black Hawk Down Incident in which the Somalis shot down an American helicopter with RPG fire.

7

The Complexities of Unconventional Warfare in Urban Environments

Come on you sons of bitches! Do you want to live forever?

(7.1) The Necessity and Objectives of Urban Combat in Various Situations

Have a plan. Have a back-up plan, because the first one probably won't work.

Urban warfare is described by the Americans as UO (Urban Operations) or MOUT (Military Operations in Urban Terrain); the British use the terms FIBUA (Fighting in Built-up Areas) or OBUA (Operations in Built-up Areas). All of them refer to combat conducted in urban areas such as towns and cities. The term close-quarter battle (CQB) refers to the micro-management factor—namely, how a small squad of infantry troops should fight in urban environments and/or inside buildings in order to achieve its goals with minimal casualties like weapons and ammunition most suitable for the mission; extra gear, such as bullet-proof vests and night vision devices; accurate explosives; routines and drills for engaging the enemy, securing a perimeter, clearing a room, etc; and team manoeuvres, etc. In other words, CQB is a sub-set of UO. You can use the generic term urban combat loosely for both.

Urban guerrilla warfare is a perfectly viable option on its own for groups wanting to fight an unconventional war with a governmental power as it is for terrorist groups. It could be the primary means of fighting an insurgent war; as terrorism, it could also be a means in a larger insurgent war. Further, if such groups are supported by a hostile foreign power, and if a war breaks out with that power, the terrorist or guerrilla groups might simultaneously open up an urban front in support of the foreign power as fifth columnists or as independent combatants striking the forces in the rear. The guerrilla force may also lead to cause commitment of friendly forces, best used in the close battle, to the battle in the rear.

The objectives of a guerrilla force in an urban armed conflict would include:

Disruption: The guerrilla force would seek to disrupt command, control, communications, and logistics operations and facilities of friendly forces. They may accomplish this by attacking key installations such as headquarters, communications sites, supply depots, maintenance facilities, and airfields. The guerrilla force would also seek to cut lines of communication and supply by interdicting supply columns, bridges, highways, and communications lines.

Confusion: By destroying key facilities and interdicting lines of communication and supply, the guerrilla force can cause confusion within the friendly force rear areas. The greater the amount of confusion created, the greater the ability of the main enemy force to discover and exploit weaknesses of the friendly force.

Harassment: The guerrilla force remains a source of harassment as long as it operates in the rear area. It may not have to conduct continuous operations to achieve its goal. The mere knowledge that the guerrilla exists within the rear area, even though undetected, may be enough.

Support: By disrupting, confusing, and harassing vital areas, the guerrilla supports the main enemy force by tying up friendly combat units in countering the threat.

The guerrilla and terrorist operations in Santo Domingo, Caracas, Belfast, Managua, and Beirut have all been characterised by urban combat. In urban combat in Grozny, Chechnya; Jenin, West Bank; and Mogadishu (Somalia), irregular forces were able to inflict disproportionate casualties on regular army troops. In many Iraqi cities under occupation, the rebels indulged in urban combat with the US forces. Ever since Stalingrad, battles have shown that a competent and motivated defender can take advantage of his knowledge of the ground and the fact that cities force short-range combat under such conditions, to inflict major casualties on the enemy. Hence, you must be prepared to fight regular as well as irregular forces in urban areas.

You must expect even regular forces indulging in urban combat like irregular forces on purpose. Conventional forces that may conduct guerrilla warfare include forces that have been cut off or that intentionally stay behind as their main force withdraws or retreats. Another type of force may be an armoured and/or mechanised unit with a mission to penetrate friendly rear areas and cause disruption, confusion, and harassment. Airborne, heliborne, or waterborne light infantry forces may also fight like a guerrilla force if they have been inserted to conduct precisely that type of operations. Special units trained for guerrilla warfare usually have a primary mission to conduct guerrilla warfare operations against targets of opportunity with a follow-on mission to train an indigenous guerrilla force. These special units may enter a friendly area through the use of high altitude, low opening (HALO); high altitude, high opening (HAHO); or low level parachute techniques. The tactics used by both conventional and unconventional guerrilla forces remain the same. They are characterised by elusiveness, surprise, and brief, violent action.

(7.2) Unique Features of Urban Combat

Anything worth shooting is worth shooting twice.
Ammo is cheap. Life is expensive.

Urban combat is one of the deadliest and most decisive forms of combat. General Charles Krulak has described the landscape of future urban operations as a "three block war". He was laying emphasis on the fact that armies used to fighting in great spaces and manoeuvres, must get used to the idea of intense and bloody fighting in spaces as small as just three blocks! You might be in a much smaller space but the fighting is much more intense and varied. There are three conditions of urban operations that span the full spectrum of offence, defence, stability, and support. The first condition, 'Urban Operations Under Surgical Conditions', comprises special-purpose raids, small precision strikes, or small-scale personnel seizures. This is the condition the IRA operated from most often, where day-to-day business and life go on in the urban area in a close to permissive environment. The second condition, 'Urban Operations Under Precision Conditions', is essentially a semi-permissive environment in which the threat is thoroughly mixed with non-combatants. The Mujahideen operated against the Soviets in the Afghan cities within these conditions. Life in the cities, although affected by the Soviet occupation, still maintained a modicum of normalcy, but large numbers of Soviet forces were present and security conditions were heightened. Lastly, 'Urban Operations Under High-Intensity Conditions', is the condition usually thought of when discussing military operations on urban terrain. It involves combat actions against enemy forces occupying prepared positions or conducting planned attacks on built up areas. The Chechen defence of Grozny in 1994 and 2000 are perfect examples of this condition of urban operations, which is characterised by seizing, clearing, or defending urban terrain and defeating the enemy using whatever force is necessary.

The most important characteristic of unconventional warfare in urban environment is that it is three-dimensional. Combat in urban areas can occur on the surface, above the surface, and below the surface, as well as inside and outside of buildings.

Urban terrain is a truly unique battlefield providing both the attacker and the defender numerous and varied avenues of approach and fields of fire. In addition to fighting the enemy at street level, fighting may also be conducted on roofs and in the upper stories of buildings and below street level in sewer systems, subways, and other underground structures. Tactics are complicated by limited fields of view and fire because of buildings, enhanced concealment and cover for defenders, and the ease of placement of booby traps and snipers. Other complicating factors also include the presence of civilians, and buildings of all sorts. Some civilians may be difficult to distinguish from combatants such as armed militias and gangs.

The three-dimensional terrain also gives the guerrilla tactical advantages. Sometimes this has been manifested in methods of concealment or withdrawal from objectives that the built-up areas provide. Often the three-dimensional terrain allows the guerrillas to get very close to their enemy during combat operations and eliminate the advantage in firepower and range the conventional forces usually enjoy. Another advantage for the guerrillas is that since in urban combat conventional forces are obliged to fight in small units as the terrain restricts the movement, visibility, and communications of their enemies; it significantly affects the force ratios. In fact, this takes care of one of their major handicaps, that is, numerical inferiority and allows them to even the odds to a great degree. It can easily nullify the overwhelming advantage that high-tech militaries have (in terms of firepower) and shift the advantage over to small, well-armed squads of regular infantry or even militia. Casualties for forces involved in urban combat are often extreme, usually bordering 40-50 per cent. Operating from, within, or through urban areas isolates and separates units of conventional forces and since traditional fighting conditions them for fighting in situations where they come to depend heavily on other units, they tend to get baffled when fighting as small units on their own and which places much greater demands on the individual soldier's and small-unit leader's initiative, skill, and fortitude. In possibly no other form of combat are the pressures of battle more intense. Continuous close combat, high casualties, the fleeting nature of targets, and fires from a frequently unseen enemy produce severe psychological strain and physical fatigue particularly among small-unit leaders and soldiers.

From the point of view of conventional forces used to operations entailing high mobility and heavy combat firepower, a serious problem is that of limited mounted manoeuvre space—buildings, street width, rubble, debris, and non-combatants all contribute to limited mounted manoeuvre space inside urban areas. Armoured vehicles may therefore find it difficult to operate inside urban areas without infantry support and *vice versa*. Firing RPGs on tanks from rooftops is fun and easy. Who knows it better than the Israelis and it is reflected amply in the design of their tank Merkava. Following Israel's incursion into Lebanon in 1982, and the battles in Beirut, they realised that fighting in urban areas calls for some fundamental changes in tank design. The Israelis cannot afford losses in men—as simple as that! The Merkava has therefore been designed for crew survival; the power plant is placed at the front of the tank, increasing frontal mass, while the crew is able to escape from a disabled Merkava via doors in the rear of the hull. The large rear doors of the Merkava also enable quicker reloading of ammunition. The armour is also modular so that when the tank is hit, only the damaged armour plates need replacement. It also carries an internally operated 60 mm Soltam mortar—once again a proof of their concern about the possibility of finding the tank in an urban environment where delivering indirect fire will be necessary. The Merkava-3-Baz was developed with only urban warfare in mind—it

Rear view of the Israeli Merkava tank: the large rear door enables faster reloading of ammunition and faster exit of crew if the tank is hit; the engine is also in the front for extra protection – design changes made specifically with urban combat in mind

features one Browning .50 caliber machine gun that can be fired from inside, extra-protection against grenades and netting that protects optics and ventilators, and a rear camera for better navigation in narrow streets. Some of the Merkava tanks were fitted with ambulance capabilities also. The Merkava ARV, called Nammer is an armoured recovery vehicle based on a Merkava chassis. It is capable of rescuing stuck tanks and carries a back-up power plant for the tank.

The third problem is that of collateral damage. Significant collateral damage can occur during combat in urban environments. This can be non-combatant collateral damage as well as structural or environmental, and can have very complex effects. The Indians were obliged to use tanks when they found it difficult to reduce the terrorist positions during their 'Operation Blue Star' in 1984 on the Golden Temple complex in Amritsar with infantry alone. That was the first time when the Indian army had to fight in an urban environment and they failed miserably. Dumb as they are, they were quick to call in the tanks.

While it is firmly established that urban guerrilla warfare and urban combat are contemporary and viable realities, adequate analytical studies have not been carried out to discuss the difficulties faced, and how tactical operations can be improved upon. Hence, this chapter.

(7.3) Operation Blue Star: How the Indian Army Fumbled in Urban Warfare

Situation normal; all fucked up. One who does not expect the worst shall, of course, be disappointed.

(7.3.1) *Ad Hocism and Lack of Institutional Knowledge*

Beware the lollipop of mediocrity. Lick once and suck forever.

It is worthwhile to study how the morons of the Indian army had fumbled in this operation. I am not interested in the politics of the conflict nor am I commenting on that. I am interested only the tactics part of it as a military scientist and in showing that for want of a comprehensive doctrine with details of tactics for combat in urban areas, the army fared so badly. For all the tall stories they tell about themselves over their *chhota* pegs, the fact is that they had no idea what they were doing. Yes, they did fight valiantly and gave up their lives too but it was sheer *ad hocism* all the way—they improvised as they encountered a situation. There was no institutional knowledge of urban combat behind their plans and actions—how would you react if you encountered such-and-such situations, and the like. No operational manuals worth their name existed that dealt with the complexities of urban combat. In fact, they could not even foresee the sort of opposition they were going to encounter, and were taken by surprise at almost every step. Nobody, given the limited intellectual capacity of the army officers at all levels, could think beyond the simple bullets and shells. The prevailing concept was: try to shoot your way through because they knew little else—as if bullets would flatten all opposition. And when they could not, they grew desperate. I am making a special point of this because, as we saw earlier, in the Moscow theater siege, the Russians did use fentanyl gas to incapacitate the terrorists instead of just barging in with all guns blazing—an excellent idea. They did so because they were alive to the possibility of extensive collateral damage. The Indian army, as I have shown a little later, utterly failed to contain collateral damage both in terms of human casualties on both sides and in damage to structures—something which was to have terrible consequences for the nation later. This analysis is necessary because most Indians, even amongst the security forces, are not aware of the facts.

(7.3.2) The Overall Plan

A sketch showing an overview of the Golden Temple complex is given below.

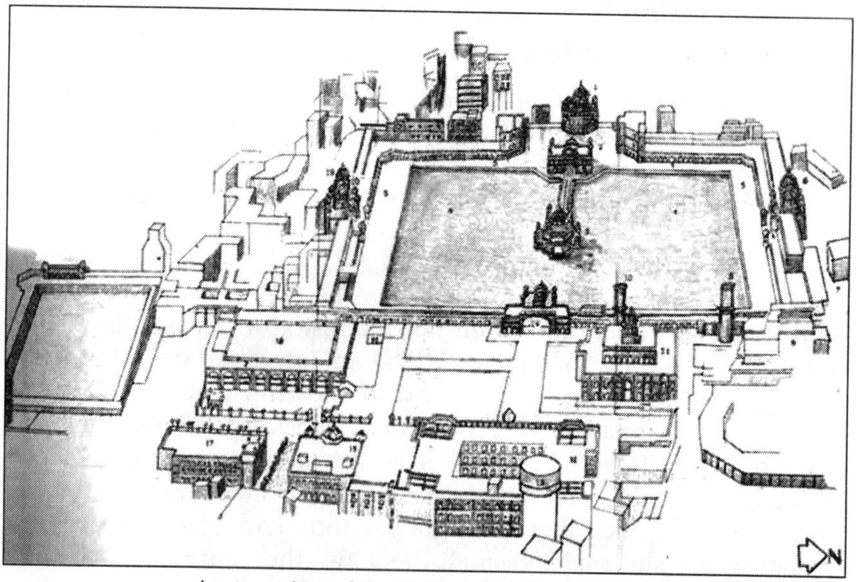

An overview of the Golden Temple Complex

The sequence of events is as follows. Men of the 12th Bihar Regiment fanned to take positions across the roof tops around the

Temple complex. Soon they realised that they were vulnerable to grenade attacks from the top of the 18th century towers and water tank. The Biharis moved to sand-bagged windows in vacated houses. Similarly, men from the Garhwal Regiment and the brigade of the Guards were moved on the other side of the Temple. Tanks fanned out to guard sensitive villages to prevent communal killings.

By June 3, the Biharis watched the area of the clock tower, the main entrance and Brahm Buta Market, the Garhwalis, the Guardsmen and the Punjabis overlooked the Chowk Parag Dass, Chhati Khui, Atta Mandi, Baba Atal and Buddhi Lutt Bazaar. The terrorists poured automatic fire from the top of water towers and elsewhere.

106-mm jeep-mounted RCLs were brought into fire at the terrorists' fortified positions. But apparently they could not do the job. Then a 3.7" howitzer gun was brought in. That took care of the fortified positions. The subsequent plan was as follows.

I - Initial Operations

1. BSF to secure Hotel Temple View by 9 p.m., June 5th.
2. CRPF to secure Brahm Boota Akhara by 10 p.m., June 5th.

II - Phase 1

1. 10 Guards to secure Northern Wing of the Temple Complex by 1 a.m., June 6th.
2. Para-commandos to:-
   - Secure a foothold in the Akal Takht at the earliest and not later than 1 a.m., June 6th.
   - Secure a foothold in Harmandir Sahib with divers and neutralise demolitions, if any, by 11:30 p.m., June 5th.
3. Special Frontier Force (SFF) to isolate Akal Takht and secure western flank by 1 a.m., June 5th.
4. 26 Madras to secure southern and eastern wings by 1 a.m., June 5th.
5. 9 Kumaon to secure Guru Ram Das Serai and SGPC building by 1 a.m., June 5th.

III - Phase 2

Mopping up all areas secured in Phase 1

IV - Phase 3

1. 9 Kumaon - extend operations to secure the rest of hostel complex.
2. Units of 10 Guards, SFF and 1 Para-commando to secure rest of Temple Complex and check prisoners.

Others

12 Bihar was to continue to cordon off the Temple with CRPF units under its command and provide fire support to any target within its span of observation.

Mechanised Units

Armour: 16 Cavalry

1. Three tanks to enter through the main temple entrance, initially for close protection for 10th Guards but thereafter provide support to infantry, paras and SFF with machine gun fire.
2. Three tanks to enter the *langar* area and provide machine gun fire to 26 Madras.

Mechanised Infantry: 8 Mech Bn

1. 4 BMPs to carry para-commando/divers.
2. 4 BMPs and 3 Skot APCs to support 26 Madras and the Paras.

Reserves: 15 Kumaon - 2 companies as backup for 9th Kumaon and 2 companies for any contingency tasks.

Central Rendezvous and Logistics Control: City Kotwali.

Divisional Tactical HQ: Roof Top outside Temple complex.

Initial operations went through as planned with both the Hotel Temple View and Brahm Boota Akhara secured with little resistance. It was however not surprising as they were isolated and only existed to provide early warning of the army's approach. However, the battlements on the top of the clock tower were proving harder to knock out and thus the H-hour was postponed by half-an-hour. At 10:30 p.m. the first phase of Operation Blue Star commenced.

(7.3.3) *How the Operations in the Temple Complex Ran Aground?*

Beauty is only skin deep but ugliness goes right to the bone.

Main Entrance - North Side

At H-hour, the leading elements of the 10 Guards moved in through the main gate. Immediately, they came under heavy and accurate machine gun fire, cleverly sited through wired enclosures on either side of steps. For those who made it across the steps, another nightmare awaited. For the couple of minutes they were caught in the open, before taking the cover of the Parikrama, they were fired upon from the Parikrama itself. Twenty soldiers were mowed down in the initial assault itself.

The troops started inching their way towards the Akal Takht but were fired upon from the southern side. Meanwhile each room had to be cleared along the Parikrama. Terrorists would come out and lob a few grenades and rush back in. Unknown to the army, was an elaborate structure of concealed manholes and underground passages connecting the rooms. Meanwhile a machine gun sited about 12 inches from the ground opened fire. This low-siting of the machinegun meant that even the crawling troops were hit.

While this was going on, the objective of the Para-commandos, the so-called elite unit of the Indian army, was to get a foothold in the Akal Takht and a foothold in Harmandir Sahib with the help of divers. As they slipped in and made a dash across the Parikrama they met a fate similar to the Guardsmen. The Parikrama was exposed to fire from all four sides. Realising their predicament, the Commandos dashed from pillar to pillar trying to cut off the oppressing fire. As they reached the Akal Takht their misery was compounded by the devastating machine gun fire from the fortified Akal Takht, as well as the Harmandir Sahib and the area of Darshani Deori-Toshakana. The mission of the divers to slip across the Sarovar was aborted as they would have not survived the murderous fire.

The Guardsmen were asked to bring down fire on the northern side from whatever portions of the northern side they had secured. By midnight the Guards had secured the eastern half of the North Wing but on the Western side only 75 per cent was secured. Due to the severe casualties suffered by the first two companies, the third company was pressed in. Rather than wait for the complete clearance of the ground floor they were asked to secure a foothold on the first and second floor. This was deemed necessary to provide some sort of fire to the bogged down Para-Commandos and the SFF.

One platoon climbed to the first floor using aluminium ladders. They then went about clearing the rooms. Another platoon likewise moved from the first to the second floor and started clearing the rooms. Troops moving up from the ground floor were suddenly fired upon by terrorists through an opening in the wall next to the stairs. Some casualties resulted, but the troops quickly wiped them out. By 1 a.m., the Guards had secured their objective and could provide covering fire to the beleaguered commandos.

The commandos were still inching their way to the Akal Takht. This five-storied building was heavily fortified with all windows, balconies and other openings closed with brick masonry and sandbags, with small loopholes through which machine guns were being fired and grenades being lobbed. Together with a double storied building, the Nishan Sahib building and the Darshani Deori, they transformed the quadrangle into an ideal killing field. The leading team of Para-Commandos made a desperate dash for the Darshani Deori. The foothold was needed to launch the CS canisters. Of the 35 men, only 12 made it. The remainder were cut down. The SFF started with 50 men, had already suffered 17 casualties (3 dead).

With midnight approaching, casualties mounting and the objectives far from being achieved, the situation was desperate.

Serai Entrance - Eastern Side

On the eastern side, the 26 Madras was expected to enter and then sweep the southern side of any resistance. The entry from the southern side was ruled out because of the narrow passage not allowing for entry of any vehicle. But two companies of 9 Garhwal were stealthily brought in, as backup near the Southern entrance. But they had been delayed by a steel gate which was much more formidable then expected. It needed a tank to ram it down.

At H-hour, 26 Madras started to move in but came under a withering fire from atop the Langar, Guru Ram Das Serai, SGPC building, Manji Sahib and Gurdwara Baba Atal Rai. In addition, the steel gate was proving difficult to break. Thirty meters from the gate they came under fire from medium machine guns from the Deori itself. A section went ahead to lob grenades and clear it, but could not succeed. The plan was changed and they moved some troops in an opening on the south-west side. This gave some relief but progress was slow as they had to fight it room by room, like the Guardsmen on the other side.

At 11 p.m., with 26 Madras behind schedule, the Garhwalis were asked to move in from the south side and secure a foothold on either side of Atta Mandi. They could then assist 26 Madras by laying down suppressive fire and allow 15 Kumaon to launch an attack on the Akal Takht from the south west. The committing of the reserves was decided based on the fact that the Guards were now more or less in control of the northern side. Garhwalis moved with little difficulty and by 1:30 a.m. had secured the ground and upper floors of the southern gate.

(7.3.4) A Frustrated Army is Left with no Option but to Use Tanks

No matter where you go in the world, there never seems to be a shortage of idiots.

At 2 a.m. the overall picture was as follows:

1. The 10th Guards after suffering heavy casualties, had more or less secured the northern wing. Sporadic militant activity from concealed chambers was still a problem.
2. 26 Madras operation had stalled, but was now gaining ground between the eastern and southern wings. However, there was still heavy opposition.
3. Two companies of 9 Garhwal had secured a foothold in the southern gate.
4. 1 Para-Commando and SFF operation had bogged down within reach of the Akal Takht.

It was at this juncture that the Indian army officers grew desperate and sought permission to open tank fire on the Akal Takht.

In the meantime, in order to help the SFF and Paras, a tank was brought in and asked to switch on its search light. It was hoped that this would temporarily blind the defenders as well as allow the SFF and Paras locate some of the defences. But unfortunately this move failed as the Xenon lamps filament burned out in a couple of minutes. When this happened, another tank was moved in followed by a third. Thus, all 3 tanks were in the Parikrama. At about 4 a.m., a Skot APC was moved in. Since it is a wheeled vehicle, the tank had to roll back and forth on the steps and crush the marble slabs. Only then could the APC be safely brought in. The APC was supposed to take a squad right up to the Akal Takht.

The Guards were asked to fire a few 84 mm Carl Gustaf anti-tank warheads at the Akhal Takht to precede the arrival of the APC. As the APC was approaching the Akal Takht, it was hit by an RPG-7 anti-tank rocket from the Akal Takht. This came as a complete shock to the poor Indians. As the APC squad dismounted and retreated, the driver was shot.

By then dawn was approaching and soon the troops in the Parikrama would become sitting ducks. At 5:10 a.m. the clearance to use tanks came from Delhi. At first they tried tank machineguns.

The first assault was led by 'A' Company of 15 Kumaon. A group of men reached the footsteps of Akal Takht, the first group to make contact. As they climbed the stairs, a machine gun opened up from the inside and all seven men were mowed down. More machine gun fire rained from the base and the buildings on both side and the Kumaonis were thrown back with heavy casualties.

It was clear that the tank machinegun fire was not enough. The Kumaonis fell back to reorganise, having suffered seven killed and 23 wounded. Two companies of 26 Madras were now asked to pick up where the Kumaonis left. In the darkness there was confusion as Kumaonis and Madrassis got mixed up. It was realised that the two machine guns at the entrance had to be eliminated for any chance to move in on the Akal Takht. A section of troops was asked to volunteer for this dangerous task.

As the groups reached the Akal Takht, some 8-9 fortified machineguns opened up. One group was cut down to the last man. In the second group all were killed except two wounded who managed to crawl back. It is said that one Subedar sahib was captured alive, was dragged back, attached with sticks of dynamite and blown up in full view of the other troops. 26 Madras had suffered 14 dead and 49 wounded.

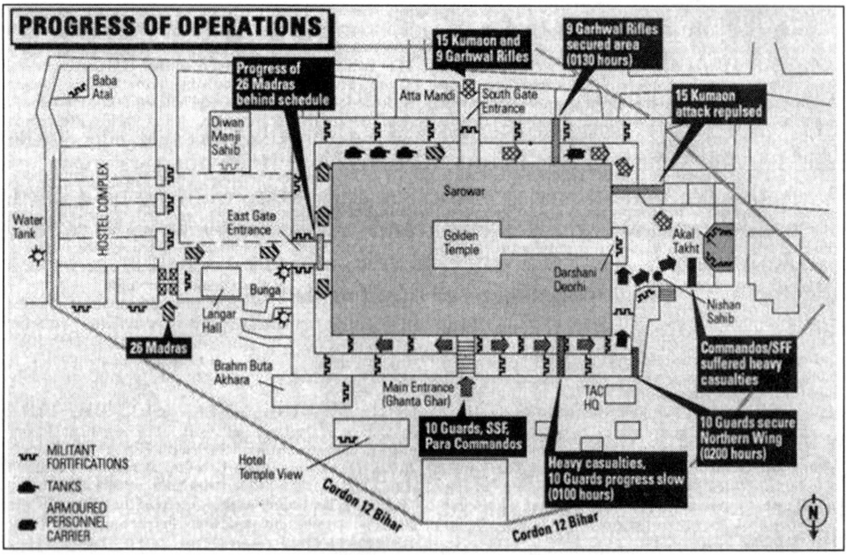

Operation Blue Star: The progress of operations

It was 7:30 am and daylight was well upon the troops. The frustrated Indian army men had finally to use the 105 mm main guns of the tanks. This, at long last, subdued the machine guns. Akal Takht was finally taken.

The Hostel Complex.

The main buildings of the Hostel Complex were:-

(A) **Guru Ram Das Langar** - Double storied heavily fortified building commanding a view of the side entrances and open area leading to Parikrama.

(B) **Guru Ram Das Serai (Akal Takht Rest House)** - Three storied building, 228 rooms and seven halls.

(C) **Teja Singh Samundari** - The office of SGPC, and was occupied by Longowal, Tohra, Ramoowalia and others.

(D) **Guru Nanak Niwas** - Four storied building with fortified roof tops, 85 rooms and one hall.

(E) Other buildinds in the complex were Guru Nanak Niwas, Manji Sahib and Baba Atal Gurdwara.

As mentioned earlier, the operation was in the hands of 9 Kumaon. The operation was to commence at 10 p.m., with the simultaneous launch of the Paras and SFF. It had three Vijayantas, six BMPs and three Skot APCs. In addition they were to break open the gates to help 26 Madras to enter the eastern gate. On schedule, 9 Kumaon moved into the Guru Ram Das Serai. A company was deployed on each of the three floors with the fourth held in reserve. The troops encountered opposition from each of the floors although it was lighter than the Temple complex. By 1:30 a.m. the building was isolated from the rest of the complex. A large number of devotees and Akali leaders were supposed to be in the building. On call, there were some surrenders. It is believed that when surrenders were taking place from the Teja Singh Samundari Hall, the terrorists threw hand grenades in the crowd and sniped at them – about 70 people got killed or injured in the process. A similar incident took place in Guru Nanak Niwas also. There were terrorists holed up in manholes, tunnels and concealed basements. The only area of resistance continued to be the *langar*. The terrorists continued to pour machine gun fire and hurl grenades. The Kumaonis fired back with everything at their disposal. At one point the wheat and kerosene caught fire sending huge columns of smoke. Gas cylinders caught fire and exploded intermittently. This fighting however was a rearguard action allowing some 40 Babbar Khalsa activists to escape. By the early hours of the morning on 7th, June the fighting suddenly died down.

Mopping Operations, 7th - 9th June

At this stage the job of clearing the many rooms, concealed tunnels and basements began. The snipers continued to take potshots. A group of terrorists emerged from a concealed tunnel and grabbed an officer and two soldiers of 10 Dogra. Eventually when the SFF blew up a grill and charged in killing seven terrorists, they found that the soldiers had been killed and their limbs chopped off.

(7.3.5) Collateral Damage and its Terrible Consequences

Life is like a fart; you never know how long it's going to last or how bad its gonna stink.

Martyrs are honoured alright but the fact remains, as the very dear General Patton had said: "No bastard ever won a war by dying for his country. He won it by making the other poor, dumb bastard die for his country". I am aware of the habit of the army officers cooking up *post facto* explanations as to how tough the fighting was, but as a professional I know that precious lives could have been saved had the Indian army known something about the complexities of urban combat. There were a large number of civilians inside when the operation took place and the army had no idea how to go about the operation in such a peculiar situation—in fact 1592 people were officially apprehended after the operation out of which 433 were claimed to be terrorists, which gives some idea of the crowd there. There is considerable dispute regarding the exact number of casualties. Many sources (such as the site bharat-rakshak.com) maintain that the army suffered casualties to the extent of 83 dead and 248 wounded, and the number of 'terrorists and others' killed was 492. The Government White Paper on Punjab Agitation says the same. Martha Crenshaw, and Pritam Singh, in their independent works, put the figure of casualties on the other side at up to 1,500! The British journalist and their India specialist Mark Tully puts it at 2093. That would indicate a very high collateral damage but even 492 is quite high particularly when you do not know the exact number of terrorists amongst them—you must compare it with the operations of the security forces of other nations and how they strive for clinical precision.

The tanks did the job but not without very significant collateral damage. As we know, Khushwant Singh was extremely livid and graphic about it in his speech in the Parliament. The damage to their religious structures was one of the reasons that led to widespread resentment among the Sikhs in India and a most unprecedented incident took place. The Indian army has historically been apolitical since 1857—the British groomed them so. But the psychological impact of damage to their most respected religious structure was so great that a large number of recruits at the Sikh Regimental Center at Ramgarh, Bihar revolted, killed their officers and fled with their arms and ammunition. According to globalsecurity.org, a large part of 9 Sikh which was in the Ganganagar area of Rajasthan also mutinied. This battalion was disbanded on April 1, 1985. The mutineers of Ramgarh could be intercepted only after they had moved well over a thousand kms across several states. And why only that? The then prime minister was assassinated by her Sikh guards some months later due to that only! That led to the anti-Sikh riots in November 1984 in which thousands of Sikhs were killed and property worth billions was destroyed—all because of a botched up urban warfare operation!

(7.4) How the IRA Made Best Use of its Limited Resources to Confound the British?

(7.4.1) Skilful Avoidance of Direct Combat

If everything is as clear as a bell, and everything is going exactly as planned, you're about to be surprised.

The strength and capabilities of the military and security forces facing the IRA and the limited assets available, in terms of manpower and weapons, drove the IRA to avoid direct confrontation at the tactical level. Command-detonated bombs, mortars, and sniping were their primary means of prosecuting their attacks as raids and traditional ambushes proved too costly to their limited manpower pool. Small, highly decentralised teams acted with an emphasis on dissociating the guerrilla with the action taken in order to avoid criminal prosecution. Collaboration with the local populace facilitated this dissociating as the auxiliary provided high levels of reconnaissance, transportation, weapons placement and concealment, and exfiltration means for targets. The most common urban combat operations employed by the IRA were sniping, bomb ambushes (usually command detonated), mortar attacks, and RPG attacks. Mortar attacks were a common means of attacking British and RUC (Royal Ulster Constabulary) patrols. Many varieties of homemade mortars had been developed by the IRA over the years. They were often mounted in vans with their roofs cut out, positioned within range of their target, and then remotely detonated. Small arms and explosives had been the mainstay of IRA weapons since the beginning because they were easier to procure, train on, and transport. Raids were rare. There was a period of time in the early 1980s when the IRA attempted some raids on RUC stations and British military outposts, sometimes using homemade armoured vehicles designed to penetrate the outer defences of the outpost. These raids were rarely successful primarily due to either the security apparatus around the target or a loss of operational security on the part of the IRA when planning a large operation that involved a greater number of personnel to execute than normal. Essentially, raids involve too much risk because of the direct engagement necessary with the security forces.

(7.4.2) Emphasis on Secrecy, Intelligence and Decentralisation

IRA combat actions were conducted by active service units (ASU), usually composed of four persons who most often know each other, but who had no natural connection (i.e., not related, did not work together, were not neighbours, etc). Although the IRA's General Headquarters issued broad guidance on operations and would sometimes designate and plan specific high-value targets, it was the local commander and ASUs who planned and executed the majority of IRA operations. The ASU was very decentralised and the members might actually be in contact for only the few minutes of the action they were conducting. Their movements to the objective, equipment pick up, movement from the target, and equipment drop off was all conducted individually.

Security for IRA guerrillas was maintained primarily through tight operational security of the information concerning the attack and an ability to dissociate the perpetrator from the action taken. The members of the ASUs travelled separately to their objectives and after an operation would withdraw from the objective separately. Clothes were changed or dropped off to separate the possible forensic evidence from the guerrilla who would then melt back into the population. Any weapons or equipment used in an attack were taken by someone else to dispose of or hide. Reconnaissance of the objective or target would have been performed by a person or persons separate from those who would execute the action to maintain operational security and dissociation. Collaboration with local populace was certainly an IRA strength that had allowed it to maintain urban guerrilla combat operations for many years. The IRA had a sophisticated network of human intelligence collection capabilities perfected through years of operations. All manner of support came from different sections of the Catholic populace inside and out of Northern Ireland's borders. Most significant to their urban guerrilla warfare combat operations were reconnaissance and surveillance support. British forces and the RUC were constantly under observation by someone in the IRA's network to keep them informed of their movements. One of the more obvious civilian IRA supporters encountered by security forces were the 'dickers': teenage boys with cell phones who loitered around security forces' barracks and on the streets, calling in locations and actions of the patrols. The IRA ensured those who conducted surveillance and reconnaissance were not part of the ASUs and they fell generally into two categories. The first were those who were members of the cause and regularly engage in auxiliary duties, whether they were logistical or intelligence gathering, short of active combat. The other category was simply the sympathetic population, who offered their services or information when asked, but were not truly members of the organisation.

The highly decentralised structure of the IRA, with local commanders and ASUs deciding upon and executing operations themselves, lent greatly to their ability to surprise British military and RUC units. Gaining intelligence and prior warning on small unit, independent action by the guerrillas was almost impossible. Some reports described the use of 'front' organisations, like the Falls Taxi Association in Belfast which the IRA used both for the support of operations and as a source of income. The 'black taxis' were considered a kind of Catholic Mafia by the British who occasionally supported the IRA with transportation to and from objectives. A more common use of the taxis was the transportation of weapons and equipment. The IRA very rarely concentrated its forces for urban operations as this would decrease their element of surprise in the bustling streets of Belfast or Londonderry. Rather, all combat operations were conducted by small, highly mobile teams.

The IRA themselves never wore uniforms except for promotional purposes such as in pictures, on posters, or briefly at funerals for one of its members. This uniform was composed of a 'black balaclava', a British-type combat jacket, and black pants. There were no incidents of using British or RUC uniforms for deception, perhaps because it was considered a dishonourable method of deception. Otherwise, both sides being white people and of the same build and features, an intelligent guerrilla would have taken it as a useful method and adopted it frequently. It seems wisdom dawned on them rather late. In 2002, a pair of guerrillas gained access to a police barracks using fake or stolen identity cards on a Sunday morning, overpowered a lone guard inside and stole several police files on IRA members.

(7.4.3) Ambushes Baited by Bombs and Snipers

Powder is scarce and must not be wasted. Fire low!

Bomb ambushes followed a common pattern. The first step was to create what the British called a 'come-on,' basically a ruse or bait of some sort to get the soldiers to come into the kill zone. This could be a civil disturbance of some kind or even a small device that appears to be a bomb. Once the soldiers or RUC responding got to the designated area the guerrilla detonating the bomb waited to initiate until à predetermined amount of personnel or vehicles entered the kill zone. He often had some type of mark on a wall or feature of the street that designated where the majority of targets should be in order to initiate the explosive. Finally, the guerrilla would detonate the device, which depending on the size and composition of the intended targets, could vary in size from a small canister to a vehicle packed with shrapnel. ANFO-based bombs were the most common, initiated with Semtex.

Snipers were often employed in the come-on role to bait British and RUC forces into a bomb ambush. Sniper specific ASUs would be comprised of a shooter, two watchers to maintain security and observation, and one person to move the weapon after the shots were fired. At times, even children were used in the role of 'weapon-mover'. This meant that the sniper himself only had physical possession of the weapon for about twenty minutes. When employed as the primary method of engagement, the sniper would take one or two shots and then withdraw. When used in the come-on role to bait security forces, it was actually better not to hit their target. An injured or killed soldier or policeman meant the patrol would be occupied with the casualty and unable to attempt pursuit and continue on into the real engagement area or kill zone.

(7.4.4) *Exploitation of the Limited Mounted Manoeuvre Space and Three-Dimensional Terrain*

The limited mounted manoeuvre space and three-dimensional terrain of the urban areas were not significant issues to the IRA as highly covert, small operations avoided direct combat as well as large numbers of security forces. The limited mounted manoeuvre space of the urban environment was certainly utilised by the IRA but not to the same degree as the guerrilla movements elsewhere. This was primarily due to the fact that the IRA did not normally contend with large numbers of armoured vehicles. The IRA would occasionally target the civilian vehicles used by the British military for general transport and logistics activity. They would block the front and back with other vehicles and simply walk up and shoot those inside. This tactic was not used very long because it exposed the perpetrators for later identification.

The three-dimensional terrain of the urban environment, with its multi-storied buildings, rows of housing units, and small streets and alleyways, was used by the IRA in a passive sense in that it made British operations more difficult. British communications, reconnaissance, manoeuvre, and organised pursuit were all degraded in urban areas. Most actions by the IRA were conducted on the surface and street level because a very rapid withdrawal was necessary to avoid direct contact and capture. The IRA used underground firing ranges in the rural areas but there was no specific use of subsurface areas in the urban environments aside from burial caches of explosives, weapons, and other equipment. Buildings above the street level were primarily used for observation and occasionally for sniping, but the nature of the conflict, essentially permissive with much civilian activity, made prolonged engagements and rapid withdrawals from roofs or upper floors of buildings problematic.

(7.4.5) The Issue of Collateral Damage

Collateral damage to civilian property and persons were very often involved in their plans and specifically targeted if deemed profitable. However, at times they did hurt their legitimacy when the target strayed too far from the military and political areas. Some bombs were planned to go off around the maximum number of civilians, primarily for the psychological effect of showing what they were capable of doing. The IRA gave warnings to the media for civilian infrastructure bombs but the time frame between the warning and the bombing would often be very short. This allowed the IRA to moralise themselves in later propaganda by attesting that they had given a warning of the bombing. Many innocent bystanders as well as security forces had been maimed or killed by IRA bombings. Sometimes this was due to mistakes such as premature detonations or warnings given too late, but at times the risk of non-combatant casualties was considered acceptable because of the importance of the target. The political effects to the IRA could often be damaging when a bombing killed or injured civilians. One example is a bombing in Omagh on a busy street of the town that caused several civilian casualties. The IRA lost much legitimacy and was forced to place the blame on a splinter group to lessen the damage to themselves.

The issue of conducting operations on non-military targets was really a question of vulnerability. The rationale for targeting what appeared to most as non-military targets, such as store or hotels, was that they would degrade the British economy. Criminal activities to finance operations range from extortion and drug-dealing to bank robberies. As the British military and the RUC improved their force protection and intelligence gathering over the years the IRA was forced to focus on more and more vulnerable, yet less military, targets.

The IRA operated in an essentially permissive environment, but with enough British military and RUC presence to keep them outgunned and thus focused on combat operations that did not overly commit their ASUs to direct engagements.

(7.5) Combat Tactics of the Afghan Mujahideen Against the Massive Soviet War Machine

When you take action, you are not going to fire a two million dollar missile at a 10-dollar empty tent and hit a camel in the butt. It must be decisive.

(7.5.1) Mujahideen's Emphasis on Raids and Ambushes

Urban combat for the Mujahideen most often consisted of small raids or ambushes that had more political or psychological effect than military value. As with much of the war in Afghanistan, most urban targets had a tactical focus and there seems to have been no effort or plan to tie the targets together with an operational plan. However, at the tactical level different guerrilla bands would conduct combined operations, even between Shia and Sunni guerrillas. The guerrilla operations conducted in the larger Soviet and Afghan government controlled cities like Kabul or Kandahar displayed the tactics and methods of the Mujahideen urban guerrilla. These tactics focused on small raids, ambushes, and bombings with extensive reconnaissance and a heavy emphasis on security. Congruent with all successful guerrilla operations, the element of surprise was the decisive factor in the Mujahideen's ability to conduct successful combat operations in urban environments. This was primarily through the use of civilian contacts and auxiliary to prepare the area for operations, either through reconnaissance or actually aiding in the execution of the action. The Mujahideen were very adept in planning for their infiltration into and exfiltration away from their objectives. Ambush and raid sites were often selected in conjunction with the routes to and from Mujahideen bases and safe houses to ensure concealed movement. Infiltrations were most often made through the suburbs with their knowledge of the city's friendly, enemy, and neutral areas to guide their planning. Most movements were made on foot even on their approaches into the cities from rural areas. Once inside the suburbs they were able to move quickly through the streets because of their knowledge of the areas and the enemy rarely ventured into these areas which were considered unsecure. When necessary, the Mujahideen were able to quickly gather large numbers of guerrillas (up to 130) for missions that required it, sometimes from different guerrilla bands. The guerrillas rarely stayed on target very long after the attack for fear of quick reaction forces.

Afghan Mujahideen lying in ambush.

Their rapid withdrawal capability came from their route security and prior reconnaissance of the objective area. The guerrillas used outlying villages as mission support sites to consolidate, gather and prepare equipment, and finalise plans before moving to the target area.

Soviets viewed the Mujahideen operations in urban areas as terrorism and sabotage, mostly targeting infrastructure and political objectives. They considered the urban guerrillas who carried out these operations as 'diversionary-terrorist' groups, trained across the border in Pakistan to conduct sabotage and terrorist acts. Whichever way they viewed them, the fact is that the Mujahideen were a pain in the ass for the Soviets. The Mujahideen had great freedom of action in the suburbs and off the main thoroughfares within the cities, but were often unable to exploit successes due to either their small numbers or lack of organisation and planning. Some urban actions occurred in villages and towns that were not occupied by Soviet or Democratic Republic of Afghanistan (DRA) forces. These encounters tended to be under high-intensity conditions, characterised by intense street fighting to maintain control of the terrain. In these situations the guerrillas would often use a type of 'baited ambush' to lure Soviet forces into the confined streets and passage ways of the villages by establishing initial firing positions on the outskirts and withdrawal into pre-planned defensive positions in and around the adobe walls and buildings. The Soviet army positioned outposts along all major roads and was especially active in pacifying the Northern provinces between Kabul and Termez. Even so, the Kabul regime faced enormous difficulties in ensuring the personal security of its own officials, who were often subject to attacks within the capital itself. The resistance network in Kabul repeatedly carried out shootings, bombings, and assassinations.

Operational security hindered effectiveness during the rare large-sised raids, such as the raid on the Kabul Metropolitan Bus Transportation Authority which involved 120 Mujahideen fighters, where only the sub-commanders knew the plan or final target to preserve security. The bulk of the guerrillas were informed of the plan and their individual duties once they were placed in position. This led to the Mujahideen having detailed plans to get to and from the target but not for actions on the objective.

Security for the Mujahideen urban combat operations played a predominant role in their planning. Heavy security was used on the routes into and out of the objective areas, sometimes consisting of as much as 70-80 per cent of the total force available as they were deeply worried about the possibility of being ambushed or surprised during operations in the urban areas. However, many cities had curfews at various times during the conflict which could make large numbers of security personnel stand out during the night. During withdrawals the Mujahideen would separate into small groups and move by different routes to assembly areas. Detailed reconnaissance, often for several days, gave the Mujahideen knowledge of the enemy's movement and security arrangements and contributed to their ability to conduct many missions in the heart of Soviet or DRA garrisoned areas. As opposed to their rural guerrilla counterparts, the urban guerrillas were able to spend more time in reconnaissance and surveillance of their targets to determine patterns and vulnerabilities. Their ability to move about in the local urban populace gave them this advantage whereas the rural guerrilla was forced to remain in hiding while not conducting operations. Isolation of the objective areas was almost always taken in consideration. Many of the security forces that took up the bulk of the manpower on operations were kept as security and blocking forces on the objective. Many of the garrisoned targets had security posts on their exterior or along the route to them. The Mujahideen would post security details at each of these posts to ensure they were not revealed on their way into the target or ambushed on their way out. Small teams of security were placed along the routes of infiltration and exfiltration. Larger security teams were placed as blocking positions in the vicinity of the target against any reaction forces.

(7.5.2) *The Mujahideen's Advantage in Intelligence*

The urban Mujahideen's collabouration with the local populace and also with Afghans within the government or DRA provided much of their access to Soviet and government installations and offered essential information concerning security forces, guard schedules, and the like. The use of contacts inside government buildings or enemy military garrisons often meant that contact had to leave and join the Mujahideen as their assistance was often direct (bomb emplacement, letting guerrillas in while on sentry duty for the DRA, etc.). The Mujahideen used civilians who worked in target buildings to emplace and arm bombs. Contacts within military (Soviet or DRA) and government (Communist party) buildings were used to provide essential information on the inside of target buildings such as the number of security forces or the schedule of the work force. Local civilians were occasionally used as guides but most often the guerrillas knew the cities well enough that guides were not needed. Local contacts, essentially auxiliary members, often provided security for small missions such as a five-man assault team. Local auxiliary would also provide safe houses for movement through the cities.

The urban Mujahideen wore no uniforms or distinctive insignia and intentionally blurred the line between combatant and non-combatant to deceive the Soviets and Afghan government forces. Elderly citizens were used to carry messages and explosives and civilian workers, sometimes even females, planted bombs in government offices. The use of enemy uniforms for deception was used in some circumstances. During one example a guerrilla was dressed as a DRA officer in order to kidnap a Soviet advisor. One group even dressed as civilian farmers and sold fruit and vegetables from a cart to Soviet advisors at a bus stop for several days. The cart was outfitted with a false bottom and loaded with explosives and timed fuzes that detonated when a crowd of Soviets was around it.

(7.5.3) *Exploitation of the Limited Mounted Manoeuvre Space in Attacking Soviet Armour*

The Mujahideen were able to capitalise on the limited mounted manoeuvre space of the cities through careful reconnaissance. Ambush sites were picked at suburban *bazaars* known to be frequented by Soviet soldiers upon their departure and return into their base. Often the guerrillas used small teams, consisting of perhaps four men, outfitted with only one RPG. Regardless of whether the plan was to destroy vehicles or not, the Mujahideen always seemed to carry RPGs or other anti-armour weapons with them on urban missions in case they encountered vehicles during their raids or ambushes. The RPG was not merely an iconic weapon. It seemed to assure the Mujahideen more than the AK-rifle that they could take on bigger things with that. No evidence from Soviet or Mujahideen accounts point to any significant use of obstacles by the guerrillas to further degrade vehicular movement in urban areas.

The RPG-7 was the signature weapon of the Mujahideen's war against the Soviet behemoth: how lovely to use one of their famous weapons against them!

There was no significant use of three-dimensional terrain by the Mujahideen as most of their urban operations remained on the surface and first floors of buildings.

During some of the larger urban battles in cities and villages they focused on keeping the fight in the streets to avoid armour, artillery, and air attacks. The use of any sub-surface areas, such as sewers or sub-basements, does not appear in either side's accounts. When possible, some Mujahideen urban guerrillas attacked or infiltrated buildings from the top down. Since many target compounds were surrounded by adobe walls, ladders and ropes were used to scale the perimeter walls then move to the roofs of buildings for entry. When city fighting was expected in the outlying, unoccupied villages and towns the Mujahideen would place crew-served weapons, especially DShKs, on roofs and upper floors. The guerrillas displayed no apparent tactics for the clearing or securing of buildings.

(7.5.4) Indifference to Collateral Damage

Collateral damage to civilian property and persons was avoided, unless associated with the Communist government, which was considered as much an enemy as the Soviets. Since it was an all-out war situation with the Soviets bent upon exterminating them outright, no quarters were given to or expected from the adversary. Non-military targets were often attacked when considered necessary to display the Mujahideen's control over the urban situation or when it would have some impact on Soviet or DRA command and control in the cities. Examples such as the attacks on a bus terminal and the telephone exchange center were conducted to disrupt daily life in the city and show that the Soviets and DRA were not able to stop them. The possibility of collateral damage, most often from bomb attacks, seemed to be an acceptable risk to the Mujahideen. Most targets for bombings or RPG attacks on buildings were Soviet, DRA, or Communist party officials. Grau points out in his commentary of an urban bombing attack in 'The Other Side of the Mountain', the only real difference between bombing attacks and aerial bombardments is the size of the bomb and the means of delivery. Although most non-combatant casualties that did occur happened as a result of the bombings, aimed at Communist party officials and their office workers, other incidents did happen. During one failed raid on a telephone exchange center the Mujahideen attacked the compound's security force with small arms during their chaotic withdrawal and learned later that they had killed some of the sentries' relatives that were staying with them.

Although snipers were the most likely used by urban Mujahideen guerrillas to some degree, there is almost no mention of them in either Mujahideen or Soviet accounts. This leads to a conclusion that, if used, they were of very small effect on operations for either side. This could be due to a lack of sufficient marksmanship training necessary to develop a proficient sniper.

(7.6) The Chechen Rebels in Grozny Make the Russians Bleed Through their Nose

When you earnestly believe you can compensate for lack of skill by doubling your efforts, there's no end to what you can't do.

Mujahideen posing with two captured Soviet field guns: Oh, boy! What a wonderful fight it was!

(7.6.1) High-Intensity Combat Using Small Units

The battles for Grozny, especially in 1994-95, were high-intensity urban combat the likes of which the Russians had not seen since their World War II battles against the Germans. Many Chechen rebels were veterans of the Soviet Army and understood the Russian tactics, capabilities, and weaknesses. The Russians had not envisioned the level of conflict to be as violent as it became and had put together *ad hoc* units to move into Grozny to disarm the Chechen rebels. Whereas the Russians fought to control and hold the territory, the rebels fought to make controlling and holding the territory as unpleasant as possible—a very different mission, and one far more difficult both to grasp and to counter. Although the Russian experience in Chechnya would eventually spread out to include the rural areas, it began under high-intensity urban combat in Grozny. The Chechens were extremely effective during small unit battles with the Russian forces by utilising methods with which the Russians were either unfamiliar or unable to counter. Operations were predominantly conducted by small units of three to eight personnel, growing up to seventy-five man groups for planned large-scale ambushes. Some exceptions existed, such as Shamil Basayev's "national guard," composed of some 500 battle-hardened veterans of the Abkhazian-Georgian conflict, who sometimes operated in groups as large as 200.

Chechen command and control was very loose and although the presidential palace was fortified and heavily defended the rebels did not concentrate forces in the center of the city. The defensive preparation of Grozny had begun three to four months prior to Russian operations commencing and the defence of Grozny was composed generally of three concentric zones. The inner zone consisted of the fortified presidential palace and the immediate one to two kilometers around it. A middle zone extending up to an additional five kilometers focused on strong-points covering key terrain and avenues of approach to the center of the city. The outer zone consisted of the perimeter and outskirts of the city for reconnaissance, surveillance, and harassment of Russian forces. The loose command and control structure emphasised small, mobile groups able to quickly react to Russian operations.

(7.6.2) *The Novel Tactic of 'Hugging' to Reduce the Effectivity of Russian Fire Support*

Using the tactic of 'hugging', the rebels would stay close to the Russian units as they moved to avoid indirect fire and keep at close range. The guerrilla mortar crews would also move constantly, firing three to

The Chechens fought with great skill and tenacity: It was urban warfare at its best

four rounds then displacing to avoid counter-battery fire. Both of these techniques significantly reduced Russian fire support as an effective tool against the guerrillas when in direct contact. Although the rebels had some night vision equipment, either left behind by the army earlier in the 1990s or stolen from Russian units, it was not commonplace among the guerrillas. Yet the Chechens were able to operate effectively at night while the Russians preferred not to.

(7.6.3) Harassing the Russian Armour in the Limited Mounted Manoeuvre Space

The Chechens had some tanks and artillery pieces most of which were used at various strong points to counter Russian armoured attacks. RPGs were the primary anti-armour weapon and seemingly every unit, from a three-man team to the 75-man planned ambush units, carried them in large amounts. At the various strong points and especially around the presidential palace obstacles such as destroyed vehicles and debris were used, primarily to funnel the Russians into engagement areas. These areas were covered by the tanks and direct-fire artillery. In the 2000 battle a lot of time was spent digging anti-tank ditches. Mobile detachments in civilian vehicles or jeeps transported supplies, ammunition, weapons, and troops throughout the city.

The Chechens were able to capitalise on the limited mounted manoeuvre space to defeat the Russian advantage in armoured vehicles. Due to their familiarity with the equipment, the rebels targeted the fuel cells and engines of the Russian armoured vehicles. They focused their fire on the top, sides, and rear to avoid the reactive armour. The rebels used multiple RPG teams against Russian vehicles to overcome the problems of back blast signature and reloading time while simultaneously disorienting the Russians as to the direction of the attack. Small anti-tank 'hunter-killer' teams, armed with several RPGs, roamed the city listening for engine noise. They would then converge on the vehicles and volley fire from multiple directions, including above. Lack of Russian infantry support, especially early on in the battle, contributed to this success.

(7.6.4) Skilful Exploitation of Three-dimensional Terrain

The Chechens' masterful use of three-dimensional terrain was a constant problem for Russian progress in the city. The rebels boarded up or blocked first floor entrances to buildings to deny their use by the

Russians, allowing them little or no cover once an engagement began on the street. Passages through the buildings were made for manoeuvre and withdrawal routes. Below the surface the rebels constructed and used a network of underground passages, sub-basements, and bunkers. Basement window positions would be used to attack armour since their guns tubes could not depress enough to engage the attackers. These positions would be reinforced into bunkers and car jacks were used to raise and lower concrete slabs and other reinforced roofing material, allowing the rebels to fire on passing vehicles and troops and then avoid the retaliatory indirect fire by lowering the slabs. It is unclear whether the city's sewer system was used by the rebels. Russian reports say it was, but the Chechens deny its use. Roofs and top floors were generally left empty for fear of air attacks and artillery. The rebels then attacked from the middle floors and used pre-planned withdrawal routes. Buildings were used for strong points when defending key terrain. In other areas the Chechens occupied buildings as needed to escape concentrated Russian fires or to draw them into engagement areas and kill zones. Except for perhaps the Presidential Palace, defended buildings were not seen as crucial to the Chechen defence. Rather, making the Russians suffer a disparity of casualties and damage for a small piece of terrain was the objective.

No quarters given, no quarters asked for: they fought with everything they had

(7.6.5) Sniping

Sniper operations played a dominant role in the Chechen defence of Grozny and were greatly feared by the Russians. Sniping was so important to the guerrillas that the basic unit of the Chechens, the three to eight man team, always had at least one sniper on it. They often targeted radiomen and officers. The basic fighting unit of three to eight personnel almost always included a sniper, meaning almost every engagement the Russians had included having to deal with a sniper. They were positioned and fired from deep within rooms to avoid detection, and were used as scouts as much as for sniping. One tactic would be to shoot Russian soldiers in the leg then engage those who attempted to help, further complicating Russian casualty evacuation and often forcing it to be conducted only at night. The psychological effect of the snipers was just as great, or greater, than their physical contribution. They were highly feared by the Russian soldiers and operated in both the day and night. Snipers were often used to draw Russian forces into baited ambushes. They were also used to control the approaches to specific intersections from roofs or upper floors. Interestingly, the Chechens did not use tracers as they felt it revealed their locations. The Russians eventually adapted this also as Chechen snipers were able to target them in the day and night by their tracer fire.

(7.6.6) Surprise, Deception and High Mobility

Surprise was achieved primarily by the Chechens operating in small, mobile groups that could react to Russian movements and operations as they chose. Deception planning became a key to maintaining surprise by monitoring Russian movements and drawing them into the center of the city by offering little or weak resistance. Street signs were taken down or repositioned to confuse Russian movements. The rebels were able to move into and out of Grozny quite freely in 1995 since the Russians did not seal off the city until late into the battle. This ability was severely lessened in 2000 as the Russians had learned their lesson and sealed off the city in the beginning. The Chechens maintained their speed of movement and mobility by not having many strong points and consistently moving in small groups, harassing the Russians when opportunities arose. Civilian vehicles with mounted 23 millimeter cannons or 12.7 millimeter heavy machineguns were used to quickly position air defence assets around the city. The guerrillas demonstrated the ability to rapidly concentrate their forces when needed to counter Russian operations even with their loose command and control. Even though their small teams of three to eight personnel often operated independently, the rebels seemed to be able to mass when necessary or when in anticipation of a particular Russian operation, to include maintaining interconnected fire positions. The Chechen guerrillas communicated with civilian off-the-shelf radios using their native language, for which the Russians had few translators, which added to this capability to concentrate forces quickly. The rebels always had preplanned escape routes from firing positions. Some mortars were mounted in civilian trucks to improve their tactical mobility and defend against counter-battery fire. Tunnels between buildings and hidden sub-basements also allowed the rebels to move quickly between positions or wait and hide as the Russians moved through, surfacing later behind the Russians in areas considered cleared.

Security for the Chechens was their mobility. The confusion of urban combat allowed them to drift into and out of contact with the Russians almost at will. Unlike urban combat in less intense conditions where a guerrilla's movements must be more covert to avoid detection by the populace as well as the enemy, most of the population left in Grozny was ethnic Chechens and not a threat to the rebels. When necessary they would blend in with civilians having been moments before, engaged in a firefight with Russian troops. Their ability to maintain constant reconnaissance and surveillance throughout the suburbs gave them early warning of most of the Russian movements. The Chechens would also isolate critical points when conducting large ambushes. They would use two-thirds of the force for security with one twenty-five man element conducting the ambush and two twenty-five man elements sealing off the objective and engaging follow-on forces.

The Chechen use of uniforms was haphazard and varied between the different bands that made up the rebels. Some rebels had Russian uniforms from their time in the Soviet or Russian military, and were used more out of necessity than intent to deceive. Generally, the rebels rarely wore uniforms and were difficult to distinguish. Reports from the 2000 battle said that rebels dressed as Russian soldiers for night raids on Russian positions, but there is little corroborating evidence of this. Other accounts had Russian-dressed rebels committing atrocities against civilians to discredit the Russians. Chechens sometimes disguised themselves as Red Cross workers, donning the armbands and moving freely among the Russian soldiers. The rebels would also offer themselves as civilian guides and lead the Russians into ambushes. The high-intensity combat conditions meant that they predominately carried their arms openly during military engagements. The Chechens therefore operated at a less covert and clandestine role than in other

A Russian Mi-8 helicopter shot down by Chechen fighters near Grozny – note the vulnerability of the helicopter in urban combat

cases. Direct confrontation and engagement of Russian forces was necessary to defend Grozny, and the urban guerrilla tactics offset the imbalance the Chechens faced in manpower and conventional weapons and equipment.

(7.6.7) Support of Local Population

Since most of the civilians in Grozny were ethnic Chechens and sympathetic to the rebels' cause, their collabouration with the local populace was complete from the beginning. The rebels even moved their operations to successive cities after Grozny to maintain the urban advantage and keep the population on their side because the Russians destroyed property and killed non-combatants in their efforts to secure urban areas. Initially, when the Russians were trying to minimise civilian casualties, the rebels were able to use the population actively by stopping Russian convoys, puncturing tires, and generally interfering with their operations, but the Russians eventually caught on and increased their security. The rebels routinely used the population for information gathering and young women proved especially useful since they could easily move throughout the city and make contact with the Russians. The guerrillas' collaboration with the local populace increased their combat effectiveness, but was less of a crucial factor than in the earlier case studies. The nature of the high-intensity combat of the battles of Grozny meant a smaller role for covert use of civilians because, although useful, it was not required to get close or gain access to the Russian targets.

(7.6.8) Exploiting Collateral Damage Caused by the Russians

Collateral damage to non-military targets and personnel did not appear to overly concern the Chechen rebels. They would deliberately deploy near a school or hospital, engage the Russian forces, and then quickly move away. The Russians would shell the area from which they received fire, inevitably destroying the non-military targets. The Chechens would then later use this as propaganda against the Russians. Most of the collateral damage to the city was done by the Russians through artillery fire and airstrikes, especially in the 2000 battle, when the city was essentially levelled in an effort to avoid the brutal street fighting that was encountered in 1994. The Chechens also targeted Russian aerial and ground medical evacuation vehicles. Some reports say rebels took Chechen hostages to coerce their family members to serve as artillery spotters in the Russian rear.

(7.7) How Urban Warfare Eventually Turned the Tide in Favour of the Nepalese Maoists

The war was started by the Communist Party of Nepal (Maoist) on February 13, 1996, with the aim of overthrowing the Nepalese monarchy and establishing the "People's Republic of Nepal". It was started in the classical fashion of a communist insurgency from deep rural areas. However, the tide turned for the Maoists only when they took the fight to the critical urban areas. It ended with a Comprehensive Peace Accord signed on 21 November, 2006 which is now monitored by United Nations Mission in Nepal. More than 15000 people were killed (6000 by Maoists and 9000 by the government) and an estimated 100,000 to 150,000 people were internally displaced as a result of the conflict. How did they win? Was it only on the strength of what they had achieved in the rural areas? No. The fact is that the Maoists had easily controlled the rural areas where the presence of the government was, in any case, notional. Yes, there were numerous pitched battles also fought with the security forces in which up to 5000 rebels had taken part. But still it was far from the glare of the media and the world. It was not able to turn the tide in favour of the Maoists.

The Nepalese Maoists were able to exploit all the intrinsic weaknesses of the regime in Nepal methodically. The people had tired of monarchy—traditionally the stupid Nepalese had been supporting monarchy as it gave them a lofty object to latch their aspirations on—if you do not have something; you can at least be happy that your king has that. However, the palace coup in which Birendra's family was wiped off, wrenched whatever respect the monarchy commanded. The brutal murders did not go well even with the stupid Nepalese and the way Gyanendra foisted himself upon the throne was repulsive even to dumb people. The monarchy wrote its epitaph that very day. Secondly, the elected government was weak. The overall military potential of the Nepal government was very small in any case. The Maoists knew that while they could control the rural areas, perhaps the government would not bother much—who bothered about the rural areas in Nepal anyway? Had anyone bothered, Nepal would not have been in a situation where in many of its 75 districts, not a single government official had ever been seen in them in several decades. Nobody would have cared even if hundreds of villages would have been burnt to cinder. The government would buckle only when the cities became prone to Maoist depredations.

Unrest reached Kathmandu in 2004, when the Maoists announced a blockade of the capital city. That really signalled the turning point that even the urban areas were not safe and the crumbling of the government started. The Soaltee Hotel, a popular luxury hotel in Kathmandu, was bombed, after refusing a demand from the Maoists to close the hotel. On September 10, 2004 a bomb exploded at the United States Information Service office in Kathmandu. The US Peace Corps suspended operations and non-essential US embassy personnel were evacuated from Nepal. Later, in November, 36 people were injured when suspected Maoist rebels exploded a powerful bomb at a under-construction government office complex, the Karmachari Sanchaya Kosh Office Complex in the heart of Nepalese capital Kathmandu. In December, Maoist forces launched a blockade of Kathmandu. In January 2006, Maoists launched co-ordinated attacks of five military and paramilitary targets in the Kathmandu valley. This was the first demonstration of their ability to organise violence within the Valley, prompting curfews at night for the next several days. A general strike followed in April, and the government was already showing signs of buckling up. In May, the cabinet announced that the Maoist rebels would no longer be considered a terrorist group. Rebels were also encouraged to open peace talks. In November, peace talks ended with the signing of the Comprehensive Peace Accord between Prime Minister GP Koirala and the Maoist leader Prachanda. The deal allowed the Maoists to take part in government, and place their weapons under UN monitoring.

(7.8) Flexibility and Adaptability in Unconventional Warfare

If you are on death row do they sterilise the needle before your lethal injection?

The guerrilla, if he has to survive and operate for some time, shall be adaptable, keeping his own and the enemy's strengths and weaknesses in mind. As we saw, the IRA had a small manpower pool in the cities to attack the British military and RUC forces, which always had nearby units for backup, and had to contend with the police forensics that could connect them to attacks after the fact. In order to avoid direct engagement with security forces and escape criminal prosecution if captured, they developed and utilised tactics that dissociated the guerrilla from the act of violence. Hence, their use of the bomb as a primary means of attack and also the extensive use of mortars and snipers. The Mujahideen had to overcome the large numbers of Russian and DRA military forces in the urban centers who were often enclosed in secure compounds. Hence, bombing was not a very profitable option. Therefore, a large per centage of their combat operations were both small and large raids and ambushes. They countered the threat of enemy quick reaction and security forces in the cities with extensive security of their own, often utilising the majority of forces available, and close collabouration with the local population to gain access to enemy compounds.

The Chechens seemed to utilise very little bombing and predominately engaged in direct combat through ambushes and sniping. As the Chechen rebels prepared to defend Grozny they correctly identified the Russians' tremendous advantage in firepower and their ability to destroy or seize defensive positions as their strength. To overcome the imbalance in firepower, the Chechens operated in small, mobile teams that struck the Russians quickly and then just as quickly dissipated into the depths of the city. During firefights they stayed close to the Russian units to avoid indirect fire and close air support. That was very clever. Even in jungle warfare, the Americans had found to their horror that quite often the Viet Cong got so close to them that aerial bombardment or artillery fire inflicted casualties on their own troops as well. The three-dimensional terrain allowed the Chechen guerrillas to get very close to their enemy during combat operations and eliminate the advantage in firepower and range the conventional forces usually enjoyed. Reconnaissance was much easier in the urban environment and hence getting knowledge of enemy installations and command organisations was also easier. Another advantage for the guerrillas was that the urban combat was predominately conducted by small units as the terrain restricted the movement, visibility, and communications of their enemies. This aspect significantly affected the force ratios facing the guerrilla fighters and enabled them to even the odds to a great degree.

The guerrilla shall decide the course of his movement depending on the situation unique to the country. One must understand this very carefully. The guerrilla, if he knows his business, shall never attempt to hold territory or defend a position. A guerrilla, insurgent or terrorist will never suffer from an inflated sense of 'honour' either. The classic guerrilla simply melts away in the face of stronger forces and continues to do so till such time that their total military potential becomes comparable to that of the government—does not matter even if it takes decades. Before that, if he, by any chance, decides to hold ground or defend a position, he writes his epitaph. The LTTE was excellent as a terrorist organisation with some brilliant terrorist attacks to their credit in the history of terrorism. However, when they decided to hold territory and even administer it, they were utterly destroyed. The reason is simple. Then they were obliged to fight on the terms of the enemy. As long as they were attacking the government targets sporadically, they had the government on its toes, because they were fighting on their terms. The moment they held some territory in some grandiose dream of having 'liberated' it, they were forced to fight on the terms of the government. Then they had to contend with the superior firepower, artillery and air force of the government for which they had no answer. Nothing could have been more foolish for a guerrilla force with inferior weaponry to dig up trenches and wait for the mighty assault of the enemy infantry and artillery. There was no way they could ever win that war. The superior firepower of the government rolled them up very cheaply and almost made the Sri Lankans forget how the LTTE had bled them all those years with their hit-and-run terrorist strikes. Fighting pitched battles was as terrible a folly as could be imagined. How stupid of Prabhakaran! Back home in India, terrorism in Punjab could have gone on for quite some more time had Bhindaranwale not committed the blunder of taking up shelter in the Golden Temple. His own fate was sealed that very day even if the operation cost the Indians dearly.

The ideal guerrilla does not aim for a decisive victory—rather he bargains from a position of strength. How that position of strength is to be obtained depends on how well he exploits the psychological weakness of the target government. This is precisely what the Nepalese Maoists did. They exploited the weaknesses of the Nepalese government brilliantly. Although they wielded considerable influence in the rural areas, they did not waste time and energy in holding territory and administering it. Instead, they mounted attacks in the urban areas, built up pressure on the government and made them yield to their demands without having to fight an all-out war. A clever guerrilla always keeps an eye on the achievable and does not waste his energies in chasing an unrealistic dream. The Nepalese Maoists' purpose was served by being able to take part in the government.

Nations fighting guerrillas must realise that a guerrilla does not lose anything by abandoning a location and leaving some items behind—he also does not bother about a few casualties here and there. He is not at all intent upon taking us on militarily or challenging our might—his real purpose is something else. The nation, for example, must not commit the mistake of thinking in terms of having got an area 'cleared' of the insurgents if they are found to have abandoned a location and left some heavy items like explosives, rations, generators, and the like behind. If a government starts exulting in such petty things such as recovering the left-over things of guerrilla, they are nothing but dumb. It only shows that even a nation can have the vision, perspective and intellectual capacity of a company commander. They do not bust any guerrilla camp—they merely find what the guerrilla abandoned of his free will. An intelligent guerrilla is not bound by any territory. Having been obliged to run from one place, he simply goes to another place and operates from there. He will carry the critical items with him and knows that he can always replenish what he has left behind. The guerrilla knows that the governments would find it enormously difficult to hold all the grounds at the same time and he will never be short of places from where to operate.

8

Some Tactical Aspects of Urban Combat

Anything you do can get you killed, including nothing.

(8.1) Fighting in the Streets

The first shot is for the Devil, the second for God, and only the third for the King.

(8.1.1) Pie Technique of Visually Clearing an Area

This technique is used to visually clear the area inside open doorways, windows, and around corners. There is no way for you to sneak past an opening or around a corner without exposing yourself. Since you have to expose yourself, you should visually clear the area first. If you are clearing an area to your left, hold your weapon right-handed. If you are clearing an area to your right, then hold your rifle left-handed. Place the butt of the rifle in your shoulder and aim in like you do in the off-hand position. The only difference is that you must keep the elbow of your shooting hand down. In other words, don't hold it up and away from your body as this will become visible to the enemy as you pie around the corner. By holding the rifle in this manner (normal stock weld), you will present the smallest possible target to the enemy. As you move forward, pivot your body so you can see the area to your direct front as it comes into view. If you have to move away from the wall, the man behind you will cover your back. If you are at the corner of a building, you will have to pie for 90 degrees until you see the entire wall on the other side of the corner.

Approaching a corner

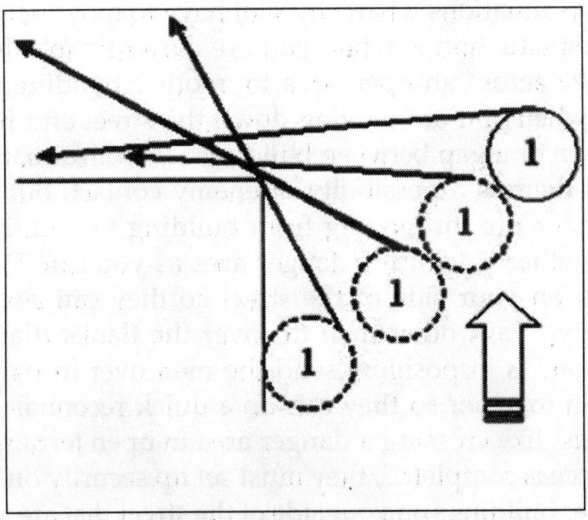

Pie-slicing a corner

(8.1.2) Unit Movement Down a Street

When moving down a street, your unit can either move down both sides simultaneously or just down one side. When moving your unit down both sides of the street, do not split your individual units up. Keep each individual fire team together on the same side of the street. This will help your fire team leaders keep control of their men. The point men on either side of the street must stay abreast of each other as they move. The advantage of this technique is that you can designate men to cover the windows and openings of the upper level floors of the buildings on the opposite side of the street. Moving down one side of the street gives you better control of your unit. If you get into a fire fight, you don't have to worry about getting everyone to the side of the street where the action is. The point man is responsible for covering low (first floor level) and to the front. When he comes to any doors, windows, or other openings, he uses the pie technique to clear the inside of that room. He also pies corners of buildings. The second man covers high (i.e. the second floor level and above) and to the front. The third and fourth men cover the flanks. If there are men on the other side of the road, they both cover second floor and above openings. If there is no one else on the other side, one of them covers first floor openings. The responsibilities of the first four men are repeated until the second to the last man of your formation. The second to the last man covers high and to the rear. The last man covers low and to the rear.

(8.1.3) Crossing Danger Areas

There are two situations when you will have to move across a danger area. The first situation is when you are currently in a building and need to move across an open area to another building. The second situation is when you are moving down the street and need to cross an intersection or a gap between buildings. In both situations we will assume that there is a possibility of enemy contact, but you are not currently under fire. In moving from building to building, cover as much of the other side of the danger area as you can. Place security into position on your side of the street so they can cover the front (front security). Task other men to cover the flanks (flank security). When everyone is in position, send the men over in pairs. Send the first two men together so they can do a quick reconnaissance of the other side (just like crossing a danger area in open terrain). When the reconnaissance is completed, they must set up security on their side so they can cover buildings on your side of the street that are not occupied by friendly forces. Move the rest of your men across the danger area one at a time.

In crossing a danger area while moving down a street, the following techniques are adopted. In the high-low technique, when the point man comes up to the corner of a building which borders a danger area, he uses the pie technique to clear around the corner. After completing his pie, he gets into either the kneeling or the prone position and covers low. The second man comes up to the corner and gets into a position over the point man. He brings his rifle around the corner and covers high. He tells the point man, 'Set', to let him know he is in position.

Begin sending men across the danger area. The first two men across the danger area assume the same 'high-low' position around the corner of the other side so they can cover the back side of the danger area. The third man across assumes the point man's position and continues the movement down the street. In the high-low bump technique you follow the same procedure as the high-low technique until the point where you start sending men across the danger area. The third man in the formation gets right behind the second man (high man) and tells him, 'Set', to let him know he is ready. The high man tells the point man (low man) 'Go'. At this signal, the low man crosses the danger area. When he leaves, the high man crouches down and assumes the previous man's position while the third man assumes the high man's position. When the previous low man gets across the danger area, the second relief man assumes a position right behind the first relief man and the procedure is repeated. The rest of the procedure remains the same as for the high-low technique. The advantage of the high-low bump technique is that each man gets a chance to see what the danger area looks like before he actually crosses it. This lets you pick out your route as well as the likely enemy positions.

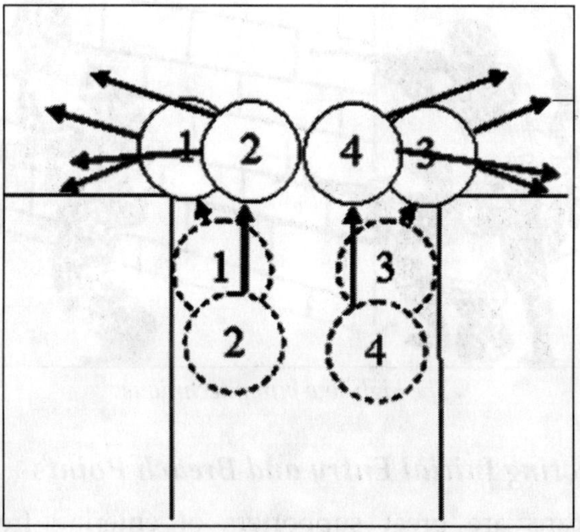

An example of high-low technique

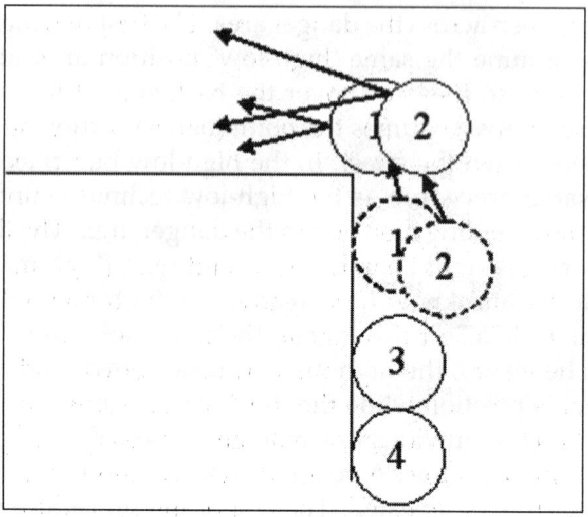

Another example of high-low technique

The high-low bump technique

(8.1.4) Selecting Initial Entry and Breach Points

The Americans are great supporters of entering from the top. Insertion by helicopters is considered a very glamorous thing. The logic of entering from the roof or the highest point possible is that it minimises the amount of upstairs fighting where you are at an obvious disadvantage. The logic is correct but you must see whether insertion from the top is feasible or not. They also say that clearing a building from the bottom up may force the enemy into a corner where he will fight like a caged animal. But American theories may not always work for you. You could very well come across only a two-storied building and the other guys might already be on the first floor! Or you could come across a three-storied building with a tin, wooden or thatched roof on the top floor on which you may not land from a helicopter. Before you decide to enter from the top, you must see the availability of access to upper stories and the cover and concealment in the area that may have a bearing on your ability to enter the building above the ground floor. Conversely, you must also evaluate the risks of scaling the side of a building or clearing upward from the ground floor. Since the enemy may have the doors and windows booby trapped and since in the middle of a firefight, you would not like to get bogged down in clearing booby traps, it is always advisable to blow up a part of the wall with explosive charges, special warheads made for the purpose or even anti-tank rounds and make your own entry points. Using a warhead designed for the purpose is always better because the problem with using explosives is someone has to move up to the entry point to set them. In any case, if you have no option but to use explosive charges, here is how you go about it. Assuming that all outer walls are constructed of reinforced concrete and are about two feet or less thick, a good rule of thumb for breaching is to use nine one-quarter pound blocks of C-4 placed against the target between waist and chest height. We presume that you know how to tamp the charge. If your point of entry is a wall, you will have to use a thick board or timber to hold the sandbag(s) against the explosives. This will normally blow a hole large enough for a man to get through. If this charge is not elevated at least one wall thickness above the base of the wall, the charge will not create the desired effect. If your point of entry is a roof, you must place the sandbag(s) on top of the charge.

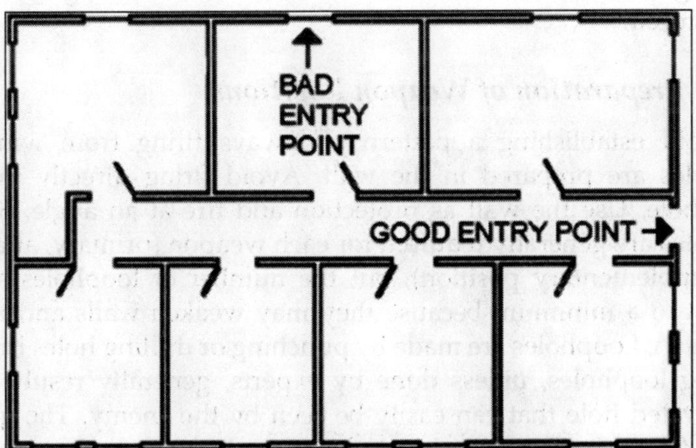

Examples of good and bad entry points

(8.1.6) Techniques for Clearing a Building Between Floors

Besides the initial entry into a building, movement between floors may be the most difficult part of your clearing operation. No matter how you move from floor to floor, the cover party must keep up with the search party. Members of the cover party are deposited along the way to cover doors, windows, mouse holes, and avenues of approach into areas that you have not yet cleared of the enemy. In moving from an upper floor to a lower floor using stairs, the procedure is the same as clearing a room. If the stairs are around a corner, line up in a stack formation, throw in a hand grenade, and enter the stairs. In moving from a lower floor to an upper floor, clear the stairs in the same manner as you clear a hallway. Do not throw a hand grenade up a stair well; it could very well roll back on you. If at all you have to throw, use the underhand throw to minimise the chance of its rolling back. Once the first grenade has detonated successfully, another grenade should be thrown over and behind the staircase banister and into the hallway, destroying any enemy hiding to the rear. Also, remember the stairs may be booby trapped. The enemy could even have them knocked down to deny you their use. Should that be so and movement between floors be impossible, you may have to consider blowing up the building.

(8.1.7) Clearing a Basement

The procedures for clearing a basement are much the same as for clearing any other room or floor of a building. But remember that basements may be connecting points for sewers and tunnels that the enemy could use for escaping and infiltrating troops back into a cleared building. For that reason, a basement must be thoroughly cleared and secured.

(8.1.8) Preparation of Weapon Positions

To avoid establishing a pattern of always firing from windows, loopholes are prepared in the wall. Avoid firing directly through a loophole. Use the wall as protection and fire at an angle. Several loopholes are generally required for each weapon (primary, alternate, and supplementary position), but the number of loopholes should be kept to a minimum because they may weaken walls and reduce protection. Loopholes are made by punching or drilling holes in walls. Blasting loopholes, unless done by experts, generally results in an exaggerated hole that can easily be seen by the enemy. The general rule to follow in preparing loopholes is to place them where they are concealed and where they are unexpected. For example, you could have them in missing or removed roof tile; in wall; between boards in window shutters; in chimneys; concealed under eaves; behind vines; behind bushes; in dark areas of sign; in bottom of doors; or in mail drops or concealed by name plates. Loopholes must be cone-shaped to enable engagement of targets above and below the firer's position and to reduce the size of the exterior aperture. The edges of a loophole, especially in brick walls, splinter when hit by bullets. Wherever possible, protective linings, such as an empty sandbag held in place by wire mesh, will reduce splintering effects. When not in use, loopholes must be covered with sandbags to prevent the enemy from firing into or observing through them. Loopholes are also prepared in interior walls and ceilings of the building to enable fighting within the position when necessary. Interior loopholes should over-watch stairs, halls, and unoccupied rooms. Interior loopholes are concealed by pictures, drapes, or light furniture. Loopholes in floors permit the defender to engage enemy personnel on lower floors with small arms and/or to drop grenades. These holes must be covered when not in use.

When using window positions, you must use the wall on either side of the window to provide a protected kneeling or standing position. To provide the ability to fire downward from upper floors, tables or similar objects placed against the wall should provide sufficient elevation. When using an elevated platform it must be positioned to prevent the weapon from protruding through the window. Prone positions do not always permit sufficient freedom for firing at widely varying angles or at targets above the position.

(8.1.9) Communications

Due to the Line of Sight (LoS) nature of the unit TO&E FM radios, and the decentralised nature of combat in urban terrain, the use of a NLOS radio for improved communication capabilities should be considered. This type of radio may also be able to provide the user with hands off capabilities, minimum body movement for operation, and remote channel/frequency changing. If fielded to each soldier, it may provide the capability of a unit intercom. Because of their lack of secure capability, however, transmissions on these radios must be considered to be monitored by enemy forces, news media, and any entity with a minimum of technology.

(8.2) Roadblocks and Vehicle Check Points (VCPs)

Whenever you have plenty of ammo, you never miss. Whenever you are low on ammo, you can't hit the broad side of a barn.

(8.2.1) General Principles

Terrorists have to use wheeled transports to move weapons, explosives, supplies and other equipment to safe hiding-places, from which they will have to move them again when they intend to use them. The best way to counter this threat is to create a permanent infrastructure of roadblocks, or vehicle checkpoints (VCPs) as they are called in Northern Ireland, upon which you can superimpose as many extra snap or temporary roadblocks or VCPs as the operational situation demands. You can use either snap or permanent roadblocks; the purpose of both is to check traffic going through a particular point or to completely block a road to prevent its further use. Roadblocks and VCPs should in general:

- Dominate the area, deterring terrorist activity and movement.
- Prevent reinforcements of enemy or terrorists reaching sensitive areas or riotous gatherings.
- Deny contacts between terrorists and local inhabitants.
- Prevent supply of arms, ammo, food and medical supplies to the enemy.
- Facilitate other operations against the enemy or terrorists.
- Gain information and intelligence.

The siting of the roadblock is important. Preferably, it should be around a corner or behind the crest of a hill so as to take the driver by surprise, and should be flanked by hedgerows or ditches so that it is difficult or impossible for a car to turn round or reverse out without being noticed by the VCP. Sharp bends or dips in the road are the places to go for.

(8.2.2) Permanent Roadblocks

The basic, permanent VCP will impose restrictions on the terrorist. Even though he knows it is there and the surprise element is lacking, it forces him to use other routes, thereby reducing his options; it also reduces the number of routes upon which you need mount snap or temporary VCPs. Permanent roadblocks or VCPs must be well-defended, permanently manned and well-equipped. The smallest practical unit that can look after itself is a section: this is just big enough to run a shift system 24-hour a day. The position should provide safe accommodation for those not on duty and reliable communications to your HQ. Remember that a permanent roadblock is vulnerable to attack and therefore its security must be carefully planned. Your perimeter should be well-defended with wire to prevent attack or fire, and with concrete bollards to prevent terrorists leaving a car bomb alongside your position. Surveillance aids such as remotely-controlled CCTV cameras can monitor approaches that you may not be able to see all the time. Your roadblock will probably be sited on a busy road or border crossing, and your job will be to check the identity of all those passing through your position and also to search them. Clearly, if the road is very busy you will not have sufficient men to search all vehicles without causing a major traffic jam. Either you will have to select vehicles at random for checking, or you will need additional police or military manpower. If your roadblock is to be effective at night, floodlights will be necessary.

(8.2.3) Snap Roadblocks

When you mount a snap roadblock you are under fewer constraints. Because you will be in position only for a short period, the enemy is unlikely to have the time to organise and mount an attack upon you, unless you compromise him in a roadblock and he tries to evade it or crash through it. Snap VCPs can be set up by foot patrols, by vehicle patrols or by patrols dropped from a helicopter. This latter technique is known by the British Army in Northern Ireland as an Eagle Patrol. Snap roadblocks can be mounted by section-strength foot or vehicle patrols whenever and wherever the moment is right. The technique is to half-block the road with your vehicle and, if you have two vehicles, to create a chicane effect by blocking alternate sides of the road at an interval or perhaps 25 meters. This will force traffic to slow down to be checked. If you are on foot or have been dropped from a helicopter, you won't have any vehicles to help you. You may have a portable Caltrop (an extendable arm with upward-pointing spikes designed to cause punctures to car tyres), but this is normally used in an emergency to stop an escaping vehicle.

(8.2.4) Layout and Checking

At least two members of your patrol will need to carry out the job of stopping and checking passing vehicles, and at least another two men should be employed to cover the checkers. These men should be far enough back so as not to get in the searcher's way, but close enough to be able to see what is going on. When to fire and when not to fire is a difficult issue. Your government will have to be clear on this. Are you supposed to fire on a car that refuses to stop, crashes through the barrier; or does everything short of opening fire at you—it is a question that your government must answer. There are not too many options open to you for halting a car that is quite determined not to stop. Caltrops can be effective if you can deploy enough of them it in time, and armoured vehicles are even more effective if you are part of a vehicle patrol. Giving a pursuit is best left for films or the regular police. You must have a communication link with the police for this. You will also need to position 'long stops' in both directions down the road on each side and well clear of the search area so that they can watch approaching traffic, prevent vehicles or people evading the VCP and watch out for snipers or other enemy forces moving into position. Their task is to cut off anyone who approaches the roadblock, sees it, thinks better of going through it and turns round to go back the other way. Alternatively, they can attempt to stop someone who has crashed the roadblock or fire at him. Ideally, it should not be possible to drive round the VCP, so it must be sited with ditches or obstacles on each side of the road. Vehicles placed in an arrowhead formation will make it impossible to drive through at speed, while permitting a slow through flow of traffic.

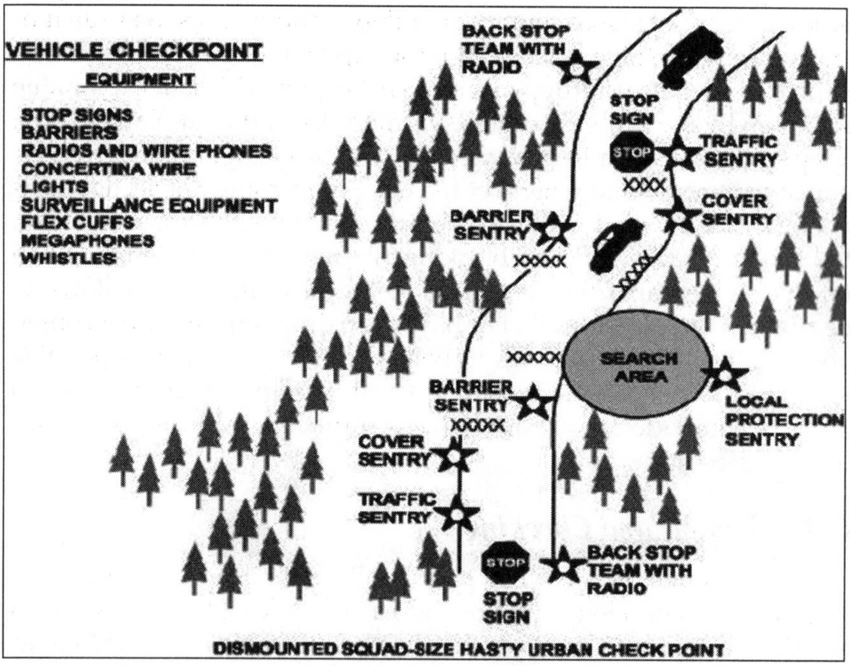

Layout of a typical hasty urban vehicle checkpoint

(8.2.5) Searching Vehicles

Searches are carried out for two reasons; the first is as a deterrent. The purpose here is to put the terrorist off carrying out his clandestine activities. Even random searches of vehicles at road checkpoints help to prevent the regular smuggling of arms or drugs, as long as the searchers are efficient at their job. The layout is one man forward, one rear, one man standing in the road to stop traffic, and the fourth covering him. Specialised training is needed to search a car properly, having stopped a vehicle in a roadblock. The second is obviously to find weapons or explosives. There are three types of vehicle search: quick search; thorough search; and workshop search. Normally, you will carry out quick or thorough searches. Workshop searches involve stripping down a vehicle completely, which is specialist's job requiring special equipment. As always, what you will do depends on the circumstances. There is a wide range of specialist terrorist devices, but you must look for the following:

- Evidence of recent activity.
- Ask yourself where you would hide something. Keep thinking where the spaces are and how to reach them.
- Strong smells of talc or perfume may be hiding the smell of explosives.
- Start with the outside of the vehicle and keep the owner with you to watch the search. Get the driver to open the bonnet and the boot; don't try it yourself. Let him take out any luggage, the carpet and spare wheel inside. Grenades can easily be concealed in the space between the boot carpet and the floor or sides.
- The simplest way to carry out a search is to break down the areas of examination into five stages: exterior bodywork; underneath; interior; boot; and engine. It is vital that you proceed logically so that no part of the vehicle is left out.
- Look carefully at the driver—is he or she nervous? There are some clever 'police' techniques that are very useful in searching vehicles. For example, ask the driver where the spare wheel is. If he has to look before answering, he may be driving a stolen vehicle—a terrorist is more likely to plant a bomb in a stolen vehicle than in his own vehicle.
- The absence of the normal/presence of the abnormal.

  Ask yourself, "Does the car look right"? Do the carpet fit properly, or have they been lifted recently? Why?
- The sophisticated booby trap. A release switch, for example, could have been placed under the hollow of the front seat, and will be activated the moment the seat is lifted. So is a pressure switch.

- The lavishly-laid booby trap. A heat-activated device can easily be tied to an exhaust, and the effect of the engine heat will be fatal if the bomb remains undetected. A device like this could be planted in seconds. A tilt switch is set off by a tilting movement and so is quite suitable for attacking around axles. It will be detonated when the car is jacked up to look underneath.
- If your search reveals an explosive device or something that looks like one, clear the area immediately. Then hand over to civilian or military bomb disposal units, who will attempt to render the device harmless.
- If the terrorist has been clever enough to install a remote controlled device and his buddy activates it from a safe distance, there is little that can be done.
- In searching bikes, look out for the following surprises: false partitions in petrol tanks; anything concealed in tubular framing, especially under the saddle; saddle and tool bags concealing explosives; electrical devices connected to lamps and bells or horns; and wires taped to underside of mudguard and crank case.

9

Fighting Guerrillas Holed Up in a Building

Wars may be fought with weapons, but they are won by men. The real hero is the man who fights even though he is scared.

(9.1) The Intrinsic Complexities of the Job of House Intervention

We, the willing, led by the unknowing, are doing the impossible for the ungrateful. We have now done so much for so long with so little, we are now capable of doing anything with nothing.

House intervention is undoubtedly the riskiest job that a soldier is ever called upon to perform in anti-terrorist operations. Normally, unless you have Through-The-Wall Imaging Radars on the spot, you have no idea of who the guys are inside and what stuff they have with them. For all you know there could be three guys in a room with their automatic rifles and machine guns pointing at every possible point of entry and fingers ready to unleash bursts of automatic fire. You never know the guys could be fanatically suicidal, willing to die irrespective of what you do. For all you know, every foot of the building could be booby-trapped. In other words, entering a house full of terrorists is an insane thing. But unfortunately, if we are into counter-terrorism, we have to do it anyway. Your general objective is to overwhelm the opposition before they can prepare an effective defence or mount a counter-attack. This could, however, be easily complicated by the fact that the terrorists could well have a contingency plan that could cause your assault to flounder, such as detonating booby-trapped bombs, falling back into an already prepared stronghold or a couple of guys making a suicidal charge much before you expect any such act. Well, that's what makes it so risky a job!

The problem has often baffled the military men. Most morons in the Indian armed forces know of only one way—approach the house in an armoured vehicle, lob explosives inside and blast the house! Unfortunately, life is not so simple. This is a hangover of the method adopted by the Americans fighting in Germany. As Ralph Zumbro, a tank sergeant had said famously "Shove the muzzle of a main gun in through the window, or directly through the wall, and fire it. Room is cleared". The Americans were fighting an all-out war and they were not bothered about the consequences. In unconventional warfare, you may not have the luxury of tanks firing in your support or even if you have the tanks, the sensitivity of the situation or the location may demand that tanks be not used—you may recall the terrible consequences that befell the Indians following the use of tanks in Operation Blue Star in Punjab! In almost every anti-terrorist operation they have undertaken in Kashmir in over two decades, the Indian army invariably ends up blasting the whole house and which has added greatly to the alienation of the Kashmiris with India. The usual explanation offered is that the house was gutted in the exchange of fire. Informed people, however, know better. Anybody who has seen any operation, knows the truth and also the simple scientific fact that bullets cannot start fires!

The problem of house intervention in anti-terrorist operations has baffled the best experts in the field across the world. And mind you, the solutions found feasible and workable are vastly different from what you see in films and which has distorted the perception of millions. House intervention in Hollywood films is a most thrilling affair with the SWAT (Special Weapons and Tactics) teams in their swanky gear working with clockwork precision and eliminating the opposition without as much as even the mirrors in the room cracking. Real life is, however, vastly different from reel life. Most of the SWAT procedures that have been developed by American police forces are good only for them and the situations that they encounter most of the time. They do not expect heavily armed crazy terrorists willing to die in the first place. They expect handgun wielding criminals who might be holding hostages. That's why they lay so much emphasis on a regulated use of force so as not to harm the hostages or other innocent persons trapped therein. That's why even when breaching by a shotgun, they emphasise that buckshot and rifled slug may go inside and harm the occupants of the room. That's why they talk of using frangible bullets also. Leave such amateurish stuff for those dumb guys who copy the Americans blindly—they have no relevance in anti-terrorist operations where real terrorists operate. You shall not use frangible bullets in anti-terrorist operations even if there are hostages. The reason is simple. A frangible bullet also kills—if you take aim at a terrorist and by mistake your shot hits a hostage, he will be killed even if you have fired a frangible bullet. Then why should you use it at all? Because frangible ammunition disintegrates upon impact with any surface harder than the projectile itself, eye protection should be worn to protect against fragments. That adds one more item on your body. Most importantly, the use of frangible ammunition can and will prevent firing through objects (furniture, walls, etc.). This could place you at a severe disadvantage if your enemy is shooting regular bullets and is able to hit you through such things.

SWAT teams are usually shown to dwell at length, among other things, on building plans. Remember that in an anti-terrorist situation and that too in a God forsaken country like the one in which you may be obliged to work, you are not likely to find building plans—think of building plans for houses in Kashmir or Waziristan! Ha, ha! In such places you will not have the luxury of poring over building plans as they show in Hollywood films. In real life you will have to operate on the assumption that you are venturing into a blind alley. American SWAT teams dwell considerably on surprise. That is to say, stealth movement and noise/light discipline to get as close to the targets as possible, hopefully putting themselves in a position to engage an enemy from the moment he becomes aware of them. Some teams use subsonic sniper rifles for their initial shots on sentries or dogs. They also dwell at great lengths on how an assault should come at a time when least expected, taking into consideration fatigue, normal sleep periods, and other factors that detract from the target's alertness. Diversions are an essential element in achieving surprise. Staged emergencies, such as a mock auto accident, fire, or explosion near the crisis site, can divert the target's attention away from the assaulting elements. Explosive breaching and diversionary devices, such as flash bang, smoke, or gas grenades can be employed to distract and disorient the targets. Negotiators can try to manipulate the defenders into a more vulnerable position or convince them that their position will not be stormed. Such niceties have no place in real situations of anti-terrorist operations in India, Pakistan, Afghanistan, Iraq, Latin America, or in most places in the Far East. The terrorist hiding in a house would come of know of you the moment you start laying the cordon. The moment you fire the first shot or they fire, all element of surprise is lost. They know that you are after them and that's the end of it. The Americans would also advise you to use multiple simultaneous attacks from different entry points to overload the target's ability to react effectively. The idea is that the more entry points the attackers can choose from, the better their chances. The teams actually entering the objective usually have to synchronize with snipers, negotiators, power technicians, perimeter guards, and others who assist from the outside. Once again, leave it to them or their Hollywood films. They sound well in theory but are impossibly difficult to execute flawlessly in real life. Managing entry through even one place is complicated enough. In real life, you are more likely to mess things up than achieve some spectacular surprise. When even your cordon may not remain covert, managing entries covertly in anti-terrorist operations are almost impossible.

House intervention is one field where training and scientific methods evolved after endless hours of research and practice must take precedence over your natural reactions. Those who try to imitate films end up very seriously dead; those who go by natural instincts also follow them. Remember that there are no failsafe methods of house intervention; there are, however, better, scientific, logical and more correct methods. The purpose of this chapter is therefore to enunciate those vital principles that will help save your life and take away the bad guy's life. It was absolutely necessary to do so because an unfortunate thing about the Indians, the Pakistanis and many other dumb forces of the world is that they are aware of only the flashy aspects of house intervention that they have plagiarised from Hollywood films or popular articles on the business. They never developed this as a scientific discipline. Worst of all, they have had only individual's notions about it. Everybody who has spent some time in areas affected by terrorism, claims to have his own wisdom of how it is to be done—the system as such has never had anything substantial on it.

(9.2) How You Must Prepare?

The Cavalry doesn't always come to the rescue. When you are in deep shit, you will have to fend for yourself.

Before you venture into house intervention, you must ensure the following.

- Every man going anywhere near the house must have body armour and bullet-proof helmet.
- You must never fall short of ammunition in any cordon; all the more so in the inner cordon. Sufficient number of loaded spare magazines must be kept ready. If necessary, you may even depute a couple of men to reload magazines that are emptied.

It may seem obvious but the fact is that in crucial moments, there should be no fumbling.

- You should also have a sufficient supply of hand grenades ready. Men must be specifically deputed to prime them on location so that the inner cordon and the assault party are not obliged to waste its time doing that.
- In an urban situation where vehicles may go up to the house, you must have at least one bullet-proof vehicle. The vehicle will be required for going close to the target house and firing.
- Portable generators must be kept ready for being taken to the operation's site for lighting up the area in the night. There should be about 100 m of flexible wire and about 6-7 halogen lamps with reflectors. Reflectors are vital so that light is thrown only to one side. If any light comes towards you, the terrorist will fire on you. If you do not have readymade proper reflectors in some situation, improvise them on the spot.
- Concertina coils for using in the outer cordon.
- You must also carry night vision devices and thermal imaging devices—they are best used by the outer cordon party in the night.
- Sufficient first-aid material must be available on the site from the beginning of the operation.
- Arrangement for casualty evacuation must be in place with earmarked vehicle. No time must be wasted in doing a management exercise on the spot or in any improvisation.

(9.3) Step-by-Step Basics of House Intervention

Don't ever be the first...don't ever be the last...
and don't ever volunteer to do anything.

It is presumed that you are familiar with the drill of how to get the house vacated of its legitimate inmates with the help of the local police before you attack—we are not wasting time on that. The five basic steps of house intervention are: gaining access; making entry into the space; securing the space; moving to adjoining spaces and; command/ control of the team and the subsequent actions. Remember that it is not going to be a free-for-all. Strict fire discipline is required. Poor armies like the dumb Indians fall into a habit that everyone who has a view of the target house starts firing and the contribution of the individual is judged by the number of magazines one has emptied. This is very bad. Fire discipline must be rigorously enforced.

(9.3.1) Probing and Weakening the Defences of the Terrorists

Laying a Cordon: The moment the target house is identified; the first step is to lay a cordon around it. This will be the outer cordon. The purpose is only to prevent the escape of any terrorist from inside the house. You must keep concertina coils ready for this purpose and deploy them to block possible escape routes. No man fires at this stage unless they find someone trying to escape.

Reconnoitering the house: The next step is to reconnoiter the house properly from all sides. Reconnoitering must not be done casually. Many casualties have resulted in this process. Do it carefully. Reconnoitering has two purposes. The first is to find out the number and dispersal of openings in the house, that is, windows and doors etc. The second is to find out the places in nearby houses or structures from where fire may be delivered effectively on to the target house. The essential point to be remembered in house clearance operations is that there could be terrorists hidden in houses other than the target house also and they could inflict casualties unexpectedly. Hence, you must try to have some sort of cover all the time—never expose yourself unnecessarily.

Probing fire: After this you must deliver what is known as probing fire. Probing fire means that you want to probe the defences of the terrorists hiding inside. If they are dumb, they will return fire and reveal their numbers and/or position (does not matter that they can change it later). If they are smart, they will keep mum and keep you guessing. Take your chance. But since you will be inviting fire, it is imperative that the probing fire be delivered from proper cover.

Stripping the windows and doors of their cover: The next task is to strip the windows and the doors of the target house. The basic purpose is to deny the terrorist the cover of the windows and the doors. He will then be not able to either fire from their cover before you try entering the house or surprise you when you make entry. Many casualties have resulted from the terrorists firing from behind closed windows. Once you have stripped the cover, it becomes easy to pour down suppressive fire through them even if someone is standing well back in the shadows. Secondly, when the windows and the doors give way, it would make it eminently easy for you to lob grenades through them or place rifle grenades through them. Depending on how a window or door is located, you may also fire tear gas shells through them. Since the men who will eventually form the inner cordon have to conserve their ammunition, the stripping fire must be delivered by the outer cordon.

Should you have the specially designed door-breaching grenades (such as Rafael's Simon door-breaching grenade), you must use them to breach them. If you do not have them, pour down controlled bursts of 7.62 x 51 mm LMG automatic fire on the windows and the doors so as to remove as much of the cover as possible. The full-length 7.62 mm cartridge is any day better for the job than the intermediate cartridge of the AK. You will have to assign duties for this—for example, such-and-such LMG will fire at such-and-such window. The effect of the fire will have to be assessed continuously. Fire say, 10 rounds and see the effect. Then fire another burst, and so on. Many of the windows and doors that you are likely to encounter will give way under such fire. However, depending on the stuff they are made of, it may not be possible to strip them completely. But whatever can be done would pay great dividends.

What to do if the windows or doors resist machinegun fire?: If a door or window resists stripping or if there is a wall or some other structure coming in the way, you must use a specific weapon, the bunker-defeat munition like the American M141 BDM or at least the M72 LAW. If you do not have that, bring in the anti-tank weapon that you might have, even though it was not specifically designed for the purpose. Remember that an anti-tank warhead like that of the CGRL round takes about 20-25 meters of flight just to arm the fuze of the warhead. Never fire it at distances less than that. Otherwise it will either fail to explode or will simply go through. Many people have committed the mistake of firing it from a short distance and then they think that the warhead was a dud. Before firing the CGRL please ensure that the other side is clear from both friendly forces and civilians. Wait to ascertain the effect.

Weakening the defences of the house: It is necessary to weaken the defences of the house, and perhaps kill some terrorists in the process of firing on it. This should, however, not become an excuse for wasting ammunition. Many people have fallen into the habit of just firing on the house, little knowing the effect of the fire. Aggressive fire means that we pour the fire through some opening only when we have a reason to suspect that the fire could reach someone. For that it is important to take up positions in such places which are very suitably located. Such places may be in the open behind some cover or even in nearby houses. Throughout the course of history of anti-terrorist operations, it has been seen that many operations have dragged for several days or have been ineffective because they do not select the positions carefully—they just take some positions and fire from there. How much and how long you will fire from such positions depends on the fire from the other side. The purpose is to make the terrorist exhaust his ammunition in return fire. Some of them might get killed in the process, but don't count on it.

Rifle Grenades: You must realise that bullets follow a straight path and you cannot hit a man who has some cover. Yet if you drop a rifle grenade behind him, the splinters would get him in spite of the cover. If you have multi-shot launchers like the Milkhor, very good, otherwise, even single-shot grenade launchers are excellent. Do not forget that the 'Thumper' M-79 served the Americans faithfully for several decades. There is nothing like a rifle grenade fired from a shoulder-fired weapon.

The role of suppressive fire in making a dash to enter: Once you have decided that more aggressive fire is not serving a useful purpose in the sense that the guy inside is either injured/killed and not responding, or is too clever to waste his ammunition, or hiding in some hideout, it is time to take him by entering the house. For entering, you have to reach close to it—to start with you must try to reach a distance from where grenades may be thrown. You reach close to it under the cover of suppressive fire. Suppressive fire, as the name indicates is intended to prevent the man who could be actually watching your moves from a safe and hidden position, from firing on you. It shall be directed simultaneously on all the openings.

Great care must be taken to ensure that the suppressive fire does not hit the men who are trying to make a dash for the building under their cover. It should be carefully controlled. If you reach a place or places from where grenades may be lobbed inside the house, lob them freely. There is nothing better than a grenade. Grenades must be lobbed through as many openings as possible. Wait to ascertain the effect of grenades. There is no hurry.

(9.3.2) Methods of Entering the House

You, you, and you ... panic. The rest of you, come with me.

Once you are sure that no more fire is likely, it is time to get into the house. Do not forget that the men going to enter need to be in constant radio contact with the men outside through hands-free wireless sets. It has happened in the past with dunderhead armed forces that some people went inside got trapped there or were killed and those outside had no idea of what happened to them. They waited for two-three days before they could make up their mind to blast the entire house. Select the intended place of entry carefully. Also ensure that just before the men dash out; the intended place of entry is sprayed with bullets.

The dash is made only after the firing stops. Before making a dash for the house ensure that you have space out there to make a foothold. A foothold means a place where you are not likely to come under fire from inside the house. At least four men must make the dash in two columns. The place should be so chosen that you may throw grenades from there too. The rule of thumb in house intervention is that a grenade precedes a man—as simple as that. No man enters any room whatsoever without throwing a grenade inside. Now, you may encounter two situations. The door could have been breached, or the door could not have been breached.

Ballistic, explosive, and mechanical breaching: If you have a door-breaching grenade designed specifically for the purpose, the job becomes easier. First breach the door and then proceed to put a couple of grenades inside. There is another excellent method of breaching. You can easily breach single brick walls with that and that too from a safe distance. The full-length 7.62 x 51 mm cartridge comes in handy here. You must fire a couple of hundreds of rounds from a LMG or MMG on the wall and you can easily make a hole big enough for two men to enter together. I had used the MMG in breaching the wall of the Punjab Hotel in Lal Chowk, Srinagar in which two terrorists were hiding—both were eventually killed without any loss on our side.

If you do not have them, the remaining three major methods of breaching are ballistic, mechanical and explosive breaching. Generally speaking, breaching is nothing more than attacking the weakest link of the entry point to gain positive access to the space. Exterior doors are likely to present more difficulty than the interior doors, but you must be prepared to deal with breaching problems after the initial breach also. Even a solid door will still be attached to the frame with hinges and secured with some sort of locking mechanism. It is these locations that represent the weakest part of the entry point and where the focus of the breaching method should be directed. What method is to be used depends on the situation and the condition of the door. In a rural situation, where light level is low and hostile fire could come on you from more than one direction, the best is to fire automatic bursts from a distance. You may have to waste some ammunition but getting close could be dangerous. Regardless of the method of entry, the application must be well-rehearsed with the team to ensure co-ordination between the breaching element, the assault element and the security element that gives covering fire. Do not commit the horrible mistake of entrusting all the jobs to one team. During the planning phase, it is important that the teams identify a primary and secondary entry point, as well as a primary and secondary method of entry. If, for whatever reason, an attempt to breach fails to gain access, a contingency plan must be ready to immediately take the next action. Whether that is going to be an alternate method of entry or an alternate entry point, it must be planned, rehearsed and expected.

Shooting the lock

Ballistic breaching is the use of a ballistic projectile that when placed correctly destroys either the locking mechanisms or the hinges and is usually accomplished with automatic fire, shotguns and special purpose ammunition. Ballistic breaching is done using a 12 gauge shotgun and a special round that has gone by several names including a Hatton, Shok-lok, Lockbuster or Avon round. While many of these are trade names used by the companies that manufacture and sell them, they are in effect all very similar in their construction and are identical in their use. Most of these rounds are made using compressed zinc powder or dental ceramic. Designed to be fired into the locking mechanism or hinges of a door, the round is designed to expend all of its kinetic energy into the locking or hinge mechanism completely disintegrating in the process. Note that for horizontal bolts, the locking bolt is what is targeted, and not the locking mechanism itself. It is the bolt that holds the door shut; if only the locking mechanism is destroyed the bolt will still hold the door closed. If you do not have these specialised loads, you may use SSG load to shoot at the hinges. Since you cannot waste one man to wield only the shotgun, that man will have to carry this extra in addition to his rifle. In any case, one advantage of firing at the door is that it may provoke the guy inside into firing prematurely and thus give away his presence. Once you are sure that he is inside and firing, you may make up your mind to use heavier weapons.

Explosive breaching is the precise application of high-explosive charges to destroy the weak links of the entry point with the added benefit of violence of action to help retain the element of surprise. This has become virtually a science in itself. For details on explosive breaching, readers may refer to our treatise on explosives, namely, "The Ultimate Book Of Explosives, Bombs and IEDs". A problem with explosive breaching is that you have to come close to the door to fix the explosives and during that period you are vulnerable. It is not to be tried when you suspect that fire could come through the door.

Mechanical breaching is the use of various tools such as rams, sledge-hammers, mallets, the Halligan Tool, an oversize combination of pry bar, claw hammer, and pick-axe, Quickie Saws and torches to attack the weak parts of the entry point to gain access. Sledge-hammers and rams are for doors that open inward; Pry bars and Halligan tools are for those that open outward. If you have these tools, fine. If you do not have them, some sort of improvised ram would be required. The simplest improvisation is a jack-hammer or a heavy mallet wielded from the side, depending on what sort of door you have. When you wield the hammer or the mallet, you can't fire, as both hands get busy. It is then for your buddies to quickly lob grenades inside. A heavier door would require a steel jack-hammer; lighter doors are best opened with a heavy mallet as then they open clean instead of getting shattered or worse, the hammer head just making a hole. But be prepared that the door could well be booby-trapped. You hammer it and it explodes. Hence, it is to be tried only when you do not have any other option of doing it from a distance. The drill is that the door is hammered open and the man hammering it steps back. The man who uses the mallet cannot use anything else for the moment. It is for two or at least one man to quickly lob a grenade inside from the side and very swiftly slide back to the side. The remaining two persons keep rifles at the ready and wait a few moments.

In Hollywood films or even in American training films, you see them kicking the door. That's utterly foolish. There could be a guy right behind the door or in the shadows and you could get completely shot up in your leg at least. Never try to give the door a front kick. At most you can deliver a 'pivot kick' to the door from the side when you have none of the above methods to use.

A terrorist hiding well behind the door could still deliver fire in a straight line or worse, make a suicidal dash towards the door. We cannot help his firing from where he is. But we can deal with that eventuality by positioning a man well outside that door in prone position. The man firing from inside would not normally expect a man in a prone position several meters away. It is necessary for this man to have cover. The cover could be natural and he could fire from the side of the cover or it could even be an armour plate high enough to cover his head. He must ensure that he does not hit the party that has dashed to the door. Very accurate fire is required here. However, since he is deployed for an extreme eventuality he will fire only if a terrorist from inside makes a suicidal dash outside.

The Stack-up: A simple stack up is shown below.

A simple stack-up

In real life you will practice more advanced methods. After the breaching element has withdrawn, two men take position on either side of it. Others remain stacked up behind them in two lines on both sides—the basic idea of stack-up is to present a small target. It is not unusual to have even four men each in both lines, depending on the degree of opposition expected.

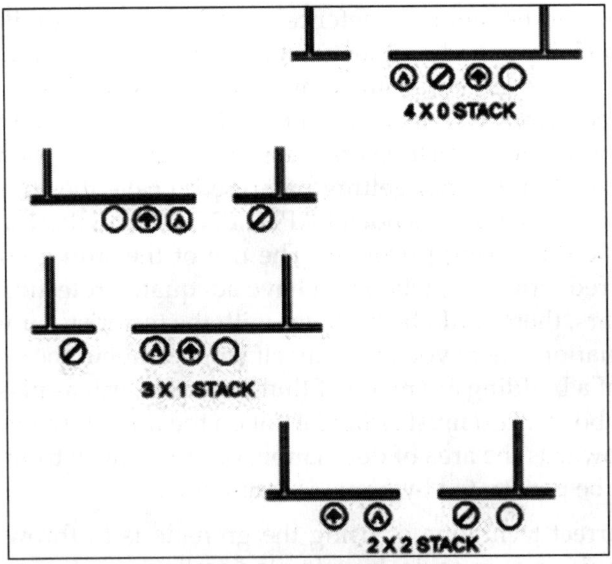

Various stacking positions

When you are approaching a room always keep a sharp eye out for booby-traps. Never touch everyday household objects such as light switches or door handles. Terrorists may not be very intelligent but it does not take much mind to fix a booby trap. Watch your feet: a favourite location for booby traps is where you have to walk—the treads of a staircase, for example. Other favourite places are in footpaths, behind doors, under thresholds, and under some rubble. In the heat of battle you cannot afford to waste time neutralising a booby trap. If you do find a booby trap, mark its position with tape, chalk or aerosol paint, and give it a wide berth.

The proper use of grenades: Soldiers are taught in basic training that their rifle is the best friend. However, when the soldier is clearing a house the grenade replaces the rifle in his affections. When you're inside a house where terrorists are installed, the grenade takes over from the gun as your first-line weapon. When clearing buildings there's no time to wonder how the enemy's going to react. You have to do it to them before they do it to you. And do it quickly, safely and surely, risking your life and those of your team as little as possible. A grenade therefore precedes entry in any room.

Much has been made of the stun grenades (flash and bang grenades which produce a blinding flash of light and also a deafening sound which is supposed to disorientate the man) in uninformed circles. I am not impressed by this. You cannot risk your life on a stupid stun grenade and hope that it will disorientate the guys inside so badly that they would be rendered defenceless. What do you do if they had muffled their ears or had goggles or were simply looking the other way, or had their eyes closed, or in some unknown way, did not register the expected effect. Or what do you do if you, in the first place, do not have these devices? There are recorded instances of people taking even a Taser shot and not getting paralysed. Leave the stun grenade to Hollywood films. This is not a LAPD or NYPD situation and we are not interested in taking prisoners. The use of the stun grenade is to be considered; however, when you have adequate protection for your eyes and ears, there could be hostages with the terrorists, or when you are in a situation where you are yourself worried about the splinters. If the walls of a building are made of thin material, such as plasterboard or thin ply board, you must either lie flat on the floor with your helmet pointing towards the area of detonation, or move away from any wall that might be penetrated by grenade fragments.

The correct technique of using the grenade is to throw it inside and then quickly step aside, hugging the wall. Grenades must not be lobbed. If they are lobbed, a desperate character may try to grab it and lob it back. Throw it as hard as possible. Never mind if it rebounds inside the room—in fact we want it to skip and bounce. It will make it all the more difficult for him to grab it. The technique of cooking off a grenade that is, holding on to it for two seconds after the pin has been pulled and the safety lever allowed to fly off, once again looks exciting in films. Do no try it in real life. Grenade fuzes are after all mechanical devices and may not be as perfect as you think.

Non-verbal or verbal alerts are used, as appropriate, prior to throwing a grenade. This consists of a visual showing of the grenade to assault party members with a visual acknowledgment from them. In other words, show the grenade, get a nod, then let loose! A non-verbal alert will ensure the enemy is surprised when the grenade is thrown. If the situation demands, a voice alert can be used, but the element of surprise may be lost. When, or if a voice alert is used, the voice alert is 'frag out'! When an enemy grenade has been identified, friendly forces shout 'grenade'!

It is absolutely necessary that such grenades must be offensive grenades like the Pakistani P2A1 or the Austrian Arges 84 which produce a large number of small splinters and may hit as many men as possible. Armies, such as the Indian armed forces, that still use defensive grenades like the HE 36 are simply dumb beyond redemption. The HE 36 is a copy of the Mills bomb the British made during the First World War. It is a defensive grenade suitable for the infantry warfare of that era in vast open spaces. A defensive grenade means that the splinters would go much farther than you can throw and hence you have to necessarily take cover after throwing it. Moreover, it breaks into a few (about 45-52) large fragments of its cast iron shell, thereby reducing the probability of a hit. Above all, we do not require such a big bang when we are throwing the grenade just a few feet away. The HE-36 is simply not suitable for anti-terrorist or anti-guerrilla operations. For anti-terrorist operations you need offensive grenades. Offensive grenades produce splinters that do not go farther than the distance to which they can be thrown and hence taking cover is not always necessary. They have a plastic body. The splinters are produced by a wire-wrapped around the explosive that is nicked at intervals. When the explosive explodes, the wire breaks along the nicks and they become the splinters—the small size makes the aerodynamics poor and they do not go far. Since the number of splinters is much higher, they increase the probability of a hit. Hence, they are ideally suited for urban combat. What the splinters of a grenade can do, perhaps a hundred bullets cannot do—particularly for a man who is hiding behind some cover that is not in direct line-of-sight of a bullet.

Example of offensive grenades: Pakistani P2A1 and Chinese Type 86 grenades

The Hollywood and the American police training method is that people enter inside right after the grenade. I ask you to wait a little after throwing the grenade. Why? There are two reasons for it. There could be a guy inside who has some protection. Thus, he may not be knocked out completely by the grenade. By waiting a few moments, you have to chance to see how he reacts. Is he going to get up and make a suicidal charge? Or is he going to open fire from where he is? The second reason is that the grenade may kick up dust or similar things in the room, thus reducing visibility. Let the dust settle down. To reduce the possibility of someone surprising you out of the dust or darkness, it is advisable to have a flashlight taped to the barrel of the rifle. It may appear a small thing but can make the difference between life and death. If the guy inside is not knocked out and reacts, you must first respond to that threat. Maybe it would be necessary to throw more grenades.

Dropping the grenades through holes made in floors: If the enemy is in a room below and you are up, you could consider dropping a grenade through a hole made in the floor. At times the floors are such that he can shoot up through them and you would find bullets coming to you from underneath—a frightening situation. Theoretically, you could also shoot down, but you might be worried about ricochet of bullets on to you—the enemy too could be bothered but he is desperate and you are not. Making the hole quickly is a problem though. You could use crowbar but that too takes some time and makes noise that would alert him. A chain saw cutter has the same drawback. An ideal solution for making a hole in a wooden floor without a warning would be a Blunderbuss sort of weapon which we could just place on the floor and fire to make a hole—shaped charges are also suitable for stronger floors—but you have to have them made specifically for this purpose. Remember the tripod in your chemistry lab under which you keep the Bunsen burner? You need a thing like that. Keep some of them with you. That will give you the stand-off distance for the shaped charge. The shaped charge may be placed on the rim as you used to place a beaker on it in the chemistry lab. You need not have a factory-made shaped charge for it. All you need beforehand is a copper cone with the apex angle of 42 degrees. Get some made in any workshop. Pat some plastic explosive on its back and it is ready. In a pinch, you could use a simple charge placed on the floor which is tamped with a heavy sandbag on top of it so that most of the explosive force is directed downwards.

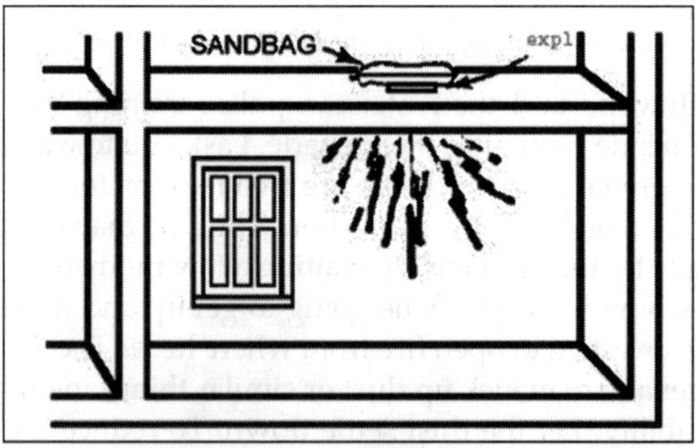

Tamping the charge to make a hole in the floor

Carrying the rifle: 'low ready' and 'high ready' positions: There are two ready/entry positions. The first, called 'low ready', requires shouldering of the weapon and then keeping the muzzle down to allow a clear view of the killing area. The muzzle of the weapon is raised only when engaging a target. This allows for extremely fast sight acquisition since the weapon is already in a shooting position. When the sights cannot be seen, say for example, in darkness, this position allows for very accurate point-shoulder shooting. The alternative is a modified port-arms patrolling position called 'high ready'. The weapon is held in a shooting grip, thumb on safety, but with the stock resting inside of the right elbow and the muzzle held at chin level but angled well-forward. The operator looks across the top of the muzzle as he scans an area, then mounts the weapon to the shoulder in one smooth motion when a target comes into view, much the same way as a shotgun shooter mounts his weapon on the trap range.

Rifle at low ready position

Rifle at high ready position

The Ballistic Shield: The ballistic shield could be an extremely valuable tool. But you must have practice of using it comfortably. The most popular ballistic shields with the Western SWAT teams are those which provide Level IIIA protection, that is, protection against handguns. Then you can hold the shield in one hand and use a handgun in another. They are of no use in anti-guerrilla operations because the terrorists will be using rifles or machineguns which will not be stopped by Level IIIA protection shields and in any case, you are also using rifles and both of your hands are occupied. They realised this problem and made shields with Level III protection also. They are reasonably light and also have grips which enable you to hold the shield as well as hold the rifle in two hands. Many makes are available in the international market. The ballistic shield of Security Pro-USA weighs only about 13 kg in size 20″ x 34″. It is made of Dyneema. The Patriot Company has produced the so-called Minuteman-III, Folding Ballistic Shield in 2002 and for that they claim that a shield of the size of 19″ x 34″ weighs only 09 kg. The Protech NATO Armour Shields company makes shields of advanced composite polyethylene fiber in the weight range 12.5 (16″ x 32″) to 15 kg (20″ x 34″). Other products like the Armour Express Raider Ballistic shield are also available.

(9.3.3) Room Entry Techniques

Stiffen the sinews, summon up the blood.

The moment of truth: Having done all this, the moment of truth arrives. Now, is the time to enter the room and face what is dreaded the most in anti-terrorist operations. Ensure that you never enter a room alone. Two personnel are the minimum room-clearing team. If the door is not wide enough you shall enter one after the other, step inside and instantly move to the side. Not a moment is to be wasted standing in the open. The door is the focal point of anyone inside the room. It is known as the fatal funnel, because it focuses attention at the precise point where the individual team members are the most vulnerable. Moving into the room quickly reduces the chance anyone will be hit by enemy fire directed at the doorway. The Point man (first man) going left is therefore a good idea, though this may be changed based on what is known of the room's layout or the situation that the Point sees as he enters. Another strategy is to head for the hinge side of the door if the door opens outward and for the handle side of the door if it swings in. This is based upon the presumption that if the hostile has to hide, he would naturally hide behind the door panel.

The first man in must get his back to the wall; the second man does the same. It is also important to note that the arc of fire is decided in advance. The man on the left will fire from the center of the room to the left corner—that is the barrel must start spraying bullets the moment it points to the center and then swings to the left; the man on the right will fire from the center to the right corner in exactly the same fashion. In other words, the man to the left must practice to swing his barrels anti-clockwise, and the man on the right must swing his barrel clockwise. For God's sake do not mess up the firing sequence—you may hit your own man. It is important to note that their rifles start firing after their barrels are pointing inside. Practice it till it becomes second nature. This fire has to be on full automatic. Nobody must fire single shots or three-round bursts inside a room. Firing single shots here would get you a ticket to the other world. You have got to literally spray bullets inside irrespective of whether you see anybody or not. It is a life and death situation. You do not think about wasting ammunition at this juncture. The question of firing single shots or aimed shots or three-round bursts arises only when you know that there could be hostages inside. Some of the SWAT manuals will teach you about clearing a corner first and then placing your back to that corner so that you may then focus your attention on the remaining area. This does not work in situations where the bad guy inside has an automatic rifle and he is equally free to swing his barrel. Ensure that if you fall down while entering the room, you stay down and do not move. Do not get up until a team member places his hands on you and lifts you up. If a team member arbitrarily gets up, he may become an impediment to the rest of the team's movements. Another possibility is that he would rise into the path of a team member's bullet.

And remember one more thing. You could have decided that the Point man takes the left side. Some unexpected problem could arise that could make him take the right side. Do not get flummoxed by it. Be prepared for it. It does not matter if the person in front of you goes the wrong way when entering the room. Just go the opposite way of the operator in front of you and it will work out. For God's sake, do not stop in the fatal funnel. The number three and number four soldiers are especially prone to stopping in the funnel. The 'fatal funnel' is the dangerous area where the attacker is silhouetted against his own entry point from the perspective of defenders inside the room. It is imperative that all of you clear the fatal funnel, which is a zone that exists not only outside the door but also inside the doorway, in a rapid fashion. This area is the ultimate choke point where you are the most vulnerable. As an instructional tool for those men who are unfamiliar with what area the fatal funnel actually would encompass, it is easy for instructors to construct a visual representation. Darken a room and at the same time leaving the lights on in the adjacent hallway. With the door to the room open, the fatal funnel is represented by the cone of light that spills into the room. This lighted area represents the funnel on the inside of the room. Darken the hallway and light the room to achieve a representation of the representation of the funnel cn the exterior of the room.

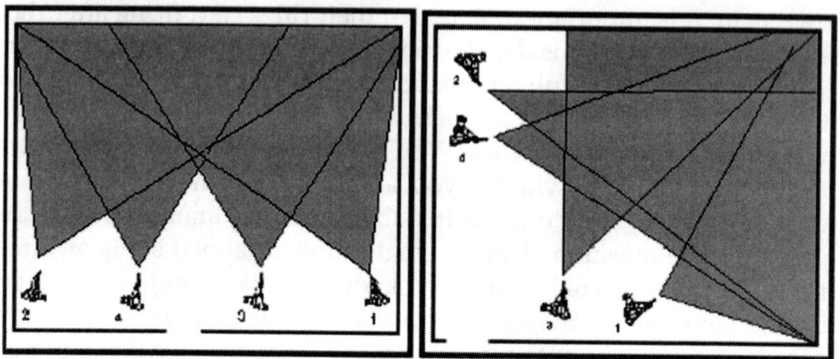

(Center door) (Corner door)

Points of domination and sectors of fire

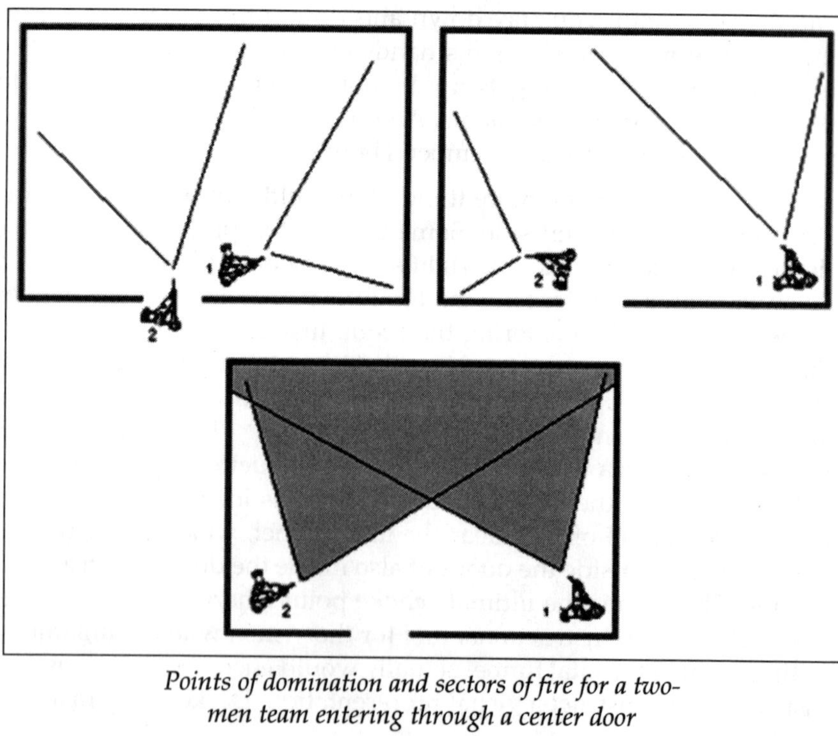

Points of domination and sectors of fire for a two-men team entering through a center door

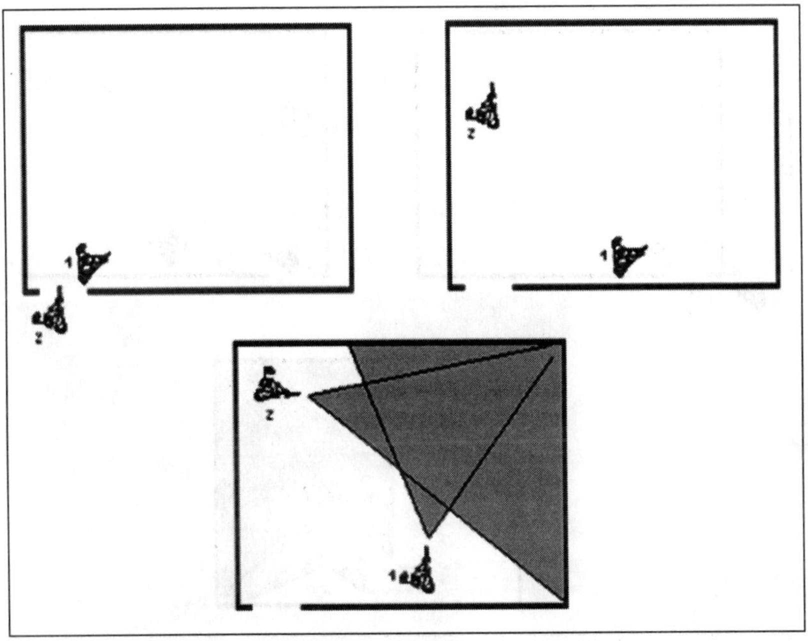

Points of domination and sectors of fire for a two-men team entering through a corner door

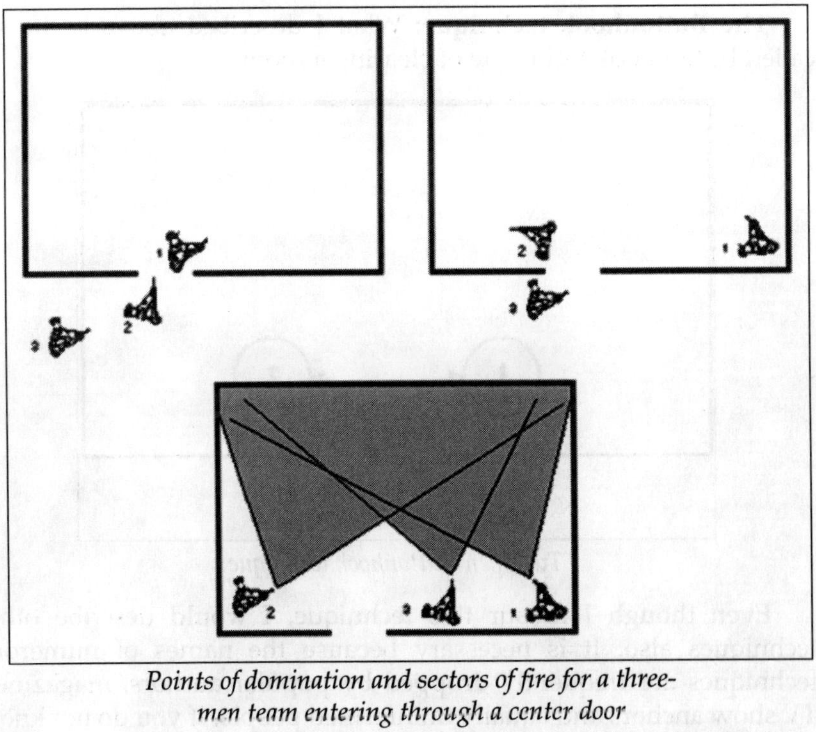

Points of domination and sectors of fire for a three-men team entering through a center door

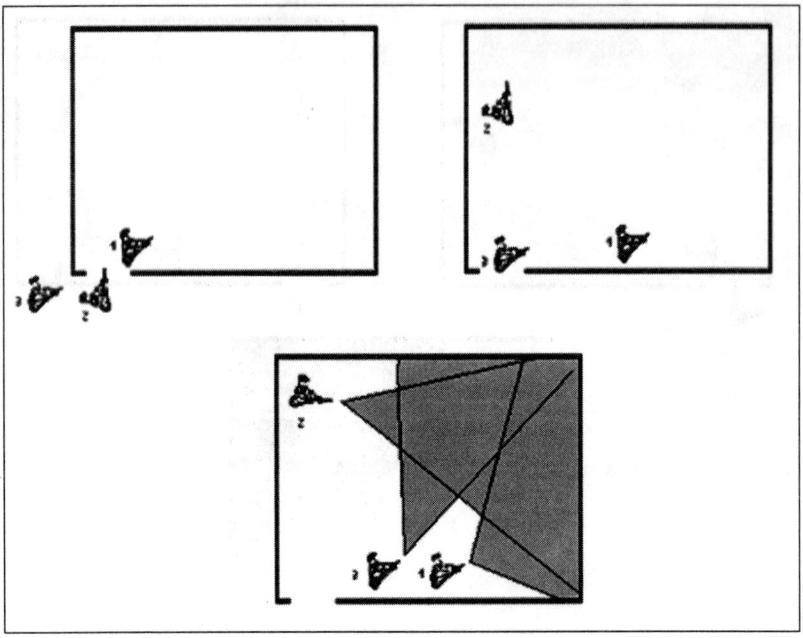

Points of domination and sectors of fire for a three-men team entering through a corner door

The Buttonhook technique: What I described above is the so-called Buttonhook technique of clearing a room.

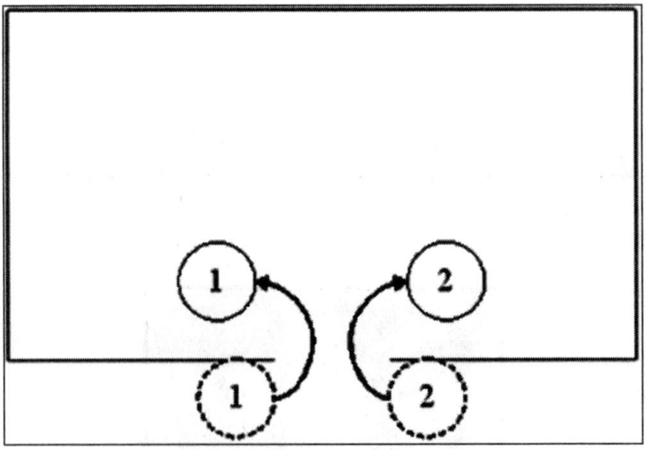

Two-men Buttonhook technique

Even though I favour this technique, I would describe other techniques also. It is necessary because the names of numerous techniques are frequently dropped by popular authors, magazines, TV show anchors and equally uninformed people. If you do not know them, you could be left wondering. The buttonhook is a very fast technique because the two operators go through the door at the same time and they are clear of the fatal funnel in a very short time.

Its limitation, however, is that the opening has to be big enough to allow both of them to go at the same time. Otherwise, they have to stagger the entry or run the risk of bumping into each other. It is risky no doubt but the fact is that in what we are advocating you are entering after a couple of grenades. When the LAPD calls it risky, they are not using grenades.

The Crossover technique: In this technique, as the name suggests, you crossover to the other side to a position inside, and opposite of where you began your entry. They say that if the door is not wide enough for buttonhook, this could be used. We do not find much merit in it. If you are entering through a door, the most natural thing is to slip to the side—why move across the fatal funnel?

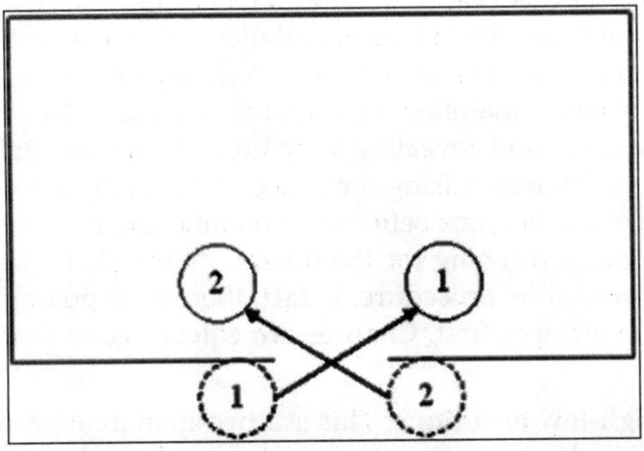

The Crossover technique

The Modified technique: The 'modified' incorporates a combination action of the 'crisscross' and the 'buttonhook' techniques. This technique may be of use when operators must enter the doorway from the same side. It is performed with one operator traversing across the entry point (fatal funnel) to an inside doorway position opposite from the outside door facing where the movement began. The other operator executes a buttonhook manoeuvre inside the same side door facing from his original position, or *vice versa*. The problem with this technique is that it demands much practice and is slower in any case.

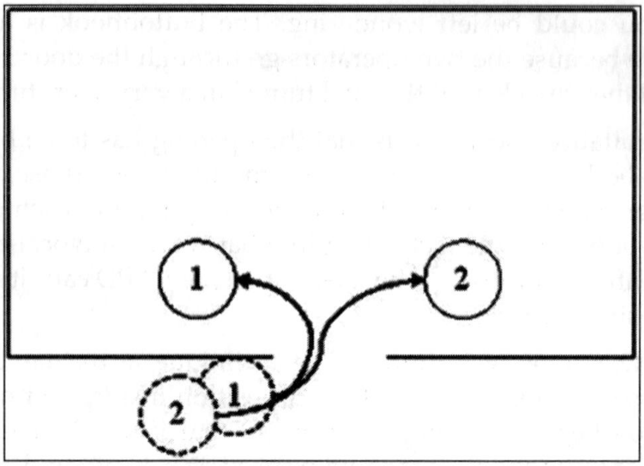

The modified technique

The Pie-slice technique: It is a manoeuvring procedure that allows gradual observation around a comer or other obstacle where a perpetrator might be hiding in ambush. This technique permits the slow, cautious viewing of an uncleared area involving an angular obstruction while maintaining a margin of safety for the operator. By staying quiet and revealing very little of himself (only head and weapon) and by maximising the space between the operator and the corner the operator gains better reaction time and minimising the risk of a perpetrator reaching for the operator's weapon. The problem is that it is a very slow procedure. In fact, there is no guarantee that you will see the terrorist first. Chances are equally good that he will see you first.

The high-low technique: This is a two-man dual protective cover technique in which one operator stands upright and directly behind a second operator who is in a crouched position. This clearing procedure allows firearms coverage in either moving or stationary positions with the operators' weapons focused simultaneously upon one point or area. This technique is suitable for clearing a corner. The advantage is that even if the terrorist spots them, he is forced to shoot at one of the operators; he can't engage both at the same time, this hesitation helps the operators. This technique is also used when a team needs to clear a T-intersection.

The limited penetration technique: This variation of the pie-slice technique can be used where operators don't initially enter the room. Each operator is positioned on either side of the door frame, then they pie around the door frame, into the door opening (fatal funnel) to engage and neutralise any threats that may be present in the room.

This tactic is often utilised when there is a high probability that a threat does exist inside. The limited penetration method exposes only a very small portion of the soldier's head and upper body to the potential threat. The problem with the technique is that it cannot ensure that the bad guys inside are killed. You have to enter the room anyway.

Other techniques: I maintain that techniques like the so-called Wedge, Delta Wedge, Running The Walls, Two-Man Wall Flood, Four-Man Wall Flood, Two-Man Penetration, Four-Man Penetration, On Line Flood, Power Shift Flood, Four-Man Leapfrog, and Saturation Techniques, etc. are of no practical use in anti-terrorist operations. They don't work when you have guys armed with assault rifles or sub-machineguns sitting inside.

(9.3.4) Clearing Operations

There is nothing more satisfying that having someone take a shot at you, and miss.

Clearing more rooms inside the house: Should you encounter another door in the room the entire sequence will have to be repeated depending on whether it is open or closed. Once we have the foothold and the first room, we must replenish their ammunition but people should not rush and crowd. In fact, replenishment is to be done after every room clearing. The doors inside that are closed spell danger as fire could come from behind them. The task of at least one member of the team is to peep and see where the other doors are and pour fire on them. Worse, they could be so positioned that if you wanted to strip them by firing at them, you would have to come in front of it and someone hiding inside could fire through them on you. More importantly, as long as you were firing from outside, you had the luxury of firing at will. Once you are inside, it is you and your two or three magazines. Hence, you cannot afford to waste ammunition in stripping doors. You must get a fresh supply as inner doors are not likely to be strong enough to withstand a short burst of automatic fire on the lock or jamb. Simply shoot up the door. Hence, you must arrange to get extra ammunition. Otherwise, the mallet or the jack-hammer would have to be used again.

Ensure that clearing teams mark cleared rooms with IR chemlight disks over entrance. In addition, clearing teams mark the outside windows of rooms with chemlight bundles to allow support by fire elements outside to track progress of assaulting squads. If the room has an adjoining room, it will either be on the same wall as the entry team or a separate wall. When the door is on the same wall, it will generally require a team member to focus his attention on the door and turn over responsibility for the rest of his zones to the team. Once the room has been cleared of threats, the team will realign on the new door, usually behind the team member holding security on the door, and start the process again. If the door is on a separate wall, the team can either request for more team members to enter the space and move directly to the new door, move to the new door with the team members in the space, or a combination of the two.

Clearing hallways: Once the initial space has been secured, the team will need to move from one space to another; usually through some sort of portal. Depending on the architecture, the team will usually make entry into either the first space or possibly a hallway. Inside the house, the danger zones are found in hallways and corridors. The rooms opening on to those are useful hideouts for terrorists who can then ambush the forces clearing the building. If you are forced to use an entrance hallway or upstairs corridor, always present yourself as the smallest target possible by flattening yourself against the wall. If you come to a turning, treat it as you would do for a room. Never make any assumptions until you have seen for yourself.

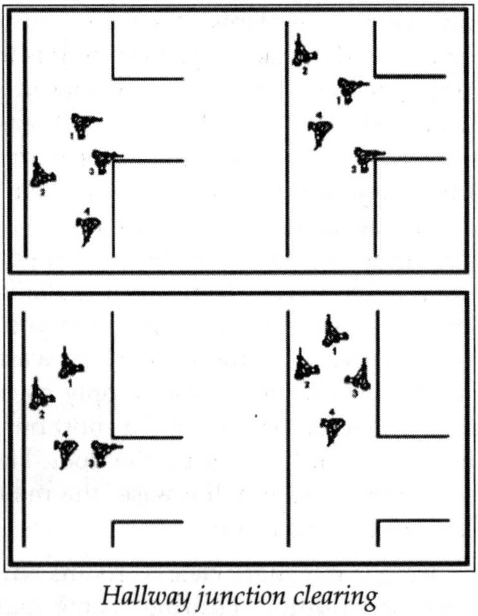

Hallway junction clearing

If the team makes its initial entry into a hallway, it will have to consider using a different approach. Hallways can be classified as being wide or narrow with pros/cons for both. If the hallway has no adjoining rooms attached, then the team will move down the hallway, emphasising security, remembering that the hallway is nothing more than an extended fatal funnel. If the hallway has adjoining rooms, then there will have to be an element responsible for maintaining security down the hallway as another element prepares to make entry into the space. The security element can be one team member or two, but usually no more. The worst case is a long hallway with opposing doors such as in a hotel or school. Doors in general can be classified as either open or closed, and this will determine the tactic to employ. If one of the doors is open, it poses the greater threat and should be cleared first in most cases. If both doors are closed, then the team has the option of sending one team into one room to wait for the space to be cleared before making entry into the opposite door. Another option is for both doors to be attacked simultaneously, but this option will be difficult in a narrow hallway. Probably, the worst case is opposing doors that are both open down a long hallway; here the solution will, more than likely, be to make entry into both open spaces simultaneously preferably behind diversionary devices.

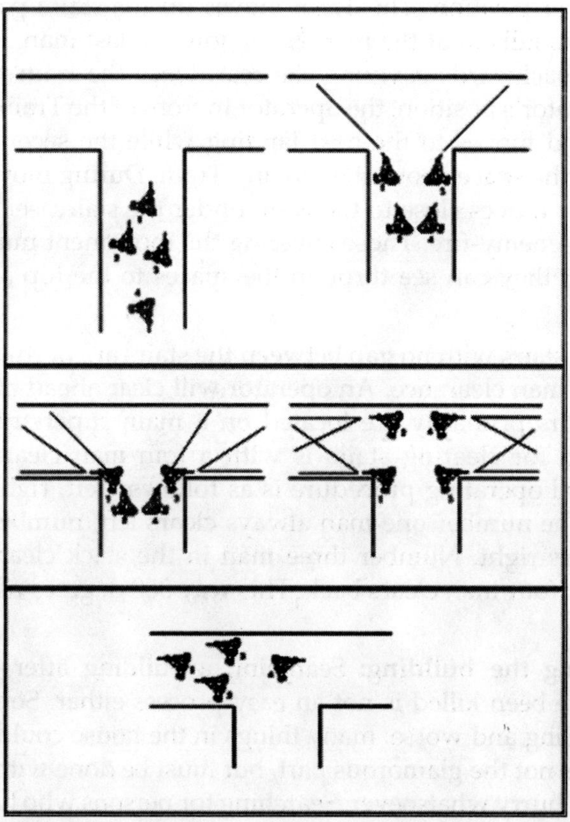

Clearing positions for a 'T'-Shaped hallway intersection

Clearing stairways: When multi-level structures are encountered; stairs become an added obstacle that requires manoeuvring. One of the more dangerous stair situations that a team is likely to encounter is a stairway with a turn between floors. Besides the blind spot at the turn, these stairways often have a loft that overlooks the bottom portion of the stairway. If the team is ascending, the number one soldier (as always) provides security to his direct front. Soldier number two secures the top row of stairs. Soldier number three secures the loft area. If a loft area does not exist, soldier number three secures the top of the second row of stairs. If the team is descending, each soldier has the same area of responsibility, except that the bottom of the stairway is secured, as opposed to the top. Stairs with split level landings that have a space allowing one to see up through to the top from below should be cleared in the following manner. Let us treat the stack-up like a Train. The first operator stands on the first level looking up covering the space between the stairs as the second operator takes Point and clears ahead of the Train to the next landing, where he stops and also takes up an upward cover position. The Train moves up the stairs past the first operator who falls in at the rear. He is now the last man. He will fall in walking backwards covering the rear. Once the train reaches the second operator's position, the operator in front of the Train takes over the Point and moves to the next landing while the second operator now covers the space above the moving Train. During movement, the Train always moves close to the wall, under the staircase, to stay out of sight and enemy-fire. Those covering the movement must stand in view so that they can see through the spaces to the top and bottom of the stairs.

Internal stairs with no gap between the stairs are normally cleared using a one man clearance. An operator will clear ahead of the Train. External stairs primarily are located on a main superstructure. The best method for clearing stairs is with a four-man clearance team. The standard operating procedure is as follows: Left, right, forward, and back. The number one man always clears left; number two man always clears right. Number three man in the stack clears forward. The number four man clears back. This way 360 degrees of security is maintained.

Searching the building: Searching a building after the visible hostiles have been killed is not an easy process either. Some of them could be hiding and worse; many things in the house could be booby-trapped. It is not the glamorous part, but must be done with great care without any hurry whatsoever. Searching for persons who have hidden themselves in areas such as closets, crawlspaces, and attics is done after the known suspects are in custody and the location is firmly under the control of law enforcement. After the structure is secure, a methodical search should begin for anyone who may have been able to hide himself during the initial entry. Here, it is very important that the utmost in officer safety practices be observed. The search should begin in the area that is furthest away from the initial breach point. The theory here is that it is much more likely that individuals deeper within the structure would have had more time to secret themselves somewhere than those that were caught unaware and were confronted by the entry unit.

(9.3.5) Insertion Through the Roof by Helicopters and Entering through Windows by Rappelling

The difficult we do immediately; the impossible takes a little longer.

In an urban scenario, the images of commandos rappelling down from a hovering helicopter are fixed in the minds of millions of people and they tend to think that it is the ideal method or the only method. Unfortunately it is not so. Unless the house is so built or located and the terrorists so positioned that even approaching the house is difficult, it is not the method of choice or the only method. For example, the house could be in a narrow lane that is covered by their automatic fire and you cannot take a bullet-proof vehicle inside the lane. Then your only option is to go from the top by a helicopter. Obviously, that cannot be done in a rural setting where the terrorists could be hiding in a house with brick walls but having a thatched roof. Entry through the roof looks very exciting in films. In a rural setting where the floors are weakly built, the chances of getting surprised by bursts of fire from beneath you are higher than your surprising them. Leave that for the films unless you are left with no other option. Similarly, any attempt to use ladders or grapple hooks may result in your getting shot up. Leave that to films and dumb criminals.

Always keep it in mind that if the guerrillas are not utterly dumb, they would expect an insertion by helicopters—they would have the roof covered with fire from a nearby building or from some cover on the same roof. Do not be under the fond delusion that everywhere you would get a flat-top roof for an unopposed landing. The helicopter itself could be fired upon or the soldiers rappelling down could be fired upon. Further, once you have landed on the roof, your element of surprise lasts only as long you have not fired the first shot or thrown the first grenade. There is no reason to believe that they would be only on the lower floors and you would be firing on them from the top floor. For all you know, they could be on the top floor as well. Once you reach the floor they are hiding in, you are on the same terms on

Insertion on roof by helicopter

which you would have been had you reached there in some other way. Rappelling from a helicopter should therefore only be taken as a method of insertion of troops and nothing else. The same argument applies to entry by rappelling through the windows. You will be dead before you land inside the room.

Blasting the house: Blasting the house is the very last option that you must exercise because of its obvious repercussions in a counter-insurgency. It may so happen that with the resources at your disposal, you are not able to neutralise the terrorists. They could be in a fortified hideout inside and the risk of casualties could be very high if you persisted with the methods described above. It could also happen that you have already suffered enough casualties and the opposition still seems to be going strong. In a war situation, tanks would have been called in. In anti-terrorist operations, you may not get tanks but you can destroy the house altogether so that the terrorists are buried in the debris. The best option in such situations is to use the bunker defeat munitions. If you do not have them, then you have to use explosive charges. You must make the charge carefully. Provide for a sling to lob it and wire it in such a manner that the wires do not get pulled out when you lob the charge. Make the packet in such a shape that it does not tumble much after landing. Wires must run on spool. The place is to be approached in an armoured vehicle; a man dashes out with the charge and lobs it in the room and jumps back into the vehicle. The vehicle retreats to a safe distance from where the charge is detonated.

(9.4) Fighting Terrorists in Special Situations

When in a fire-fight, kill as many as you can, the one you miss may not miss you tomorrow.

(9.4.1) Fighting Terrorists in Buses and Trains

By assaulting the bus from the front or rear you have many targets in line, some hostile and some friendly. By assaulting from the side with short ladders, or pick-up trucks, several operators can engage several hostile targets simultaneously. After that entry is then made through the conventional door—this is at least a four-man job. The first two operators who enter the bus from the front, fall to the sides into a seat, and provide cover down the rows. The other two advance down the aisle covering left and right, and hope to engage the terrorists. Trains are very similar to buses except that the windows are usually higher. A moving train may have to be assaulted by helicopter, with the team using ropes and sledge-hammers to gain entry.

(9.4.2) Fighting Terrorists in Aircrafts

Some nations have sky marshals in aircrafts. They have never been put to test. Till such time they remain only a hope. It remains to be seen whether they can ever put up a credible fight when there are several terrorists and they have taken hostages—after all one can very easily stand near the cockpit door and have a gun on the head of a crew member there—what can the stupid sky marshal do to that sitting in the tail or elsewhere? Fighting in flying aircrafts is admittedly very difficult for the simple reason that if bullets do penetrate the skin of the aircraft or the cockpit door, the aircraft may lose control. All cockpit doors are not bullet-resistant. Nations continue to be dumb. The marshals are given frangible bullets that won't penetrate the skin of the aircraft, but who said that the terrorists are also obliged to keep such bullets? Further, they may have explosives also.

Fighting on a parked aircraft is relatively easier but still fraught with serious risks. There could be two situations. In one you are allowed entry under some ruse; in the other you force entry. Real life is vastly different from reel life where commandos wearing only underwear have been allowed entry and then they fight the terrorists with some impressive tae-kwon do kicks. Leave that bullshit to films. In real life if at all someone is allowed entry whether disguised as janitor or paramedic, they will have a gun on his head first. For forced entry, pre-formed, shaped cutting charges could be used. Those teams, that know planes well, may be able to open the doors from the outside. Help of airline engineering staff may be required for this. The actual shooting problem is different from that of a bus, in that the windows are too small and too strong to breach. Entry must be made through several points simultaneously and the hostage-takers engaged in that manner. Warnings must be yelled to the passengers to duck, and the team members should try to stay out of the aisles. Fall to the side, into a seat, and shoot over or around cover. Advance down the aisle only to engage the terrorists in hiding. Things become difficult if the hijackers insist that the tarmac be lighted to reduce the element of surprise for them and if they keep the door open for a lookout. You cannot attack a plane with armed men inside and hope to overcome them without collateral damage to the passengers. Be mentally prepared for some innocent lives to be lost if you have decided to storm the plane after all.

10

Proper Weaponry for Urban Combat

These pants may not look like much, kid, but they've got it where it counts.

(10.1) How Improper Weaponry Flummoxes the Troops?

The only time suppressive fire works, is when it is used on abandoned positions.

The armed forces of many countries including India have no weapon available specifically for dealing with guerrillas who could be hiding behind a built-up structure in a populated area. In fact, the dimwits do not have any tactical doctrine for this either. This is a classic example of the 'pandemic of ignorance' and 'intellectual bankruptcy' that has engulfed this world. In the absence of any tactical doctrine or specific weapon, they deal with the situation in the crudest manner possible. They run into rough waters when the usual rifle fire and grenades do not work. Then the troops are left with their own improvised solutions. They may set fire to the structure if there is something combustible in it. This has been done with things as simple as throwing a burning rag to special pumps that squirt a high velocity jet of fuel to some distance. It is hoped that the terrorist could be burnt alive or forced to run to some other place. Or they fire anti-tank warheads into the house. This is done without knowing the intrinsic limitations of the weapon. Those who fire it, hope to bring down the structure by it. Sometimes the warhead explodes, sometimes it does not. Quite often they are obliged to fire many rounds of the weapon. Once again it is hoped that if the structure collapses as a result of the repeated holes created or the effect of the blasts of the warhead, the terrorist would be buried in the debris or his cover exposed. Flooding the structure with water has also been tried if it is lower than the ground so as to drown the terrorist. Blowing up the building with explosive charges is the last resort.

The problem is that all these methods have their own limitations. You can set fire to only that structure which has got something combustible in it. If it is a purely masonry or concrete structure, the method would fail. There is a serious systemic limitation of anti-tank weapons like the Carl Gustav Recoilless Rifle which most people do not even seem to understand. This is because of the 'pandemic of ignorance' we talked about. When it is fired at a short range encountered in anti-terrorist operations, the fuze of the warhead does not get enough flight to arm itself. This explains why many of them fail to explode at close ranges and simply go through the wall(s). Even at proper range, the warhead of a CGRL cannot distinguish between a brick wall, a layer of sandbags, and a concrete wall. The result is that you do not get detonation of the warhead where you need it.

(10.2) Addressing the Problem of Breaching Structures Scientifically

(10.2.1) The Difference between Anti-tank Munition and Anti-bunker Munition

Other nations of the world have applied R&D mind to it and have developed specific weapons for dealing with built-up structures that could be or could not be fortified. In other words they have understood that an anti-tank round cannot be properly used in anti-bunker role, so to say. In fact, they call such munitions, BDM or Bunker Defeat Munitions as against anti-tank munitions. For dealing with structures, as against armour, we require a warhead that, in the first place, is not moving very fast. This will ensure that it will not penetrate through several houses and inflict unwarranted collateral damage. Then it requires a special fuze so that it explodes after penetrating the wall and not merely on impact. Thirdly, it should be possible to fire it at small ranges that are likely to be encountered in anti-terrorist operations.

(10.2.2) The M141 Bunker Defeat Munition of the US

The M141 BDM addresses the specific need to destroy hardened targets, such as bunkers and other fixed enemy positions, and incapacitate the enemy personnel located within these targets. Optimised for the close fight in the environment of anti-terrorist operations, the M141 BDM is effective at distances ranging from 15 to 300 meters. The muzzle velocity is only 217 m/s. Maximum range is 500 m. Effective range is 300 m. The minimum arming distance is 15 m. It can be employed effectively against double-reinforced concrete walls up to 8 inches thick, triple brick structures, and standard earth and timber bunkers. The M141 BDM can incapacitate threat personnel when employed against cave complexes. Should the need arise, it can also perforate up to 20 millimeters of rolled homogenous steel, which provides a capability against lightly armoured and thin-skinned vehicles also. It is classified as a SMAW-D (shoulder launched multi-purpose assault weapon—disposable). The M141 BDM is a disposable, lightweight, self-contained, man-portable, shoulder-fired, high-explosive, multi-purpose weapon that contains all gunner features and controls necessary to aim, fire, and engage targets.

The weapon system consists of an unguided free-flight rocket, which is packed in an expendable, telescoping launcher that also serves as the storage container. It provides water resistant protection for the rocket during weapon storage, transportation, and use. All propulsion unit operation occurs within the launch tube. The M141 BDM is issued as a round of ammunition, requires no maintenance, and can only be fired from the gunner's right shoulder. The M141 BDM utilises the 83-mm high-explosive, dual-mode assault rocket. The dual-mode rocket consists of three major components: a high-explosive warhead containing 2.38 lbs of A3 composition, a dual-mode fuze, and a rocket motor. The rocket is ignited by electrical power from the launcher firing mechanism. This signal initiates an electric match in the igniter, which in turn ignites the rocket motor propellant. The rocket motor propellant is completely burned out before the rocket leaves the muzzle of the launcher, which protects the gunner from adverse propellant exhaust effects. As the rocket leaves the launcher muzzle, eight spring-loaded fins automatically deploy to aerodynamically stabilise the rocket in flight.

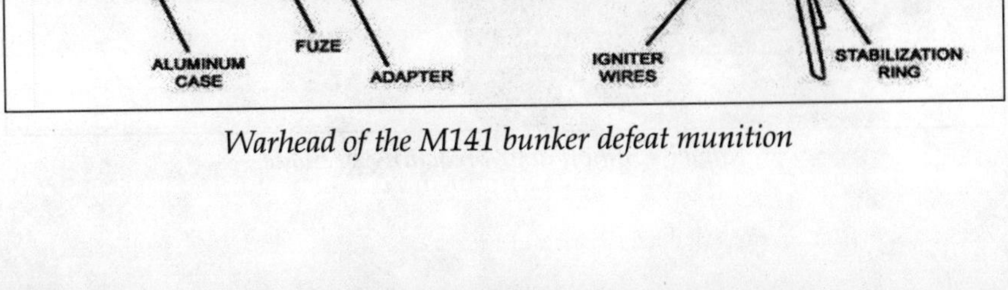

Warhead of the M141 bunker defeat munition

The dual-mode fuze is the key to beauty of the M141 BDM. The warhead function, in quick or delay mode, is automatically determined by the fuze when the rocket impacts a target. The M141 BDM is fired at hard or soft targets without any selection steps required by the gunner. This automatic feature assures that the most effective kill mechanism is employed. Warhead detonation is instantaneous when impacting a hard target, such as a brick or concrete wall, or an armoured vehicle. Impact with a softer target, such as a sandbagged bunker, results in a fuze time delay that permits the rocket to penetrate into the target before warhead detonation.

(10.2.3) Other Systems and Technologies

Many nations of the world have developed other systems also specially for urban anti-terrorist operations where collateral damage is sought to be minimised. Even a small country like Spain has made the Alcotan-100 system which has a configuration especially for the anti-bunker role. Israel's Rafael has made a special door-breaching rifle grenade called Simon. The purpose is self-evident from the name itself. Weighing only 640 g, the grenade slips on the muzzle of 5.56 mm rifles like the M4. It uses bullet trap technology to propel itself to 15-30 m. The 40 cm long nose that you see provides stand-off distance so that the blast of the 150 g explosive covers a large area of the door.

Rafael's Simon door breaching grenade

Other technologies include:

Follow Through Grenade (FTG) Technology: It has a 'Fused Follow Through Grenade' which provides incapacitation behind walls. It utilises a forward shaped charge to create a hole for a follow through grenade providing incapacitating fragments to defeat the target. Very clever, indeed.

Explosively Formed Projectile (EFP) Warheads: EFP warheads are designed to breach brick and reinforced concrete walls. In a 24"x24" reinforced concrete column, it can remove 65 per cent of the concrete.

Confined Space Propulsion Technology: It is based on the 'Davis Gun Counter-mass Principle'. This technology leads to a significant reduction in the noise and the extent of the back blast danger zone. It can therefore be safely fired from small or enclosed spaces. This is vital because the back blast of conventional weapons like the CGRL requires a clear space of 10-15 meters for the back blast or else serious injuries could result.

(10.3) The Quest of Infantry Support Weapons Especially Suited for Urban Combat

Modern infantrymen need more than rifles, machine-guns, and hand grenades to overwhelm their enemies. The combat threats facing infantrymen, that is, the targets to be engaged and destroyed may have changed during the past 90 years, but the basic support weapon issues have not. The key to the puzzle is providing effective firepower that can be used and moved by men on foot. Why it has been difficult? The reason is that traditionally, the armies have been thinking on a different axis. In the era of massive ground force deterrence in Europe (1945-1989), most war-fighting organisations such as the NATO and the Warsaw Pact planned for the worst. Thus, from the 1960s to the 1980s, US Army planners saw their infantry forces, riding aboard combat vehicles, fighting alongside 50 to 60-ton main battle tanks to counter similar forces attacking from the East. Soviet military thinkers viewed their problem in a similar fashion. Their infantry forces would accompany armoured units to engage NATO units.

While a grand clash between NATO and Warsaw Pact ground forces never materialised, actual fighting elsewhere, during the era of deterrence, revealed a very different scenario. From the Falklands to Grenada, from Angola to Panama, real wars of the post-1945 era have generally been fought with 'light' as opposed to 'heavy' ground forces. Although in the aftermath of the 'Revolution of 1989' commanders of NATO and Warsaw Pact armies still may be slow to change their doctrinal mindset, the challenges facing them have altered significantly. Infantrymen have been in need of several types of support weapons to supplement their personal weapons. These include:

- Heavy machine-guns (12.7 mm to 15.5 mm) for direct fire against enemy emplacements and lightly armoured vehicles.
- Heavy caliber sniper rifles (12.7 mm to 14.5 mm) for long-distance precision fire against enemy communications, electronic and other high-value equipment.
- Bursting munition systems for use against exposed or lightly protected enemy forces at ranges between that of the farthest reach of the hand grenade (30-40 meters) and the middle range of smaller caliber mortars (300-400 m).
- Shoulder-fired anti-armour/anti-bunker systems for use against heavier armoured vehicles and built-up structures.

Though its utility is not in doubt, the problem with the heavy machinegun is its weight. Urban combat demands considerable mobility by small units. The demand becomes greater when you are fighting irregular forces. The HMG becomes difficult to use in such situations. The sniper rifle has no such handicap and excellent sniper rifles are available. The problem of bursting munitions has been addressed in various ways. Under Barrel Grenade Launchers attached to rifles and firing 40 mm grenades have been made both by the former Soviet Union and the USA. From the soldier's perspective, however, the necessity of a special launcher has been the greatest shortcoming of 40 mm grenade cartridges. Only a man with the launcher could fire those grenades, and when his ammunition was expended his launcher was dead weight. The attachment has an adverse effect on the ergonomics of the rifle also. Hence, after several years in limbo, renewed emphasis has been given to rifle grenades.

The first of the new-generation rifle grenades were a family of 35 mm to 40 mm Bullet Trap Rifle Grenades (BTRG) developed by MECAR of Belgium. BTRGs allow riflemen to launch grenades with standard ball cartridges instead of requiring use of a special blank cartridge. Carrying blanks for the traditional rifle grenade is a pain. You have to keep them separately and load them one-by-one; and the rifle becomes useless as long as you are using it for launching the grenade. The bullet trap, an alloy plug in the launch tube, halts the projectile before it reaches the explosive payload. When NATO standardised the exterior diameter of rifle muzzle devices at 22 mm, grenade makers could develop families of grenades launched from the muzzle of any modern rifle. Success with MECAR's grenades led

Israeli Military Industries (IMI) to develop their own family of BTRG munitions, which on average are heavier than either MECAR's or Luchaire's. The greater weight allows IMI grenades to deliver larger payloads to the target, but the tradeoff is heavier recoil impulses to the rifle.

(10.4) What the Future Holds in Store?

Currently, the United States military is testing a system called the 'Urban Warfighter 2025' system. Future high-speed urban operations require a radically new land combat capability. While to many it will likely appear to be an evolutionary offspring of the existing Land Warrior concept, the 2025 Urban Warfighter System will be a revolutionary new man-machine fighting system with self-contained C4ISR, lethality, mobility, survivability, and sustainability far exceeding those of the current and near-term systems.

C4ISR: The core of the Urban Warfighter System will be a body suit with integral C4ISR (Command, Control, Communications, Computers, Intelligence, Surveillance and Reconnaissance), engagement, and active survivability systems. It will provide immediate access to a variety of non-line-of-sight munitions and contains mobility enhancements allowing operation in horizontal and vertical dimensions at speeds greatly exceeding today's maximums. Individual sensors will provide constant physiological readings both to the soldier wearing the suit and to appropriate monitoring entities. The Urban Warfighter System will provide the individual with a comprehensive situational awareness capability. This implies easy-to-use, integrated communications and navigational systems that can provide real-time updates to the soldier and to relevant friendly elements. The system will also be able to connect with and employ a wide variety of robotic systems, UAVs (Unmanned Aerial Vehicles), and other sensor systems to determine who or what is in the buildings or streets around him—day or night. He needs to be able to communicate and 'see' through walls. This capability will dramatically increase survivability and allow a very small number of soldiers essentially to 'occupy' a large building or even a city block.

Lethality: The Urban Warfighter will have an unprecedented level of lethality across a broad spectrum of capabilities. In addition to precision lethal fire provided by his next-generation individual assault weapon, he will be able to access digital, voice, or possibly even thought-activated fires from a variety of robotic systems operating semi-autonomously within the urban battle space. He will also have direct access to precision fire support from distant platforms when larger engagement opportunities present themselves. Additionally, the future Urban Warfighter needs to possess non-lethal weapons to assure crowd control and minimise collateral damage in certain situations.

Mobility: In addition to that provided by the advanced urban combat vehicle, the individual soldier will require enhanced individual mobility in both the horizontal and vertical dimensions. Some of this capability will be provided by UGVs (Unmanned Ground Vehicles) that will carry much of the load currently borne by the soldier. Small, individual aerial assault systems will also be used to provide soldiers with a dramatically improved ability to move vertically and horizontally. The 2025 Urban Warfighter System may include a Vertical Assault Urban Light Transporter (VAULT) that will give a soldier the ability to 'leap' to the top of three- or four-storey buildings and 'jump' long distances over rubble at speeds of up to 30 knots. At a minimum, the individual fighting load must be dramatically lightened by severely reducing the inherent weight of the load components and by reducing logistical needs. For instance, ammunition could be made of lighter materials and less of it may be needed because of reliance on precision fires from UGVs and UAVs.

Survivability: Because of the relatively small numbers of soldiers that will be available to the commander for urban operations, each one must be extremely survivable. By 2025, uniforms themselves will help guarantee survival. They will be light, non-bulky, and offer protection from bullets, CB (Chemical-Biological) agents, cold, and heat; they must also offer low signature and 'chameleon' camouflage. They will have immunisations and antidotes that will protect against the diseases often associated with urban squalor and a wide variety of CB agents. In the event that a soldier is wounded within the urban area, the system will have robotic aerial and ground evacuation vehicles that allow for immediate extraction with only minimal soldier assistance. Finally, fratricide will be made a thing of the past. The Urban Warfighter will be able to quickly and accurately identify friendly personnel, the enemy, and non-combatants. 'Smart' munitions may be developed to assist in this effort.

Sustainability: The Warfighter will need to carry lighter and more concentrated rations, enabling him to subsist for at least a week when operations preclude stopping for re-supply. Individual water purification will be a must because the potability of city water supplies will always be suspect. Batteries cannot continue to slow the warrior down in terms of both their weight and their efficacy. Lightweight, long-duration, high-energy power sources will be found. At the macro-level, an anticipated revolution in logistical distribution systems needs to occur. New systems designed to support forces engaged in urban operations will incorporate the technologies that UAVs and precision cargo airdrop systems have to offer.

The Human Component: Just as the technology of the 2025 Urban Warfighter System will be radically different from that of the Land Warrior, the human component of the system will look much different from its 1999 counterpart. Biotechnology holds numerous promises for making that happen. New biotechnical processes will allow accurate screening for an array of potential qualities—e.g. leadership, decision-making, memory, courage, and susceptibility to stress, disease, or even CB agents. While they cannot alone determine who will be the next generation of successful warriors, these biotechnical assessments would assist in identifying areas that individual training programmes should focus on. Finally, while training and simulations can be used to develop both inherent and learned skills, "performance enhancers" would also play a distinctive role when and where appropriate.

11

Urban Guerrillas and Nuclear, Biological or Chemical Weapons: A Reality Check

There is always a way, and it usually doesn't work.

(11.1) Can Guerrillas Make Nuclear Weapons?

(11.1.1) The Unfounded Fears of Nuclear Terror

The minimum acceptable level is perfection.

The USA changed the history of the world by launching a war upon Iraq, based on a completely false accusation of Iraq having made the so-called 'weapons of mass destruction'. Well, none were found in Iraq. But the media has to churn some sensational material for its survival. Hence, the fear of nuclear terror—what Saddam and Osama could not do, maybe Hafiz Saeed would be able to do. The specter of the terrorists unleashing nuclear, biological or chemical weapons upon hapless people is a nightmare that frightens all but the most informed people. Before we debunk the myths, we must explain how these myths have come to stay in the first place? The reason is that nuclear weapons, like dieting and dating, have been a field where non-scientist popular authors have written a great deal of over-simplified and non-sensical trash over the decades. Most of the material on nuclear weapons you would usually come across in encyclopedias or even nuclear physics text-books is very sketchy and of a fairly low standard. That makes the subject somewhat esoteric and leaves scope for all sorts of imaginations. Many people are genuinely led into believing that if the terrorists could somehow place their hands on a few kilograms of uranium from somewhere—stolen or purchased—they would have a nuclear bomb ready in no time! It is not so, and it cannot be done. Even high school kids might have some knowledge of the basics of nuclear fission and fusion—this does not impart them with any knowledge of nuclear weapons, however. Nuclear weapons are an entirely different thing—as Edward Teller had said during the Manhattan project, making a nuclear bomb is an engineering problem, not a physicist's problem! As far as nuclear weapons are concerned, a host of misconceptions abound among people from all walks of life as nuclear weapons entail things much more complicated than the basics of nuclear fission and fusion, and about which they do not know anything. It is this ignorance which leads to wild speculations by half-baked journalists and knee-jerk reactions from politicians who keep on imagining that terrorists would be able to make nukes in their backyards! Unless you learn this, you will remain vulnerable to popular myths. For detailed information on the subject, interested readers may refer to our treatise on weapon systems 'The Ultimate Book Of Weapons'.

(11.1.2) Technical Sophistication, Theoretical Knowledge and Engineering Skills required in making Atom Bombs

The theory of a nuclear chain reaction sounds very simple. In practice it is not so simple. If you wish to make a bomb, you must ensure that the sub-critical pieces do not fly apart as a result of the energy produced in the first instance and thus end the progression of the chain reaction prematurely—you have to keep the supercritical mass together for about a micro-second and it is not easy because the tremendous energy released tends to throw everything apart with tremendous force. Also you must ensure that before you want to explode, stray neutrons should not be creating any mischief. The majority of the technical difficulties of designing and manufacturing a fission weapon are based on the need to both reduce the time of assembly of a supercritical mass to a minimum and reduce the number of stray (pre-detonation) neutrons to a minimum. There are basically two techniques for assembling a supercritical mass. Broadly speaking, one brings two sub-critical masses together and the other compresses a sub-critical mass into a supercritical one. Compressing from all sides is called 'implosion'. The first is used with uranium and the second with plutonium. Since the amount of uranium in the world is very little, most of the bombs have been made with plutonium only. We will, therefore, discuss only the plutonium bomb.

How will they get Plutonium-239? For getting Pu-239 you have to depend on production reactors in which U-238 is bombarded with neutrons. They are purpose-built and not really efficient for electricity production because of the low burn-up restriction for production of weapons grade plutonium. Nations can afford this. How will the terrorists get it? Do not count on pilfering.

Then even you are given all the fissile material you need, it is unlikely that you will be able to make a system that could implode it, or compress it uniformly with such tremendous force that the plutonium metal would behave like a fluid and get compressed to nearly 2.5 times its normal density. This sudden but uniform compression is achieved by an extremely clever design called 'explosive lenses' invented by John von Neumann. Making explosive lenses is a challenge in both the chemistry of explosives and precision mechanical engineering. The lens system needs to be made to very precise tolerances. The composition and densities of the explosives have to be accurately controlled and extremely uniform. The pieces must fit together with an accuracy of less than 1 mm to prevent irregularities in the shock wave. Accurate alignment of the lens surfaces is even more important than a close fit. Not only that, for making the design work, you must understand the physics of the fissile material under implosion and have the capability of doing the intricate calculations and predict how a metal being compressed that way would behave.

Now even if the appropriate explosive lenses could be produced, they would have to be set off simultaneously to create a symmetrical implosion. This means the implosion must start at essentially the same time over a large part of the surface of the explosive material. In other words, the detonators must be very precise, time-wise—capable of giving a synchronicity of about + 10 nano seconds. This is accomplished by novel devices called exploding-bridgewire (EBW) detonator, and slapper detonator etc.

For a reliable weapon you require a strong source of neutrons which produces a burst of neutrons at the very appropriate time—neither a moment earlier nor a moment later—it should be activated by the arrival of the implosion shock wave at the center of the pit.

It is difficult to pull off all of this by a bunch of guerrillas and whatever scientists they may possibly muster in their support. If they are intelligent, they would not waste their time trying to make a nuke; the best shot for them would be to somehow get a readymade nuke. How they get it is their problem—there are many vulnerable places in the world such as some of the former Soviet republics. Nations that are worried about terrorists getting hold of nukes must keep their antennas extended in that direction.

(11.2) Low Efficiency or Crude Bombs: Can They be Made?

People generally refer to them as terrorist bombs. Technically, a more proper usage is to call them low efficiency or crude bombs. Let us see how far they are feasible. If someone could somehow get a sufficient quantity of HEU (Highly Enriched Uranium), making a decent gun-type nuclear weapon is not very difficult. But getting HEU is more or less impossible for non-state actors. Plutonium presents a similar problem. Reactor-grade plutonium appears to be a possibility though the bomb will face the problem of pre-detonation problem. As we saw, making explosive lenses for a spherical implosion system would be rather difficult for the technical people available with the terrorists. But developing linear and cylindrical implosion systems fast enough to produce a highly destructive terrorist bomb appears to be feasible. The flying plate line-charge approach is sufficiently simple, and testable—a low resource group could develop a workable system. Even plane or cylindrical explosive lenses are not out of the question, although they are probably more difficult.

Illicitly obtained plutonium would most probably be in the form of plutonium oxide, possibly as mixed oxide fuel. If the material were purified oxide powder, then it could be used directly in a bomb design. Fuel material, fabricated or not, would require chemical separation. People sophisticated enough to attempt chemical processing would probably go on to reduce the plutonium to metal which is much more desirable for bomb making. Since the density of plutonium oxide is much lower than plutonium metal, considerably more plutonium in this form would be needed. How much would depend on how highly compacted the plutonium oxide was at the moment of criticality. Although the crystal density of plutonium oxide is 11.4, the bulk density of unconsolidated oxide powder is only 3-4 (possibly even lower). To raise it to as high as 5-6 would require it to be compacted under substantial pressure. The pressures generated by shock waves are much less efficient at compacting porous materials, compared to static pressures. If it is assumed that a bomb builder could compress the powder to a density of five with moderate pressure, and that a density of 10 is achieved during implosion, then something like 50 kg of plutonium in the form of oxide would be required for a bomb without a reflector. Assuming a fairly good, readily available reflector (a few inches of iron or graphite), this could be reduced to 25-30 kg. Taking into account the explosive required, such a bomb (with a reflector) would be large—weighing about a ton. That's not a very attractive proposition for a terrorist—the bomb would have to be loaded onto a truck!

Using plutonium metal would greatly reduce fissile material requirements, and lead to a much smaller bomb. A design might use the cylindrical collapse of a hollow ring of plutonium metal (as the *delta* or *alpha* phase), or cylindrical compression of a solid *delta*-phase aluminium-plutonium alloy disk. No more than about 10 kg of plutonium would be required in such a design, if a reasonably good reflector were used. Such a weapon might weigh as little as 200 kg.

Given that the system will disassemble well before compression is complete, an accurate symmetrical implosion is not really a necessity. Simply imploding the fissile material at a high rate even if imperfectly (that is, without a true plane or cylindrical shock wave), could produce the necessary rapid compression. For this to work, the fissile material would have to be fairly close to critical at the beginning of the implosion since an imperfect implosion would create unacceptable distortions if the compression factor were very large. But manufacturing a device that is close to critical is extremely hazardous and itself requires substantial sophistication.

All said and done, the explosive power of a low efficiency or crude bomb could be anywhere between 100 tons to maybe a couple of kilotons. Now, the question is whether it is really worth the trouble. It depends on the target. A pusillanimous nation like India would perhaps buckle with the very name of a nuclear weapon, even if it is a 100 ton device. The very sight of a mushroom cloud would make the Indians shit in their pants—the actual destruction is immaterial. The media will go ballistic—today they have flattened Connaught Place, tomorrow they can take out the seat of government on Raiseena Hill—save India; save Indian business; save foreign investments in India; save our monuments; save our children, the future of this country, and so on!

(11.3) Radiological Dispersal Device or 'Dirty Bomb'

The bad news is they are capable of making a nuclear bomb.
The good news is they have to drop it from a camel.

A radiological dispersal device or a 'dirty bomb' has generated considerable paranoia in the minds of the people, courtesy once again the dumbos in the media. The essential idea is that someone could spread radioactive material in the air with the help of conventional explosives. This could have some value as a panic weapon particularly against the people of a country like India where people love to panic and where the TV channels have nothing else to do than to make a fool of those who are already fools. Technically the idea is very simple.

If someone could get suitable radioactive material in sufficient quantities, he can easily make a radiological dispersal device or a 'dirty bomb'. We emphasised the words 'suitable' and 'sufficient'. The radioactive material should have a reasonably high-level of radioactivity and the half life should not be too short.

From this angle only the following nine industrial isotopes qualify: Americium-241 (Am-241); Californium-252 (Cf-252); Cesium-137 (Cs-137); Cobalt-60 (Co-60); Iridium-192 (Ir-192); Plutonium-238 (Pu-238); Polonium-210 (Po-210); Radium-226 (Ra-226); and Strontium-90 (Sr-90). They are legitimately available for medical teletherapy; industrial radiography; radiothermal generators; and well-logging devices. Out of these nine also, only three are gamma ray emitters: Cs-137, Co-60, and Ir-192. They are dangerous for the targets but equally dangerous for the terrorists also because handling them would require all the protective gear. Sr-90 is a beta emitter and is dangerous and would be capable of causing harm even when not ingested. The remaining are alpha emitters and since their penetration is very poor, they will have to be ingested or inhaled to cause harm. Am-241 can, however, be mixed with beryllium to become a neutron emitter and then it is dangerous.

The isotope should lend itself to easy dispersal in the form of a very fine dust; they have to be pulverised to micron-size particles and mixed with something that could increase the chances of inhalation. Cobalt, iridium, and polonium generally exist as solid metals and would not be readily dispersible. Several of the others, including americium, californium, and plutonium, are typically oxides that could exist as a powder. Cesium is typically found as cesium chloride, which is also a powder and is quite soluble in water. Radium and strontium are used in various forms; strontium fluoride in certain sealed sources is sintered such that it is essentially insoluble and non-dispersible. Even considering the forms in current sources, the specific physical and chemical characteristics of radioactive materials that could be in an RDD is uncertain because the original material could be chemically or physically altered (weaponised) to enhance dispersal. If the dispersal method is explosion via a dirty bomb, that would also likely physically and chemically alter the materials to produce a mixture that could include oxides as well as nitrates (from the explosives) over a range of particle sizes.

Then it should be in sufficient quantities for dispersal over a fairly large area to make sense as a weapon—now that's a real problem. Remember that in a built-up area the dispersal would be poor and in an open area one requires suitable weather conditions. When all these requirements are taken together, making a RDD does not appear to be that easy though quite possible. Pilfering from the radioactive sources used in radiotherapy and in industry is not going to help much, the quantities involved being rather small; the best they can do is to go for radioactive waste from commercial nuclear reactors. But their disposal is carefully controlled. It may be kept in mind that even if a 'dirty bomb' does not cause many casualties, the cost of de-contaminating the buildings exposed may be very high, or you may have to demolish them—you will also have to monitor a large number of people afterwards for possible exposure. Since the media people do not understand such things, they spread all sorts of misconceptions. In dumb nations like India, the very mention of the word radioactive in some attack, even if the material is in very small quantities, would provide enough spice for the third-rate TV channel to spread large-scale panic—therein lies its strength.

A Chechen leader had threatened to turn Moscow into an 'eternal desert' via radioactive waste. To demonstrate their potential for doing so, the Chechens directed a Russian news agency to a small amount of cesium-137 (a highly radioactive material used for industrial and medical purposes) in a shielded container that the news agency found in a Moscow park. According to a subsequent assessment by the US Department of Defence, at least the park would have been contaminated by low level radiation if that small amount of cesium-137 had been dispersed in a bomb blast.

(11.4) Feasibility of Chemical Warfare by Terrorists

(11.4.1) The Basic Chemical Warfare Agents

The Americans tell a great deal of lies about chemical weapons. Poor Saddam Hussein was killed in the name of chemical weapons that were never found. I will just bust the myth of chemical weapons but before that you must know what they are. Depending on how they act, chemical agents are classified into several types. Non-persistent agents lose their effectiveness within minutes to hours. Persistent agents may remain in the environment for even a week.

The Pulmonary Agents: Pulmonary agents include Chlorine, Phosgene, Diphosgene and Chloropicrin—old stuff. All of them are gases and present inhalation hazard. Effect is immediate. They act by damaging and flooding the respiratory system. The result is choking and suffocation. They are non-persistent agents. Gas masks will offer a fairly good degree of protection against them.

The Vesicants (Blister Agents): They are usually poorly volatile liquids and thus are persistent agents—again old stuff. They include

Mustard Gas (a liquid in pure form at room temperature, in spite of its name—when they used it in the First World War they made an aerosol of it with other chemicals for easy dispersal), Lewisite, and Phosgene Oxime etc. They penetrate ordinary clothing and cause blisters on the skin which heal with difficulty and may get infected too. The effect is, of course, more severe on eyes and lungs—eyes develop conjunctivitis and blindness may result; lungs develop edema. They act rather slowly, taking a couple of hours to a day or more. If more than 50 per cent of the body surface is exposed to them, fatality may result. Gas masks are of little help against them but effective decontaminating agents are there.

The Blood Agents: Usually they are Cyanides or Cyanogens—who has not heard of them? Chemically very simple compounds yet extremely toxic, they act very quickly by preventing the transfer of oxygen from blood to the body tissues, thereby disrupting the functioning of vital organs and result in death in a matter of minutes—the action is a sort of internal chemical asphyxiation. In gaseous form hydrogen cyanide is a classic example—it smells like bitter almonds, in case you want to recognise it before it is too late. Antidotes are available these days.

The Nerve Agents: They are the new stuff. Nerve agents are hundreds of thousands of times more toxic than pulmonary agents, vesicants or blood agents. They are neurotoxins. Several of them have been made. Some are non-persistent posing inhalation hazard; some are persistent. The action time varies from seconds to hours if the entry is through skin. Initial symptoms include runny nose, constriction of pupils, excessive production of tears, drooling, and tightness in chest. Death eventually results by asphyxiation as control is lost over respiratory muscles. Antidotes are available. There are two main classes of nerve agents, namely, the G-series and the V-series. The Western nations made, tested, and stockpiled a whole lot of them for decades before they claimed to have become holier-than-thou.

The G-Series Nerve Agents: Famous G-series agents include Tabun, Sarin, Isoman, and Cyclosarin. Agents of the G-series were discovered before those of the V-series. Among them, GA (Tabun) was the first to be synthesised in 1936, followed by GB (Sarin), GD (Soman) and GF (Cyclosarin). Tabun was discovered accidentally by Dr Gerhard Schrader in Germany while he was working towards developing an improved insecticide. A drop of a chemical got spilled accidentally on a bench and everybody in the lab suffered from dizziness and shortness of breath for three weeks! It was later identified and named Tabun. Though production on a military scale was made during the War, the

Germans refrained from using it in War apparently fearing that the Allies might also have made it and could use it in retaliation against them. That was poor intelligence, as the Allies had not been able to make it. They learnt of it only after Germany was over-run towards the end of the War. You can easily imagine the course of the War as well as human history had the Nazis used it successfully! Thus in a way, poor intelligence cost them the War! Sarin caught the attention of the general public in 1995 when the Aum Shinrikyo group in Japan released some quantity of this in the Tokyo subway system.

The V-Series Agents: Agents of the V-series were discovered a little later. There are four of them, namely, VX, VE, VG, and VM. All of them are persistent agents, posing a greater skin hazard and can also be used as area-denial weapons.

(11.4.2) Practical Problems in Terrorists' use of Chemical Agents

There are no weapons of mass destruction in Iraq or Iran; Chuck Norris lives in Oklahoma.

Making good chemical warfare agents like the Nerve Gas in small laboratories is difficult. It does not appear possible that terrorists would be able to make the advanced chemical agents. The simpler ones can be made, however. More than their actual killing potential, it is the psychological impact of having used a 'chemical' which will be more important. In countries like India where stupid TV channels vie with each other in sensationalising things, the use of even rat poison by some fool would be described as a terrorist chemical warfare.

Contrary to popular notions, use of chemical agents in such a manner as to cause a large number of casualties is not that easy. Effective dissemination is a major problem and then you require considerable quantities of the agent for large areas. It is not that a little quantity produced in a college lab or one's backyard will be enough for two blocks. Life is not so simple. Remember, there is a great deal of difference in disseminating even simple compounds like cyanides in air or water and someone biting a cyanide capsule! A little quantity of chemical agents available with the terrorists may serve the purpose of a small attack only—that will have more of propaganda than military value. Dissemination in air is always dependent on prevailing atmospheric conditions. If you are close to the target then you have to be very cautious and study the weather very carefully lest you expose yourself too! If you are not efficient in disseminating then you will be wasting a great deal of the agent. The technique to be adopted also depends on the properties of the agent. The military technique is to use artillery shells or bombs with sub-munitions that cover a larger area per shell than a single-payload shell. One single-payload 155 mm artillery shell exploding in still air, on a sunny day, and with light wind is good only for a radius of 24 feet! The other is aerodynamic dissemination. Aerodynamic dissemination is the non-explosive delivery of a chemical weapon agent from an aircraft, allowing aerodynamic stress to disseminate the agent. If a line of less than four miles is to be exposed by aerodynamic dissemination, the aircraft will have to spray about four tons of the chemical for ensuring 50 per cent fatalities in a depth of a little over half a mile. Making chemical shells or bombs is difficult for terrorists? That's why some terrorists keep on toying with the idea of using a crop-duster plane to disperse it—but the problem is from where will they get tons of chemicals?

(11.5) How about Biological Warfare by Guerrillas?

Scientists in Washington have recently conceded that, if there were a biological war, all that would remain are cockroaches and Chuck Norris.

(11.5.1) Now that is quite Feasible

Making and using biological agents for warfare is not as easy as it is made out to be in popular writings and in the media. Still, it is infinitely easier and cheaper than making a nuclear bomb and in the long run, biological agents could do nearly as much damage to the population, resources and morale of the target as the nukes! One who has not fully appreciated the horror potential of biological warfare is a fool. Watch out for biological terror—this is the thing of the future for the intelligent terrorist! In the triad of nuclear, biological and chemical weapons, biological weapons come closest to becoming a reality in the hands of terrorists. Remember the paranoia that was caused in the USA by anthrax? How the Americans were shit scared? Imagine something like that in a country like India. The moment a suspicious envelope lands in a government office, these guys would find yet another excuse for absenting from the offices for weeks!

(11.5.2) The Problem of Weaponising Biological Agents

The intrinsic features of biological agents which would make them suitable for use as weapons include: infectivity; virulence; toxicity; pathogenicity; incubation period; transmissibility; lethality; and stability. There are about 25 of them but the important ones are anthrax,

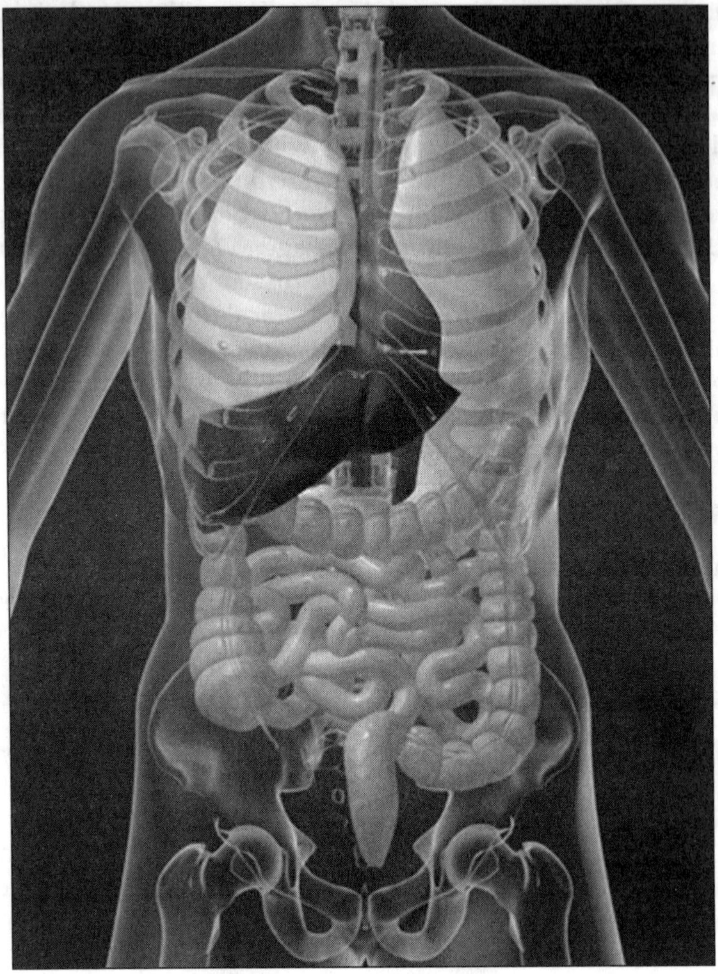

Bio-terrorism is indeed feasible

Ebola hemorrhagic fever, Marburg hemorrhagic fever, Congo-Crimean hemorrhagic fever, plague, botulinum toxins, Clostridium Perfringens toxins, Ricin, Saxitoxin, Tricothecene Mycotoxins, smallpox, Rift Valley fever, Tularemia, Brucellosis, and Staphylococcal Enterotoxin B.

Let us first understand the technical issues and problems involved in 'Weaponising' biological agents. What would be the objectives of a terrorist? The first objective is to get the right strain of the organism. Why? The reason is that the modern man has immunity against a large number of diseases and medicines are easily available for many diseases. A terrorist would not be helped by an organism that caused only diarrhea, so to say. Hence, first he will have to develop or isolate the right strain of the organism for which the majority of the target people would not have immunity or which is a more virulent strain of some existing pathogen. Then it should be such that it should be difficult to diagnose the disease quickly from the symptoms. Finally, even if diagnosed, the disease should be such that medicines are not easily available for it. For this, he may have to genetically modify some strains. Then for the purpose of warfare, one must have them in sufficient amount. Then they need to be stabilised. For example, if they lend themselves to spore formation, they could be made into spores for storage. They should also survive the environmental stresses when they are released. For example, one may have to add nutrients to improve chances of survival in aerosols. The spores must be of the right size (1-3 microns) for proper dissemination. Finally you need a dependable release or delivery mechanism. One can't possibly use a crop-duster aircraft in a military situation and it should be kept in mind that crude methods like contaminating water supplies are suited only for small terrorist attacks. Nations will be able to deal with them quickly.

The specific technologies used in realising these capabilities include (1) cell culture or fermentation; (2) organism selection; (3) encapsulation and coating with straight or cross-linked biopolymers; (4) genetic engineering; (5) active or passive immunization or treatment with biological response modifiers; (6) monoclonal antibody production; (7) genome data bases, polymerase chain reaction equipment, DNA sequencers, and the rapid production of gene probes; and (8) the capability of linking gene probes and monoclonal antibodies on addressable sites in a reproducible manner. They are all sophisticated technologies, though not secret. Because they are not military secrets like nuclear technology, that's why it is easier for the terrorists to make biological weapons in comparison to making nukes

Interestingly, the biological technology industry of this field is more information intensive than capital intensive. Information on technologies involved in this field is widely available in published literature. These technologies are dual use, with applications in the pharmaceutical, food, cosmetic, and pesticide industries. While laboratory-scale capability for production of biological agents is sufficient for achieving most terrorist purposes, large-scale production for military purposes can be achieved easily in dual-use facilities. All of the equipment needed for large-scale production of offensive biological agents is dual use and available legally in the international market. Even if somebody cannot afford a full-scale vaccine plant, the purpose could still be served by a less elaborate fermentation plant costing much less. You may also note that for terrorists' purposes or even for warfare, one does not have to worry so much about purity of the strain being developed as he has to when he is producing a vaccine! And finally, one need not observe the rules of biosafety so rigorously when he is producing agents for weapons.

(11.5.3) Possible Ways in which Terrorists Could go about Making Biological Weapons

Obtaining from natural sources and isolating: With the exception of the smallpox virus—an eradicated disease agent that is currently stored in only two official repositories in the United States and Russia—the roughly twenty-five infectious micro-organisms considered suitable for bio-terrorism could be obtained from natural sources, such as infected animals, patients, or even contaminated soil (in the case of anthrax spores). Nevertheless, because natural pathogens vary widely

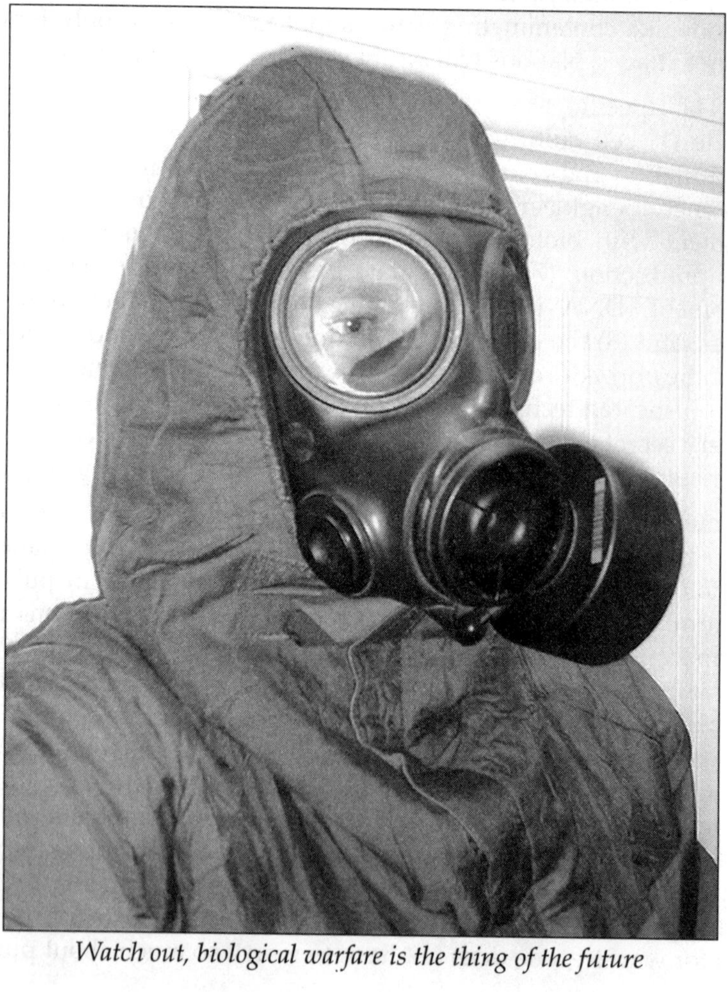

Watch out, biological warfare is the thing of the future

in virulence (that is, the degree to which a micro-organism can cause disease), many strains isolated from nature may have low virulence. Micro-biologists have catalogued more than seventy different strains of Bacillus anthracis, only a minority of which are highly virulent—the Ames and Vollum strains of anthrax, for example, are known to be highly virulent. Thus, a terrorist would almost certainly have to isolate many different strains before finding one that was sufficiently potent to serve as a weapon.

Stealing and the issue of biosecurity: Stealing biological agents is possible. Given the technical hurdles associated with obtaining virulent micro-organisms from nature, it would probably be easier for terrorists to steal well-characterised strains from a research laboratory. Bio-terrorists might also seek to purchase known pathogenic strains from a national culture collection or a commercial supplier under false pretences by claiming to be engaged in legitimate bio-medical research. That's what leads us to the concept of 'bio-security'.

Enhanced bio-security is, however, not a panacea for the problem of bio-terrorism. Since a skilled microbiologist could isolate pathogens and toxins from natural sources, the goal of bio-security measures is to make terrorists' acquisition of deadly agents more difficult, albeit not impossible; by ensuring that legitimate research activities and facilities remain off-limits. That leaves the terrorists with two options. The first is to infiltrate the research facilities. The second is to obtain dangerous pathogens from natural sources, a route that demands greater technical skill and is considerably less reliable.

Bio-security cannot be as strict as the security adopted for nuclear materials. Pathogens have certain characteristics which make them qualitatively different from nuclear materials. The characteristics of pathogens that limit the applicability of the nuclear safeguards model include the following: they occur naturally; they are dual-use; they are highly diverse; they can reproduce; they are not detectable at a distance; they are present in many types of facilities; they can be present at multiple locations within a facility; and they can be derived from benign microbes or even made 'from scratch'. The fact that microbial pathogens exist naturally in the environment and that small samples can be grown into large quantities means that biological materials cannot be controlled as effectively, or in the same manner, as fissile materials. Since no technology or procedure can ensure the quantitative accounting of pathogens, applying controls based on nuclear safeguards to biological labouratories would create a false sense of security while seriously impeding legitimate research. In any case, all this would fail if they decide to make their own agents.

12

Other Myths Associated with Terrorists

Never attribute to malice that can be ascribed to sheer stupidity.

(12.1) Can the Terrorists Blow Up Dams?

Against stupidity, the gods themselves struggle in vain.

This is one of the popular fantasies of the media and a nightmare of the intelligence agencies who are as dumb as the media people, if not dumber! Frightening though it may be, the specter of the terrorists blowing up huge dams and the terrible deluge resulting from it inundating hundreds of thousands of people is a fantasy in which only those people indulge who have neither historical nor technical knowledge.

Dams are enormously big and tremendously strong structures. Though there are several types of dams, we will limit ourselves to concrete gravity dams for obvious reasons. Historically, dams have been targeted using explosives only during the World War II. The Royal Air Force had attacked Mohne, Eder, Sorpe, Lister, Ennepe, and Diemel dams of Germany. And how they did it? The problem was solved by the brilliant scientist Barnes Wallis. He calculated that if the dams were to be attacked in a straightforward manner using high explosives (that's the only way a team of saboteurs could do it at that time, and it is still the only way in which terrorists can even think of doing it in this age also) it would require an impractically high (about 30,000 lbs!) amount of explosives. The amount was so high that it was not even to be considered. It needs no imagination that when the RAF had found it absurd, the ISI would not be fool enough to even think of it. Wallis, however, proved that if the dams were desired to be breached by a smaller amount of explosive, the explosive would require to be emplaced in a very special way—if you do not emplace the explosive in that special way, it would not be able to breach the wall. For this purpose he developed what is known as the Upkeep bouncing bomb. This was a great invention. The Upkeep was a perfectly cylindrical bomb. It was slung beneath a Lancaster bomber outside its bomb bay and given a back spin of about 500 rpm. The bombers had to fly as low as 60 feet so that the released bomb would strike the surface of the water at about 7 degrees. The spinning Upkeep bounced on the surface of the water till it struck the dam wall and then sank along the surface of the wall when it detonated at a predetermined depth at which the tamping by the water above it would maximise the explosive effect on the wall. With all these brilliant innovations, the Upkeep was still a monstrosity at 9,250 lbs! It must be kept in mind that this specially designed weapon also required great care in placement and flying the heavy bomber aircraft at just 60 feet which resulted in many Lancasters being shot out of the sky. Can we reasonably expect that the ISI would design the Upkeep bomb for the terrorists? Even if they do, how can the terrorists carry a nearly 10,000 lbs heavy monstrosity and where and how would they transport and conceal it in the hinterland. The ISI avoids giving even 81 mm mortars to the terrorists for similar reasons. Who can even

Don't worry, terrorists carrying explosives in rucksacks would not be able to do anything to gigantic structures like dams!

think that they would give them such huge bombs? As we saw, even if they give them 10,000 lbs of explosives instead of the bomb, and even if the terrorists are able to beat all the security measures at our dams, merely planting the explosive would not result in a breach. Perhaps people should learn from history. Even those Upkeep bombs which had exploded just a few feet away from the dam walls but not exactly in the manner designed, had failed to breach the dams.

(12.2) The Myth of the Naval Commando Training of the Terrorists

In the wake of the 26/11 Bombay attack, popular fantasies and cheap sensationalism ran amok. An article in *India Today* claimed: "The terrorists are given one year to one-and-a-half year's training in three phases: swimming lessons; handling large boats; laying mines on coasts and planting explosives under bridges and ships. In the last phase, they are taught sea navigation—using GPS, reading the wind, waves, tides and currents, rescue operations, surveillance and concealing explosives". Sounds impressive to the uninitiated, isn't it? But there are obvious loopholes in it. It appears as if swimming is an esoteric art and before the introduction of this course by the Lashkar-e-Taiyyibah/ ISI/Pak Navy for the terrorists, they had no idea of swimming at all! Looks like young able-bodied terrorists in a country like Pakistan which has 37 rivers and may be thousands of ponds, have never had an opportunity to learn swimming on their own till they joined the ranks of terrorists? Quite a novel find by the Lashkar-e-Taiyyibah/ ISI/Pak Navy!

Then the terrorists are said to have been trained in the art of seamanship—the whole enchilada! If a training of such a little period is enough to make them not only complete seamen but also expert saboteurs, we could rather emulate it. Why do we waste so much money and time on maintaining the huge training establishments of our armed forces? They could be trained at infinitely lower costs! The journo would have you believe that the Lashkar-e-Taiyyibah/ISI/Pak Navy have discovered some secret training courses which nobody else in the world had been able to find out. Well, now that the cat is out of the bag, we might learn from them! Garmin GPS costing as low as Rs 15,000 are used by thousands of fishermen even in India. What is so special about using a GPS?

We are told that the terrorists are taught to operate large boats. Once again alert readers should be able to notice that it amounts to speaking in vague and imprecise terms. What is a large boat and how does it differ from a small boat? Who has defined a large boat? Or for that matter, what is a small boat? Knowledgeable people must speak at least in terms of displacement of vessels, materials used in construction and the power of the engines fitted therein if not the electronics of the navigational aids deployed. As far as crossing the sea to reach India from Pakistan is concerned, this is no big deal. We may remind the media that in the world famous Kon-Tiki expedition Thor Heyerdahl had been able to purposefully cross 4300 miles of the Pacific Ocean in nothing but a raft (a mere raft and not a boat) made of balsa wood, reeds and other native materials without any engine or navigational aid at all merely to prove the point that it is possible to do so and that's how the ancients must have done it! If we accept that our waters are so insecure and the coasts so porous that anyone can come in crafts of various sizes with almost complete impunity, such vulnerability should have been always there. How is it that someone hostile to us woke up to the possibility of exploiting this vulnerability only now?

Whoever speaks of the possibility of the terrorists laying mines on coasts, obviously does not know a word about naval mines. Naval mines are large and heavy affairs. They come in a great variety of shapes and sizes. But because they were designed to attack ships with displacement in the range of say 2400 tons and much above, factory-made naval mines used by navies of the world typically range from 440 lbs to 3000 lbs! Almost all of them require to be laid by warships if not special minelayer ships, submarines or aircrafts—the process of laying mines takes time too. It is difficult to both carry and conceal such mines in boats of the type used by fishermen and even more difficult to deploy them from such crafts. Had it been possible, navies of the world would not have been wasting their time and resources on specialised ships, submarines and aircrafts for that purpose! Further, for conventional HE naval mines to be effective, whether they are floating, moored, magnetic or whatever, they have to be deployed in very large numbers. Mines are not miracle weapons or weapons like heat-seeking missiles that latch on to their targets. Mines simply lie in wait for a target to come near them. Precisely for this reason they are more effective in a defensive role. One mines a certain stretch to render it difficult for enemy ships to negotiate it—that's all. How are the terrorists going to get mines in such 'militarily' large numbers? Are they going to bring them in their so-called 'large boats'? Is it practical? It is inconceivable that the terrorists would be able to infiltrate our coastal zones with such complete impunity in the sense of taking their time and hauling their equipment that that would not only be able to lay a large number of mines which would be able to inflict considerable damage on our naval ships or merchant ships—after all they would not be interested in targeting boats of fishermen! That leaves limpet mines which frogmen attach to the hull of the ships. To be afraid of this possibility would amount to saying that the ships of our navy lying in our harbours are so helpless that some terrorists would be able to take out our warships by the few mines which in some untold or unimaginable way the terrorists would be able to bring in. This stuff is suitable for cheap novels sold from railway book stalls! One who knows even a bit about naval warfare knows that had it been possible to inflict any significant damage on the ships of an enemy by such commando action, navies of the world would not have been spending trillions of dollars on maintaining warships and armaments of diverse types. Naval ships have mechanisms to deal with such threat. A great deal of research has been done into the so-called anti-frogman techniques and scores of technologies are available, ranging from diver-detecting active sonar system; remotely operated underwater vehicle (ROV); sound weapons; and trained dolphins to counter-offensive frogmen. If all that the terrorists plan to do is to attack private crafts in the manner of frogmen, what exactly would they achieve by this wasteful exercise? Limpet mines can be used profitably once in a special operation. One cannot use them repeatedly for the target would be alert. One must learn to think in terms of feasibility and profitability of a terrorist operation. No terrorist would undertake an operation simply because it is feasible. The operation must be cost-effective and it should be profitable to the overall objectives of the terrorists. Sinking a few private crafts at great effort and expenditure would not help them in any way.

(12.3) The Hoax of the Aircraft 'Toilet' Bomber

The western media has been full of utterly irresponsible and speculative reporting about two explosives, namely, TATP and HMTD following the July 2005 bombings in London. The impression sought to be generated was that the terrorists have hit upon a secret formula using which they can make deadly liquid explosives from everyday chemicals. Not only that those everyday chemicals could be carried easily on board aircrafts because they are not explosives to start with, the actual explosive would be made on board by simply mixing them there in the toilet of the aircraft and then the aircraft would be blown up. Such was the paranoia that the morons had banned all sorts of liquids on flights for quite some time and their utterly imbecile followers back home, having no knowledge or intellect of their own, had done the same. Mothers were made to taste baby food in front of airport security guards to prove that it contained no liquid explosives. Liquids and gels were banned from flights. Travellers repacked their luggage in airports, stowing all but the most necessary items in the hold.

TATP is triacetone triperoxide; HMTD is hexamethylene triperoxide diamine. In the first place, we must state that liquid explosive is actually a misnomer given by the media. The explosives are not liquids. The ingredients used to make them are liquids. Both TATP and HMTD appear as white crystalline substances, and may be indistinguishable from one another without laboratory analysis. TATP is formulated from acetone, hydrogen peroxide, and a strong acid. It is a primary explosive. HMTD is formulated from hydrogen peroxide, a weak acid (such as citric acid), and hexamine solid fuel tablets. HMTD is also a primary explosive. It is slightly more stable than TATP. The misconceptions took hold quickly because people did not care to verify facts. They thought that since acetone is a common solvent found in hardware stores, hydrogen peroxide is also easily available, and the acid used in car batteries could serve the purpose of the strong acid, there was nothing easier than making TATP. So was the case with HMTD. They thought that since hexamine fuel tablets, commonly used to fuel camp stoves, could be found in many outdoor recreation stores and thus making HMTD was also child's play.

An improvised method of preparation of TATP is an impractical proposition for the simple reason that the proper procedure cannot be resorted to under the field conditions, that is, on board an aircraft! Further, it would result in a product that would, in all probability, explode right there in the preparation and handling process. TATP is an explosive alright in the sense that it is a highly unstable compound, but it does not produce heat when it decomposes explosively. TATP actually undergoes an entropic explosion, each molecule of TATP collapsing to produce three molecules of acetone and one of ozone—very little heat is produced when it explosively decomposes. Setting it alight with the batteries of mobile phones, iPods, etc. (as the western security agencies suspected) is very much possible, given the extreme sensitivity of TATP but it is utterly puerile to even suggest that it could burn through the skin of a plane and bring it down. The heat produced is simply not enough for the job! In all likelihood the bomber would injure himself and nothing else. Similarly, a hasty preparation of HMTD in the field or on board an aircraft would also not be practical.

(12.4) The Myth of the LPG Cylinder Bombs

This is a dream which fools all over the world have been chasing with regularity and, of course, without any success. Anyone who thinks that he could create a fuel-air explosive (FAE) by taping a stick of dynamite to the LPG cylinder is sadly mistaken. The onslaught of ignorance is universal; be it the matter of TATP or the LPG cylinder bomb, the ignoramuses are too eager to believe that the terrorists have stumbled upon a cheap, simple and yet absolutely devastating formula. How people love to delude themselves! For the LPG cylinder to be converted into a bomb all the gas must burn simultaneously. This would require that all of the gas be released in one go, allowed to mix with the proper amount of oxygen, and then the mixture ignited simultaneously throughout its volume. The entire process must take place very rapidly as against accidents which take quite some time to develop. Is it possible to achieve this? For all practical purposes and within the limitations of amateur bombers, no! For a LPG cylinder bomb you cannot have the luxury of a mixture that has already been prepared and kept ready for ignition as it happens with the LPG cylinder in the kitchen that has been leaking all night. For a bomb you require the mixture to be produced instantaneously on command. And that is not possible. The mythical LPG cylinder bomb would therefore fail to explode. Yes, the gas will burn and there will be a lot of fire—quite impressive to watch but no big boom and things blown to smithereens. But there will not be any explosion of the type you get with a FAE bomb. This is precisely what happened at the Glasgow airport in 2007. All that the bomber succeeded in was burning himself to death.

Precisely for the reasons discussed above, and against what they have been showing you in films, even if somebody shoots through LPG/Propane cylinders, LPG tankers, or gasoline tankers, they would not explode. A bullet will result in only a small leakage in the first place. Secondly, the bullet is so small that the total amount of heat carried by it is very low. Thirdly, the bullet is moving at a very high speed. Hence, if it passes through the tanker's skin, it will be in contact with the gas for a very short time. In that short time of contact, it can deposit only a small fraction of the little heat it is carrying. Thus, a bullet or several bullets also will not be able to heat up the great volume of gas substantially. If the bullet is an incendiary or a tracer which gets lodged with its tracer composition still burning then the chances of a fire are increased. But that too only for the fuel which is leaking. You see, oxygen is available only to the gas which is leaking from the holes created and not to the entire tank! A small tanker also carries about 12,000 liters of gas! Even if the bullet gets lodged, there is simply not enough heat in it. If a tank is full, there is simply no oxygen in it. Even if is not full, the amount of oxygen available is not enough for the fuel present. You cannot fire so many bullets into the tank that it practically gives way. Thus, it is only the leaking gas which could burn if the incendiaries or tracers have deposited enough heat at the leakage point. An explosion can take place only if there is fire at several holes simultaneously and the fire from the punctured holes is allowed to be there for such a long time that a BLEVE (Boiling Liquid Expanding Vapour Explosion) can take place.

Had it been so easy to make gas tanks explode by shooting and considering that there are hundreds of thousands of tankers that ply across the length and breadth of any country absolutely unprotected, the terrorists would have been utter fools to not shoot them from hundreds of yards away and watch the flames leaping? And yet those who close their eyes to reason think that this is indeed possible.

13

Dealing with a Hostage Crisis

Remember that the enemy is just as frightened as you are, and probably more so. They are not supermen.

(13.1) How Nations must Respond when Hostages are Taken?

(13.1.1) Why a Hard-line must be Maintained?

Urban guerrillas and terrorists also like to capture large numbers of hostages at once as and when they seize an embassy, hijack an airplane, or take possession of a public building like a school, hospital, or maternity home. Such 'spectaculars' usually generates considerable publicity, provides a forum for making the group's demands widely known, offers a chance to free jailed fellow travellers, and may leverage important concessions from the government. The seizure of the Japanese ambassador's residence in Lima by the Tupac Amaru Revolutionary Movement (MRTA) in December of 1996 exemplifies this method. The group initially captured 500 people during a party at the ambassador's residence, including eight US officials, numerous foreign ambassadors, six Peruvian supreme court judges, two government ministers, several high-ranking members of the Peruvian police and military, as well as important members of the Peruvian and international business communities. It is a different thing that, sans the resolve to kill many people and the preparedness for that, such large hostage taking is risky since the group's demands are seldom met. Often the hostage-takers come away with little but their skin, and sometimes not even that as the MTRA found out. The execution of the operation may not have been professionally sound but still, the incident generated a great deal of news.

During the last thirty years international hostage taking has transformed itself from an era of hijackings in the early 1970s, to the rise of the so-called Islamic extremism in the 1980s with embassy sieges, to the 1990s with the advent of narco-terrorism. Today, and during the recent war in Iraq, terrorist organisations are using hostage taking as the coercive weapon of choice, trying to level the playing-field against superior forces. Terrorists are kidnapping civilian workers and soldiers alike, beheading them for the world to see on television. In terms of Game Theory, it is a game of chicken against an opponent that parks his vehicle in the middle of the road and walks away. Only when the hostage taker's location is known, can we apply the waiting game. Otherwise, it is a race against time to try to find the hostages before they are executed. To counter this tactic, counterterrorist forces must rely heavily on a robust intelligence network that can provide actionable intelligence, pin pointing the exact location of the hostage takers, and destroy them immediately. Simultaneously, diplomatic and informational levels of national power should focus on a theme that seems to devalue the hostage, preventing the 'theater of terror' effect from rising, while at the same time allowing the military arm to pursue these terrorists aggressively. Giving in to terrorist demands encourages more acts of terror, strengthens the terrorist's agenda, and reinforces that their strategy works.

Therefore, regardless of the difficulties involved in trying to maintain a hard-line against terrorists, it is better than to give in to their demands. The dominant strategy for any country with a competent rescue force must be to conduct the rescue attempt, whether the terrorists decide to kill the hostages or not. This strategy reinforces the 'no negotiations' policy of most countries towards terrorists. The terrorists will thus have to make a decision-based on this knowledge. The Nash Arbitration Method tells us that there is a better solution to the Hostage Dilemma than the Status Quo Point. To achieve this, immediate communications must be established between the terrorists and the country's government where the crisis is taking place, in order to prevent a catastrophe. It is up to the targeted country to decide whether to meet the demands of the terrorists, or to cheat the system by deceiving the terrorists and conducting an assault.

(13.1.2) *Effective Crisis Management*

The more stupid the leader is, the more important missions he is ordered to carry out.

It is critical to understand how the policy makers' image of the opponent and the policy makers' general beliefs about bargaining strategy and the danger of escalation influence decisions. In addition, it is important to understand how crisis-induced stress and fatigue have a detrimental effect on the performance of decision-makers and their advisers. Effective crisis management requires policy makers to develop and employ strategies and tactics that are sensitive to both diplomatic and military considerations. The use of military force in these situations must be carefully employed as an instrument of last resort. The use of SOF (Special Operation Forces) and counterterrorist forces should be looked at carefully so as not to 'burn out' these valuable assets on 'hyper-conventional' targets of opportunity; these forces are in a critical high demand and constitute only a small per centage of the armed forces. The commitment of national level assets to 'take down' a target or handle a crisis could have tremendous implications for a government and could influence world opinion. These forces are usually tasked with the most critical and sensitive target sets. These failures lead to political repercussions and blowback that cannot be taken lightly. Careful crisis management will help prevent some.

No one afford to make mistakes as a nation, causing irreparable damage to both foreign policy and reputation. Careful handling of a hostage crisis, weighing every possible option, informing all those responsible in the civilian/military leadership is crucial. The crisis manager as well as the administration should take a hard look at the developing crisis before committing SOF or national assets as a quick fix. The risks vs. benefits of committing these forces must be weighed and war-gamed carefully between all civilian/military leaders prior to committing the military arm.

(13.1.3) *The Bio-rhythm Model of Hostage Crisis*

The bio-rhythm model describes how initially, the hostage rescue force is not prepared to conduct the operation and how the terrorists have the upper hand controlling the crisis area. The rescue force has not developed a deliberate action plan or any accurate intelligence on the situation. Furthermore, it has not conducted any rehearsals or gathered any special equipment requirements specific to the target area. The terrorists, on the other hand, are taking advantage of the shock value of their most recent violent action, and are exploiting this window of opportunity to maintain their relative superiority over the hostages as well as any opposing force that might be in or around the target (police forces or security guards). As time goes by, the readiness level of the rescue force increases as well as the intelligence picture and information on the target area. In contrast, the situation degrades for the terrorists. They begin to feel fatigue due to their static posture while in a high stress environment and their knowledge of the target area has reached its limits. They must now rely on outside information, most of the time provided by a negotiating team. The security posture and readiness of the terrorists begin to degrade significantly; their close proximity to the hostages will weaken their will and make them second-guess their intended cause. The only way for the terrorists to recapture some of their initiative is by killing a hostage or by taking some other kind of drastic measure that will help them regain some relative superiority. This will allow them to re-establish a new culminating point and increase their chances of success. When this occurs, there is a 'switch back' in favour of the terrorists, and the rescue force must wait until the next window of opportunity.

(13.1.4) The Dynamics of an Effective Response

Never draw fire, it irritates everyone around you.

Hostage rescue aims at recovery of hostages or sensitive material from terrorist organisations. The operations are much more difficult than any other anti-terrorist operation because the safety of the hostages and preventing destruction of the sensitive material is an essential mission requirement. Should the hostages get killed in the operation; the purpose of the operation will be defeated. They require speed, shock, surprise, and violent action. In the first place, the terrorists could be keeping in an unknown location. Even if the location somehow becomes known, they are very likely to have barricaded themselves in, fortifying their location and blocking its access from any outside contact. Barricades include explosive booby traps, alarms, and any other equipment that will aid the terrorists in securing themselves from any outside intervention. For obvious reasons, the special equipment requirements for an assault force to breach an entrance into these target areas vastly differs from those not fortified. Hostage rescue forces should be employed only after the careful implementation of the hostage rescue principles and the close monitoring of the hostage crisis bio-rhythm. Maintaining the pulse of the crisis through the bio-rhythm model will allow commanders at the strategic, operational, and tactical levels to decide the best execution time, exploiting the enemy's culmination points. This implies having patience in the negotiations process and trusting the intelligence apparatus to do its job.

Although it might seem that an early attack on a terrorist organisation before it settles into a routine is the most suitable option, early execution of a rescue operation is not often feasible. Executing the operation early does not allow for the natural degradation inside the target—a fundamental aspect to ensure surprise for the rescue element. Waiting permits the situation to develop and it allows for the negotiations process to take effect, intelligence to be gathered, and for the rescue force to prepare a skillful recovery plan. Alert sequences for counter-terrorist forces must take into consideration the benefits of waiting for later execution. Timelines that set the battle rhythm for these forces must reflect and focus on preserving operator's skills, and not allow for the natural degradation of the force as the siege continues. Spinning up and alerting CT forces to prepare an emergency plan of action en route to the target when the situation has not been developed will only tire and degrade the quality of the force. These forces are already at a peak state of readiness; the focus during the initial stages of the siege should be on getting the intelligence apparatus into action to exploit the target. This will lay the foundation for a good deception plan, which will in turn give the operators their much-needed element of surprise. Only then should the CT force be readied to initiate their battle rhythm. Prolonging the siege can also set the stage for an explosive confrontation between the hostage takers and their victims. Therefore, the art of solving the crisis rests on the skillful manipulation of the negotiations process to buy time, through a synergistic approach encompassing all the instruments of national power to influence the siege. Unless a trigger is met early in the crisis, the rescue must wait. However, the waiting game must focus on finding the best windows of opportunities to send in the rescue force.

(13.2) Prerequisites for Hostage Rescue Operations

(13.2.1) Intelligence and OPSEC

The intelligence requirements for a hostage crisis are very specific and often very different from conventional or SOF (Special Operations Forces) missions. The target intelligence details such as the specifics of possible breaching points, blueprints and diagrams of the structure, exact location of the hostages and terrorists, established routines, all demand very accurate and real time intelligence that uniquely serve the operator on the assault force. Technical intelligence collection during the hostage siege focuses but it is not limited to audio and video surveillance devices, which can collect and provide real time information on what is happening inside the target. The issue at hand is being able to plant these devices inside the target location in order to receive accurate data on the hostages, the terrorists, and the target area configuration. To bridge the intelligence gap when these devices cannot be used, it is essential to employ HUMINT assets in and around the target area, to collect and report the details not answered through TECHINT means. Both collection means must be monitored constantly to pick up any changes inside the crisis site such as movement of hostages from one location to another and the condition, weapons, strength, and capabilities of the terrorists. Sniper-observer teams provide another excellent means of reconnaissance and surveillance of the target area, and can serve as the emergency assault element in case any triggers are set off during the initial stages of the siege. These teams are force multipliers around the target area, in that they can provide expert advice on the tactical situation by technical and human surveillance means; at the same time, they give an additional course of action for an emergency assault option.

Operational Security (OPSEC) is another critical aspect of the intelligence principle in hostage rescue operations that is closely tied to deception and surprise. The rescue force must constantly be thinking about operational security measures to protect the force and the plan from being compromised. Strict OPSEC is a force multiplier for hostage rescue forces and cannot be overlooked. Operational security measures were very sloppy during the failed attempt to rescue the Israeli athletes during the Munich Olympics of 1972. There was no control over media or any security cordon of the area, causing the German police forces to expose their plan on national television as they were attempting to conduct a hasty assault against the Black September terrorists. On the contrary, a perfect example of strict OPSEC is Operation Chavin De Huantar in Lima, Peru. Throughout the 126 days of planning and preparation prior to the assault, the rescue force and the tunnel diggers were kept in an undisclosed location in total secrecy, while rehearsing and preparing for the daring assault, on a full size replica of the target area.

(13.2.2) Surprise

Rescue operations are the only type of military operation in which complete surprise is a pre-condition. The critical element is always the feasibility of a surprise assault, for the key to success in any rescue operation is the ability to achieve complete surprise. SOFs must achieve surprise to the extent that the enemy cannot react effectively prior to mission accomplishment. Surprise means being able to use creativity and agility, not just violence and explosiveness.

Take for example Operation Winter Harvest—the rescue of Brigadier General James Dozier in January of 1982. After nearly a month of captivity, a US surveillance team reported the exact location and guard patterns of the Red Brigade terrorists that were guarding the General to Italian authorities. A team of ten men from the Italian Carabinieri was on alert, waiting for the right opportunity to enter the apartment and conduct a rescue. When there were only two guards from the Red Brigade guarding the General, the Italians simply walked up to the apartment and knocked on the front door. As soon as one of the guards opened the door, ten Carabinieri stormed the room, subduing the two terrorists and safely rescuing General Dozier. In a hostage rescue situation, a few seconds can mean the difference between success and failure; a terrorist can shoot a hostage or can detonate an explosive device inside the target area. Absolute surprise is necessary to allow the assault force those critical seconds to neutralise the threat. The loss of surprise will almost automatically mean aborting the plan. Rescue forces must rely heavily on the element of surprise to gain relative superiority. The element of surprise is closely dependent on a good deception plan, excellent timing, and exploiting the enemy's weaknesses.

(13.2.3) Operators' Skills

Hostage rescue operations are the most difficult type of special operations missions. They require absolute precision and demand a specific type of force with attributes and capabilities that distinguish them from conventional forces or even regular SOF. The special skills required by a rescue force are even more technical and sophisticated than those required of regular SOF units. Specialised shooting techniques, breaching, technical and tactical surveillance, and close quarter battle, are all special skills specific for hostage rescue. A competent rescue force takes months to create and requires resources and capabilities not encountered in a regular unit. The following qualities and attributes are described as the SOF 'truths': (1) Humans are more important than hardware; (2) Quality is better than quantity; (3) SOF cannot be mass-produced; and (4) Competent SOF cannot be created after emergencies arise.

The most important part of a rescue operation is the physical act of actually saving the hostage. Hostage operations involve the use of surgical precision fires from snipers as well as from every operator and breacher in the assault force. An error while taking a shot or calculating a charge to blow a door is not an option. This can lead to disaster for the entire operation. Assaulters are required to be able to shoot at a terrorist with exact precision, while moving through obstacles, and be able to discriminate between the terrorist and the hostage being held at gunpoint. Each rescue member must be able to engage a terrorist with killing shots on his very first try, with two rounds to the chest (known as the 'double tap') followed by one to the head, if required (usually if the terrorist is wearing body armour). If the rescuer misses, the terrorist will have time to either shoot back or, even worse, kill the hostage, causing the operation to fail.

Fourteen *Movimiento Revolucionario Tupac Amaru* (MRTA) rebels had taken more than 400 people hostage at the residence of the Japanese Ambassador in Peru on December 16, 1996 and kept them hostage for 126 days. The rescue assault was made on April 21, 1997. Major Felix Diaz of the Army Special Forces recalls that they had rehearsed and trained on a full size replica of the Japanese Ambassador's residence for four months. They got to a point where they could walk the whole assault blindfolded. They knew exactly who would be to their left and right, how many steps they had to take to a door, and how many seconds it would take them to walk from one room to the next. Eventually when the assault was made, only one hostage and two commandos were killed. They could kill all of the mainly MRTA rebels, including their leader, Nestor Cerpa Cartolini. In spite of this preparation, there was a surprise for them in store. During the actual assault, a full size brick wall crumbled on top of him; a breaching charge was placed on a door that was booby trapped by the MRTA with a large amount of explosives causing a tremendous explosion, knocking down the entire brick wall. The explosion sent Major Diaz flying approximately 30 feet and covered him in bricks, but he was able to regain his composure and continue the assault.

The very nature of the CQB fight takes combatives to a new level, making the operator's psyche critical for his survival. If the operator has any second thoughts as he enters a room or a structure during the assault, he will second-guess himself allowing the enemy just enough time to fire a shot back at him or at the hostage. He might even stop the flow of the assault force, creating chaos and confusion inside the target area, allowing the terrorists to regain their initiative. When an operator dons his protective body armour and special equipment, a "switch must be turned on" in his mind—he must believe that he is indestructible and can face any odds.

(13.2.4) Deception

Hostage rescue operations require a very different type of approach to help the rescue element reach the entry without being compromised.

Deception affords the rescue force the much-needed element of surprise. When used properly, it can direct the terrorist's attention from the assault, or delay their reaction long enough for surprise to be gained at the crucial moment. During the famous Israeli rescue at Entebbe in July 1976, the Israeli assault force disguised their approach to the target by riding across the airfield in Mercedes sedans (typically used by Ugandan dignitaries), successfully delaying the initial actions of the Ugandan guards.

The deception plan must be considered at the strategic and operational levels of the operation. At the strategic level, the negotiations must maintain the focus of freeing the hostages by diplomatic means at all cost, even in the face of a mounting rescue attempt. On the operational level, the deception plan might give the impression to the hostage takers that the military preparations have nothing to do with the rescue of the hostages. The volatility of the situation, the political implications, the media coverage, and the national test of will, all provide a degree of complexity that must be tampered by any means possible. It is therefore critical to introduce the deception plan at the strategic, operational, and tactical level of the rescue operation. The deception plan can, on one hand, hide military preparations and rehearsals from the negotiations process or the media, or, on the other hand, it can help promote the fact that the country is steadfast in its resolve not to negotiate and rescue the hostages. More importantly, the deception plan can be used to catch the enemy completely off guard, distracting their attention during the initial few seconds of the approach and assault on the target. A drawn out negotiations process can also be a great deception tool to masque an impending assault. The analogy of the frog in a boiling pot applies here; if a frog is thrown in a boiling pot, he will immediately jump right out of it. However, if he is slowly brought up to a boil, he will die before he knows it. The terrorists will not know if things are slowly heating up because of a good deception plan.

There are five categories of deception plans. First, strategic deception is planned and executed by and in support of senior military commanders to result in adversary military policies and actions that support the originator's strategic military objectives, policies, and operations. Second, operational deception is planned and executed by and in support of operational-level commanders to result in adversary actions that are favourable to the originator's objectives and operations. It is planned and conducted in a theater of war to support campaigns and major operations. Third, tactical deception is planned and executed by and in support of tactical commanders to result in adversary actions that are favourable to the originator's objectives and operations. It is planned and conducted to support battles and engagements. Fourth, service deception is planned and executed by the services that pertain to service support to joint operations; service military deception is designed to protect and enhance the combat capabilities of service forces and systems. Fifth, deception in support of operational security (OPSEC) is planned and executed by and in support of all levels of command to support the prevention of the inadvertent compromise of sensitive or classified activities, capabilities, or intentions; deceptive OPSEC measures are designed to distract foreign intelligence away from, or provide cover for, military operations and activities.

(13.3) Anatomy of a Rescue

The most important consideration prior to the start of any rescue preparation is the question of operational feasibility: Does the country responsible for handling the crisis have a dedicated unit capable of responding to such incidents? Does the political environment allow for the use of military action to resolve the crisis? Are the rescue unit's operational and/or tactical limitations too great, preventing them from executing the rescue? The success criteria of any hostage rescue operation can vary depending on the operation and the uniqueness of the incident. For our purposes, success for the hostage rescue operation is defined by these three specific conditions:

- The safe rescue of all hostages alive
- Minimal damage to the rescue force's personnel or equipment (any casualties should be restricted to the terrorists)
- The politico-military ramifications at the completion of the operation do not outweigh the risks involved in launching the rescue

Hostage rescue operations, for the most part, can be broken down into three major phases: Phase I, the planning, preparation, and rehearsals; Phase II, the approach and assault; and Phase III, the post assault. These phases vary depending on the type of hostage scenario; barricaded hostage takers, hostage takers out in an open area or in a hijacked plane, or a lone suicide terrorist, but essentially remain the same throughout.

(13.3.1) Phase I: Planning, Preparation and Rehearsals

At the onset of the hostage taking, the designated rescue force must be summoned at once, to start developing an emergency plan for action. This plan is utilised if the hostage takers decide to start killing or moving the hostages. From this initial plan, a further more refined deliberate plan of action is developed, to be conducted in the event negotiations fail. This plan is never finalised; it is updated and refined continuously as new information and intelligence come in that can aid in the rescue. A third option developed in the rescue planning sequence is the emergency-deliberate plan of action; this plan is a variation of the deliberate plan of action. It is a contingency plan in the event that the terrorists detect the rescue force during their approach to the target, while conducting the intended deliberate plan of action. For example, the rescue force can be moving to the target area surreptitiously and a terrorist might be out for a walk outside of the target area. The rescue force can be compromised at this point and be forced to change their original plan and rush to the target. The new plan now becomes the emergency-deliberate plan of action. These three plans become the essence of the rescue order. This is why it is so essential that the operators get intimately involved in the planning process, aware of all the changes and contingencies, able to execute it when the time comes.

Not only is it critical that planning occurs at the operator level, but the planning and rehearsals must fully integrate all participants involved with the rescue operation. This was a critical mistake during Operation Eagle Claw in 1980 – the failed rescue attempt to recover the hostages in Iran. Throughout the six-month preparation and rehearsal process, none of the individual operational elements planned or rehearsed their portion of the operation as one group. Staff planners isolated themselves from the operational element in a futile effort to preserve operational security, failing to disseminate the plan properly. This caused mass confusion once the helicopters departed with the assault force, leading up to the disaster at the Desert One.

(13.3.2) Phase II: Approach and Assault

Never get into a fight with a guy having more ammunition than you.

The safe rescue of all the hostages means success for the operation. In order to accomplish this, each phase of the hostage rescue plan must be planned, rehearsed, and executed with surgical precision. The approach and assault phase of a rescue operation are the most volatile parts of the rescue attempt because the assault force must remain undetected in order to maintain the element of surprise. Once the assault begins, they must immediately neutralise the threat and control the hostages. During the approach, the rescue force must be ready to execute all contingency plans rehearsed as part of their emergency-deliberate plan of action, in case they become compromised. Full synergy of all command and control elements is required during the approach, in order to positively control the flow of forces into the target and de-conflict from those already there (such as sniper-observer teams). The breach must be calculated with exact precision to ensure the explosion will not hurt or kill any hostages inside, while at the same time allowing for a positive entry of the rescue force into the target. Once inside, the rescue force must be quick, precise, and deliberate in their use of accurate and discriminate fires, while at the same time safeguarding any hostages encountered. The rescue party must be ready to protect the hostages during the assault. Initially, the effects of breaching, explosions, and firing will shock hostages; they will not know how to react, and sometimes they might even want to help by attacking some of the terrorists. Some hostages might be confused and want to stay behind in the comfort and security of what used to be their own 'little world'. Others might want to go and retrieve some of their own personnel belongings before leaving the target site. All these factors complicate the mission of the assault force. For these reasons, all personnel inside the crisis site must be considered dangerous until properly identified by other authorities during Phase III.

(13.3.3) *Phase III: Post Assault*

Upon the completion of the assault phase, the first immediate reaction of the hostages and the rescue force will be a state of overconfidence and euphoria. The operation at this stage is far from over, and the rescue force must remain in complete control by focusing on returning the hostages to the proper authorities. The first step should be to secure the target area from any outside intervention until it has been deemed safe by the assault force commander. The sniper-observer element must be notified that the target is secured in order to minimise the chance of fratricide. Only when the assault force commander has stated that he is in complete control of the crisis site can follow-on agencies enter to conduct a handover. All hostages must be carefully identified and accounted for properly. If there are any leaders within the group of hostages, those must be singled out to aid in the process of further identifying the rest of the hostages. The wounded and the dead should then be identified. The rescue force must pay particular attention not to leave any of the hostages behind during the exfiltration, or take a terrorist with them instead. The terrorist can be hiding a grenade or some sort of explosive and set it off inside the exfiltration vehicle or aircraft, ruining the whole operation. The decision to repair or leave behind broken equipment is also critical during these moments.

Contingency plans should address destruction procedures in the event something has to be left behind or repaired in place. If the rescue occurs in enemy territory, the main priority for the rescue force will be to treat the wounded, either while waiting for the exfiltration or during their transit. If the operation takes place in friendly territory, then the duty to treat the injured lies with other agencies designated for this task; the assault force's primary purpose is the safe handover of the hostages to other competent government agencies. Regardless, no personnel should be allowed inside the target area until it has been deemed safe by the assault force commander. The handover element must have capable forensics experts and legal personnel that will immediately take control of the site and treat it as a crime scene, not letting media or curious personnel enter the target area. Government officials must be ready to issue a public affairs statement to the press, in order to begin the process of quality control of information to protect the rescue force and enforce OPSEC measures.

(13.4) Deterrence, Coercion and Crisis Management During the Hostage Crisis

(13.4.1) Deterrence

Hostage crises are unique in that they involve the effective manipulation of three key elements—deterrence, coercion, and effective crisis management. In order to deter future acts of hostage taking and the states that sponsor them, we must devise and engage in a new overarching deterrence strategy that encompasses strategic, operational, and tactical goals other than our current deterrence options. This strategy must clearly send the message out to terrorists and their sponsors that the costs and risks of engaging in such actions far outweigh the benefits. It must be a credible strategy making the terrorists believe that the nation concerned will use force, and it must make it clear to them that it can use that force by having the capability. It is possible to deter terrorists or potential terrorists and their sponsors from pursuing hostage taking as a strategy; however, deterrence will not work every time. Terrorists are hard to deter because they have very little to lose and have very little that they value; the odds are always in their favour.

(13.4.2) Coercion

Coercion by denial: The second aspect critical in the dynamics of a hostage siege is the ability to coerce an opponent. In his book 'Bombing To Win', Robert A Pape argues that a denial strategy is the strategy most likely to succeed when trying to coerce an opponent. This strategy must be directed towards military and not civilian vulnerabilities. Coercion by denial operates by using military means to prevent the target from attaining its political objectives or territorial gains. The object is to wear down the opposition government's political authority gradually, and thus its ability to field military forces, rather than to destroy their forces in battle. Denial may require stopping the opponent from either gaining or holding territory, depending on whether the threatening assailant's goal is to prevent an attack, stop an ongoing attack, or force territorial concessions.

Coercion by punishment: Pape says that punishment operates by raising costs or risks to civilian population. It is not limited to hitting civilians in population centers. Pape considers surrender long before complete military defeat as an outstanding coercive success. Coercion fails when the coercer stops his coercive military actions prior to concessions by the target, or when the coercer imposes his demands only after complete defeat of the target. This is why punishment rarely works. Punishment generates more public anger against the attacker than against the government. Heavy punishment does not produce disruptive behaviour; it induces political apathy. Light punishment equals popular anger toward the attacker and demands reprisals. Punishment strategies attempt to raise the costs of continued resistance. They inflict suffering on civilians by damaging the target state's economy. Blockades are indiscriminate instruments because they affect the target's economy as a whole, as in the case of the 40-year economic blockade on Cuba.

Coercion by risk: This is like the punishment strategy; it inflicts suffering on civilians and raises the probability of suffering costs. It is the same as punishment, but gradual. The coercer puts at risk essentially the same targets as in punishment strategies, but the key to risk strategy is to inflict civilian costs at a gradually increasing rate rather than destroying the entire target (kill the hostage concept). Operations are slowly escalated in intensity in order to convince the opponent that much more severe damage will follow if concessions are not made. Punishment or risk strategies fail because outcomes of conventional coercion are determined mainly by the target state's powers of resistance.

Coercion by decapitation: This strategy strikes at key leadership and telecommunications facilities. It is partly punishment and partly denial; it is punishment if the attacker's intent is to destroy coercive control so that the effect of punishment (coup, rebellion, etc) can work better. It is denial if it is part of an effort to produce strategic paralysis.

There are three types of decapitation: leadership, political and military. Leadership decapitation is attacking specific leaders on the assumption that they are keeping the war going. This will not work because it is very hard to find and kill key individuals. In addition, because idiosyncratic wars are rare, it is not just one group of leaders who are the cause. Finally, succession is very hard to predict. According to Pape, political decapitation is attacking the regime's instruments of internal control, so that punishment can work, resulting in successful coup or rebellion. There are several reasons why this will not work: conflict generates loyalty to the regime; internal monitoring of the people by a regime is hard to stop; and finally, the Army is usually the key and conflict increases its loyalty to the regime. In military decapitation, you are attacking national command and control to induce strategic paralysis. This does not work because military operations do not require lots of command and control (C2); C2 cannot be disrupted for too long. Pre-delegation of command makes strategic paralysis difficult.

14

The Problem that Defies a Solution

Having all your body parts intact and functioning at the end of the day beats the alternative...

(14.1) The Americans Learn it the Painful Way

The easy way is always mined.

It happens without warning—one minute you're driving along doing your job and the next minute, BOOM! Some soldiers live to tell the tale. Some soldiers, well... In Iraq and Afghanistan today, death is measured less by the accuracy of bullets than by the cleverness of bombs. Every conflict eventually develops its own nomenclature, its own slang, and in the postwar occupation of Iraq and Afghanistan, IED is easily the most used and most distinctive word. If someone is hit by an IED, it is described as having got 'IED'd'. And while the Marines don't generally get scared easy, if you press hard enough, just about every grunt will admit that, deep down, he fears them. "IEDs are the one thing I worry about over here," says Staff Sgt Gary Pokorny, "You want to fight me face to face, fine, bring it on. But blow me up while I'm just driving by—from out of nowhere? Yeah, I'll admit it: IEDs scare me". For the US Marines now in Iraq and Afghanistan, IEDs are an inescapable fact of life. They have to spend an inordinate amount of their patrol time looking for them and the people who make them—all the while hoping that the IEDs don't find them first. The situation is not very different in those parts of the world where intelligent terrorists are to be found.

An American journalist who accompanied the Marines described his experience in the following words. On the long patrol of the 1st Platoon of Alpha Company, 1st Battalion, 5th Marine Regiment, near Fallujah, Iraq, an IED does just that. It's a Saturday night, and the Marines are driving in a 10-vehicle Humvee and truck convoy on a two-lane blacktop road. After two days of hot food and warm showers and relative safety in a rear area, they're heading back to 'Fort Apache', Alpha Company's forward base at a remote abandoned chemical factory, to begin an exhausting 48-hour vehicle and foot patrol through the Iraqi countryside. It's a beautiful night. The road takes the convoy through lush green fields and date palm groves, lighted by a billion stars and the slim crescent of a rustler's moon. And yet, to the Marines, this place is sinister. "I hate this road,'' Cpl John McFarling, says with a combat veteran's sixth sense for danger. "There's always IEDs here". And sure enough, as the Marine vehicles round a curve, toward the rear of the convoy there's a sharp, hard blast and a shower of light and sparks; even from 100 yards ahead, you can feel the concussive power of it. A dense cloud of smoke and dust instantly envelops the last few vehicles in the convoy. The Marines in the lead vehicles have no idea if their buddies will come out of that cloud alive or whole. "It flipped us out," Lance Cpl Kenneth Dooley, who was in one of the vehicles closest to the blast, would say later. After spending most of the night on 'over-watch', lying up on a sand berm and watching a road for IED planters, at morning light the platoon returns to the scene of the IED attack. They find a 3-foot-wide-and-deep crater, and dozens of pieces of shrapnel from an exploded 155-millimeter artillery shell. Just before the explosion, an Iraqi civilian car passing the convoy in the opposite direction had flashed its high-beam headlights. The suspicion is that it was a signal of some sort, a way of identifying the darkened convoy's position. The problem is that while the Marines can shoot when there's a direct threat, but they can't shoot on vague suspicion. You encounter the same problem everywhere in a similar situation.

By the end of January 2012, the coalition forces had suffered as many as 2888 fatalities in Afghanistan. The maximum number of soldiers killed in a year was in 2010 when 711 soldiers were killed. The year 2011 came in second at 566 fatalities. More than half (up to 75 per cent) of these fatalities have been caused by IEDs. For Iraq also, a similar conclusion was arrived at in a landmark study by Cary Wilson published as a Congressional Research Service (CRS) report for the US Congress titled "Improvised Explosive Devices in Iraq: Effects and Countermeasures in Iraq".

In the Second World War, losses to mines were just 2.5 per cent of the total casualties. In Vietnam, the figure rose to 23 per cent in respect

The IED strikes and the mighty Stryker AFV bites the dust

of mines and booby traps. In Iraq, it crossed the 50 per cent mark and in Afghanistan, it touched 75 per cent at times! With few paved roads, Afghanistan is even more fertile territory for IEDs than Iraq, where hard pavement often forced the rebels to leave bombs in the open. Not so in Afghanistan, where it is relatively easy to bury a device in a dirt road and cover the tracks. Even when the IEDs do not wound or kill troops, the threat restricts and complicates the movements of forces. American convoys often wait for bomb-detection teams that move at three miles per hour. Helicopters are limited, and most troops travel in mine-resistant, ambush-protected vehicles known as MRAPs (Mine Resistant Ambush Protected), which are lumbering and hard to manoeuvre. Though the heavily armoured MRAPs are effective in shielding soldiers from explosions; two turret gunners died recently when one flipped over after hitting IEDs.

(14.2) IEDs: The Iconic Weapon of Our Times

So let's not talk of love and flowers; and things that don't explode.

The IED is the ideal weapon of the intelligent terrorist. The purpose of the IED is to demoralise, to create a feeling of insecurity and to make people timid and cautious, not to destroy a fighting force – precisely what a terrorist ought to do. A terrorist, who starts dreaming of militarily defeating a nation's army, will eventually get frustrated. The IED, regardless of its effectiveness, causes apprehension among the forces, consumes or occupies major amounts of resources and, most importantly, gives the insurgent exposure in the media and information battle. Short of an all-terrain, all-weather 100 per cent effective IED counter, the IED will remain the terrorists' primary weapon for the foreseeable future. They are easy to assemble, the components are plentiful and the risks of a failed attack are low. From a cost/benefit perspective, the IED has a much higher expected value than more conventional attacks and has the benefit of little risk to the terrorist. It does not require a large, well-disciplined force. It is perfect for a loosely knit insurgency.

What matters most to the terrorists is not a tactical victory or a few casualties inflicted on the enemy, but his continued survival in spite of all the military might that the nations pitch against them. What the terrorists intend to produce is a war-weariness among the target forces if they are operating in their own country, and also among the target populace if the forces of their nation are fighting elsewhere, as the Americans are fighting in Iraq and Afghanistan. IEDs have filled that role—not for the harm that they do but for the steady casualty rate they produce and the repetitive broadcasts that they get in the news. For example, the Mujahideen in Afghanistan and the rebels in Iraq are attempting to attack the US on the operational level by demoralising the forces with the threat of the IED and on the strategic level by sapping the will of the US population through a protracted conflict. The problem of the target nation is that it almost always fails to understand the implications of the double-pronged attack. The US, for example, is responding to the IED threat on a purely tactical level alone, treating it as a force protection issue.

(14.3) How far the USA is Correct in Attempting a Purely Technological Solution to the Problem?

When all else fails, simply revel in the absurdity of it all.

Americans think that because the United States is the technology powerhouse, the solution to the problem of IEDs would come from technology. The attitude was: "All we have to do is throw technology at it and the problem will go away". Unfortunately, it did not. Their tendency, verging on blind faith, to view all problems as being solvable by technological means is probably their single worst strategic defect. It reminds us of the old urban legend of NASA spending millions of dollars and hours designing a space-pen that would work in zero gravity. The Soviets faced with the same problem adopted the use of the pencil!

Over the last few decades American armed forces slowly convinced themselves that something fundamental had changed in warfare; that the conduct of warfare would become as clean as fighting a war in a war game; and that the 'Fog of War' would no longer apply; that information technology would give them perfect knowledge of the battle space; and with that they would be immune to the vagaries of chance—war-fighting would become a matter of administrative planning as straightforward and reliable as Wal-Mart ensuring adequate supply of frozen turkeys and tinned cranberry sauce for late shoppers on Christmas Eve. In other words, they would force the other guy to fight their kind of wars and so the future would consist of more and easier righteous ass-kicking by the Western world of, well, whoever does not kowtow to them. It turns out that the other guy wasn't merely an inert 'target' waiting to be 'negated' but a living, thinking opponent with some tricks of his own up his sleeve. Result? Well, as we saw above, it's the American ass that's getting kicked because, to their horror, they are found to be fighting the other guy's kind of war.

The simple scientific fact is there are fundamental limits to combating IEDs in a cost-effective and practicable way. This is the catch. Yes, we can indeed develop most exotic technologies to detect explosives and IEDs. But they are not likely to be cost-effective or practicable. The US may afford a terrible waste of money in such pursuits, as they once did with the Strategic Defence Initiative (SDI—popularly known as the Star Wars Project)—poorer nations like India would simply buckle under the load. Then it has to be practicable. You cannot fight in the jungles if your IED detectors take half-a-day to clear a stretch of half a kilometer. You can't spend billions and research your way around this fundamental problem. They invested billions to develop counters to remote controlled IEDs, usually radio triggered—the terrorists countered it by using either RCIEDS or IEDs that are hard-wired. Simple! When they made highly sophisticated detectors to detect even the most advanced high explosives, the terrorists countered them by using low explosives in rather large quantities. MPVs (Mine Protected Vehicles) was designed to withstand shattering blast waves of high explosives; the terrorists countered it by using low explosives that heaved the entire vehicle several feet up in the air—the vehicle remained intact and no shrapnel penetrated the hull, but the occupants were killed or injured as a result of the impact of the vehicle falling on the ground. They have constructed IEDs powerful enough to kill soldiers inside 22-ton Bradley Fighting Vehicles. In one incident in 2004, after a Bradley ran over a large IED, the armoured bottom plate of the vehicle was reportedly found some 60 yards from the site of the explosion. Then they switched over to the 19-ton Stryker medium-weight armoured vehicle, hoping that with its maximum speed of more than 60 mph, it could perhaps dash past ambushes and roadside IEDs that might catch the slower moving Abrams tank and Bradley Fighting Vehicle. Unfortunately, it did not happen so. In this battle of wits between the IED bomber and the vehicle designers, the bomber has won all the rounds so far.

This is the fate that befell this heavily protected vehicle in Logar, Afghanistan – incidentally, the vehicle was doing road clearance patrol ahead of other vehicles and got hit itself.

Engineering effective IED countermeasures has proven to be a formidable task as innovative attackers continually adapt their methods. Over time, the rebels have successfully adapted to many US countermeasures, and IEDs have grown more lethal. Recent news reports indicate that they have now resorted to kidnapping victims for the purpose of secretly booby-trapping their cars. The unknowing victims are then released, and their vehicles are detonated by remote control when they reach a certain location. IEDs have been used to draw US soldiers into a co-ordinated ambush. For example, when first responders arrive to give aid to initial IED victims, or when a medevac helicopter touches down on a nearby temporary landing zone, they sometimes then trigger other pre-placed bombs, or begin a follow-on attack with rifles or grenades. Coupling is a method of linking one mine or explosive device to another, usually with detonating cord. This technique is often used to defeat countermeasure equipment. A heavy mine roller will pass over the initial, unfused device and set off the second fused device. This in turn detonates the over-passed device underneath the clearing vehicle. In boosting, buried mines, or other explosive devices are stacked on top of one another. The topmost explosives are non-metal, and only the device buried deepest from the surface is fused. This reduces the probability of detection, and it increases the force of the blast. In daisy chaining, IEDs may be linked together along a roadway with trip wire or detonating cord. When the initial mine is detonated; the other mines also detonate.

The Joint Improvised Explosive Device Defeat Organisation (JIEDDO) was established as an organisation on February 14, 2006. JIEDDO was initially formed as the IED Task Force under the US Army's Brig Gen Joseph Votel as an extension of their Explosive Ordnance Disposal initiative with an obvious focus on IEDs in the fall of 2003. The organisation was then extended to include the larger intelligence and defence communities as the Joint IED Task Force in July 2004. The highly classified and diverse group was finally made the Joint IED Defeat Organisation by DoD Directive 2000 in February 14, 2006. The JIEDDO is now a joint entity and jointly manned activity of the US Department of Defence established to reduce or eliminate the effects of all forms of improvised explosive devices used against US and Coalition Forces. Its mission is defined as: "The JIEDDO shall focus (lead, advocate, co-ordinate) all Department of Defence actions in support of the Combatant Commanders' and their respective joint task forces' efforts to defeat IEDs as weapons of strategic influence. The JIEDDO is directed by retired Army Gen Montgomery Meigs, and works with various national labouratories, the Department of Energy, contractors, and academia—requests for proposals are regularly posted to private industry participants. The agency has issued a request for proposals that covers just about every element of the bomb-fighting problem, from mitigating against bomb damage to detecting explosives to training what to do when you find an IED. Most (but certainly not all) of the time, when a government research group issues a "Broad Agency Announcement", it is to ask for assistance on a specific subject or two. For example, the DARPA asked for an "Electromagnetic Pulse Tolerant Microwave Receiver Front-End". But JIEDDO's latest announcement is different, asking for help on just about every aspect of their work: capabilities and tools that integrate and exploit intelligence to contribute to a clearer understanding of enemy personnel, equipment, infrastructure; tactics/techniques/procedures, support mechanisms or other actions in order to forecast specific enemy IED-focused operations directed against US interests; capabilities that enable the targeting, interdiction, and elimination of enemy personnel, the associated infrastructure and logistics required for using IEDs as a weapon against military and civilian personnel; a low-cost, low-profile sensor capability that can rapidly and reliably detect (with a goal to identify) explosives chemical vapourous or aerosolize molecules of the energetic compounds; a vehicle-mounted system to simultaneously detect and neutralise Command Wire and Pressure Plate triggered IEDs from operationally safe standoff distance; a single-vehicle system capable of detecting and neutralising [remotely-triggered] IEDs by disrupting or disabling the electronics from a threshold distance of 50 meters and an objective distance of 100 meters; lightweight armour (transparent and opaque) solutions that are significantly lighter than current expedient designs that protect against emerging anti-armour IED threats; a high-quality, comprehensive training programme that all units can utilise to address everything associated with Tactical Site Exploitation; and so on.

(14.4) A Review of the Exotic Technology to Defeat Elementary Technology

(14.4.1) The Approach of the JIEDDO and the US Army

The JIEDDO has been spending at the rate of about $ 2 billion per year with few tangible results in sight. In fact, so much was the investment in it and so much was the hype associated with it that it was hailed as a "Mini Manhattan Project" or a "Later-day Manhattan Project" when it was established. Alarmed by a spike in deadly roadside bombings

The US Marine Corps has not realised that a sniffer dog does not lend itself to be used in operational situations where large distances are involved and where an IED could lurk anywhere

in Iraq and Afghanistan, the Pentagon enlisted an early critic of the US war strategy to re-evaluate the controversial organisation that has spent billions of dollars but failed to curb the biggest killer of American troops. In 2007, the DoD ordered the creation of a special task force to analyse the effectiveness of the struggling JIEDDO. It is essentially because of the cult of secrecy that an organisation like this has been able to survive without producing results—partly it is due to the fact that there are few people left in the US who would raise their voice publicly against its war-mongering and the paranoia associated with Islamic terrorism.

The JIEDDO and the US army have established "five tenets of IED defeat" (predict, detect, prevent, neutralise, and mitigate) and continues to seek solutions based on these tenets. Each current countermeasure focuses on one or more of the five tenets, yet each has its weaknesses. Countermeasures are tested at the National Training Center at Fort Irwin, California. The technologies being evaluated include electronic jammers, radars, X-ray equipment, robotic explosive ordnance disposal equipment, physical security equipment, and armour for vehicles and personnel. A weakness common to all of these countermeasures has been the terrorists' ability to learn about them and adapt to them. Through public websites and media reports they can discover the number of countermeasures deployed, how they work, and even their performance specifications.

To Predict IEDs: They have developed unmanned air vehicles (UAVs) to conduct surveillance. UAVs equipped with GPS and high resolution digital cameras identify changes in the terrain along travel routes and give the location of suspicious roadside objects to within 10 meters; however, they cannot positively identify the objects as explosive devices. We will explain you how easy it is to beat it. The Americans, being the morons they are, think that if an IED is to be planted on a road with asphalt surface, the surface has to be broken first and, however hard they try to restore the original position, it is likely to betray itself. Poor guys do not know that in most parts of the developing world, particularly where agricultural fields are to be found by the sides of the road, the road surface is at a considerable elevation from the fields and there are sloping dirt surfaces on both sides. Intelligent terrorists simply bore through the sides and plant the IEDs under the surface of the road, without disturbing it. Since the sides of the road are unpaved, it is easy to restore them.

To Detect IEDs: They have developed a variety of sensors. A detailed exposition of sensors and their limitations can be found in our treatise "The Ultimate Book Of Explosives, Bombs, And IEDs". Some sensors such as the GE Vapour tracer electronically sniff out trace amounts of explosive particles. These sensors, however, can only be used at very short range to screen suspected IEDs and people suspected of planting them. It should be easy to see that they are of use only in places like airports. As such they are of little use in the field because you could not possibly be sniffing the whole length of a road! Another approach is the use of microwave imaging. A Pentagon microwave project codenamed PING claims that it can find large weapons caches hidden inside buildings. The microwaves or terahertz waves penetrate buildings easily but unfortunately can only detect explosive devices that contain large amounts of metal. The high energy levels in the explosive's chemical bonds create resonance patterns in the reflection of the microwaves. Terahertz imaging can detect non-metallic weapons, but it is still very expensive and sensitive to environmental conditions. Both of these imaging technologies have potential, but much research is required before they could autonomously detect an explosive device at a stand-off distance. In any case, it too has little application for IEDs on roads.

Using devices like Remote-Controlled Counter-IED Robot is cumbersome – they are not suitable for a large theater of war

To prevent: There is little which could be done about it by way of technology.

To neutralise IEDs: They have developed electronic jammers and remote detonation devices. Jammers such as ICE (IED Countermeasures Equipment) and Warlock emit low power radio frequencies to block the detonation signals from cell phones and other radio frequency devices. Quite expectedly, the terrorists obtained information about how the jammers function and have adapted their triggering mechanisms to get around them. It is not rocket science. The range of frequencies covered by a jammer is not a state secret. The US has spent over $ 370 million on radio frequency jammers since 2003, yet soldiers complained that the devices worked for only six months before the other guys whom the American soldiers derisively describe as savages, found ways around them. Companies making the jammers, eager to highlight their engineering accomplishments, had described the devices on their public websites. Through these websites and investigative media reports, they learned details about the jammers that could be used to counter them, including their operating frequencies. All they have to do is to make their trigger in such a manner that it does not use those frequencies, or use something else—one could use ultrasound, laser, speed radars, anything! Furthermore, jammers cannot prevent manually detonated IEDs. Devices emitting an electromagnetic pulse are sometimes able to prematurely detonate an IED at a safe distance or destroy the electronic circuitry in its triggering mechanism. For safety reasons, however, this type of device is typically only used after a suspected IED has been identified. The 'Talon' is a bomb-disposal Unmanned Ground Vehicle (UGV), or robot, that comes equipped with a mechanical arm to pick up and inspect dangerous objects, such as suspected IEDs. Another robot, called the 'PackBot' has also been used by the Army to clear bombs and explore suspected terrorist hideouts.

To mitigate the damage: For this they have developed armour for soldiers and their vehicles. Unfortunately, the other side has responded by drawing on their seemingly limitless supply of unexploded ordnance to make even more powerful IEDs. They have also begun using shaped charges, which direct the energy of the explosion into a projectile that penetrates easily through armour plating. The US military has increased the quality of armour used for vehicles in Iraq, including up-armouring the High-Mobility Multi-Purpose Wheeled Vehicles (HMMWV, or Humvees). However, as an apparent response to use of more heavily armoured vehicles, the rebels have developed even more powerful IEDs, along with more sophisticated methods for deploying and triggering them.

(14.4.2) A Critical Appraisal of the JIEDDO Products

Right now they are pretty much the ham in a bad ham sandwich.

Actually there's not much in JIEDDO's public grab bag that's revolutionary— nothing that quite lives up to the organisation's initial billions as a "Later-day Manhattan Project". Some devices could be decades old, like Kevlar liners for a Humvee's interior, or World War I era mine rollers—wheels attached to the front of a vehicle, to trigger pressure-sensitive devices before a vehicle does. A backpackable version of the jammers is an interesting device though as it can be carried even at those places where the jammer vehicle would not go. There is nothing novel about an explosives detector rigged up to one of the standard robots used to handle IEDs. Then there's the stuff, already on the shelves, which has been pre-purposed for the bomb fight: blimps and drones, watching for explosives-planters; and dogs specially trained for the IED mission, etc. Finally, the JIEDDO shows off a more mysterious device: the 'Rhino,' used for 'IED pre-detonation' developed at a cost of $ 37 million! Listed in budget documents as a 'defeat system' for bombs with 'passive infrared' triggers, the Rhino features a long spindly arm attached to the front bumper of a Humvee. At the end of the arm is a black box, which is believed to engage any infrared tripwires (either physically, or with light of its own) before the Humvee gets hit. The whole thing is rather impractical. One need not design a passive infrared trigger always with a tripwire. The Americans thought of it because infrared tripwires are commercially available for as low as $ 15. One can always design a passive infrared trigger that looks for the infrared rays from the heat of the engine of a vehicle. Admittedly, the simplest of this kind would not be vehicle-specific and would go off with the first engine that came its way. However, the 'infrared trip wire' also does the same thing. Sensors could be based on lead sulfide (PbS), indium antimonide (InSb) and mercad telluride (HgCdTe), etc. While their performance does improve by cooling, it is not really critical for a sensor which has to work only as a trigger. Hence, one should not be under the delusion that terrorists would find it difficult to make cooled systems and hence cannot use heat sensor based triggers. Passive IR sensors are commercially available for as low as $ 5. In any case, uncooled thermal sensors are also available that work by the change of resistance, voltage or current when heated by infrared radiation and are mostly based on pyroelectric and ferroelectric materials. And if it comes to that, what is so difficult about making or procuring cooled sensors. Above all, even with a trigger based on commercial infrared tripwire, it is always possible to introduce a delay in the circuit—the spindly arm will trip it alright, but the bomb will explode only after the main body of the vehicle comes over it.

Researchers at the Naval Surface Warfare Center's Dahlgren Laboratory in Virginia are working on a device called Neutralising Improvised Explosive Devices with Radio Frequency (NIRF). The device is supposed to produce a very high-frequency field at very short range that can neutralise an IED's electronics by literally burning out their circuitry. Get the catch? It requires solid state electronic circuits that are vulnerable to induced electromotive force. The terrorist will not use a device that is based on solid state electronics. Simple wire-controlled devices or electro-mechanical devices would beat it. For example, they could use vibration sensors or even buried microphones to pick up vibrations and which could trigger a device.

The IED humbles the latest and mighty Cougar MRAP (Mine Resistant Ambush Protected) vehicle

Sensors, such as the Laser-Induced Breakdown Spectroscopy system (LIBS), are being developed to detect traces of explosives used for IEDs from as far away as 30 meters. Get the catch? The device requires traces of explosives on the packing material or other parts of the device. The traces come as a result of contamination or improper handling. All the terrorist has to do is to ensure that there is no surface contamination while making and packing the explosive in the device, and seal the explosive hermetically. No trace, no detection. Intelligent terrorists can devise a completely hermetically sealed assembly of the explosive and the detonator which is a separate unit altogether and that only needs to be wired to the firing circuit.

A problem has been discovered with jammers. Much of the Radio Frequency (RF) spectrum in the combat theater is unmanaged and can sometimes cause dangerous interference with radio communications on the ground. Sometimes IED radio jammers can lock onto other new electronic combat systems because of a lack of co-ordination for spectrum usage. Unmanned Aerial Vehicles (UAVs) can sometimes lose their radio control links due to ground-based radio interference once they are far away from their control base. Therefore, DoD is now obliged to develop an "Electronic Warfare Co-ordination Cell" to help sort out problems that can impede friendly operations, or endanger Explosive Ordnance Teams as they disable IEDs on the ground—yet another costly overshoot of a costly solution. With passive radio direction finding equipment, such vehicle mounted jammers could also betray the movement patterns of patrol or convoy vehicles, over a large distance, given the easy availability of portable computers and software capable of plotting such signals rapidly and automatically onto a map.

After billions and billions spent, the US military still can't overcome a loose collection of do-it-yourself, low-dollar, no-tech weaponeers. That illustrates how vexing the problem of the IED is. Fact is, the bombers shall one day rule the world.

Even after the billions of Dollars spent, the JIEDDO has not been and cannot be successful in defeating the IEDs – here a Humvee is the victim of the IED in spite of its 105-Kmph speed

(14.5) Innovations being Tried for Protection from Landmines

(14.5.1) Limitations of the V-shaped Hull Design

Landmines designed for vehicles (AVLs—Anti-vehicle Landmines) cause damage to both vehicles and occupants in a number of ways.

The blast pressure generated may cause the vehicle's hull to rupture, thus allowing blast overpressure and heat to enter the cabin. Fragments generated by a mine may penetrate the hull. The blast pressure and fragments may cause severe impact to the vehicle, resulting in direct-impact injury, or injury due to excessive body acceleration of the occupants. If the impact to the vehicle is excessive it may cause the vehicle to overturn or become unstable, resulting in injuries similar to those incurred in traffic accidents. Landmines may cause damage in other ways, such as fire, toxic fume, and so on. In order to protect vehicles against AVL attack, a number of countermeasures have been utilised. These include most famously a V-shaped hull, deflection panels above the wheels, higher ground clearance, higher strength hulls and relatively large vehicle mass. These measures may reflect and deflect shock waves, facilitate ventilation of explosive combustion products, prevent entry of fragments, overpressure and heat into the cabin, and reduce overall acceleration and displacement of the vehicle in the event of an AVL incident.

However, in order to optimise vehicle design and guaranteed occupant protection, the seating and flooring need special design attention. Hirsh investigated the response of an unrestrained adult human male to a rapidly applied motion, or shock delivered upward through the feet. He found that the subject would receive compressive injuries in the body-supporting bones near the point of load application when subjected to a peak velocity change of 3 to 4 m/s for a pulse duration shorter than 10 ms (or an average acceleration higher than 30 g). In a medium-sized armoured vehicle, localised floor average acceleration and peak velocity change may typically exceed 100 g and 12 m/s respectively under AVL attack.

(14.5.2) The False-floor Approach

Scientists are therefore trying to develop a practical solution that would effectively limit load transmission through the vehicle's floor, thereby affording enhanced lower-limb protection for the occupants. In the so-called 'false-floor approach' the load-limiting and energy-absorbing materials are inserted under the false-floor surface to limit or decouple the impact load. The following mechanisms are being considered:

- Soft-spring suspension;
- Load limiter; and
- Energy-absorbing materials.

The soft-spring mechanism may reduce the impact load by way of an impedance mismatch (similar to how an earthquake gauge works), which may be used as a footrest for seated occupants. A typical example of a load limiter is a hydraulic damper with its relief pressure threshold appropriately set. Once the load pressure exceeds the preset value, the piston will move in response, and further load increases will be prevented. Similarly, either a friction damper or a collapsible material may also be used to achieve load limiting. Energy-absorbing materials consume energy during deformation thereby resulting in a plastic impact. In an ideal case, a plastic impact may reduce the peak velocity change by as much as 50 per cent when compared with the alternative elastic impact. Any candidate decoupling mechanism must take into account the floor's essential functional constraints. Hence, the proposed mechanism needs to provide sufficient rigidity to withstand the occupant's weight during normal operational conditions. The structure, which sits on top of the vehicle's 'natural' floor, also needs to be relatively thin in order to retain the internal ergonomic clearances. Satisfactory results on a commercial scale are yet to be seen, however.

15

Can Terrorists Wage War Through the Internet?

Never underestimate the ability of the top brass to foul things up.

(15.1) What is Cyberterrorism?

(15.1.1) How it all Started?

Public interest in cyberterrorism began in the late 1980s. As the year 2000 approached, the fear and uncertainty about the Y2K millennium bug heightened and interest in potential cyberterrorist attacks also increased. Since then the pseudo-scientific write-ups and ignorant media people have been feeding on the fears of the people. "We are at risk. Increasingly, America depends on computers. They control power delivery, communications, aviation, and financial services. They are used to store vital information, from medical records to business plans to criminal records. Although we trust them, they are vulnerable - to the effects of poor design and insufficient quality control, to accident, and perhaps most alarmingly, to deliberate attack. The modern thief can steal more with a computer than with a gun. Tomorrow's terrorist may be able to do more damage with a keyboard than with a bomb". Thus, began the opening chapter of one of the foundation books in the computer security field called 'Computers at Risk: Safe Computing in the Information Age'. This book published in 1991, commissioned by the National Research Council, was the product of twenty-one experts in their field and was a proposed blueprint for future computer security in the United States. In the 17 years since this was written, computers and information technology has exploded. But most people, including those in the computer field, believe the above statement to still be true. Many authors such as Winn Schwartau and John Arquilla had considerable financial success selling books which described what were purported to be plausible scenarios of mayhem caused by cyberterrorism. The sensationalism needs to be busted because that has distorted the perception of many.

(15.1.2) What can be done by Cyberterrorism?

The term cyberterrorism was coined by Barry C Collin. There is considerable dispute regarding its definition. We agree with the definition given by Kevin G Coleman of the Technolytics Institute who defines it broadly as follows: "The premeditated use of disruptive activities, or the threat thereof, against computers and/or networks, with the intention to cause harm or further social, ideological, religious, political or similar objectives, or to intimidate any person in furtherance of such objectives".

The scenario which the media and popular authors have painted is frightening. Imagine an enemy able to knock out the power in some sizable chunk of the country by means of fast-spreading viruses inserted into our computer systems. Or think of an adversary who can gain remote access to and then crash highly automated controls that run many sensitive operations, from hydroelectric dams to gas and oil pipelines and robotic chemical plants. The most popular term that is doing the rounds is 'digital Pearl Harbour' – a name which strikes a very sensitive chord deep in the collective subconscious of the Americans. In a News Factor article, "Fanatics With Laptops: The Coming Cyber War", Tim McDonald warns that a "fanatical individual can, if we do not defend against it, use a laptop to do unimaginable damage at no personal cost whatsoever". Cyberterrorism has fascinated novelists and film-makers also. It was featured in Dan Brown's Digital Fortress and in Amy Eastlake's Private Lies. In the movie Live Free or Die Hard, John McClane (Bruce Willis) takes on a group of cyberterrorists intent on shutting down the entire computer network of the United States.

The basis of all such apprehensions is the fact that the critical infrastructure in most developed countries depends vitally on the Internet and computer networks. Power, water, transportation, etc maintain a certain reliance on the Internet for communications. The Cassandras say that a terrorist cyberattack could cripple this infrastructure, disrupting, for example, flight patterns or causing a failure in emergency response due to power or communications loss.

(15.2) How Far the Fears of Cyberterrorism are Justified?

(15.2.1) Fictional Scenarios are not Realistic

Decisions made by someone over your head
will seldom be in your best interest.

Many critics claim, and we are amongst them, that such scenarios are unrealistic in their assessments of whether the attacks described (such as nuclear meltdowns and chemical plant explosions) are possible. A common thread throughout what critics perceive as cyberterror-hype is that of non-falsifiability; that is, when the predicted disasters fail to occur, it only goes to show how lucky we've been so far, rather than impugning the theory. It has also been pointed out that there have been accidental disruptions that caused the same types of widespread outages the Cassandras warn cyberterrorists could affect, but the consequences were not as catastrophic as predicted by the cyberterrorism theorists.

According to Steve Gibson, president of the Gibson Research Corporation (GRC.com) and creator of the popular (and free) firewall checking application Shields Up!, "Perhaps the best way to think of the Internet is as being extremely robust and essentially invulnerable

Cyberterrorism: more hype than reality

on a global scale, but quite vulnerable" prone to attack, and forced outage on a local scale. Consequently, taken as a whole, the Internet is in little, if any, danger from 'cyberwar' or 'cyberattack'. But specific 'sub-nets' of the Internet are indeed vulnerable to attack and make easy targets'. Regarding the likely attack scenario, Steve surmises, 'It is impossible to know exactly what the mind of the terrorist is planning. Certainly no one could have predicted that the World Trade Center towers – specifically – would be the target of suicide pilots. Therefore, it is impossible to speculate usefully about the possible targets of a cyberattack without knowing the full and complete plans of a terrorist attack. What we can say, however, is that if any cyber attack were to occur, it would most likely not be the main thrust of a terrorist plot, but would most likely be an ancillary component of a larger scheme. For example, critical communications infrastructure could be temporarily shut down by a cyber attack in a co-ordinated effort against some other non-cyber physical target".

Ralf Bendrath, author of "The Cyberwar Debate: Perception And Politics In US Critical Infrastructure Protection", describes cyberwar as "a growth market in the US" and notes in his study that the risks are "especially open to political interpretation and instrumentation". Ralf goes on to note that, "compared to the traditional security threat, which consists of the dimensions actor, intention, and capabilities, 'cyberwar' threats cannot easily be categorised". Specifically, with a range of tools and exploits available, attacks can as easily originate from bored teenagers with no specific agenda to hardened hackers with a terrorist agenda. Such attacks also rely on opportunity, that is to say, the ability to locate and exploit 'compromisable' systems. It is vital to understand the difference between cyber pranks and cyberterrorism – hackers are aplenty and their skills might surprise us – it, however, does not necessarily follow that they could 'take over' vital computer systems and run them at will without anybody being able to do anything except watching helplessly. Whenever a system controlled by computers is designed, it is always anticipated that the computer could malfunction some time and then there should be some other way of controlling the system. It is not that you entrust a system to a computer and forget about it. There are in-built mechanisms to detect malfunctioning at any stage, after which corrective action may be taken or the system may be shut down. In other words, a malfunctioning computer is not allowed to become uncontrollable! Hackers may cause, at best, mass disruption; it is unlikely that they can cause mass destruction.

Ralf's research delves into the history of the many agencies spawned by the federal government in an attempt to justify and address the threat of cyberterrorism. He also questions the futuristic scenarios laid out by paranoid officials, first asking "How plausible are these scenarios"? and then humorously compares it to a scene in a legendary series, "like a member of the Syndicate once said to Agent Fox Mulder in the TV show, The X-Files: The best way to predict the future is to invent it".

Barry Collin, the original proponent of the 'fear of cyberterrorism' paints the following scenario: "Suppose a hacker takes over the process control computers on a cereal manufacturing line. The subject then alters the amount of iron supplement added to a fatal dose. Boxed cereal then sickens and kills a nation of children". Frightening, isn't it? There are a number of fallacies concerning this script, however. The quantity of an additive providing nutritional benefit is extremely small. The quantity necessary to change the nutritious additive to become toxic is greater by several orders of magnitude, if it is even possible! Presumably, when the usual quantities of additive run out on the production line much faster than usual, someone will notice the increased consumption. Most food manufacturers conduct routine product testing for just such eventualities. It is a business necessity in this litigious world. It is also likely that the taste of the altered product will be changed, and not for the better. It should be obvious that while a hacker could tamper with the computer and may be even alter the composition of the product, but the consequences are not likely to be as catastrophic as predicted. Modern assembly line production controlled by computers does not mean that there is no notice taken of what is happening.

Another commonly offered scenario involves the air traffic system. The world's air traffic control system is highly computerised. It is imagined that the 'terrorist' either obtains control of the system or alters the system in such a fashion that airplanes are flown into each other, resulting in mass death. This scenario requires that the entire human element and the structure of the rules involving the control of aircraft are ignored. It is not true. The computers used in the air traffic control system do not control anything. They merely provide an aid to the human controller. Even if he/she were deceived by the computer, there are other human beings in the loop. A basic tenet of pilot training is 'situational awareness'. From the first day of training, pilots are taught to be aware of not only their location, direction and altitude, but those of all other aircraft. Pilots routinely catch errors committed by air traffic controllers. It is the spectacular human failures that result in aircraft collisions, and the errors of some computer! Further, the "rules of the road" for aircraft operations anticipate the complete failure of the air traffic control system also. In fact, the rules are designed to work where there is no air traffic control at all! Thousands of flights are conducted each day in bad weather, around the world without the benefit of an ATC system at all!

(15.2.2) Cyberterrorism has become Big Business

The Cassandras have succeeded in one thing. The US government is spending money big time on this. Budgetary allocations have typically exceeded $ 50 billion since 2003 for Homeland Security Information Technology. Art Jahnke, Editorial Director for CSO magazine, gives food for thought in an editorial. "Cynical readers won't be surprised to learn that the BSA, a group of nineteen powerful hardware and software manufacturers, recommends the immediate establishment of 'true private-public sector partnerships'. In other words, the government should hire BSA members to help. And fast".

16

Physical Security of Important Facilities

Fixed fortifications are a monument to the stupidity of man.
Anything built by man, can be destroyed by him.

(16.1) Objectives of Physical Security

Physical security is defined as a part of security that is concerned with physical measures designed to safeguard personnel; to prevent unauthorised access to equipment, installations, material, and documents; and to safeguard against espionage, sabotage, damage, and theft. The objectives of a terrorist with respect to static locations could include: inflicting injury or death on people; destroying or damaging facilities, property, equipment, or resources; stealing equipment, material, or information; and creating adverse publicity. The terrorist or the aggressor has a wide field of choice to achieve these objectives and the security systems must be designed to protect against each one of them.

Moving Vehicle Bomb: He drives an explosive-laden car or truck into a facility and detonates the explosives. His goal is to damage or destroy the facility or to kill people. This is a suicide attack.

Stationary Vehicle Bomb: He covertly parks an explosive-laden car or truck near a facility. He then detonates the explosives either by time delay or remote control. His goal in this tactic is the same as for the moving vehicle bomb with the additional goal of destroying assets within the blast area. This is commonly not a suicide attack. It is the most frequent application of vehicle bombings.

Exterior Attack: He attacks a facility's exterior or an exposed asset at close range. He uses weapons such as rocks, clubs, improvised incendiary or explosive devices, and hand grenades. Weapons (such as small arms) are not included in this tactic, but are considered in subsequent tactics. His goal is to damage the facility, to injure or kill its occupants, or to damage or destroy assets.

Stand-off Weapons: He fires an explosive warhead at a facility from a significant distance. These weapons include direct Line-of-Sight (LoS) (such as anti-tank weapons) and indirect NLOS weapons (such as mortars). His goal is to damage the facility, to injure or kill its occupants, or to damage or destroy assets.

Firearms: He fires various firearms from a distance. His goal is to injure or kill facility occupants or to damage or destroy assets.

Forced Entry: He forcibly enters a facility using forced-entry tools (such as hand, power, and thermal tools) and/or explosives. He uses the tools to create a man-passable opening or to operate a device in the facility's walls, doors, roof, windows, or utility openings. He may also use small arms to overpower guards. His goal is to steal or destroy assets, compromise information, injure or kill facility occupants, or disrupt operations.

Covert Entry: He attempts to enter a facility or a portion of a facility by using false credentials or stealth. He may try to carry weapons or explosives into the facility. His goals include those listed for forced entry.

Subversion: Taking help of authorised personnel who has been subverted to somehow bypass the regular checks. The aggressor may also try to carry weapons or explosives into the facility in this tactic. His goals are the same as those listed for forced entry.

Visual Surveillance: He uses ocular and photographic devices (such as binoculars and cameras with telephoto lenses) to monitor facility or installation operations or to see assets. His goal is to compromise information. As a precursor, he uses this tactic to determine information about the asset of interest.

Acoustic Eavesdropping: He uses listening devices to monitor voice communications or other audibly transmitted information. His goal is to compromise information.

Electronic-emanations Eavesdropping: He uses electronic-emanation surveillance equipment from outside a facility or its restricted area to monitor electronic emanations from computers, communications, and related equipment. His goal is to compromise information.

Mail-Bomb: He delivers bombs or incendiary devices to the target in letters or packages. The bomb sizes involved are relatively small. His goal is to kill or injure people.

Supplies-Bomb: He conceals bombs in various containers and delivers them to supply- and material-handling points such as loading docks. The bomb sizes in this tactic can be significantly larger that those in mail bombs. His goal is to damage the facility, kill or injure its occupants, or damage or destroy assets.

Airborne Contamination: He contaminates a facility's air supply by introducing chemical or biological agents into it. His goal is to kill or injure people.

Waterborne Contamination: He contaminates a facility's water supply by introducing chemical, biological, or radiological agents into it. These agents can be introduced into the system at any location with varying effects, depending on the quantity of water and the contaminant involved. His goal is to kill or injure people.

(16.2) Design Approach Against Various Types of Threats

Stay alert. Everything seems to happen when you are tired.

Developing technical protective systems requires a close co-operation between technical and physical-security personnel. Physical-security personnel need to understand the basic approaches the engineers will take in laying out protective systems; engineers must understand the issues involved with ensuring that anything they lay out is compatible with security operations and the operations of the asset users.

(16.2.1) Protection Against Vehicle Bombs

General-design strategy: Blast pressures near an exploding vehicle bomb are very high, but they decrease rapidly with distance from the explosion. The design strategy for these tactics is to maintain as much stand-off distance as possible between the vehicle bomb and the facility and then, if necessary, to harden the facility for the resulting blast pressures. Barriers on the perimeter of the resulting stand-off zone maintain the required standoff distance. The difference between moving and stationary vehicle-bomb tactics is that the aggressor using the moving vehicle bomb will attempt to crash through the vehicle barriers; the aggressor using the stationary vehicle bomb will not. Therefore, vehicle barriers for the moving vehicle bomb must be capable of stopping a moving vehicle at the perimeter of the stand-off zone. For a stationary vehicle bomb, vehicle barriers must mark the perimeter of the stand-off zone, but they are not required to stop the moving vehicle. They only need to make it obvious if an aggressor attempts to breach the perimeter.

Levels of Protection: There are three levels of protection for vehicle bombs—low, medium, and high. The primary differences between the levels are the degree of damage allowed to the facility protecting the assets and the resulting degree of damage or injury to the assets. Low level of protection means that the facility or the protected space will sustain a high degree of damage but will not collapse. It may not be economically repairable. Although collapse is prevented, injuries may occur and assets may be damaged. Medium level means that the facility or the protected space will sustain a significant degree of damage, but the structure will be reusable. Occupants and other assets may sustain minor injuries or damage. High level means that the facility or the protected space will sustain only superficial damage. Occupants and other assets will also incur only superficial injury or damage. The two primary types of site-work elements for vehicle bombs are the stand-off distance and vehicle barriers. The vehicle's speed must also be taken into consideration.

Stand-off Distance: The stand-off distance is the distance maintained between where a vehicle bomb is allowed and the target. The initial goal should be to make that distance as far from the target facility as practical. Do not allow vehicles to park within the established stand-off distances. You must keep in mind that this restriction can result in significant operational and land-use problems.

Exclusive Stand-off Zone: When an exclusive standoff zone is established, do not allow vehicles within the perimeter unless they have been searched or cleared for access. The zone's perimeter is established at the distance necessary to protect the facility against the highest threat explosive. All vehicles should be parked outside the exclusive stand-off zone; only maintenance, emergency, and delivery vehicles should be allowed within the zone after being searched.

Non-exclusive Stand-off Zone: A non-exclusive stand-off zone is established in a location having a mixture of cars and trucks (with relatively few trucks). A non-exclusive stand-off zone takes advantage of the aggressors being able to conceal a smaller quantity of explosives in a car than they can in a truck. Therefore, a non-exclusive stand-off zone includes inner and outer perimeters. The inner perimeter is set at a distance corresponding to the weight of explosives that can be concealed in cars. The outer perimeter is set at a distance associated with the weight that can be placed in trucks. With these two perimeters, cars can enter the outer perimeter without being searched but they cannot enter the inner perimeter. Trucks cannot enter the outer perimeter, since it is established based on what they can carry. The non-exclusive stand-off zone provides the advantages of allowing better use of the parking areas and limiting the number of vehicles that need to be searched at the outer perimeter.

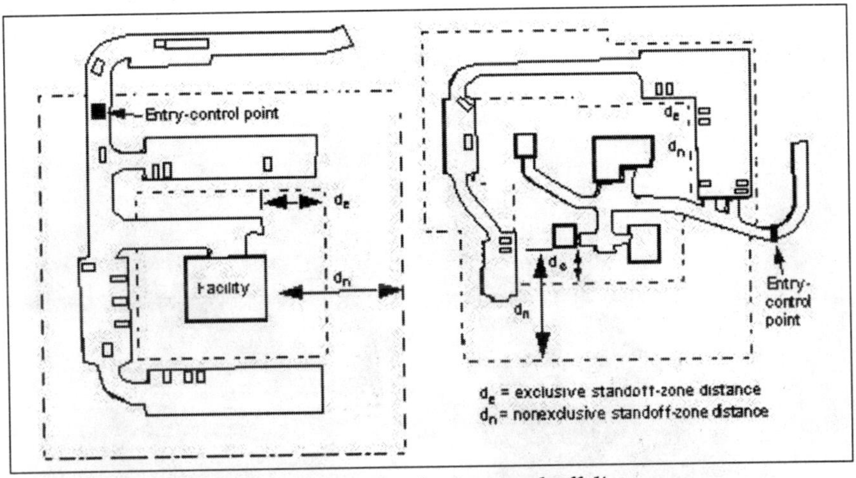

Exclusive and non-exclusive stand-off distances

Vehicle Barriers: Two types of vehicle barriers are used for vehicle bombs—perimeter and active barriers. The type of barrier used for a moving vehicle bomb differs from the barrier used for a stationary vehicle bomb. The barrier used for a stationary vehicle bomb does not have to stop a vehicle's motion. The goal for that barrier is to make anybody driving through the barrier noticeable. The assumption is that the aggressor's goal in the stationary vehicle bomb is to park the vehicle and sneak away without being noticed. Crashing through a barrier would be noticeable. Barriers for the moving vehicle bomb need to stop the vehicle's motion; they must be much more substantial.

Perimeter Barriers: Perimeter barriers are fixed barriers placed around the entire perimeter of a stand-off zone. Anything that presents a fixed obstacle will work for the stationary vehicle bomb. Common applications include chain-link fences, hedges made of low bushes, and high (over eight inches) curbs. Aggressors driving through such barriers are likely to be noticed. Barriers capable of stopping moving vehicles include chain-link fences reinforced with cable, reinforced concrete 'Jersey barriers', pipe bollards, planters' ditches, and berms. When barriers such as the Jersey barriers and planters are used to stop moving vehicles, they must be anchored into the ground to be effective. The cables in the reinforced fence also have to be anchored into the ground or partially buried. Spaces between barriers should be no greater than four feet. The Hesco bastion is made of a collapsible wire mesh container and heavy duty fabric liner, and is used as a temporary to semi-permanent dike or barrier against blast. We now also have Bremer walls of T-walls (12 feet high RCC wall sections with a 'T' shaped cross-section); and 20 feet high Alaska barriers.

Bremer wall sections at a factory producing them in Gopala, Iraq

Active Barriers: Active barriers are placed at openings in perimeters where vehicles need to enter or exit. These barriers must be able to be raised and lowered or moved aside. For the stationary vehicle bomb, barriers can be as simple as chain-link, pipe, or wooden gates that can be raised and lowered. Aggressors crashing through any of these or similar obstructions will likely draw attention. For the moving vehicle bomb, the barriers must be heavy and strong structures and have many construction and operation considerations associated with them. These barriers must aim to stop vehicles weighing up to 15,000 pounds and travelling 50 miles per hour. But remember that terrorists can muster really powerful vehicles and even use improvised armour on them to enable them to crash through barriers unless you impose great restrictions. They can also use subterfuge—concrete mixers have been used to carry explosives in great quantities.

Speed Control: It is important to control the speed of a vehicle approaching a barrier used for a moving vehicle bomb. Since kinetic energy is proportional to the square of speed, it is necessary to control the speed of a vehicle. You do not have any control on the mass of the vehicle, but you can control the speed. If you can decrease the speed of the incoming vehicles, you would require smaller and less costly barriers. The best way to limit a vehicle's approach speed to perimeter barriers is to place or retain obstacles in potential approach paths. The vehicles are forced to reduce speed when going around these obstacles. The same principle applies for road approaches. Placing obstacles in a serpentine pattern on the road forces a vehicle to reduce its speed. If the vehicle hits the obstacles instead of going around them, they are still slowed down. Other means to slow vehicles include forcing them to make sharp turns and installing traffic circles.

A cleverer idea is to make a triangle of two sections of the Bremer Wall so that they resist a speeding vehicle better

Building Elements: Once the stand-off distance is established and the site has been laid out, the designers can select the building components necessary to protect the assets against the threat explosives at the stand-off distance. The building components include the walls, roofs, doors, and windows.

Walls and Roofs: If the distances determined for the desired damage levels cannot be enforced, the building's walls and roofs will need to be strengthened. This can be achieved in new construction by using reinforced masonry or reinforced concrete in the walls and reinforced concrete in the roof. When the stand-off distance is not available for existing construction, a more detailed analysis may be required to determine what the explosion's impact will be on the structure. When the construction is inadequate, more stand-off distance should be investigated or the engineers should apply specialised techniques for retrofitting the construction to increase its strength.

Windows: Historically, glass fragments have caused about 85 per cent of injuries and deaths in bomb blasts. There are two basic approaches to mitigating the effects of bomb blasts on glass – retrofitting the windows with film or curtains and using blast-resistant glazing.

Retrofitting Windows: One of the most common means of decreasing the hazards from broken glass is to install fragment-retention film on the glass. The film is a plastic (polyester) sheet that adheres to the window glass with a special adhesive. The film does not strengthen the glass; but when the glass breaks, it keeps the fragments from spreading throughout the room. The glass fragments stick to the film, and the film either stays in the window frame or falls into the room in one or more large, relatively non-hazardous pieces instead of many small, lethal pieces. Another retrofit approach is to install a blast curtain or a heavy drape behind the window. The curtain or drape catches the glass fragments. The curtains are generally used with fragment-retention film. Another retrofit technique is to use fragment-retention film with a metal bar placed across the window. This 'catcher bar' catches the window. The designs for this and other types of retrofit devices are complicated and require specialised engineering-analysis tools. The retrofit techniques are generally thought of as providing a lower level of protection than the glazing replacement techniques. For deployed locations, removing the windows and covering them with plywood minimises the danger.

Blast-Resistant Glazing: To achieve higher levels of protection, the window glass must be replaced and the window frame should be reinforced. Because of its expense, this procedure is generally limited to new construction and major renovations. Special blast-resistant glazing and frames are available that use either tempered glass or a plastic glazing (such as polycarbonate). Another promising type of blast-resistant glazing is laminated glass, in which several layers of common glass are adhered together with a special interlayer. The resulting laminated construction is usually stronger than common glass while retaining the same thickness. The interlayer acts similarly to fragment-retention film. For deployed locations, a means of minimising the danger of windows is to remove them and replace them with plywood.

Doors: Common metal and wood doors provide little resistance to a blast. The two ways to address the problem of doors is to install them in foyers or to replace them. Glass doors or doors containing windows must be avoided. Door hazards can be reduced by installing doors in foyers during construction or by adding foyers to existing buildings. When a door is located in a foyer and the outer door fails, the outer door flies into a wall instead of the building's interior. The inner door then has a greater chance of remaining intact. This option generally provides a low level of protection. Another option is to replace the doors with specially constructed blast-resistant doors and frames. These doors are commercially available and can provide a high level of protection, but they are very expensive and heavy. The doorframe must be made of the same type of material and provide the same level of protection as the door.

Detection: Numerous devices are available for scanning a vehicle. While they increase the chances of detection, the fact remains that it is possible to conceal the explosives in a vehicle that would beat all but the most sophisticated detection methods.

(16.2.2) Exterior Attack

Because the exterior attack is directed at a facility's exterior surfaces, the general-design strategy is to keep aggressors away from the facility (at a stand-off distance) and, if necessary, to harden the facility's exterior components to resist the effects of weapons and explosives. A stand-off distance of about 50 feet from the facility reduces the degree of hardening required to resist weapons effects. Keep the perimeter about seven feet or more high and leave trees around the perimeter – this makes it difficult to throw explosives etc. over the fence. Normally, it is not expected that the aggressors would be able to use things bigger than briefcase-sised bombs at the exterior and this is not a very serious threat.

(16.2.3) Stand-off Weapons

The stand-off-weapons tactic includes the use of anti-tank weapons and mortars. In both of these tactics, the aggressor fires weapons at assets located in the protected facility from a distance. An anti-tank weapon attack requires a clear LOS to the target, while mortars can fire over obstacles and only need a clear line of flight. Stand-off weapons attacks cannot be detected reliably before they occur. Defending against a mortar attack is indeed very difficult. Protective design to resist these tactics relies on blocking LOSs to protected areas of a facility or hardening the facility to resist the particular weapon's effects.

Levels of Protection: There are two levels of protection against both mortars and AT weapons. For AT weapons, the low level of protection depends on detonating the AT round before it hits the target facility. The high level of protection avoids the risk associated with that and hardens the building to resist the direct impact of the AT round. For mortars, the low level of protection involves allowing some areas of the facility to be sacrificed. Those spaces provide a buffer to the assets to be protected. The assets within the sacrificial areas and the areas themselves may be destroyed. At the high level of protection, the building's exterior fully resists the mortar rounds and there are no sacrificial areas.

Site-Work Elements: The primary site-work element for stand-off weapons is to obstruct LOSs from vantage points outside of the site. That helps against the AT weapons, but not mortars. The LOSs are blocked by using trees, other buildings, vehicle parking areas, or fences. Another site-work element, a pre-detonation screen, applies only to an AT weapon. When using a pre-detonation screen, the AT round is detonated on the screen and its effects are dissipated in the distance between the screen and the target. The screen distances vary from less than 10 feet to almost 40 feet, depending on the building construction.

Building Elements: A building's interior layout is only an issue for the low level of protection against a mortar round. The layout issue involves designating sacrificial areas in which unimportant assets are located. The assets to be protected are located in a hardened interior layer. The sacrificial area has to be both around and above the protected area in case a mortar round comes from above. If walls have to resist the round, they would have to be at least 24-inch-thick reinforced concrete.

(16.2.4) Firearms

Protective measures to resist shooting by firearms rely on blocking LOSs to protected areas of a facility or by hardening the facility to resist the ballistic effects. The LOSs can be blocked using trees, other buildings, motor pools, or fences. This strategy focuses on assets within buildings only. Protecting people or property in the open is not possible. Important windows and doors can be fitted with bullet-resistant assemblies, should you so desire.

(16.2.5) Forced Entry

If the aggressor is using explosives, he can breach any normal perimeter that you could have erected. The general-design strategy for forced entry is therefore to detect the aggressor early in the forced-entry attempt and delay him long enough for a response force to intercept him. The combination of detection and defensive measures must provide sufficient time for a response force to intercept the aggressor before he reaches the asset or before he escapes with it, depending on the protective goals for the asset. The first goal would apply where the asset is likely to be destroyed or where access to it is not acceptable. The second goal would be applied when the idea is to prevent it from being stolen. Detection can be achieved by using an IDS (Intruder Detection System). Once a sensor detects an aggressor, the alarm annunciator communicates that event to security personnel, who then dispatch a response force. The alarm can be accessed through a guard response or via CCTV. Building elements are used to provide delay. The process for designing to resist forced entry involves laying out concentric 'rings' of delay (called defensive layers). These defensive layers can include the facility's exterior, interior rooms within that layer, and containers within the interior rooms. The individual building components for each of the layers (walls, doors, windows, floors, ceilings, and roofs) provide the delay time.

(16.2.6) Covert Entry and Entry by Subversion

The general-design strategy for both the covert-entry tactic and entry by subversion is to keep people from entering areas they are not authorised to enter. Covert entry is defeated by a strict application of basic security measures like access control. It becomes more difficult when a subverted insider is throwing his weight to assist an unauthorised person to enter. Eventually it falls on the persons entrusted with access control as to how much pressure they can resist. A common design goal would be to limit the number of entrances into controlled areas because there will be need to control access at each entry. Further, the controlled area may be compartmentalised, and each compartmentalised area may have separate access requirements.

Detection Elements: Detection elements vary based on the aggressor's goal. For theft, the detection elements are mainly related to access control. For destruction, the detection elements are used to detect weapons, explosives, or incendiary devices. The main detection elements for theft or compromise are access-control devices. These can include procedural systems (such as guards checking ID), mechanical systems (such as keyed or combination locks), or electronic entry-control elements (such as electronic card readers, keypads, and biometric devices). The sophistication of these elements and the number used varies with the level of protection. When destruction of the assets is the goal, detection is oriented toward detecting weapons, explosives, or incendiary devices. At the lower levels of protection, it is sufficient for guards to search for carried-in items. Achieving higher levels of protection requires the application of such equipment as metal detectors, X-ray machines, and explosive detectors.

(16.2.7) Surveillance and Eavesdropping

Surveillance and eavesdropping tactics include visual surveillance, acoustic eavesdropping, and electronic-emanations eavesdropping. In these tactics, aggressors remain outside of controlled areas and try to gather information from within those areas. The tools used for these tactics include ocular devices for the visual-surveillance tactic and listening devices and electronic-emanations-eavesdropping equipment for the eavesdropping tactic. The general-design strategy for these tactics is to deny the aggressors access to information assets. The kind of information (objects, operations, or files; secure conversations; or electronically processed data) and how it can be compromised differs for each tactic as do the specific protective strategies. Defeating visual and acoustic surveillance is not difficult. Protection against electronic-emanations eavesdropping involves the application of Terminal Electromagnetic-Pulse Emanation Standard (TEMPEST)-shielded equipment; separation between electronic circuits that handle classified information and those that do not (commonly called red/black separation); and TEMPEST-shielded enclosures (specialised, metal-shielded construction).

(16.2.8) Mail and Supply Bombs

In mail- and supply-bomb tactics, aggressors place bombs in materials delivered to a facility. Explosives used in supply bombs are significantly larger (briefcase size) than those in mail bombs (pipe bombs or smaller). Mail bombs are usually directed at individuals, while supply bombs may be used to target larger numbers of people. These tactics assume that the facility containing the asset has a mail-handling area or a supplies-handling and -receiving area. These tactics do not apply if mail or supplies are handled and screened in a different facility. The general-design strategy for mail and supply bombs is to detect delivered bombs before they explode and to harden the area where the explosion takes place. This minimises the damage to the remainder of the facility. For detection, equipment such as X-ray examining devices, metal detectors, and explosives detectors can be used. Mail rooms and supplies-handling areas should be located on the facility's exterior, away from any critical assets. The walls and ceiling between the mail room and the remainder of the building are hardened to keep the blast effects out of the facility. The exterior walls and doors should be of lightweight construction so that they may fail and vent the blast pressure away from the building.

(16.2.9) *Chemical And Biological Contamination*

When using chemical- and biological-contamination tactics, aggressors introduce contaminants into the air or water supply to a facility or a group of facilities. Both airborne and waterborne contaminants include chemical, biological, and radiological agents. Aggressors may also forcibly enter a facility to contaminate water or air using the forced-entry tactic. It is unlikely that all agents will be detected, so the general-design strategy for these tactics is to filter out suspected airborne contaminants or to shut off suspected waterborne contaminants. Also, because contaminants can easily be entered into the environment from inside a facility, the strategy includes limiting access to the facility (especially mechanical rooms, water intakes, and so forth). Protecting large water-treatment plants and water-storage structures is not really difficult. Contrary to popular perception, one would require huge quantities of the contaminants and they cannot be brought to the site covertly. Protection against airborne contamination at a facility involves making elements of the air-handling system (including air intakes) inaccessible and laying out toxin-free areas for people to be protected. A toxin-free area is an area in which the internal air pressure is higher than the external air pressure. Therefore, if a chemical, biological, or radiological device is set off outside, its contaminant will not be able to penetrate the protected area. Achieving that 'net positive pressure' requires a significant air-handling system with air filters to filter contaminants out of the air. It also requires an air-lock entrance into the area so contaminants cannot enter through the door.

(16.3) Protective Barriers

There is no such thing as a small firefight.

Common barriers such as barbed wire or concertina protect against human intrusion. A great advantage with concertina is the ability to deploy quickly. When used as the perimeter barrier for a restricted area, the concertina must be laid between poles with one roll on top of another or in a pyramidal arrangement (with a minimum of three rolls). All observation towers should be located to provide maximum observation and should be constructed for protection from small-arms fire. However, during inclement weather and during a blackout, towers lose the advantage of a greater range of observation and must be supplemented by on-ground observation. They must have appropriate surveillance, target-acquisition, and night-observation (STANO) equipment. All facilities using towers must have a support force available for emergencies. You must ensure that towers have overlapping, mutually supporting fields of observation and fire and that they are provided with a backup fortified defensive fighting position, as appropriate. When the perimeter barrier encloses a large area, an interior all-weather perimeter road should be provided for security-patrol vehicles. Clear zones should be maintained on both sides of the perimeter barrier to provide an unobstructed view of the barrier and the ground adjacent to it. If it is not possible due to whatever reason, compensate for it by increasing the height of the perimeter barrier, increasing security-patrol coverage, adding more security lighting, or installing an intrusion-detection device along that portion of the perimeter. You may also require special barriers to impede observation; as a means to defeat stand-off weapon systems (such as rocket-propelled grenades); and as a barrier to hand-thrown weapons (such as grenades and firebombs). Sewers, air and water intakes and exhausts, and other utility openings of 10 inches or more in diameter that pass through perimeter barriers must have security measures equivalent to that of the perimeter. Gates and entry-control stations should be hardened against attacks according to the type of threat.

(16.4) Principles of Security Lighting

It is necessary to discuss the principles of security lighting here because most people are generally ignorant about them. Optimum security lighting is achieved by adequate, even light on bordering areas; glaring lights in the eyes of an intruder; and little light on security-patrol routes. In addition to seeing long distances, security forces must be able to see low contrasts (such as indistinct outlines of silhouettes) and must be able to detect an intruder who may be exposed to view for only a few seconds. Higher levels of illumination improve these abilities. High brightness contrast between an intruder and the background should be the first consideration when planning for security lighting. With predominantly dark, dirty surfaces or camouflage-type painted surfaces, more light is needed to produce the same brightness around installations and buildings than when clean concrete, light brick, and grass predominate. When the same amount of light falls on an object and its background, the observer must depend on contrasts in the amount of light reflected. His ability to distinguish poor contrasts is significantly improved by increasing the illumination level. The observer primarily sees an outline or a silhouette when the intruder is darker than his background. Using light finishes on the lower parts of buildings and structures may expose an intruder who depends on dark clothing and darkened face and hands. Stripes on walls have also been used effectively, as they provide recognisable breaks in outlines or silhouettes. Providing broad-lighted areas around and within the installation against which intruders can be seen can also create good observation conditions. An open yard adjacent to a perimeter (between guards and fences) must be illuminated according to the perimeter's illumination requirements. Where lighting is necessary in other open yards, illumination should not be less than 0.2 foot-candle at any point. Decks on open piers must be illuminated to at least one foot-candle and the water approaches (extending to a distance of 100 feet from the pier) to at least 0.5 foot-candle. The area beneath the pier floor must be lit with small wattage floodlights arranged on the piling. A secure auxiliary power source and power-distribution system for the facility should be installed to provide redundancy to critical security lighting and other security equipment. Auxiliary power sources must be available for critical electrical loads and must be secured against direct and indirect fires as well as sabotage.

(16.5) Electronic Security Systems (ESS)

An ESS's basic function is to notify security personnel that an intruder is attempting to penetrate covertly, or has penetrated a protected area in sufficient time to allow the response force to intercept and apprehend him. An overall site-security system is comprised of three major sub-elements—detection, delay, and response. The detection sub-element includes intrusion detection, assessment, and entry control. Digital and analog data are transmitted from local (field) interior and exterior locations to the security center for processing. Interior and exterior sensors and their associated communication and display subsystems are collectively called IDSs (Intruder Detection Systems). An ESS is an integrated system that encompasses interior and exterior sensors; CCTV systems for assessing alarm conditions; electronic entry-control systems (EECSs); data-transmission media (DTM); and alarm reporting systems for monitoring, controlling, and displaying various alarm and system information.

(16.5.1) Intruder Detection Systems

Boundary sensors that detect penetration (such as structural-vibration sensors or passive ultrasonic sensors) provide the earliest warning of an attempted intrusion. This alarm is usually generated before the barrier is penetrated. Door-position sensors and glass-breakage sensors do not generate an alarm until the barrier has been breached. Volumetric motion sensors do not generate an alarm until the intruder is already inside the area covered by the sensors. Point sensors, such as capacitance sensors and pressure mats, provide warning of attempted penetration only if they detect the intruder before access is gained to the protected area. Because of environmental conditions, the exterior electronics must be designed and packaged for extremes of temperature, moisture, and wind. Weather and climatic conditions at a specific site can significantly influence sensor selection. For example, IR detectors are not very effective in heavy rain, fog, dust, or snow. Deep snow can affect detection patterns and performance of both IR and microwave sensors. High winds can cause numerous false alarms in fence-mounted sensors. Electrical storms can cause alarms in many types of sensors and may also damage the equipment. Tall grass or weeds can disturb the energy pattern of microwave and both thermal IR and near-IR beam-break sensors. Vegetation growing near electric-field sensors and capacitance sensors can cause nuisance alarms. Large weeds or bushes rubbing against a fence can produce nuisance alarms from fence-mounted sensors. Large trees and bushes moving within the field of view of video motion sensors can cause nuisance or environmental alarms. A clear area must be established for exterior sensors. This area must be void of vegetation or contain vegetation of carefully controlled growth.

Exterior sensors must have a high probability of detection for all types of intrusion and have a low unwanted-alarm rate for all expected environmental and site conditions. Unfortunately, no single exterior sensor that is presently available meets both these criteria. All are limited in their detection capability, and all have high susceptibility to nuisance and environmental conditions. Fence sensors detect attempts to penetrate a fence around a protected area. Penetration attempts (such as climbing, cutting, or lifting) generate mechanical vibrations and stresses in fence fabric and posts that are usually different than those caused by natural phenomena like wind and rain. The basic types of sensors used to detect these vibrations and stresses are strain-sensitive cable, taut wire, and fiber optics. Other types of fence sensors detect penetration attempts by sensing changes in an electric field or in capacitance.

Electric-field sensors consist of an alternating-current (AC) field generator, one or more field wires, one or more sense wires, and a signal processor. The generator excites the field wires around which an electrostatic-field pattern is created. The electrostatic field induces electrical signals in the sense wires, which are monitored by the signal processor. Under normal operating conditions, the induced signals are constant. However, when an intruder approaches the sensor, the induced electrical signals are altered, causing the signal processor to generate an alarm. Several different field- and sense-wire configurations are available. They range from one field wire and one sense wire to as many as four field wires and one sense wire or four field wires and four sense wires. The three-wire system has a wider detection envelope and is less costly (one field wire and associated hardware less). However, because of the tighter coupling between wires, the four-wire system is less susceptible to nuisance alarms caused by extraneous noise along the length of the zone.

Capacitance proximity sensors measure the electrical capacitance between the ground and an array of sense wires. Any variations in capacitance, such as that caused by an intruder approaching or touching one of the sense wires, initiates an alarm. These sensors usually consist of two or three wires attached to outriggers along the top of an existing fence, wall, or roof edge. To minimise environmental alarms, the capacitance sensor is divided into two arrays of equal length. The signal processor monitors the capacitance of each array. Changes in capacitance common to both arrays (such as produced by wind, rain, ice, fog, and lightning) are cancelled within the processor. However, when changes occur in one array and not the other because of an intruder, the processor initiates an alarm.

A buried-line sensor system consists of detection probes or cable buried in the ground, typically between two fences that form an isolation zone. These devices are wired to an electronic processing unit. The processing unit generates an alarm if an intruder passes through the detection field. Buried-line sensors have several significant features: they are hidden, making them difficult to detect and circumvent; they follow the terrain's natural contour; they do not physically interfere with human activity, such as grass mowing or snow removal; and they are affected by certain environmental conditions, such as running water and ground freeze/thaw cycles.

The ported-coax cable sensor consists of two coax cables buried in the ground parallel to each other. An RF transmitter is connected to one cable and a receiver to the other. The outer conductor of each cable is ported (fabricated with small holes or gaps in the shield). The transmitter cable radiates RF energy into the medium surrounding the cables. A portion of this energy is coupled into the receiver cable through its ported shield. (Because of the ported shields, these cables are frequently referred to as leaky cables also). When an intruder enters the RF field, the coupling is disturbed, resulting in a change of signal monitored by the receiver, which then generates an alarm. Two basic types of ported-coax sensors are available—pulse and continuous wave. A pulse type sensor transmits a pulse of RF energy down one cable and monitors the received signal on the other. The cables can be up to 10,000 feet long. The signal processor initiates an alarm when the electromagnetic field created by the pulse is disturbed and identifies the disturbance's approximate location. Continuous-wave sensors apply continuous RF energy to one cable. The signal received on the other cable is monitored for electromagnetic-field disturbances that indicate an intruder's presence. Cable lengths are limited to 300 to 500 feet. Additionally, the sensor is available in a single-cable configuration as well as two separate cables. The pattern typically extends 2 to 4 feet above the ground and can be 5 to 13 feet wide, depending on cable spacing and soil composition.

Sensor performance depends on properties of the medium surrounding the cables. Velocity and attenuation of the RF wave that propagates along the cables and the coupling between the cables are functions of the dielectric constant of the soil and its conductivity which, in turn, depends on its moisture content. For example, the velocity is greater and the attenuation is less for cables buried in dry, low-loss soil than in wet, conductive soil. Freeze/thaw cycles in the soil also affect the sensor's performance. When wet soil freezes, the wave velocity and the cable coupling increase and the attenuation decreases, resulting in greater detection sensitivity. Seasonal sensitivity adjustments may be necessary to compensate for changing ground conditions.

The LOS sensors, which are mounted above ground, can be either active or passive. Active sensors generate a beam of energy and detect changes in the received energy that an intruder causes by penetrating the beam. Each sensor consists of a transmitter and a receiver and can be in a mono-static or bi-static configuration. Passive sensors generate no beam of energy; they simply look for changes in the thermal characteristics of their field of view. For effective detection, the terrain within the detection zone must be flat and free of obstacles and vegetation.

Microwave intrusion-detection sensors are categorised as bi-static or mono-static. Bi-static sensors use transmitting and receiving antennas located at opposite ends of the microwave link, whereas mono-static sensors use the same antenna. A bi-static system uses a transmitter and a receiver that are typically separated by 100 to 1,200 feet and that are within direct LOS with each other. The signal picked up by the receiver is the vector sum of the directly transmitted signal and signals that are reflected from the ground and nearby structures. Detection occurs when an object (intruder) moving within the beam pattern causes a change in net-vector summation of the received signals, resulting in variations of signal strength. The shape of the microwave beam and the maximum separation between the transmitter and the receiver are functions of antenna size and configuration. Mono-static microwave sensors use the same antenna or virtually coincident antenna arrays for the transmitter and receiver, which are usually combined into a single package. Two types of mono-static sensors are available. Amplitude-modulated (AM) sensors detect changes in the net-vector summation of reflected signals similar to bi-static sensors. Frequency-modulated (FM) sensors operate on the Doppler principle similar to interior microwave sensors. The detection pattern is typically shaped like a teardrop. Mono-static sensors can provide volumetric coverage of localised areas, such as in corners or around the base of critical equipment.

IR sensors are available in both active and passive models. An active sensor generates one or more near-IR beams that generate an alarm when interrupted. A passive sensor detects changes in thermal IR radiation from objects located within its field of view. The spacing between transmitters and receivers can be as great as 1,000 feet when operation is under good weather conditions. However, conditions such as heavy rain, fog, snow, or blowing dust particles attenuate the IR energy, reducing its effective range to 100 to 200 feet or less.

17

The Myth of Fancy Weapons

Wonder weapons... my God, I don't see the wonder in them.

(17.1) How Myths are Created?

It is generally believed that the Indians are failing in their counter-terrorist mission because they do not have the latest weapons and gadgetry. Ignoramuses in the media keep on lamenting how impoverished the Indian forces are. We wish they had lamented more about their intellectual impoverishment. Indian forces are fumbling in their fight against terrorism because they are dumb, not because they are badly ill-equipped. This myth is propagated mainly by two sources. The first is the forces themselves who want to hide their tactical and strategic incompetence behind an alleged lack of fancy weapon systems. The second is an utterly ignorant media. Quite like adolescents, the media is fascinated by gadgets. When they watch foreign channels or surf the Internet, they get to see a lot of gadgets being used by foreign forces. Since they are intellectually incapable of understanding the complexities of counter-terrorism, they latch on to the catchiest objects—gadgets fit the bill perfectly. The general refrain becomes: if we had such-and-such thing, we would have wiped off these jokers a long time back. Little do they realise that fancy weapons are either simply fancy weapons or an adolescent's fancy—having a fancy weapon does not mean that you will win in all combats; not having a fancy weapon does not mean that you will lose all combats. The fact is that above a certain minimum standard, the difference they make is really very small. Nobody thinks for a moment that there is much more to counter-terrorism than hunting down bandits in the woods.

I would like to reproduce a media report as illustrative of the way in which the media keeps on dropping nuggets of its lack of wisdom: 'Mumbai Police Modernisation Generates Controversy' (*The Hindu*, April 08, 2009) and "No Bang In Mumbai Police's New Guns" (*The Hindu*, April 08, 2009) – Praveen Swami

"In the wake of November 2008 carnage, the Mumbai Police promised the people that it would soon arm itself with the equipment it needed to evolve into a credible counter-terrorism force…In the next few weeks, the police will receive the first of the new guns it desperately needs. But experts in India's elite forces and military have told *The Hindu* that the four critical weapons systems do not in fact pack much of a bang. Ordered without competitive field trials, the weapons are being criticised as technologically suspect and inappropriate to local needs…Last month, the police placed orders for four new weapons without conducting field trials to determine their effectiveness in local conditions or evaluating the competing technologies…The police planners selected the Colt M4 5.56-millimeter carbine for assault roles, the Brügger and Thomet sub-compact MP9 for close-protection duties, the Smith and Wesson Military and Police 9-millimeter pistol as a personal sidearm and the M107 50-caliber Special Application Rifle… But experts in the National Security Guards and the Army told *The Hindu* that the choices made were less than transparent…For example, the United States military Special Forces are replacing the Colt M4s with new-generation European-made weapons. And the state-of-the-art MP9 is intended to protect VIPs in environments where it is inappropriate to display guns – a responsibility the Mumbai Police do not have…The M107 SAR, a lethal weapon designed to penetrate armour and bullet-proof glass, has been selected despite the risk of collateral damage and the fact that the Mumbai Police have no range on which personnel could be trained in its use…Highly placed police sources said the weapons were chosen by a committee comprising Police Commissioner Hasan Gaffur, Additional Commissioner of Police (Protection) Vinay Khargaonkar and Joint Commissioner of Police (Traffic) Sanjay Barwe...off the record, Mumbai Police officials said the force chose to bypass testing and competitive evaluation procedures because of the urgent need for new weapons…Gaffur did not respond to phone calls and a text message seeking information on how the weapons systems were chosen…Notably, the committee did not hold consultations with the Maharashtra Police and the NSG, which have primary responsibility for counter-terrorism roles in Mumbai…

On April 2, the Maharashtra government passed orders creating Force One, a 350-man crack special weapons and tactics formation modelled on the NSG. According to the order, Force One, rather than the Mumbai Police, will have the primary responsibility of counter-terrorism operations in the city – making it possible that the expensive weapons the committee ordered will never be used...Later this year, the NSG will begin operations from a new 25-acre facility in the city's Kalina area. The NSG personnel in Kalina will be equipped with much of the special equipment the Mumbai Police ordered, including the M107 SAR and the Brügger and Thomet MP9...Union Home Ministry officials in New Delhi, who granted permission to the Mumbai Police to import the new equipment last month, declined to comment on the controversy..."It is our job to act as a facilitator of modernisation and not to sit in judgment on what equipment best meets the needs of a particular state. While we may have our concerns, we do not wish to be cast as spoilers," a senior official said.

The said media report is important for several reasons. In the first place, the reporter says that field trials were not conducted. The poor fellow does not even know how trials are conducted and how cumbersome the process is. He would not have said so had he even heard of the Great American Pistol Test (also known as the XM9 pistol trial) and how it ran into controversy in spite of being so exhaustive. Has such testing ever been done in India in any force for any weapon? Most of the trials conducted by the army get mired into controversy because they are conducted in such an unscientific and slipshod manner and which always leave scope for allegations of manipulation. For that matter, has anybody ever laid down the structure of a scientific testing? We shall be shortly discussing some of the fancy weapons which the SPG have acquired and of which the same media people have been speaking very highly of. Were they purchased after any scientific test? If so, what were the parameters of the test and was there any peer review of the same? When the so-called experts of the National Security Guard and the army are said to have spoken of the process being less than transparent, the reporter is actually obliquely hinting at or insinuating corruption. Since the media in this country is utterly irresponsible and also unaccountable, neither they felt obliged to pursue it to its logical end nor did the agency insinuated (that is, the Maharashtra police) feel obliged to clear its name and haul the reporter. In the following we will systematically demolish the ignorance of the media and the so-called unnamed 'experts' they cite about technical and professional matters related to weaponry. The simple fact is that the journos do not know anything about a weapon, its design, its merits or demerits – all they know is its name and may be what they have read in some magazine somewhere. The hype surrounding fancy weapons is nothing but unethical marketing by the companies and those who are lured by it are guilty of an unscientific approach at the best and downright stupidity at the worst.

(17.2) Why the Hype Surrounding Every New Weapon is not Justified?

Night vision devices will only fail at night. They will function perfectly once the sun rises.

(17.2.1) Combat Effectiveness as Perceived by Human Targets

The ignoramuses do not know that as far as combat effectiveness goes, there is very little difference amongst all the assault rifles that have been invented since 1944. The reason is simple. The basic technology remains the same. After all, you have smokeless powder that burns and propels a bullet—there is not really much that you can vary in it—you can change the caliber and the weight of the bullet a little, you can also get the rate of fire changed a bit. All such things bring about cosmetic changes—they become necessary because each new design has to claim something new—after all the companies have to remain in business and for that they have to employ all the usual marketing techniques and those of befooling the customers. Different weapons systems differ more in their marketing strategies than in their combat effectiveness. An automatic rifle over a bolt action rifle was a qualitative improvement. However, there is no qualitative improvement between an automatic rifle that weighs 4 kg and fires at a cyclic rate of fire of 600 rounds per minute and one that weighs 3.6 kg and fires at a cyclic rate of 700 rounds per minute—the human target in front of both will never know the difference.

The point to be understood is that when you are spraying bullets on full auto in a room, you are not firing 700 bullets. All you can fire is one magazine of 30 rounds. It does not really make any difference whether you are pouring out 30 rounds in 3 seconds (at the rate of 600 rounds per minute) or 2.6 seconds (at the rate of 700 rounds per minute)—the human targets in front of you will not be able to tell the difference—you cannot say that the target can take evasive action, if the rate of fire is 600 rounds per minute and cannot take such evasive action, if the rate of fire is higher—human reflexes are, in any case, far slower. And for the duffers' kind information, when you take into account the fact that anyone of the bullets could be fatal, the difference becomes even more insignificant.

There is no assault rifle developed since 1944 that brought any material change in the rifle or the bullet. While the controversy over the relative merits and demerits of the 7.62 x 51 mm full-length, 7.62 x 39 mm intermediate, 5.56 x 45 mm NATO, and 5.45 x 39 mm Russian cartridges rages on, the fact is that as far as an unprotected human target at 200 yards is concerned, he is likely to be killed by all of them! Yes, there are differences and it is a source of great pleasure to discuss them, but the difference is not very great. Bullets can be optimised for minimum time of flight, minimum dispersion, maximum retained kinetic energy, minimum cross wind sensitivity, minimum ballistic drop, maximum penetration, and limiting maximum range. For instance, a heavier bullet launched at lower muzzle velocity is a bullet designed to minimise cross-wind sensitivity. As the bullet gets heavier, more of the projectile body can be dedicated to give length, reducing drag. A heavier and faster bullet with lower drag is indeed desirable, but with a fixed case volume, it is not possible to improve on all of these attributes simultaneously. A bullet optimised for one parameter is often the worst solution for another important parameter. Optimising one parameter requires compromise on others.

There is no bullet that will chase its target like a surface-to-air missile and be a true 'fire and forget' bullet; there is no bullet that will kill ten men in a row either. Many new concepts were tried in the pursuit of novelty. Caseless ammunition was developed to save the weight of the cartridge case so that the soldier could carry more cartridges and also to save on the cost of the precision-made metallic case. Sounds fascinating in theory but was not successful. Modern caseless ammunition consists of a solid mass of propellant, originally nitro-cellulose, cast into shape to form the body of the cartridge, with cavities to accept the bullet and a primer, preferably combustible, which are glued into place. The completed cartridge might also contain a booster charge of powdered propellant, to help ignite the body and provide initial thrust to the bullet. While it seems a simple operation to replace the case with a piece of solid propellant, it overlooks the fact that the cartridge case provides more than just a way to keep the cartridge components together, and these other functions must also be replaced if the case is to be replaced. The first major problem, of great concern to the military, is the heat sensitivity of the ammunition. Nitro-cellulose, the primary component of modern gunpowder, ignites at a very low temperature of around 170 degrees Celsius. One of the lesser known functions of the metallic cartridge case is to function as a heat sink; the metallic case carries away a significant amount of the heat of firing, slowing the rate at which heat is transferred to the chamber. The case also acts as insulation for the propellant, shielding it from built-up heat from the chamber walls. Without a case to provide these functions, caseless rounds using nitro-cellulose will begin to 'cook off', firing from the residual chamber heat, much sooner than metal cased cartridges would. The normal solution to the problem of heat is to increase the heat resistance by switching to a propellant with a higher ignition temperature, typically, a non-crystalline explosive carefully formulated to provide an appropriate rate of combustion. Another important function provided by the cartridge is to seal the rear of the chamber. During firing of a cased cartridge, the pressure in the chamber expands the brass and blocks the chamber. This prevents gas exiting from the rear of the chamber, and it has also been experimentally shown to provide a significant amount of support to the bolt. Without the case to provide this seal, the firearm design must account for this and provide a means of sealing the rear of the chamber. Caseless rounds are limited by the fact that the cartridge body is primarily a propellant, and structural properties are secondary to the combustion properties. The primary issue is one of extraction. While caseless ammunition obviates the need to extract a fired case, unfired cases must be extracted in case of a misfire, or to unload the firearm. In metallic cases, this ability is provided by a rim or extractor groove machined into the rear of the case. Even in completely plastic bodied cartridges, such as the Activ brand shotgun shells, a thin metal ring is moulded into the rim to provide support for the extractor. All such problems made it unsuccessful. Caseless rifle grenades (such as the Russian GP-30 Obuvka, GP-25 Kastyor, and BG-15 Mukha) survived to some extent because a grenade launcher does not have to fire so many of them and thus many of the problems mentioned above are taken care of, but not caseless small arms cartridges.

(17.2.2) The Objective Individual Combat Weapon: The Failed Dream of an All-in-one Weapon

In the quest to design a novel rifle, attempts were made to incorporate many additional weapon systems in the same rifle such as a grenade launcher and much more. The OICW (Objective Individual Combat Weapon) of the USA was conceived with this idea in mind. It is still under development and there is no guarantee that the troops will like it when it is fielded. Americans have an everlasting obsession of developing technically complex things. It keeps the arms industry going, and the military and the people can always be made to feel happy that their soldiers are armed with the best gadgets available. In fact, the universities as the research agencies, the arms industry as the suppliers and the military as the consumer all fuel each other in a vicious circle. Even as the Advanced Combat Rifle programme was dragging its feet, the US Army Infantry School at Fort Benning published a paper titled "Small Arms System 2000" (SAS-2000). This paper argued that the conventional small arms had already reached their technological peak, and the only way to increase the hit probability with small arms was to introduce a weapon that will fire explosive and fragmentation warheads, combined with the smart fusing and sighting/aiming technologies. The idea was to develop a rifle that would enable targets behind cover to be attacked by using airburst munitions. The munitions were to be much smaller than the existing grenades, but big enough to function as intended. That is they projected the requirement of a combination of an assault rifle and a semi-automatic low-velocity cannon firing air-burst munitions. The US Army TRADOC (Training and Doctrine Center) generally supported it in a paper titled "The Small Arms Master Plan" (SAMP), and argued for a family of infantry 'Objective' weapons, namely the Objective Individual Combat Weapon (OICW), Objective Personal Defence Weapon (OPDW), and the Objective Crew Served Weapon (OCSW). It also argued that such weapons must utilise the latest developments in computers and visual technologies, as well as in the small arms, and combine both high explosive warheads and traditional bullets firing capabilities in a single weapon.

By the mid-1990s the winner was a team led by the US-based Alliant Techsystems Corporation (ATK), with Heckler-Koch (Germany), Brashear and Omega (both of USA) as the other team members. The prototype developed by them was called XM29 OICW and it was tested in 2002. The XM29 is a combination weapon, which has a 20 mm semi-automatic, magazine-fed grenade launcher as its primary part giving the 'kill factor', and a 5.56 mm compact assault rifle as its secondary part. Both parts are assembled into a single one-man portable unit, with the addition of the target acquisition/fire control system (TA/FCS), which is an essential part of the whole system. The data provided from the TA/FCS can be used to programme the 20 mm HEAB (High Explosive Air Burst) grenade fuzes. These electronic fuzes have multiple modes of detonation, including direct impact mode and air-burst mode.

The rifle, or the 'kinetic energy' part of the XM29 system, on the other hand, is a fairy conventional, short-barreled assault rifle, derived from the HK G36 assault rifle. The basic 'rifle' part of the XM29 has no butt stock and no sights of its own, and thus can be used separately from the whole system only as emergency, personal defence weapon. The target acquisition/fire control system (TA/FCS) is the most expensive and complicated unit of the whole system, since it must combine day and night vision capabilities, laser range-finding unit, ballistic computer and various interfaces to the grenade launcher and external systems. It is used to find the targets in any light and weather conditions, determine the range of the target, calculate and display the aiming data, so the grenade or bullet could be fired to the desired point of impact, and then supply the data to the grenade launcher, so the range could be preset into the grenade fuse. In the case of damage to the TA/FCS the 20 mm grenade launcher still can be used in the direct impact mode, as well as the rifle part of the system.

The current status of the programme is uncertain. Some reports indicate that the prototype was found to be bulky, heavy and costly with much of the cost coming from the TA/FCS. There were doubts about the lethality of the 20 mm grenade also. Some reports indicated that it had been decided to split the project into two parts. OICW Increment-I would consist of the development of the rifle called XM8 and OICW Increment-II would consist of the development of a 25 mm instead of 20 mm grenade launcher called XM25. Development of a complete system (OICW Increment-III) would be undertaken only if these two are developed successfully. Still other reports indicated that the whole OICW thing has been put into cold storage for the time being.

(17.2.3) The AN-94: Complexity Exemplified

Most people do not understand that the designer is at liberty to make a weapon system as complicated as possible but the man who has to use it is a human after all. He has preferences and not all of them be logically derived ones. Soldiers do like something and do not like some other things for whatever reason. Their opinion matters because after all, they have to use them. Wayback in 1944, the German assault rifle Sturmgewehr was capable of firing special bullet from a curved barrel, so that you could fire round a corner without exposing yourself—a great technical achievement in itself—but could it become popular? No. The AK-47 is not an ergonomically designed weapon. In that respect, it has no comparison with the M16 or M4. But still, its other features are so great that it became a legend.

Consider the Russian AN-94 (Avtomat Nikonova) rifle as an epitome of complexity. This is the latest Russian assault rifle designed by Gennady Nikonov. It is also known as 'Abakan' probably because Abakan is the place where extensive tests were held in the late 1980s to consider a replacement for the venerable AK-74 and where this design had emerged the winner. The AN-94 also illustrates how changing political and war philosophies dictate weapons design. The AK was designed in an era when the Soviet army needed a cheap and reliable weapon that could be produced in great numbers and there was no time or money to be wasted on sophistication. The AN-94 is designed in an era when they are no longer fired by the revolutionary zeal of dominating the world with vast armies and are keen to demonstrate that they too could indulge in the pursuit of complexity. It even looks futuristic. There are serious doubts whether the project has really been worth the effort. Functionally, the AN-94 offers the additional feature of a two-round burst fire in addition to the usual single-shot and full-auto. These two rounds are fired at a very high rate of fire—1800 rounds per minute—and the full auto rate is 600 rounds per minute. This means that the two bullets could be placed in the same spot. It is claimed that a repeated hit on the same spot would make them highly effective against body armour as the armour also gives in to the phenomenon of fatigue. It has got a strange-looking '8'-shaped muzzle attachment. It is said to be a special, self-cleaning muzzle brake.

In terms of construction and principle of operation the AN-94 is a very complex piece. Its principle of operation is described as 'blowback shifted pulse'. When one pulls the charging handle, the bolt carrier goes back, unlocking and retracting the bolt. At the same time, a rammer, which is linked to the bolt carrier via a thin steel cable and a large pulley, goes forward, stripping the first round from the magazine and placing it into the feed way in the receiver. Upon firing, as soon as the fired bullet passes the gas port, the traditional gas-operated action begins. Since the bolt group is relatively light and the amount of the gas pressure is carefully calculated, the bolt group rapidly goes back, unlocking the barrel, extracting and ejecting the spent case. Due to the recoil impulse, the barrel receiver assembly begins to recoil inside the gun housing, compressing the recoil spring. At the same time, the cartridge rammer quickly strips the next cartridge from the magazine and introduces it into the feed way. The bolt group, under the influence of its main spring and the return buffer spring, rapidly goes forward, chambering the second round from the feed way. As soon as the bolt group locks the barrel, the hammer is released automatically, and the second shot is fired with the theoretical rate of fire of 1800 rounds per minute. At this moment the receiver is still recoiling inside the housing, and its recoil is accumulated and not yet affects the shooter and the position of the gun. When the second bullet is fired and leaves the barrel, the recoil cycle of the receiver/barrel group is stopped, and the hammer is held in the cocked position. They call it 'shifted pulse' because at that moment the shooter feels the recoil of two fired rounds simultaneously, 'shifted in time'. The reloading cycle continues as described above, but the hammer is held until the recoiling unit is returned into the forward position. If the gun is set to the 'two rounds burst' mode, the hammer is held cocked unless the trigger is released and then pulled again. If the gun is set to the "burst mode", the hammer unit switches itself automatically to the low rate of fire, and releases itself only once per complete recoil cycle.

User opinion on the AN-94 is not favourable. The gun is five to six times costlier than the AK-74. Then it is 1.2 lbs heavier than the AK-74 and the ergonomics is decidedly poorer. The pistol grip is uncomfortable and the magazine is offset, inclined from the vertical to the right. Most strangely, the folding stock interferes with trigger operation when it is folded. The complexity of the rifle makes it difficult to maintain—one requires better trained soldiers to keep it. An obsession with the so-called 'latest' is therefore utterly childish.

(17.3) A Scientific Evaluation of the Weapons Exalted or Derided by the Media

Never forget that your weapon and other equipments were purchased from the lowest bidder.

(17.3.1) The M4

The media report says the following: "The Mumbai Police planners have chosen this assault weapon, which had been in service with militaries and Special Forces around the world just as it is being phased out...Despite its distinguished pedigree, the M4 suffers from several problems inherent to the gas-optimised system that powers its firing mechanism: among them, jamming and heavy component wear and tear...Given that the M4 will serve the Mumbai Police for three decades and more, the choice of technology is debatable. Even as the police prepare to take delivery of the Carbine, some of its users are switching to more modern systems. The United States' Marines have chosen the Fabrique Nationale Herstal Special Forces Compact Assault Rifle, while the crack Delta Force has picked the Heckler and Koch M4".

Let us see, how far it is correct. The first question is how the Americans got to the M4 in the first place. Early in 1990s the old idea of replacing the pistols in the hands of the troops with some more effective, shoulder fired weapon, rose again in the heads of the US Military. The United States Marine Corps therefore ordered its officers (up to the rank of lieutenant colonel) and Staff Non-commissioned officers to carry the M4A1 carbine instead of the M9 handgun (Beretta

92 SBF). This was also in keeping with the Marine Corps motto, "Every Marine a rifleman". United States Navy corpsmen will also be issued M4A1s instead of the M9 pistol. Now, what's wrong with that? The M4 carbine differs from the M16A2 rifle only in having a shorter barrel and a telescoped, 4-position butt stock. The fact is that length and weight are immaterial. As long as you have to hold a thing with two hands, a few inches here and there do not make any difference.

There has been some criticism of the M4 carbine, such as lower muzzle velocities and louder report due to the shorter barrel, additional stress on parts because the shorter gas system works under greater pressure, and a tendency of the fore-end to overheat faster than the M16A2. Are they justified? As with many carbines, the M4 is handy and more convenient to carry than a full-length rifle. The price is slightly inferior ballistic performance compared to the full-size M16, with its nearly 6" (15 cm) longer barrel. The question is: "Is this really critical"? A shorter barrel results in lower muzzle velocity because the chamber pressure is not fully utilised—it is simple physics and there is nothing new about it. The difference in muzzle velocity becomes most apparent only at ranges of 300 yards and beyond. Statistically, however, most small-arms engagements occur within 100 yards—it is particularly true for the Marines who are fighting in Afghanistan and Iraq. They are not the battlefields of Europe where troops could engage the enemy at greater ranges. And who cares about the slightly louder report. This means that the M4 is very much an adequate weapon for the Marines as well as anyone who has to engage the enemy at the ranges commonly encountered in anti-terrorist operations.

Colt's M4A1 is one of the best in the world and in terms of heft and adaptability of use by firers of different builds, is in fact better than the AK-47.

It may not be the ideal weapon for the regular infantry intending to fight conventional battles of the World War II type in plains. The marginal sacrifice in terminal ballistics and range, in exchange for greatly improved handling characteristics, is very much a worthwhile compromise. The specifications and performance of the M4 are as follows: cyclic rate of fire: 700-950 rounds per minute; magazine capacity 30; length 757-838 mm; weight 3.1 kg. The original M4 has semi-automatic and three-round burst (TRB) fire modes, while the M4A1 has 'semi' and 'full auto', with no three-round burst. As we have discussed elsewhere in the book, the TRB mode has no advantage in anti-terrorist operations. Good that they dispensed with it while the Indians are still sticking to that in their hopeless rifle INSAS.

As for the Heckler and Koch M4 and the Delta Force using it, who said that the Delta Force is the final word in weapon systems? Incidentally, we may add that in April 2004, Colt had filed a lawsuit against Heckler and Koch and Bushmaster Firearms, claiming acts of trademark infringement, trade dress infringement, trademark dilution, false designation of origin, false advertising, patent infringement, unfair competition, and deceptive trade practices. Heckler and Koch later settled out of court, changing one product's name from 'HK M4' to 'HK416'. The Delta Force had actually collabourated with the German company to develop this and hence they had to take it. The HK416 uses a proprietary gas system derived from the HK G36, replacing the direct impingement gas system used by the standard M16/M4. In the fall of 2007, the US Army tested the M4 against three other carbines in 'sandstorm conditions' at Aberdeen Proving Ground, Maryland: the Heckler and Koch XM8 rifle, Fabrique Nationale de Herstal SOF Combat Assault Rifle (SCAR) and the Heckler and Koch HK416. Ten of each type of rifle were used to fire 6,000 rounds each, for a total of 60,000 rounds per rifle type. The M4 suffered far more stoppages than its competitors: 882 stoppages, 19 requiring an armourer to fix. The XM8 had the fewest stoppages, 116 minor stoppages and 11 major ones, followed by the FN SCAR with 226 stoppages and the HK416 with 233. The Army rightly pointed out that even with 863 minor stoppages—termed 'class one' stoppages which require 10 seconds or less to clear and 'class two' stoppages which require more than ten seconds to clear—the M4 functioned well, with over 98 per cent of the 60,000 total rounds firing without a problem. The Army said it planned to improve the M4 with a new cold-hammer-forged barrel to give longer life and more reliable magazines to reduce the stoppages. Magazine failures caused 239 of the M4's 882 failures.

The criticism that the M4 is not fancy enough is therefore not justified. Incidentally, the Marines have not abandoned the M4 and the ignorant reporter is factually wrong on that score. As we discussed above at length, there is hardly any difference amongst all the assault rifles including the venerable AK that offer full-automatic fire facility in so far as the human target is concerned.

(17.3.2) The Brugger and Thomet MP 9

The media criticises the MP 9 for the following reasons: "In service with crack forces such as the Special Protection Group (SPG) and National Security Guards, the Brugger and Thomet MP9 is a sub-compact version of the classic MP5 A4 and MP5 A3 machine-pistols...Designed to be concealed inside the clothes of close-protection guards assigned to VIPs, the MP9 has a retractable stock and the magazine is fitted inside the grip. Like other weapons of this kind, it trades accuracy for size... The Mumbai Police planners are thought to have ordered over 200 MP9 units—a surprise number, given that responsibility for protecting the State's VIPs lies with a special unit of the Maharashtra Police. Moreover, it has ordered none of the more accurate MP5 series...Experts in the armed forces believe that the Mumbai Police ought to have evaluated newer weapons systems before making a purchase decision...For a variety of technical reasons, the 9 millimeter ammunition used by the MP5A4 is known to be less than optimally efficient at generating the neurological shock that kills or incapacitates targets. Designers have sought to compensate for the design flaws in the 9 millimeter system by creating what are known as hollow-point bullets...But many crack forces have switched over to newer ammunition systems...The SPG, for example, uses the 5.27 x 8 millimeter Fabrique Nationale Herstal P90. Built around what designers call a 'Bull-pup' frame, the P90 is compact without compromising on accuracy".

Let us examine the reporter's wisdom or lack of it. The reporter is factually wrong from the beginning. The MP9 has never had to do anything with the Heckler and Koch MP5 series. They are products of different companies altogether. The reporter has simply looked at the initial MP and imagined the rest. The MP9 sub-machine gun started its life in 1992 as the Steyr TMP. The Steyr-Mannlicher company developed it in Austria, but Austrian export licensing laws and lack of sales resulted in the decision of Steyr to drop the TMP from the product line in 2001. Then, Brugger Thomet AG of Switzerland bought all the drawings, patents and rights for the TMP design. At the present time the MP9 (which stands for 'Machine Pistol 9 millimeter') is produced and marketed by them.

The MP9 claims to offer interim solution between true 'machine pistols' such as Beretta 93R or Glock 18, and full-size submachine guns, like the Beretta 12S or H&K MP5. The logic or the concept is not new. Much before it, the Ingram MAC-10, H&K MP5K or IMI Mini-UZI had addressed the same issue. While the aforementioned SMGs/machine pistols are very compact, they full-auto fire capability is severely limited by high recoil, short barrels and high rates of fire; the full-size submachine guns, on the other hand, are big enough to demand two hands. All these weapons caught the fancies of Hollywood filmmakers, gangsters and incidentally, brainless persons entrusted with security of individuals. Since rifles were ruled out due to size and pistols had become old-fashioned, these guys, being of the same intellectual capacity, latched on to the SMGs of various types.

In all other applications, the rate of fire is never an issue. The market is full of innumerous designs of SMGs firing at a higher or lower rate. The rate of fire, as discussed above, is absolutely immaterial because the human target can never tell the difference. Hence, the question of comparison with the MP5 on account of its supposed accuracy does not even arise. Both are, as shown a little later, equally useless in the business of protecting a constitutional functionary. Next he speaks about the efficacy of the 9 mm bullet in comparison to the newer ammunition and also the P90. In the first place there is nothing called neurological shock. The poor reporter must study more. It is neurogenic shock and it is irrelevant here. We would be digressing if we start discussing the mechanism of injury by bullets as that is the subject of a separate monograph. The 9 mm is not a bullet, it is legend. As early as 1986, in the NRA's book 'Handloading' stated that "the modern science of wound ballistics has established beyond reasonable doubt that the 9 mm cartridge is highly effective".

(17.3.3) The P90

The FN P90 submachine gun (SMG) was developed in the late 1980s as a personal defence weapon for the troops whose primary activities does not include carrying of a rifle or carbine, such as vehicle and tank crew members, artillery crews et al. Standard pistols and submachine guns chambered for pistol rounds had proved ineffective against enemy soldiers wearing body armour; therefore FN designers first developed a new round with enhanced penetration, initially known as SS90. To achieve necessary high penetration while keeping recoil impulse low, FN used a small-bore approach, creating a round that looked much like the scaled down 5.56 mm NATO round. It must be noted that similar concepts were tried in other countries, most notably in USA, several decades before the FN; for example, the US Army tested M1 carbines chambered for .221 Johnson Spitfire round back in late 1950s; later on, Colt produced its .22 SCAMP and 5.6 x 30 MARS ammunition for special SCAMP machine pistol and MARS 'mini assault rifle' (a scaled-down M16 rifle) respectively. It must be noted that 5.6 x 30 MARS round was in a sense a direct predecessor to 5.7 x 28 FN SS90 round, although the latter featured slightly lighter and faster bullet. Initially the weapon was designed to use a 5.7 x 28 mm cartridge called the SS90. The SS90 propelled a 23 grain plastic-core projectile from the P90 at a speed of roughly 2800 fps. FN revised the 5.7 x 28 mm ammunition. The new cartridge, designated the SS190, used a projectile 2.7 mm shorter in length than that of the SS90. This allowed it to be used more conveniently in the FN Five-seven pistol also being developed at that time. This projectile also had a heavier and more conventional full metal, plated steel jacket, lead core and steel/aluminium penetrator. This cartridge weighs roughly half as much as a typical 9 x 19 mm Parabellum cartridge. The touted advantage was that you could carry extra ammunition and that since it produced roughly 30 per cent less recoil, the controllability of the gun was improved. One of the design intents of the SS190 variant of this cartridge (not sporting variants) was that it was supposed to penetrate Kevlar protective vests such as the NATO CRISAT vest.

The P90 (named after 'Project 90') is a bull-pup design weapon made of impact-resistant polymer to reduce weight. It uses a unique horizontally-mounted feeding system. The box magazine is mounted parallel to the bore axis and locks in place between the charging handles and optical sight, flush with the receiver top cover. It has a capacity of 50 rounds and it is of clear plastic, so the user can see the amount of ammunition remaining. Ejection is to the bottom and the controls are ambidextrous. Specification and performance: caliber 5.7 x 28 mm SS190; weight 2.54 kg empty; 3 kg loaded with magazine with 50 rounds; length 500 mm; barrel length 263 mm; rate of fire 900 rounds per minute; magazine capacity 50 rounds; and effective range 200 meters.

(17.3.4) The M82

The media criticises this weapon because "no police force in the world uses the M82/M107 SAR in counter-terrorism jobs, where civilians may be at risk. New York's police Special Weapons and Tactics team uses the SAR to blow apart vehicle engines in high-speed chases as a last resort...The Jammu and Kashmir Police, India's most experienced counter-terrorism force, use nothing more powerful than the Soviet-designed 7.62 millimeter sniper rifles".

The question is, are they the final word? Should we stop thinking for ourselves simply because the dunderheads in the J&K police or the NYPD do not use it? The rifle may not be useful in anti-terrorist operations but the reasons cited against it are absolutely wrong. The M82 (also sometimes designated by the military as the M107) is a recoil-operated, semi-automatic anti-material rifle developed by the American Barrett Firearms Manufacturing chambered for the famous .50 BMG round. It is used as an anti-material weapon and EOD (Explosive Ordnance Disposal) tool. The long effective range of over 1500 meters along with high energy and availability of highly effective ammunition such as API and Raufoss M213 allows for effective operations against targets like radar cabins, trucks, parked aircrafts and so on. M82 also can be used to defeat enemy snipers or criminals from stand-off range or when targets are behind some cover, but the anti-personnel work is not a major application for Barrett M82 or any other .50 BMG rifle for that matter. It may not be wise if it is purchased as a sniper rifle only but other applications could also be thought of. Incidentally, the reporter does not know that there is nothing called the SAR—it is SASR for "Special Applications Scoped Rifle".

Further, the very role of snipers in anti-terrorist operations in India is grossly misunderstood. Little do these officers know that sniper rifles have very little role in the kind of operations which we undertake here. Sniper rifles are used profitably only at ranges in excess of 600 meters and frequently up to 1.5 kilometers! In the sort of operations they usually have in this country, they hardly ever engage the enemy at ranges beyond 100 meters. Why do they require a sniper rifle for that? In fact, given the way in which houses are built clustered around each other and the nature of dense vegetation, nowhere in the towns or villages of Kashmir we would get even a clear line-of-sight for even 200 meters! Above all, even the best snipers in the world can shoot only at targets that they can see. In urban anti-terrorist operations, how do you shoot at a target which you cannot see even at 50 meters—such as one who is hidden behind glasses and curtains with no shadows to indicate his presence—for all you know, he could be lying behind a window sill? We do not have the rolling hills of Northern Ireland where an IRA terrorist sniper could shoot at a British army patrol from a great distance—we do not have the barren land of Afghanistan either where American snipers take shots at Taliban targets from long ranges. We know as to how these morons acquire such childish notions. The role of the sniper has been hyped greatly in many famous recent as well as old Hollywood films. Stalingrad was; for example, as everyone knows, a battle won at the cost of sheer blood of hundreds of thousands of men and nothing else. Yet in the famous film 'Enemy At The Gates' they made it into a game of two snipers of the opposing sides! Filmmakers are not military experts or have even a rudimentary knowledge of history! Yet most of such people are subconsciously influenced by what they see in Hollywood films.

(17.4) The Intellectual Bankruptcy of the Bodyguards

With their knowledge being only Power Point deep, they just realised that this war could take a whole lot longer than they thought, so they started developing a new system of hanging charts on walls to solve the problem and win the war.

(17.4.1) Show Over Substance

The job of a bodyguard is a lowly one—a completely de-intellectualised one—the dumbest of the men, in fact, make the best bodyguards. The job of a bodyguard does not really deserve comments in a serious scholarly work like this. However, since they are responsible for spreading many myths and building an undeserving aura around their stupidity, I consider it our duty to bust the myths. People must be shown their places—the bodyguards are kept to guard bodies—since when did they become authorities on weapon systems? If looks could kill, they would sure kill—white loose trousers, knee pads, swank goggles, a trademark dumb zombie-like expression and the works. The rest is all crap.

In the first place, do we really expect an attack on a VIP by terrorists wearing armour? Where on earth are you going to encounter armour wearing terrorists and why? Won't they be making themselves all the more conspicuous? The very premise is questionable to the point of being absurd! Are they not supposed to know that the standard training of VIP security anywhere prescribes at least one head shot? What protection they will have for their heads? And if they are going to get hit in the head, what use is the soft armour? OK, for the sake of argument, one might argue that with soft body armour worn inside their clothing, they could disguise themselves to look like ordinary men! If one invokes the argument of disguise, it means that he accepts that the assailants would be a part of a regular crowd. The question is how would they penetrate the outer cordon that VIP security systems necessarily put in place? Why do you have the three-tier security ring in place after all if armour clad terrorists can reach up to the isolation cordon? Well, well, next they will say that one could encounter terrorists in BP cars. Then you will start carrying RPGs also! After all it does not take anything to cook up an highly sensational and purely fictitious intelligence report sitting on the desk—they could even curry favours with the powers that be by telling them that they are so very badly threatened! Thus there could be terrorists throwing even chemical agents on a so-called VIP. By God, the bodyguards must carry NBC kit also. In a 1997 Mel Gibson-Richard Gere thriller 'The Jackal', Mel Gibson uses a Russian 14.5 x 114 mm KPV heavy machinegun in an attempt to kill the wife of the American President from over 700 meters with armour piercing bullets made of depleted uranium. The bullet-proof podium which they so very ceremoniously place in front of the protected person would simply disintegrate under these bullets leaving the muzzle at over 3264 fps. Looks like these guys haven't seen the film or else they would have stacked ten podiums in tandem! The ability to pierce soft body armour like Kevlar is nothing but a marketing gimmick. The argument that was given originally for vehicle and tank crew members, and artillery crews *et al* cannot be extended to VIP security. The tank men and the drivers are likely to encounter real enemy soldiers who could perhaps be wearing body armour, and not terrorists. The VIP is not going to be attacked by soldiers!

These guys never realised that the very rationale of using a sub-machinegun for VIP security is utterly wrong, its size being compact or big being utterly irrelevant. If you are in a situation in urban combat or even in a jungle where you want to deliver a high volume of fire in a short time but the range is not high, the accuracy is not important and if you are not concerned about the penetrating power of the bullets, then the sub-machine gun is the thing for you. In other words, the sub-machine gun is the weapon of choice when you simply want to pump in as much lead as possible on targets which are neither far from you nor are hardened. Using sub-machine guns for VIP security as you see them toted by the commandos is another example of intellectual bankruptcy of the Indian system. The so-called VIPs are generally to be found and likely to be attacked only in a gathering of people—you cannot afford to pour in a high volume of fire there indiscriminately and kill innocent persons! In fact, you need a weapon like the SIG-Sauer P226 pistol there which can deliver accurate fire. You could fire from the SMG if you are protecting a rich man and if your car is stopped by a bunch of hoods in a lonely place; you cannot fire it if you are protecting the prime minister of a country and he is apparently attacked by a man wielding a so-called pen pistol, an improvised country-made single-shot 12 bore handgun, a country-made Potassium Chlorate-Arsenic Sulfide mixture bomb or something similar from amongst the 20,000 and odd people that the protected person could be addressing in a rally. How the hell can you fire on that crowd with an automatic weapon, however great a shot you be and ensure that innocent persons are not killed?

Now, let us see whether the P90 has any intrinsic advantage over other weapons? What is the advantage of a range of 200 meters? None whatsoever! In VIP security you do not engage an enemy at this range. One who decides to attack the target at that range will take precautions to conceal himself too or make a provision to get away immediately after firing his shots. At that distance, he would not bother to wear soft armour in case it is argued that soft armour could be hidden under clothing. If he is really keen on protecting himself and if his position is disclosed, he would cover himself in steel. And if you are going to engage the enemy at say less than 50 yards, the P90 is no better than any other weapon. When it comes to its large magazine capacity and high rate of fire, we have already seen that the rate of fire is immaterial and in all probability you shall not fire on full auto, thereby rendering its large magazine capacity useless.

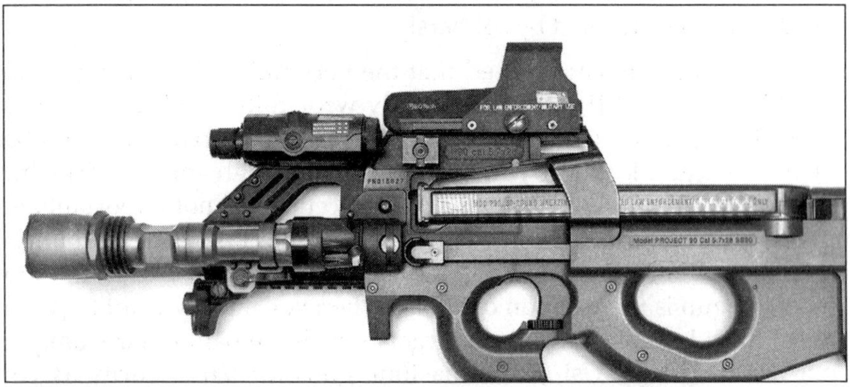

The FN P90: A good example of marketing gimmicks: bodyguards do not have to engage enemy at 200 yards and if they are firing on full auto in a crisis, they cannot have time to look at the transparent magazine – in any case you do not expect assailants to be wearing body armour!

And for God's sake, if at all you are obliged to fire on full auto for whatever dumb reason, you are supposed to concentrate on firing. Would you have the time to look whether any rounds are remaining or not? What purpose does it serve then to have a clear magazine? A manufacturer introduces some juvenile thing and the duffers are smitten by it. Could the transparent magazine of the INSAS save it from being a disaster or a poor design otherwise? Something does not become the final word simply because the US Secret Service is using it or that some small countries like Cyprus are using it. For that matter, even the US Secret Service, in spite of their obsession with gadgetry, spend more time being human shields and grabbing their principals and getting them under cover or out of the area than they do shooting back with handguns on imaginary terrorists wearing Kevlar jackets.

(17.5) Bull-pup Rifles

(17.5.1) Why People are Fascinated by the Bull-pup Rifles?

They look cool, and this is the real reason so many people are enamoured of them. Other than the fact that science fiction films and television shows like featuring bull-pups, there is no reason why bull-pups should be called the future of assault rifles. The main advantage to a bull-pup design is that you can have a much shorter weapon for the same barrel length. But there are many design disadvantages too. Bull-pup designs are mechanically more complex, requiring a long trigger linkage with the hammer mechanism, and control system linkages. That makes it difficult to design a bull-pup with a light trigger pull. This seriously degrades both control feel and reliability, and increases bulk and weight. Magazine changes on a bull-pup are much slower because they require more repositioning, and are difficult to see (if necessary) without fully dismounting the rifle. A conventional rifle is balanced in between your dominant and support hands; and there are good reasons for that. A human being naturally handles things better that balance in the palm, or in front of it. Because the weight of the receiver, trigger group, and ammunition in a bull-pup configuration is all concentrated in the stock, the center of gravity of a bull-pup gun is quite a bit further toward the rear than other designs and this has a bearing on the heft of the rifle for most shooters. Charging the rifle and manipulating the operating handle is often more difficult, and sometimes can't be done without dismounting the rifle, or reaching over with your support hand. A lot of this can be worked around with training, but what it comes down to, is that bull-pups are ergonomically incorrect for human beings; you don't train someone to do something ergonomically incorrect, you must redesign the equipment to fit human ergonomics. Until someone has shot thousands of rounds through them, had to change magazines in the dark, and in cramped conditions, had to clear jams under combat conditions etc, they can't know how unsuitable they are as anything other than a niche weapon. So far they have not seen much real action and the problems that manifest themselves in the long run are not known yet. And it is true of all the new fancy weapons. The basic question still remains: what is so great about them that you place all your hopes of crushing terrorism or winning an urban war on them.

Bull-pups are to be preferred only where OAL (Over All Length) is the most critical factor, but a SMG or collapsible or folding stock in a conventional rifle are inappropriate choices. Bull-pups, if they have not to be carried for long in which the asymmetrical distribution of weight becomes tiring, do lend themselves to urban combat because of shorter overall length.

In spite of all the hype, many armies that have fielded bull-pups have found them wanting. The British L85 has gone through a 20-year saga just to get it to function reliably, the ChiCom's QBZ-95 is being 'supplemented' by the conventional layout QBZ-03, and now we hear that the French are supposedly thinking about replacing the FAMAS. The only bull-pup that doesn't seem to garner severe criticism is the AUG, and even that rifle has not seen the kind of widespread combat deployment that brings design issues to the surface. It would be instructive to analyse the Chinese experience. In the late 1980s, Chinese designers developed a 5.8 x 42 mm cartridge, apparently designated DBP87, which was claimed to be superior to both the 5.56 mm NATO and the 5.45 mm Soviet cartridges. This cartridge develops a muzzle velocity of 930 meters per second from a standard barrel, with a bullet weighing 4.26 grams. As soon as the ammunition was ready, the PLA began to develop an entirely new and much more modern family of small arms based on the same action. This family, known as QBZ-95 ('Qing Buqiang Zu' = Light Rifles family, 1995), was first displayed outside the PLA in 1997. When China took over Hong Kong; it was observed that the Chinese guards were armed with a bull-pup rifle. For various but unpublished reasons the bull-pup Type 95/QBZ-95 assault rifle was apparently found not entirely satisfactory in PLA service. Therefore, it was decided to develop a new 5.8 mm assault rifle of conventional layout. The new weapon is known as QBZ-03 (Type 03/2003).

(17.5.2) The FN F2000

During the late 1980s and early 1990s FN Herstal began the search for its next entry into the assault rifle world. This ultimately resulted in the FN F2000 rifle, which was first displayed in public in 2001. The F2000 has a compact bull-pup layout. The specifications and performance of the FN F2000 are as follows: gas operated rotating bolt action; caliber 5.56 mm NATO; length 694 mm; barrel length 400 mm; weight 3.6 kg empty in standard configuration, 4.6 kg with 40 mm grenade launcher; magazine capacity 30 rounds. So far FN F2000 rifle has found only few buyers, including Armed Forces of Slovenia and Belgian Special Operations Forces! A unique feature of the F2000 rifle is its patented front ejection system: the spent cases, extracted from the chamber, travel from the rear part of the gun to the ejection port near the muzzle via a special ejection tube and fall out of the gun at the safe distance from the shooter's face. That makes the rifle a truly ambidextrous one as most left-handers find it difficult to use bull-pups because the empties are ejected so close to the face. It has a modular design which allows the rifle to be 'tailored' for any particular mission or tactical situation. For example, for peacekeeping operations F2000 could be fitted with less-lethal M303 under-barrel module, which fires tear gas or marker projectiles using pre-compressed air. On the other hand, the F2000 could be fitted with various 40 mm FN EGLM grenade launchers and a proprietary computerised fire control system, instead of the standard low-magnification optical sights.

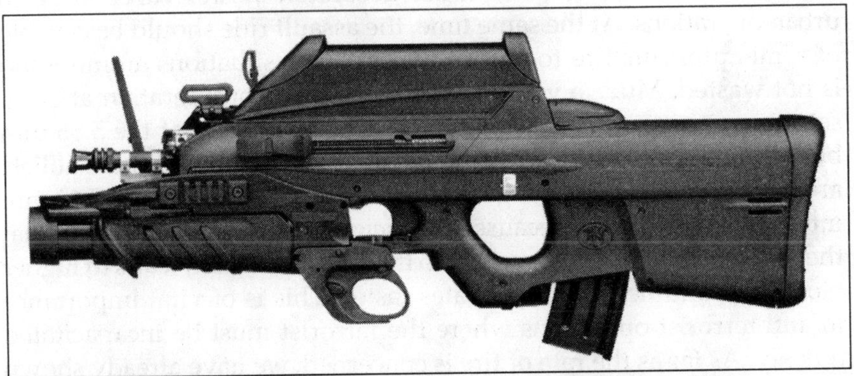

The FN F2000: interesting features but yet to be proven in combat or by a large number of users

(17.6) Selecting the Best Weapon for Urban Operations

(17.6.1) Features Needed

What sort of rifles do we need for urban operations? This question becomes important because the requirements of urban operations are obviously different from those of an infantry fighting in plains or in jungles. Remember that in urban operations, ranges are usually smaller and hence great accuracy is not on premium. Overall size and weight are obviously important considerations, however. This means that the stock has to be collapsible. When troops have to operate in built-up areas and manoeuvre themselves into tight spaces, or scale walls etc with the rifle, the rifle must not be big or heavy. In anti-terrorist operations, in stark contrast to infantry warfare, we cannot dispense with the requirement of fully automatic fire in critical situations like entering a building or a room. But you cannot keep a SMG for that. The reason is that when a unit goes into operation, it is not practical to arm different men with different types of weapons and even more difficult to expect that a man with MP-5 would be available at hand when a group has to enter a room. You may have to begin the operation by engaging the enemy at 100-200 meters and then close in on him. Even when inside a building you may have to shoot through certain obstacles which a 9 mm bullet may not be able to penetrate. Hence, SMGs are ruled out. You may have to return fire at enemy, who could be 200-300 meters away also!

All this means that you cannot dispense with rifles capable of delivering fully automatic fire. A three-round burst capability might have some (and that too questionable) relevance for an infantry soldier in regular infantry warfare—it has absolutely no relevance at all in urban operations. At the same time, the assault rifle should be capable of semi-automatic fire to ensure that in other situations ammunition is not wasted. Muzzle velocity is not a critical consideration at all in selecting an assault rifle. The higher muzzle velocity of the 5.56 mm bullet offers no additional advantage in urban operations where bullets are fired at a rather low range. My personal vote goes for the 7.62 mm intermediate cartridge because it is a scientifically established fact that the higher caliber (in comparison to the 5.56 mm bullet) leads to higher blood loss and hence incapacitates faster. This is of vital importance in anti-terrorist operations where the terrorist must be incapacitated quickly. As far as the rate of fire is concerned, we have already shown that it is not critically important. Other factors that must be kept in mind include: soundness of design as ascertained from the opinion of millions of users—the more complicated a design, the higher the chances of failure; reliability of operation under field conditions dirt, mud, snow etc as ascertained from other users in history; ease of field stripping and maintenance as ascertained from other users in history; ruggedness of use and handling as ascertained from other users in history; initial cost and the cost of spare parts; ergonomics of handling, pointing and carrying; and provision for UBGL.

Keeping all these factors in mind, there would be a tie between the venerable AK series rifles with folding stocks and the M4A1 carbine. The M4A1 has definitely better heft but the AK is more rugged and shorter. The telescoping stock of the M4 family which provides for a custom fit for shooters of different builds is another great advantage. Depending on the situation, the AKS-74U, firing the Russian 5.45 x 39 mm cartridge is also an excellent weapon in view of its great compactness. In urban combat, the stopping power of a bullet is not really critical—your purpose is served if the enemy is wounded seriously. Hence, you need not bother about which bullet penetrates more. You will have to bother about it only when your opponents are wearing body armour. Then you will have to refer to very elaborate ballistic studies. You must also keep in mind the sort of combat you are likely to have. If you are in a situation where you have to negotiate a lot of obstacles, jump over walls and fences, climb through windows, or undertake activities which might require the use of both hands, you must opt for smaller and lighter weapon, which can be easily slung over your back without snagging anywhere and which, should the need arise, may be fired even single-handedly. In such situations, you may also consider a PDW like the P90. Ruggedness should not be lost sight of. After all, you might trip, bang against stone walls or find your rifle clattering against the railing of a staircase. You do not want the plastic magazine or stock of the rifle cracking. You also do not want a rifle which has got so many magazine release catches (and that too so softly operated ones) that one of them does get pressed somewhere. The Israeli Tavor MTAR-21 bull-pup, in particular, is prone to this problem. The point being made is that there is no really universally greatest assault rifle for urban warfare. You must select your rifle in view of the specific circumstances you are likely to face.

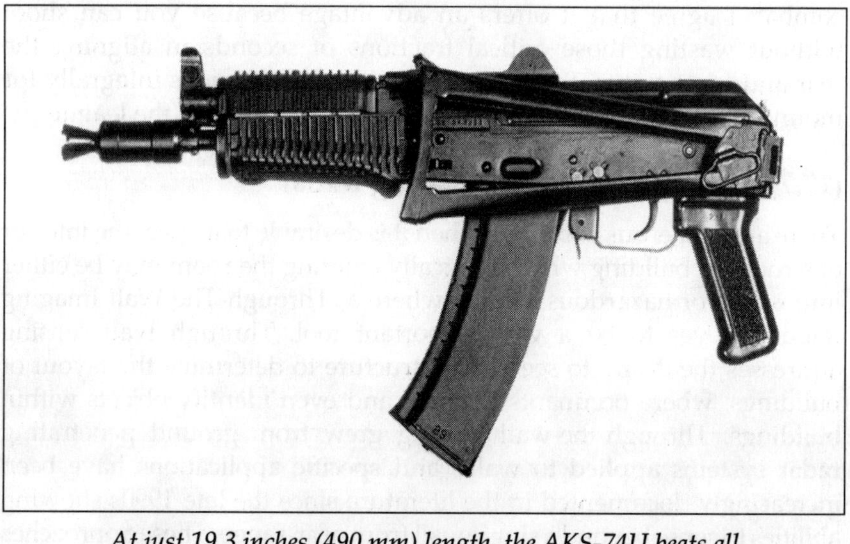

At just 19.3 inches (490 mm) length, the AKS-74U beats all others, even Bull-pups, compare with 25.4 inches of the AK-47, 27.1 inches of the FN F2000 and 29.8 inches of the M4A1

Viewed in a historical context, the Soviet PPSh-41 7.62 x 25 mm sub-machinegun was also a great weapon for urban combat with its 71-round drum magazine of huge capacity and range up to 200 yards, but it is no longer under production.

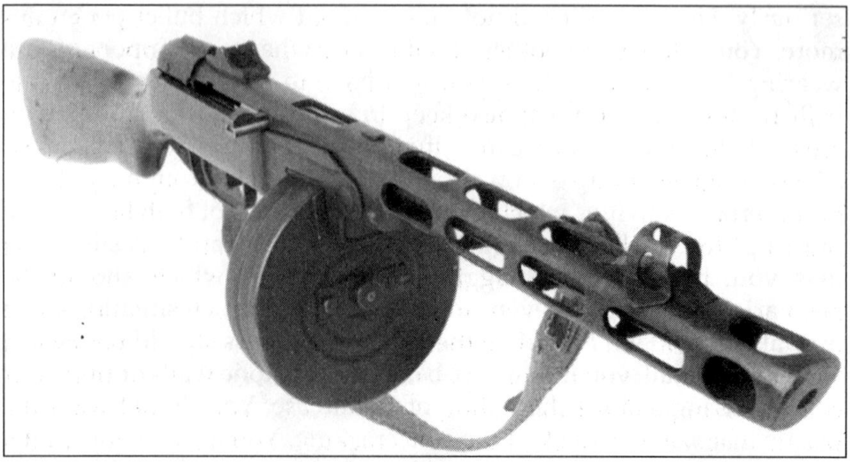

This was a great submachine gun for urban combat – 71 round drum magazine, and a small but very nasty cartridge that could shoot up to 200 yards

(17.6.2) *Reflex Sights*

A case has been made out for reflex sights of various sorts in urban combat. I agree that it offers an advantage because you can shoot without wasting those critical fractions of seconds in aligning the rear and front sights. By that logic, a rifle that provides integrally for mounting the reflex sight automatically pushes itself in the league.

(17.7) Through-the-Wall Imaging Radar

There are numerous occasions when it is desirable to inspect the interior of a room or building when physically entering the room may be either impossible or hazardous. This is where a 'Through-The-Wall Imaging Radar' proves to be a very important tool. Through wall sensing addresses the desire to see inside structure to determine the layout of buildings, where occupants may be, and even identify objects within buildings. Through-the-wall sensing grew from ground penetrating radar systems applied to walls, and specific applications have been increasingly documented in the literature since the late 1990s showing abilities to sense beyond a single wall from near-range. These approaches have generally borrowed from traditional optical, radar, and sonar image processing techniques, which begin with basic wave physics to form matched filters for every point in the imaging target space.

Radio waves can penetrate walls and it is therefore possible to use radar to image the interior of a room. While high frequency radio waves give excellent resolution and the possibility of detecting signs of human respiration, penetration depth through masonry walls is an obvious concern. For a scenario where a point target is placed behind a single layer wall, the signal at the radar receiving antenna is mainly composed of two parts: backscattering from the target; and reflection from the wall. At normal incidence, the backscattered field from the wall is very strong. Consequently, the side-lobes generated by image formation spreads on the desired image domains. In cases where the scattering from targets is small compared to the reflection from the wall, the detection of targets becomes difficult. Therefore, in order to increase the signal-to-clutter ratio the reflected signal from the wall must be subtracted. For instance, the reflection from the walls can be estimated by analyzing the time-domain signal and subtracted from the total received signals. However, the clutter may not be totally eliminated due to the multi-path effects.

In true free space conditions, this represents a mathematically accurate way to perform imaging. Imaging of structure features and contents of buildings requires 2-D and preferably 3-D systems. It cannot rely on Doppler processing for separation of desired features, so multi-lateration or Synthetic Aperture Radar (SAR) approaches have been the most common approaches. Synthetic Aperture Radar can be thought of as a coherent extension of the multilateration concept. Instead of incoherent combinations of range returns from multiple transmit/receive pairs, coherent algorithms are used to provide a complex matched filter to specific points in the target space. The general idea behind multi-lateration is to correlate range measurements from multiple sensors to specific points in the image. With sufficient spatial diversity from a large set of transmit/receive combinations, specific reflection points will start to integrate above the background interference. Tomographic algorithms are capable of making some of these adjustments for projection data through solid materials.

(17.8) Fiber Optic Snake Camera

This is another very useful device in anti-terrorist operations, particularly when you have to peep under a crack or through a small hole. Obviously, the longer the cable, the better it is. If the device can transmit the images or videos over wireless, it becomes better.

18

The Dubious Combat Value of Fancy Training

An army is a team. It lives, sleeps, eats, and fights as a team. This individual heroic stuff is pure horse shit. The bilious bastards who write that kind of stuff for the Saturday Evening Post *don't know any more about real fighting under fire than they know about fucking!*

(18.1) Whose Training is Exalted and Why?

Training is important; however, fancy training, quite like fancy weapons, is not. Most people fail to realise that fancy training is often used to showcase the organisation for vested interests. This is particularly true of the training given to the Special Forces in various armies even as they constitute but a small fraction of the total strength of the armed forces of that nation. Since they are the best, the strongest, the fittest, the smartest, have the best and the most exotic weapons and gadgets, and receive the most difficult training, they are also the most presentable face of the armed forces of a nation through which they can befool the people and further their organisational interests. And this is publicised to such a great extent in attractive programmes on the TV and in the print medium that when one thinks of the US Army, the picture of the heavily loaded US Marines automatically pops into the mind; when one talks of the Russian Army, the images of the Spetsnaz commandos practicing bare-chested in the freezing winters of Moscow crop up; and when one speaks of the British Army, one tends to think in terms of what he has seen of the gruelling training of the Royal Marine Commandos. You will often find highly exciting programmes on the Fox History Channel or the Discovery

Channel about the training given to the Royal Marine Commandos, the Spetsnaz, the US Marines and the IDF. The Krav Maga system of unarmed combat is shown so much on the TV and exalted so much that one starts wondering whether Israelis fight bare-handed only!

(18.2) What is the Track Record of the US Marines and the Royal Marine Commandos in Afghanistan?

Officers think they're businessmen. They think the principles used in business, like 'corporate vision' and 'TQM (total quality management)' can work in the Army. This is because officers spend a lot of time trying to sell things, usually grand ideas and catchy names.

The TV programmes are fine for amusement but the fact is that the actual combat value of the training given to these Special Forces, after they are deployed in real life situations like Iraq and Afghanistan, is highly doubtful. We can already hear the groans of the dumb army officers, but the truth cannot be denied. Let us get it straight, the American or the British commandos do not have a very impressive track record in either place. A rag-tag band of the Taliban has necessitated the deployment of nearly 150,000 highly-equipped troops in Afghanistan and they are keeping them on their toes. The successes which the coalition troops have achieved against the Taliban or are likely to achieve in the future are to be attributed actually to their vastly superior firepower and the exotic weapon systems at their disposal. Not one of them can be attributed to the commando training they give—eventually the Taliban are killed by the Predator drones only!

We are told that the US Marines and the Royal Marine Commandos undergo such-and-such difficult and special training and it is so very good that they are often sent direct to Afghanistan from the training. For God's sake, they never tell when was the occasion in Afghanistan when they had been able to profitably use the special aspects of their training? Let us look at it another way too. How are their opponents trained? They do not receive any training whatsoever. Not a single member of the Taliban ever receives any formal training. In a man-to-man bare-handed fight maybe a US marine would be able to take on four of them together and beat them to pulp. Maybe on a field range not a single Taliban would be able to shoot straight. Maybe only one out of hundred would be able to score a bull's eye at 300 yards in spite of the fact that they learn to handle guns from childhood. Maybe they can march up and down the hills longer than the Marines, but ask them to carry the same load which the Marines carry and they would double up under the load. They have tender boys too amongst their ranks. Yet, they do fight the legendary Marines without fear. How?

The Taliban have no training infrastructure. Even the West admits that. They accuse the al-Qaeda of having some training for their cadres but in reality they keep on showing the same video clippings that they had obtained nearly a decade ago. There has not been any addition to that old footage. In fact, if they really had any information of al-Qaeda training grounds anywhere in the world, they would have bombed it out of existence a long time back. For your information, the so-called al-Qaeda training videos that you see telecast repeatedly on the channels seem to be made for the benefit of the western viewers only. They contain the most rudimentary infantry training—the sort of which the armies of the world used to give before the Second World War. Who would accept that the al-Qaeda allegedly set out to conquer the world with that sort of training to a couple of hundreds? Gentlemen, it does not matter that on a man-to-man basis or in terms of the basic combat skills of a soldier, even the best of the Taliban come nowhere near the worst amongst the Marines—however, what matters is how they perform as a fighting force in the field in the sort of war they are fighting. Have the Taliban not been able to put up a decent fight and inflict an all-time high casualty figure of 711 in dead on the coalition forces in 2010, followed by 566 in 2011? The Americans cannot possibly argue that the Taliban are fighting a most asymmetric war and western regular armies or the Special Forces are not geared to fight that sort of war. The question is why should the Taliban fight on the terms of the enemy? They are fighting on their own terms and the Americans, in spite of the billions they spent on the war, have not been able to fight the way they love to. If the Americans could not make the Taliban fight the sort of war they are trained for, it is the failure of American strategy. The fact is they have opened up back channels for negotiating with the Taliban because deep down their hearts they know they, in spite of having wasted trillions of dollars and having bombed every inch of the land, have not been able to exterminate the Taliban!

Given the fact that a rag-tag band of ill-fed, ill-equipped, ill-trained, and almost primitive people have given a tough fight to the very best soldiers in the whole world, one must admit that real combat is infinitely different from simulated combat in training fields. Performance of an army in real combat depends on many factors other than your individual worth as a soldier. The Americans and the British would be reluctant to admit it because they are not intellectually honest people, but the fact is that practically no advantage of the highly specialised and exotic training has been demonstratively gained on the real battlefield. Eventually, you have to depend on your superior technology for your successes.

This is one of the points that we have emphasised in the chapter on fancy weapons also. As far as the unprotected human body is concerned, it will die the same way whether it is hit by the bullet of the old AK-47 or the most modern bull-pup Tavor, FN2000 or some other exotic rifle. If you are shot at and injured or killed, it does not make any difference whether the man was a good shot or not. If he is exploding a bomb under your vehicle, it does not matter whether he can do the 30-miler or not. He may not be able to even handle your fancy rifle; it does not matter as long as he can lure you into an ambush and kill you with his old AK-47. You can call them cowards; you can call them crooks; you can call them bandits! They do not mind. They have no pretension to the exalted concepts of honour or fighting fair. They never claimed it. They are fighting a war and the ethics of war is not important for them. Have you forgotten; even your pirates fought the same way? The 2009 Fox History Channel documentary 'Deadliest Warrior' made a French knight face a pirate, and the pirate emerged the winner!

(18.3) The Outcome of Wars does not Depend on the Rambos

Do not watch too many of Rambo or Arnold Schwarznegger films—wars are not won by Rambos even though all the stupid generals would love to showcase them. Do not visit those scores of Internet forums where adolescent boys endlessly discuss who is superior: SEALs, Spetsnaz, SAS, Green Berets, US Marines, or the Royal Marine Commandos—that's simply a somewhat homosexual fascination of young boys with strong, rough-and-tough men. Leave it to their adolescent banter. Let us face it; if the Spetsnaz commandos can fight bare bodied in freezing temperatures, it is their problem. Who cares and what do they expect? Do they expect that the soldiers will really have an occasion to fight bare bodied in freezing temperatures? Well, if they have to, it would only mean that their army neither takes good care of their logistic needs nor has a sound strategy! Or they think that they will force the enemy to fight in freezing temperatures where he would be frozen stiff but the Spetsnaz would beat them to pulp? It is fine for a demonstration to mesmerise ordinary people, but has no relevance for real combat. There could be a one-in-a-billion chance that soldiers would find themselves in such a condition that they do not have even a shirt on their backs and it is freezing cold. My dears, if it comes to that, it would mean that you are already in deep shit; that your entire nation has been whipped to such an extent that your soldiers do not even have shirts on their backs. You cannot expect to turn the tide of the war by having soldiers being able to fight in freezing cold without any shirts. The enemy has already whipped you naked. It means that you have already failed on several critical aspects of war-fighting. Do not waste your time, energy and resources preparing for a one-in-a-billion chance – prepare for things which are far more likely!

In real life one is never obliged to perform a back flip in the air and then throw a hatchet to kill someone – if you have an occasion to do so, it would mean that you have neglected other far more vital aspects of fighting a war

In the training of Spetsnaz soldiers, great attention is paid to their ability to engage in hand-to-hand combat and to use hand-held weapon as well as various expedients. Do they really think that the Taliban are stupid enough to grapple with them? Usually, a fighter from the Spetsnaz could have several knives: knife-bayonet for the AK-74, combat knife, all-purpose 'survival' knife, all-purpose clasp-knife, hidden knife, and the legendary 'ballistic knife' that can propel a blade to six meters at the speed of 63-km per hour! Well, sir, the Taliban have no intention of coming anywhere within several meters of you! Why you waste so much time and energy with such things? The Spetsnaz's answer was that when conducting a combat mission in the enemy rear, a sudden close engagement with the enemy was quite probable. A hand-to-hand combat could break out in the conditions of limited visibility (at night, in smoke conditions and so on), in a forest, destroyed buildings, trenches, underground communications, constructions etc. As a rule, during such engagements hostile soldiers outnumber a Spetsnaz reconnaissance/sabotage team, and therefore the hand-to-hand combat with several enemies was an important element in training a fighter of the Spetsnaz. OK, keep on training; the Taliban will never give you that opportunity! Admit it, dear, could the Russians hold on to Afghanistan in spite of the Spetsnaz? The same thing applies to the US Marines also. Their martial arts programme is famous throughout the world. Even their entrenching tool (sort of modified shovel) is of special importance; first, it is an element of a regular outfit and, second, it is a formidable weapon in close combat. Keep it, guys, the Taliban have no intention of coming anywhere close to you.

For the benefit of the Indian readers, let me inform them that rock climbing looked very fine in the Hindi film *Lakshya* (with its scene copied from the Tom Cruise film *Mission Impossible II*) on the Kargil war; it has practically no relevance in real warfare. If an army is obliged to gain a tactical victory by a couple of guys climbing a vertical rock face, it only means that the General Staff has not planned the war well. Indians have always suffered from this problem. We produced great swordsmen but not great armies and systematically lost most of the battles since 1192 AD when Prithviraj Chauhan, a great warrior by himself, lost to Muhammad Ghori in the second battle of Tarain and ushered in the era of 666 years of Muslim rule in India. Real war is a complex and unglamorous affair. No war in history has been won by commandos. The stories of commandos make for exciting reading but they do a great disservice to the terrible grind through which millions of ordinary soldiers go through and which eventually decides the outcomes of wars. War, as even the Romans had learnt, is a complex organised affair requiring much strategic planning and manoeuvres by an entire nation before the soldiers step in on the battlefield, and then the joint effort by a group on the battlefield—the physical attributes of individual soldiers do not matter. By God, if that were to be so, you could as well hire body builders, weightlifters, athletes, boxers, karatekas, kung fu artists, Muay Thai kickboxers and MMA (Mixed Martial Arts) fighters in the armies—why waste time and money in training soldiers? Remember, having strong men in your army does not mean that you will win wars. That's a very primitive logic when men fought with bare hands. Precisely for this reason, when Commodore Perry's ship landed on the shore of Japan in the first contact of Japan with the western world, the Japanese emperor lined up his sumo wrestlers on the shore to show how great his warriors were. That sort of bullshit does not help anymore. Soldiers have to do physical work more than laymen—hence they should be physically more conditioned than laymen. But you do not need super humans or 'universal soldiers' of Jean Claude Van Damme films to win wars!

(18.4) The Carefully Cultivated Myth of Elite Forces

"What! what! men, dodging this way for single bullets! What will you do when they open fire along the whole line? I am ashamed of you. They couldn't hit an elephant at this dist..".

(18.4.1) The Royal Marines Commando Course

The thirty-two week training course is divided into six modules, beginning with the Foundation Module and ending with the King's Squad Pass Out Week. The training includes fundamental things like weapon training, map reading, field craft, first-aid, survival training, navigation training, light support weapon training, communication training, CBRN (Chemical, Biological, Radiological, Nuclear) training, training in grenades, helicopter training, underwater escape drills, training in mortars, observation posts and harbour drills, tactical field patrol, fighting patrols and ambushes, Minimi light machinegun training, GPMG training, training on the multi-terrain vehicle Viking, training in fighting in woods and forests (FIWAF), training in fighting in built-up areas (FIBUA) and close quarter battle skills, dig and defence, amphibious training, sea-safety training, climbing and mountain skills, cliff assault and military abseil training, amphibious assault training, which culminates in a raid from the sea and a night cliff assault, and European Computer Driving License (ECDL) computing. That's all very fine. My observation is regarding the much-exalted physical training and endurance course which is projected as the mainstay of the entire course.

The Six-mile Speed March: This test requires the recruits to complete a six-mile route, carrying full fighting order (31 lbs including weapon) at a pace of 10 minutes per mile (60 minutes in total).

The Endurance Course: It is a six-mile course across rough moorland and woodland terrain at Woodbury Common near Lympstone, which includes tunnels, pipes, wading pools, and an underwater culvert. Starting early in the morning trainees must complete a two-mile course across rough terrain, which includes a host of obstacles including culverts, deep pools and an underwater tunnel. Then they run four miles back to Lympstone. At the camp, they then fire their weapon on the range at a 25 m target simulating 200 m. They must achieve six out of ten shots on the target; otherwise they will have to do it again. All this they must do carrying full fighting order (31 lbs including weapon) Time: Recruits 73 minutes, officers 71 minutes.

The Tarzan Assault Course: The Tarzan course is an aerial confidence test, which starts with a death slide (now called a

Commando Slide) and includes numerous obstacles high up in the trees. It culminates with trainees climbing a 30-ft wall. A zip-line (also known as a flying fox, zip wire, aerial runway, aerial ropeslide, death slide or tyrolean crossing) consists of a pulley suspended on a cable mounted on an incline. It is designed to enable a user propelled by gravity to traverse from the top to the bottom of the inclined cable, usually made of stainless steel, by holding on or attaching to the freely moving pulley. The assault course incorporates a dozen or more obstacles ending with a 12-ft wall. All this must be done carrying full fighting order (31 lbs including weapon). Time: Recruits 13 minutes, officers 12 minutes.

A Royal Marine commando salutes as he slides down the 'Death Slide' on a zip-line – good for impressing young boys and swooning girls; it has absolutely no relevance to real combat.

The Nine-Mile Speed March: This test requires the Recruits to 'speed' march a total distance of 9 miles in 90 minutes (10 minutes per mile) carrying full fighting order, both Recruits and Officers must run as a squad or troop. Time: 90 minutes.

The 30-Mile March: This test consists of a 30-mile march or 'yomp' across Dartmoor carrying full fighting order, safety equipment and weapon. Starting early in the morning both Officers and Recruits are split into teams or syndicates to complete the test in the time permitted. Time: eight hours for recruits and seven hours for officers, who must also navigate the route themselves, rather than following a DS (a trained Royal Marine) with the rest of a syndicate and carry their own equipment.

(18.4.2) US Navy SEAL Training

The US Navy SEAL training is famous because of the extremely tough standards and the fact that nearly 80 per cent of the trainees are not able to complete the training.

The SEAL training course consists of 4–12 weeks at the Naval Special Warfare Preparatory School for all enlisted men followed by a three-week Indoctrination programme for all personnel. After the initial screening, the applicants attend the 25 weeks Basic Underwater Demolition/SEAL (BUD/S) training at the Naval Special Warfare Center, Naval Amphibious Base Coronado, California. Following graduation from BUD/S is 26 weeks at SEAL Qualification Training including Tactical Air Operations, cold weather training and SERE (Survival, Evasion, Resistance and Escape). Prospective trainees are expected to exceed the minimums. The minimum requirements are 500 yards (460 m) swim using breast or combat sidestroke in under 12:30 minutes with a competitive time of 10:00 minutes or less, at least 42 push-ups in two minutes with a competitive count of 79 or more, at least 50 sit-ups in two minutes with a competitive count of 79 or more, at least six pull-ups from a dead hang (no time limit) with a competitive count of 11 or more, and run 1.5 mile (2.4-km) in boots and trousers in under 11:30 minutes with a competitive time of 10:20 minutes or less.

The BUD/S consists of a three-week 'Indoctrination Course', known as INDOC, followed by three phases, covering physical conditioning (seven weeks), diving (eight weeks), and land warfare (ten weeks) respectively. Officer and enlisted personnel go through the same training programme. It is designed to develop and test their stamina, leadership, and ability to work as a team. In the first phase, BUD/S students are divided into 'Boat Crews' which can consist of six to eight men. Although some exercises will be undertaken as boat crews (such as 'log PT', which requires boats crews to exercise with logs that weigh 150 lb (68 kg) each, and 'Surf Passage' where boat crews must navigate the Pacific surf in inflatable boats, the first phase of BUD/S also consists of a series of demanding individual physical tests including frequent sets of push-ups and sit-ups, ocean swims and timed four mile (6.4 km) runs in boots and long trousers, in soft sand (to be completed in 32 minutes). The first phase is most well-known for 'Hell Week', 132 hours of continuous physical activity, which now occurs during week three.

(18.4.3) The TACFIT Course

The TACFIT Commando programme professedly aims to develop the ability to run, jump and slide like Parkour or crazy break dance sequences. Taught by a man called Scott Sonnon, it is supposed to give you tireless stamina, extreme range reactive strength, ballistic speed, the agility and co-ordination of a free runner, and active recovery and re-habilitation—all using your own body weight and nothing else. It is said that Scott travelled behind the tattered remains of the Iron Curtain to seek out ancient martial wisdom backed by Soviet sport science. Bullshit—there is nothing called ancient martial wisdom. That's all a hoax and what is so secret about Soviet sports science that the rest of world does not know—they doped their athletes alight! It claims that TACFIT Commando course helps tactical operators recover their heart rate and breath up to 6X faster than a highly conditioned athlete—only Indian yogis made that sort of absurd claims—you cannot defy human biology. And all this is just 20 minutes a few times a week! By God, where in real warfare soldiers have to jump like Free Runners? Stop being an adolescent. Warfare is not about gimmickry of individual soldiers. It is sheer grind.

(18.4) Has Extremely Hard Physical Training been ever Critical in Wars?

The desire to select physically the very best is understood; however, my contention is that there is no evidence that one who does not acquire such exacting standards will not perform well in war—fighting in modern wars requires a certain minimum standard of physical abilities; possession of vastly superior physical abilities does not confer any significant advantage on the soldiers! Modern warfare is materially different from medieval or, for that matter, even the wars of the 19th century. The soldiers are not obliged to wield heavy weapons like broadsword, shield, battleaxe or the pike for long, nor are they obliged to grapple with their opponents in deadly combat. I mentioned wars of 19th century also because the rifles and muskets of the era were heavier than those used now and there were occasions of crossing the bayonets when bodily strength made some difference. The performance of a modern army in war depends on a myriad factors—the factor that the physical abilities of the soldiers of one army are of a very high order whereas that of the soldiers of the other army are not of such a high order (but are of an acceptable level), does not really help the former. It is all show business—designed to maintain that tag of being an elite force. Well, my dears, face it—elite forces do not win wars—the grunts do.

The simple, almost brutal, question is: "Tell me of any time when the special training of the elite force was critical in deciding the course of a war"? Yes, we have all heard of the raid by the 45 SAS men on the

Pebble Island in the Falklands War. Yes, they did destroy 11 Argentinean aircrafts there—but Argentina did not lose the war because of those 11 damn planes! Incidentally, the Pebble Island was a grass airstrip (yes, grass!) of the Argentine navy. The raid had destroyed FMA IA 58 Pucara light ground attack aircraft and T-34 Mentors. The Pucara was a puny 6800 kg twin-turboprop engine aircraft with two 20 mm auto cannon and four 7.62 mm Browning machineguns. The T-34 Mentor was a even smaller 1342 kg single engine trainer aircraft. They were not important planes for the Argentineans.

Argentina lost the war because they were fighting a conventional war against England, that is, on the terms of the enemy. The total war-fighting potential of Argentina was, in any case, painfully less than that of England—they never stood a chance! The Argentine Air Force (Fuerza Aérea Argentina; FAA) had never considered the possibility of waging a long-range naval air campaign against a major NATO power. It was not trained or equipped for such a mission. The FAA had only two tanker aircraft to serve the whole air force and navy, and its fighter-bomber Mirage-IIIs and IAI Daggers were not equipped for aerial refuelling. The FAA's training, tactics and equipment were focused on a possible war against Chile, resulting from disputes such as the Beagle conflict. Argentina's fleet of A-4 Skyhawk attack jets was in very poor condition. The arms embargo placed by the United States in 1976, due to the 'Dirty War', had made most airframes unusable.

Against this, the British had deployed nearly a division sized formation for the war. The naval fleet was massive replete with two aircraft carriers and a host of destroyers and frigates. In comparison to the primitive Argentine air force, the British had deployed 128 modern aircrafts including the Harrier and the Vulcan for air superiority and strike missions. During the war, in spite of the overwhelming superiority, Britain suffered 258 killed and 777 wounded. In addition, two destroyers, two frigates, and two auxiliary vessels were sunk. For Argentina, the Falklands War cost 649 killed, 1,068 wounded, and 11,313 captured/surrendered. In addition, the Argentine Navy lost a submarine, a light cruiser, and 75 aircraft.

The point to be understood is that with such a massive effort and investment in war, and losses on both sides, the Pebble Island raid is unnecessarily hyped in an effort to exalt the SAS—it would be an insult to the over 1000 casualties in dead and injured which were incurred by other British soldiers during the war, and the other losses that were inflicted on the enemy. The Scots Guards of the regular British infantry, for example, had fought terrible land battles like the Battle of Mount Tumbledown in the same war in which 900 British troops fought with 500 Argentine troops and could take the post only after suffering casualties in 10 killed and 53 wounded. This battle also witnessed one of the last bayonet charges in the history of modern warfare when a fortified Argentine position could be taken only after a bayonet charge—Major Kiszley got the Military Cross for that bayonet charge! The action won the units one Distinguished Service Order, two Military Crosses, four Military Medals and two Distinguished Conduct Medals.

As for Pebble Island, the fact is that the Argentines had only 31 combatant soldiers there. There was perhaps only one sentry because they never expected the airstrip to be attacked by land soldiers. The SAS fooled the sentry alright. Even after the attack, the Argentines could not engage them because the moment the explosive charges were set off on the aircrafts, the destroyer HMS Glamorgan had started shelling the airstrip with its 4.5 inch guns and an over two-ton heavy Sea Slug missile, and they had to take cover. It should also not be forgotten that two other SAS operations were earlier aborted during the war. If the Pebble Island raid would be remembered it would be for the load-carrying capacity of the SAS men—that's all! It was no big deal attacking small parked aircrafts with no defence at all!

The Taliban have refused to fight the coalition forces on their terms—now tell me what success stories have been scripted by the SAS, Royal Marines, the Delta Force or the SEALs in Afghanistan? And for God's sake, do not tell me of the killing of Osama bin Laden. Here was an old man with a rifle (that he could not even pick up) and a couple of men, women and children with him in a house—all sleeping blissfully. He was as defenceless as anybody could ever be—not even a *chowkidar* in the house, not to speak of an armed sentry! You send in a whole bunch of 79 SEALs armed to the teeth in four helicopters to kill him on pin-pointed intelligence and take them by complete surprise. There is no resistance worth its name as only one man Al-Kuwaiti is claimed to have fired—still, they killed a couple of unarmed guys and a woman too in their nervousness. And yet they take pride in that operation? Shame on you, American bastards; may your wretched souls be condemned to burn in the fire of the seventh hell forever. What is there to be proud of in that raid which you have been tom-tomming all over the world? What operation could have been easier than that? Any fool could have done that. And you had to scuttle one Cobra helicopter also in the process! Operation Neptune Star only served to bolster American jingoistic ego—it does not prove a thing for the SEALs! Go tell it to the ignoramuses of the world and in your own country—not me. We do not take any pride in killing defenceless people!

Appendix

Quite often during urban operations, it becomes difficult to communicate over wireless due to the general din. Moreover, in situations like house intervention, it may be necessary to maintain silence so as not to lose the element of surprise. This necessitates the use of arm and hand signals. I am giving some of them below.

Listen or I Hear

Watch or I See

Cover This Area

Go Here or Move Up

Dog

Cell Leader

Column Formation — File Formation — Line Abreast Formation

Pistol — Rifle — Shotgun

I Understand — I Don't Understand — Crouch or Go Prone

Door — Window — Point of Entry

Wedge Formation

Rally Point

Ammunition

Vehicle

Breach(er)

Gas

A Select Bibliography

A Military Guide to Terrorism in the Twenty-First Century, US Army Training and Doctrine Command, 2004.

Adelmann, Steve, Modern Urban Sniping, *SWAT Digest*, September 2008.

Akers, F, "Task Force Ranger: A Case Study Examining the Application of Advanced Technologies in Modern Urban Warfare," for DOE, prepared by National Security Programme Office, Y-12 National Security Complex, Oak Ridge, Tennessee 37831-8260, Available on the internet at: http://www.at.y12.doe.gov/ranger.pdf

Amis, M, Fear and Loathing, *The Guardian* 2, 18th September, pp 2-4, 2001.

An Infantryman's Guide to Combat in Built-up Areas, FM 90-10-1, US Army, 1993.

Army Special Operations Force Unconventional Warfare, FM 3-05.130, US Army, 2008.

Army Special Operations Forces, FM 100-25, US Army, 2006.

Arreguín-Toft, Ivan, How to Lose a War on Terror: A Comparative Analysis of a Counter-insurgency Success and Failure," in Jan Ångström and Isabelle Duyvesteyn, Eds., *Understanding Victory and Defeat in Contemporary War* , Frank Cass, 2007.

Arreguín-Toft, Ivan, Tunnel at the end of the Light: A Critique of US Counter-terrorist Grand Strategy, *Cambridge Review of International Affairs*, Vol. 15, No. 3 (2002), pp. 549–563.

Asthana, Dr NC and Dr Anjali Nirmal, *Terrorism and Anti-terrorist Operations*, Pointer Publishers, 2010.

Asthana, Dr NC and Dr Anjali Nirmal, *The Ultimate Book of Explosives Bombs and IEDs*, Pointer Publishers, 2008.

Asthana, Dr NC and Dr Anjali Nirmal, *The Ultimate Book of Weapons*, Pointer Publishers, 2006.

Asthana, Dr NC and Dr Anjali Nirmal, *Urban Terrorism: Myths and Realities*, Pointer Publishers, 2009.

Atran, Scott, *The Moral Logic and Growth of Suicide Terrorism*, Volume: 29, Issue: 2, The Washington Quarterly (2006).

Baldy, Tom F, *Battle For Ulster: A Study of Internal Security*, National Defence University Press, 1987.

Ballistic Resistance of Body Armour NIJ Standard–0101.06, 2008, US Department of Justice, Office of Justice Programmes, National Institute of Justice, The National Institute of Justice's National Law Enforcement and Corrections Technology Center.

Battle Drill #6: *Enter and Clear a Building (Platoon)* (7-3-D108), Sergeant's Time Training.com, October 2005.

Battle Drill #6a: *Enter a Building and Clear a Room (Squad)* (7-4-D109), Sergeant's Time Training.com, October 2005.

Battles for Grozny, *Marine Corps Gazette*. Vol 84, no. 4, April 2000.

Baumann, Robert F, *Russian-Soviet Unconventional Wars in the Caucasus, Central Asia, and Afghanistan*, Combat Studies Institute, US Army Command and General Staff College, 1993.

Bell, J Bowyer, *IRA Tactics and Targets: An Analysis of Tactical Aspects of the Armed Struggle 1969-1989*, Poolbeg Press Ltd., 1990.

Bell, J Bowyer, *The IRA 1968-2000: Analysis of a Secret Army*, Frank Cass Publishers, 2000.

Bender, Bryan, *War Strategy Critic to Review IED Office: US Effort to Quell Bombs Questioned*, The Boston Globe, April 16, 2007.

Berkowitz, BJ, *et al*, *Superviolence: The Civil Threat of Mass Destruction*

Black, Robert J, A Change in Tactics? The Urban Insurgent, *Air University*, 23, no 2 (January-February 1972).

Borer, Doug, War in Afghanistan: How it differs from the Soviet Experience, *Virginia Tech Research Magazine (Winter 2002)*, http://www.research.vt.edu/resmag/2002winter/war.html.

Brar, Kuldip Singh, *Operation Bluestar: The True Story*, South Asia Books, 1993.

Bruce Hoffman, *Inside Terrorism*, Columbia University Press, 1999.

Bruscino, Thomas A., *Out of Bounds: Transnational Sanctuary In Irregular Warfare*, Combat Studies Institute Press, Kansas, 2006.

Brush, Peter, the Helicopter Road to Vietnam, *Viet Nam Generation*, vol 6:34, 1995.

Chechnya: The Kremlin's Difficult Choice, *Izvestia, 10 December 1994* p 4, as reported in *FBIS-SOV-94-238*, 12 December 1994.

Clearing an Enemy Held Building, Combat and Survival Training, http://meltingpot.fortunecity.com/nevada/726/4b.html

Cluterbuck, R, Kidnap, *Hijack and Extortion: The Response*, Macmillan, 1987.

Clutterbuck, Richard L, *Terrorism and Guerrilla Warfare: Forecasts and Remedies*, Routledge, 1990.

Clyne, Peter, *Anatomy of Skyjacking*, TBS the Book Service, 1973.

Collins, Joseph J, *Soviet invasion of Afghanistan: A Study in the use of Force in Soviet Foreign Policy,* Heath and Company, 1986.

Collins, Joseph J, The Soviet-Afghan War: The First Four Years," *Parameters 14,* no 2 (Summer 1984).

Combat in Built-Up Areas, Subcourse Number IN0531, United State Army Infantry School, Fort Benning, GA, 1992.

Combined Arms Operations in Urban Terrain, FM 3-06.11, US Army, 2002.

Commander's Tactical Handbook, MCRP 3-11.1A, US Marine Corps, 1988.

Counter IED Smart Book (Iraq), GTA 90-10-046, USA, 2008.

Counter Improvised Explosive Device (IED) Basic Research, Office of Naval Research, Broad Agency Announcement # 05-024, 2005.

Counter Improvised Explosive Device, International Security Assistance Force, Smart Book.

CQB-Team Close Quarter Battle Tactical Education and Motivation, cqb-team.com.

Crackdown In Punjab—Operation Bluestar, *India Today,* 30 June, 1984.

Crane, David, the Israeli Anti-Terrorist SWAT School, *Tactical Response Magazine,* March 2007.

Crelinsten, Ronald D and Szabo, Denis, (Eds). *Hostage- Taking,* Lexington Books, 1979.

Crenshaw, Martha, *Terrorism in Context,* Penn State Press, 1995.

Danis, Aaron A, Afghanistan Revisited: Soviet Lessons Learned, *Military Intelligence 16,* no. 4 (October-December 1990).

De Leon, P, and Hoffman, B, *Threat of Nuclear Terrorism: A Reexamination,* RAND, Santa Monica, 1988.

Derradji, Abder-Rahmane, *Algerian Guerrilla Campaign: Strategy and Tactics,* Edwin Mellen Press, 1997.

Dick, CJ, *Mujahideen Tactics in the Soviet-Afghan War,* A102, Conflict Studies Research Center, Ministry of Defence, UK, January 2002.

Dudik, Charles E, *The Soviet-Afghan War: A Superpower's Inability to Deny Insurgent Sanctuary,* US Marine Corps Command and Staff College, Marine Corps University, Marine Corps Combat development Command, 2009.

Eisler, Peter , Insurgents adapt faster than military adjusts to IEDs, *USA Today,* 7/16/2007.

Ellis, John, *A Short History of Guerrilla Warfare,* St Martin's Press, 1976.

Experimental Collective Tasks for the Infantry Rifle Platoon and Squad in Urban Combat, MOUT ACTD Programme Handbook #2, Omega Training Group, April 1999.

Explosive Entry, *Tactical Response Magazine,* March 2006.

Ferrell, William H Ferrell, No Shirt; No Shoes; No Status: Uniforms, Distinction, and Special Operations in International Armed Conflict, *Military Law Review,* Vol 178, pp. 94-139, 2003.

Finch, Raymond C, *Why the Russian Military Failed in Chechnya,* Foreign Military Studies Office Special Study no 98-16. Fort Leavenworth, KS: Center For Army Lessons Learned. 1998.

Forces Operational Techniques, FM 31-20, US Army, 1969.

Forces Operational Techniques, TC 31-29, US Army, 1990.

Ford, Peter, Chechens' Eye for Eye Vendettas Shape War, *The Christian Science Monitor,* 8 March 1995.

Gall, Carlotta and de Waal, Thomas, *Chechnya: Calamity in the Caucasus,* New York Univ. Press, 1998.

Gallagher, James J, *Low Intensity Conflict: A Guide for Tactics, Techniques and Procedures,* Stackpole Books, 1999.

Gangle, R, "Training for Urban Operations in the 21st Century," *Marine Corps Gazette - July 2001,* available on the internet at: http://www.urbanoperations.com/training2.htm

Gelner, John, *Bayonets in the Streets: Urban Guerrilla at Home and Abroad,* Collier Macmillan Canada, 1974.

Gold, J and Revill, G (Eds), *Landscapes of Defence,* Prentice Hall, 2000.

Gonzales, Jeff, Five Pillars of Close Quarters, *Combat, Law and Order Magazine,* June 2006.

Gourley, Scott R, US Forces Break Down Urban-Warfare Barriers With Training And Technology, *Jane's (Land Forces – News Story),* February 2008.

Graham, S and Marvin, S, *Splintering Urbanism : Networked Infrastructures, Technological Mobilities, and the Urban Condition,* Routledge, 2001.

Graham, S., In A Moment : On Glocal Mobilities And The Terrorised City, *City,* vol. 5, 3, pp. 411-415, 2001.

Grau, Lester and Jalali, Ali Ahmed, *The Other Side of the Mountain: Mujahideen Tactics in the Soviet-Afghan War,* www.MilitaryBookShop.co.uk, 2010.

Grau, Lester W (Tr and Ed), *The Bear Went over the Mountain: Soviet Combat Tactics in Afghanistan,* Foreign Military Studies Office, Fort Leavenworth, Kansas, National Defence University Press, Washington, 1996.

Grau, Lester W and Thomas, Timothy L., Russian Lessons Learned from the Grau, Lester W and Thomas, Timothy L., *Soft Log And Concrete Canyons: Russian Urban Combat Logistics In Grozny.* In The City's Many Faces: Proceedings of the RAND Arroyo-MCWL-J8 UWG Urban Operations Conference held in Washington, DC 13-14 April 1999, edited by Russell W Glenn, 633-649, Santa Monica, Rand.

Grau, Lester W and William A Jorgenson, DO, *Handling the Wounded in a Counter-Guerrilla War: the Soviet/Russian Experience in Afghanistan and Chechnya,* US Army Medical Department Journal. January-February 1998.

Grau, Lester W, *Changing Russian Urban Tactics: The Aftermath of the Battle for Grozny,* INSS Strategic Forum, number 38, July 1995.

Grau, Lester W, *Russian Manufactured Armoured Vehicle Vulnerability in Urban Combat: The Chechnya Experience,* Red Thrust Star, January 1997.

Grau, Lester W, The RPG-7 on the Battlefields of Today and Tomorrow, *Infantry,* Vol 88, no 2, May-August 1998.

Grau, Lester W, The Soviet-Afghan War: A Superpower Mired in the Mountains, *Journal of Slavic Military Studies* 17 (March 2004).

Grau, Lester, and Gress, Michael A (Tr and Ed), *The Soviet-Afghan War: How a Superpower Fought and Lost,* University Press of Kansas, 2002.

Grau, Lester, *The Bear Went over the Mountain: Soviet Combat Tactics in Afghanistan,* www.MilitaryBookShop.co.uk, 2010. (Orig. Work by Frunze Combined Arms Academy, Moscow)

Grinter, Lawrence E, The Soviet Invasion of Afghanistan: Its Inevitability and its Consequences, *Parameters* 12, no. 4 (December 1982).

Handbook for Volunteers of the Irish Republican Army: Notes on Guerrilla Warfare, issued by their General Headquarters in 1956.

Heggoy, Alf Andrew, *Insurgency and Counter-insurgency in Algeria,* Indiana University Press, 1972.

Horne, Alister, *A Savage War of Peace.* Middlesex, Penguin Books Ltd, 1977.

Ijames, Steve, The Breach and Delay Tactic, *Tactical Response Magazine,* March 2006.

Infantry Rifle Platoon and Squad, FM 7-8, US Army, 1992

Joes, Anthony James, *America and Guerrilla Warfare,* the University Press of Joint Urban Operations, *The City's Many Faces: Investigating The Multifold Challenges of Urban Operations,* Rand Arroyo Center, Marine Corps Warfighting Lab, J8 Urban Working Group, April 1999.

Joseph, Max F, Doors and Corners for the Two-Man Team, *SWAT,* July 2001.

Kelly, Robert E, *US Army Forces Unconventional Warfare Doctrine: Engine of Change or Relic of the Past?* Final report, Naval War College, 2000.

Kilunin, VV, New Views on Combat Actions in a City, *Military Thought,* 7 (No. 3, 1998).

Kohl, James, and Litt, John, *Urban Guerrilla Warfare in Latin America,* The MIT Press, 1974.

Krulak, Charles C, "*The Three Block War: Fighting In Urban Areas,*" presented at National Press Club, Washington, DC, 10 October 1997, Vital Speeches of the Day, 15 December 1997, p. 139.

Kulikov, Anatoly Sergeevich, *The Chechen Operation from the Viewpoint of the Military Command, Russian Ministry of Internal Affairs in Capital Preservation: Preparing for Urban Operations in the Twenty-First Century* – Proceedings of the RAND Arroyo-TRADOC-MCWL-OSD Urban Operations Conference, March 22-23, 2000.

Kuriansky, Judy, Editor, "*Terror in the Holy Land: Inside the Anguish of the Israeli-Palestinian Conflict*" Praeger Publishers, 2006.

Lamont, Robert W, USMC, "*Urban Warrior: A View from North Vietnam,*" Marine Corps Gazette - April 1999.

Lessons from the War in Afghanistan, US Army Report (Declassification Date May 1989), Department of the Army, http://www2.gwu.edu/-nsarchivINSAEBBINSAEBB57/us11.pdf.

Lopez, Vincent C, *What the US Army Should Do About Urban Guerrilla Warfare*, US Army War College, Carlisle Barracks, Pennsylvania, 1975.

Magness, Thomas H, IED Defeat: Observations from the National Training Center, *Engineer*, 35, 28-31, 2005.

Mahadevan, Prem, *the November 2008 Fidayeen Attack in Mumbai: Origins and Implications*, Research Paper No 127, Research Institute for European and American Studies (RIEAS), Greece, January 2009.

Mallin, Jay, *Terror and Urban Guerrillas: A Study of Tactics and Documents*, University of Miami Press, 1971.

Marine Corps Common Skills Handbook Book 1b, All Marines Individual Training Standards, US Marine Corps, 2001.

McMichael, Scott R, The Soviet Army, Counter-insurgency, and the Afghan War, " *Parameters* 19, no 4 (December 1989).

Merari, Ariel, "Terrorism as a Strategy in Insurgency," *Terrorism and Political Violence*, Vol 5, No 4 (Winter 1993), pp 213–251.

Messer, John, the Art of breaking and Raking, *Tactical Response Magazine*, September 2008.

Military Operations In Urban Terrain, MCI 0366B, Marine Corps Institute, US Marine Corps, 1997.

Military Operations on Urbanised Terrain (MOUT), MCWP 3-35.3, US Marine Corps, 1998.

Military Operations on Urbanised Terrain (MOUT), FM 90-10, US Army, 1979.

Miller, Abraham, *Terrorism and Hostage Negotiations*, Westview Press, 1980.

Mitchell, James, "*Identifying Potential Terrorist Targets*" a study in the use of convergence. G2 Whitepaper on terrorism, copyright 2006, G2. Counterterrorism Conference, Washington D.C. June 2006.

Molnar, Andrew R, Tinker, Jerry M and LeNoir, John D, *Human Factors Considerations of Undergrounds In Insurgencies*, US Government Printing Office, Washington, DC, 1965.

Moore, KC Airport, *Aircraft and Airline Security*, Los Angeles

Moss, Robert, Counter Terrorism, *Economist Newspaper*, 1972.

Moss, Robert, *Urban Guerrilla Warfare*, Adelphi Paper No 79, The International Institute for Strategic Studies, London, 1972.

Moss, Robert, *Urban Guerrillas in Latin America*, Conflict Studies No. 8, The Institute for the Study of Conflict, London, 1970.

Moss, Robert, *Urban Guerrillas*, Temple Smith, 1972.

Night of Blood—Operation Bluestar, *India Today*, 15 August, 1984.

Notes on Guerrilla Warfare, Paladin Press, Boulder, CO., 1985.

Oldham, Scott, *Common Mistakes in Building Searches*, Hendon Publishing Company, 2009.

Oldham, Scott, Rapid Assault Tools, *Law and Order Magazine,* January 2007.

Oliger, Olga, *Russia's Chechen Wars 1994-2000: Lessons from Urban Combat,* Rand Arroyo, 2001.

Operation Bluestar, 05 June, 1984, http://www.bharat-rakshak.com/*LAND-FORCES/History/1972-99/283-Operation-Bluestar.html.*

Operations Against Guerrilla Forces, FM 31-20, US Army, 1951.

Operations in a low-intensity Conflict, FM 7-98, US Army, 1992.

Oppenheimer, Martin, *the Urban Guerrilla,* Quadrangle Books, 1969.

Organisation and Conduct of Guerrilla Warfare, FM 31-21, US Army, 1955.

Perez, Carlos M, *Anatomy of a Hostage Rescue: What Makes Hostage Rescue Operations Successful?,* Naval Post Graduate School, September 2004.

Porzecanski, Arturo C, *Uruguay's Tupamaros: The Urban Guerrilla,* Praeger Publishers, 1973.

Ra'anan Uri *et al, Hydra of Carnage: The International Linkages of Terrorism and other low Intensity Operations,* Lexington Books, 1986.

Rappelling Techniques and Procedures, B-GL-392-003/FP-001, Chief of the Land Staff, Canada, 2002.

Rappelling, TC 21-24, US Army, 1997.

Remsberg, Chuck, *"Slicing The Pie" Vs "Button Hook" for Room Entry,* Calibre Press Street Survival Newsline, PoliceOne.com, August 2007.

Roy, Oliver Roy, *"The Lessons of the Soviet/Afghan War,"* Adelphi Papers 259 (Summer 1991).

Sageman, Marc, *Understanding Terror Networks,* University of Pennsylvania Press, 2004.

Scheuer, Michael, *Imperial Hubris: Why the West is Losing the War on Terror,* Potomac Books, 2004.

Schreiber, Jan, *The Ultimate Weapon: Terrorists and World Order,* Morrow, 1978.

Seegmiller, Neal, *Engineering a Long-Term Solution to the Improvised Explosive Device,* Department of Mechanical Engineering, University of Texas at Austin.

Seger, Karl A, *The Antiterrorism Handbook: A Practical Guide to Counteraction Planning and Operations for Individuals, Businesses, and Government,* Presidio Press, 1990.

Selection and Application Guide to Personal Body Armour, NIJ Guide 100-01, US Department of Justice Office of Justice Programmes, National Institute of Justice, The National Institute of Justice's National Law Enforcement and Corrections Technology Center.

Shachtman, Noah, *Improvised Bombs Baffle Army,* Wired News, January 26, 2005.

Shachtman, Noah, *Pentagon Bomb Squad a Dud?,* Wired.Com, March 29, 2007.

Shachtman, Noah, *Pentagon Bomb Squad also Wages Info, Corporate War,* Wired Home, May 18, 2009.

Shachtman, Noah, *Pentagon Bomb Squad Backs Super Snipers, Mini-Bots, Secret Spy Tech, Danger Room*, September 21, 2010.

Shachtman, Noah, *Pentagon Bomb Squad's Budget Slammed, Danger Room*, November 13, 2007.

Sharabi, Hisham, *Palestine Guerrilla: Their credibility and effectiveness*, Georgetown University, 1970.

Singh, Pritam, *Federalism, Nationalism And Development: India and the Punjab Economy*, Routledge, 2008.

Sniper Training, FM 23-10, US Army, 1994.

Sokuit, Sergey, "*The `God of War' is Changing Tactics*," interview with Colonel General Mikhail Karatuyev, Nezavisimoye Voyennoye Obozreniye, 19 November 1999, 12, as translated by FBIS and downloaded from their web page.

Special Forces Operations, FM 3-05.20, US Army, 2001.

Speyer, Arthur L, *Chechnya: Urban Warfare Lessons Learned, Marine Corps Intelligence Activity*, in Capital Preservation, op Cit.

Spiller, Roger J, *Sharp Corners: Urban Operations At Century's End*, US Army Command and General Staff College Press, 2000.

Staten, CL, *Urban Warfare Considerations; Understanding and Combating Irregular and Guerrilla Forces During A 'Conventional War' In Iraq*, Emergency Response & Research Institute (ERRI), Chicago, March, 2003.

Steve Crawford, *Deadly Fighting Skills Of The World*, St. Martin's Griffin, 1999.

Stoneberger, Brett A, *Combat Leader's Field Guide*, Stackpole Books, 2000.

Styles, George, *Bombs Have No Pity: The War Against Terrorism*, Luscombe, 1975.

Surozhtsev, Sergey, 'Legendary Army in Grozny,' *Novoye Vremya*, No 2-3 (January 1995).

Taw, Jennifer M, and Hoffman, Bruce, *The Urbanization of Insurgency: The Potential Challenge to US Army Operations*, Rand Corporation, 1994.

The City's Many Faces and Capital Preservation, Compilations of Briefings and Reports from the Urban Operations Conferences Held in 1999 and 2000, RAND Arroyo Center.

Thomas, Timothy, 'The Battle for Grozny,' *Slavic Military Studies*, 10 (March 1997).

Thomas, Timothy, Grozny 2000: Urban Combat Lessons Learned, *Military Review*, July-August 2000.

Thomas, Timothy, The Battle Of Grozny: Deadly Classroom for Urban Combat, *Parameters*, pp. 87-102, Summer 1999.

Thomas, Timothy, The Caucus Conflict and Russian Security: The Russian Armed Forces Confront Chechnya, Parts One, Two, and Three, *Slavic Military Studies*, Vol 8, No 2, June 1995.

Thompson, Leroy, *Dirty Wars: Elite Forces Vs the Guerrillas*, David and Charles, 1991.

Thompson, Leroy, *Ragged War: The Story of Unconventional and Counter-Revolutionary Warfare*, Arms & Armour Press, 1994.

Thompson, Leroy, *Counter-terrorist Manual: A Practical Guide to Elite International Units*, Frontline Books, 2009.

Tolson, John J, *Vietnam Studies: Air Mobility 1961-1971*, US Army, 1989.

Training For Urban Operations, Training Circular 90-1, US Army, 2002.

Trifunovic, Darko, *Islamic Fundamentalist's Global Network-Modus Operandi-Model Bosnia,* The Center for Documentation of the Government of Republic of Srpska and The Secretariat of the Government of RS for relation with ICTY, Banja Luka, Republic of Srpska, 2002.

Trifunovic, Darko, *Terrorism – Global Network of Islamic Fundamentalist's - Part II – Modus operandi-Model Bosnia,* The Government of Republic of Srpska and The Secretariat of the Government of RS for relation with ICTY, Banja Luka, Republic of Srpska, 2004.

Tully, Mark, *Amritsar: Mrs. Gandhi's Last Battle*, South Asia Books, 1991.

Urban Areas, Chapter 8, FM 3-21.75, *The Warrior Ethos and Soldier Combat Skills*, US Army, 2008.

Urban Operations, FM 3-06, US Army, 2003.

Urban Warfare Study: City Case Studies, Compilation Marine Corps Intelligence Activity, April 1999.

Wang, J, Bird, R, Swinton B and Krstic, A, *Protection of Lower Limbs Against Floor Impact in Army Vehicles Experiencing Landmine Explosion*, Weapons, Adcon Corporation, 1972.

Weinberger , Sharon, *IED Fight = "McNamara Line"?* Wired Home, May 11, 2007.

Weinberger , Sharon, *Pentagon Bomb Squad Under Fire, Wired Home*, April 16, 2007.

White, Robert W., *Provisional Irish Republicans: An Oral and Interpretive History*, Greenwood Press, 1993.

Wilson, Clay, *Improvised Explosive Devices (IEDs) in Iraq and Afghanistan: Effects and Countermeasures*, CRS Report for Congress, September 25, 2006.

Wilson, Clay, *Improvised Explosive Devices in Iraq: Effects and Countermeasures*, CRS Report for Congress, November 23, 2005.

Winter, Phil; Meiliunas, Alex and Bliss, Steve, *Countering the Improvised Explosive Devices Threat*, United Service 59 (3) September 2008.

Yousef, Mohammad and Adkin, Mark, *The Bear Trap: Afghanistan's Untold Story*, Jang Publishers, Pakistan, 1992.

Index